CRIME PREVENTION

NOTICE

THESE PREMISES EQUIPPED WITH A
DEPOSITORY SAFE
DEPOSITS ARE MADE THROUGH
SLOT OR HOPPER INTO SAFE.
THE SAFE COMBINATION IS NOT
KNOWN BY THE ATTENDANT OR
DRIVER AND NOT KEPT ON
THE PREMISES.

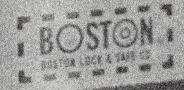

BOSTON
BOSTON LOCK & SAFE CO.

CRIME PREVENTION

Paul M. Whisenand
California State University at Long Beach

Holbrook Press, Inc.   Boston

To Doug, Paula, and Kathy—
it has been my good fortune to know
them and love them all their lives.

Photo Credits

The Department of Justice, Common-
wealth of Pennsylvania, p. 202; New York
State Department of Correctional Services,
p. 352; John Servideo, pp. xii, 42; Pat
Torelli, pp. ii, 284.

Library of Congress Cataloging in Publication Data

Whisenand, Paul M
    Crime prevention.

    Includes bibliographical references and index.
    1.   Crime prevention—United States.   2.   Criminal
justice, Administration of—United States.   I.   Title.
HV7431.W45   364.4   76–44819
ISBN 0–205–05595–8

CONTENTS

Consulting Editors for the
Holbrook Press Criminal Justice Series

VERN L. FOLLEY
Chief of Police
Bismarck, North Dakota

DONALD T. SHANAHAN
Associate Director
Southern Police Institute & University of Louisville

WILLIAM J. BOPP
Director
Criminal Justice Program
Florida Atlantic University

PREFACE

At this point in time I feel quite comfortable in predicting that the "preventing of crime" will during the 1970s and 1980s exert a dominant influence in legislative and administrative decisions pertaining to the goals and operations of our criminal justice system. Currently, we can find highly visible outcroppings of crime prevention planning, funding, and programs in the three subsystems: police, courts, and corrections. Their emerging presence today should develop into omnipresence tomorrow. For, criminal justice agencies at the local, state, and federal levels of government have and are in the process of creating crime prevention programs. While falling under the same title, there are major variances from one program to another. Nevertheless, the prediction remains—crime prevention will increase in significance and scope in the decade of the 70s.

In retrospect, one might reasonably refer to criminal justice in the 1960s as being an era of confusion, consternation, conflict, and change. This state-of-affairs was, in the main, caused by the delivery system (criminal justice) and its clientele (people in need of help) failing to accurately understand and appreciate one another's conditions. On the one hand we had an antiquated delivery system obsolesced by time, tradition, inadequate resources, and public disinterest. On the other hand we had a society comprised of millions of communities (governmental, social, racial, economic, and political) that were experiencing growing frustrations in the manifesting of their values and resolution of their problems. In summary, the *relationship* of the system to its clientele deteriorated to such an extent that what cooperation did exist was soon replaced by conflict.

Obviously all of this did not occur within the 60s, but rather should be attributed to a lengthy period of neglect that spans many decades. What did come during this particular decade, however, was the shocking recognition of the gravity of the problem. It caught nationwide attention through the criminal justice system's inability to effectively cope with a crime rate that had increased to the extent that many communities found their streets and homes less safe, and collective violence and other related acts of anarchy were on the rise. Moreover, some citizens and policy makers arrived at the disturbing conclusion that the *system* was in part culpable for these conditions. Those of a positive bent both within and without the criminal justice system decided to: (1) assume their share of the blame, and (2) take corrective action. Those of a hypercritical nature continue to this day to: (1) engage in the indictment of others, and (2) remain to one side and carp.

If you accept my thinking thus far then the first reason for writing a text on the subject of crime prevention is self-evident. Plainly, since crime prevention appears destined to either dominate or at least be carefully considered in *every* decision affecting the criminal justice system, *every* effort should be made to identify and define its parameters. What is crime prevention? How do we know it when we see it? The second reason for creating this text involves an effort to provide clarity to an operational concept. A reduction in such ambiguity, at minimum, permits us to converse about the same phenomena with an improved degree of mutual understanding. Better still, a clear understanding over the nature and dynamics of a given phenomena—in this instance crime prevention— permits us to establish objectives against which it can be evaluated. Essentially then by an improved and generally agreed upon understanding of what is denoted as "preventing crime," we find ourselves in a much better position to make rational decisions about the allocation of scarce resources to and within the criminal justice system. Most certainly a clearer picture of crime prevention is needed. Whether *this* book fulfills *this* need is left up to you the reader.

In attempting to identify that which is crime prevention and that which is not, I found it imperative to first make certain decisions that arbitrarily set parameters. It should be noted, however, that recognized benchmark sources were consulted for such differentiation. Pointedly, crime prevention extends far beyond the confines of the criminal justice system. Educational, employment, health, recreational, and a host of other such service institutions and functions are (or should be) directly involved in the prevention of criminal behavior. Second, once the limits were decided, I was confronted by the vast number of activities within the various systems that might be tagged as preventing crime. To sum up, the greatest challenge in the writing of this text centered around conceptually fencing-in the phenomena known as—crime prevention.

One final comment: you will observe that each chapter contains a "Preview," a summary of its contents, at the beginning rather than at the end of the chapter. The rationale underlying this particular format stems from a speed reading course I took in my freshman year in college. The instructor repeatedly coached us to read our texts as follows: first, read the preface; second, if present, read the summaries of each chapter; third, read the first and last chapter in the text; fourth, read the entire book from front to end. I have used this advice to my advantage over the past twenty years. It is my hope that you similarly will find chapter summaries helpful in facilitating your learning. They are positioned at the beginning of the chapter with this hope in mind.

Paul M. Whisenand

PART ONE

Toward a System of Criminal Justice
The Importance of Reducing Crime

The mounting concern over the concept of crime prevention and its practice in our society can be attributed to four primary causative factors.

- Crime is personally threatening to us.
- Crime is expensive.
- Crime is corrosive of public morals and morale.
- Crime is occurring at a socially intolerable rate.

There is a compelling and most urgent need to reduce the impact and incidence of crime within this country, and the strategies for this reduction now emphasize, and will continue to emphasize over the coming years, *prevention* as compared to *control* of crime.

Responses to the Need for Crime Reduction

Currently we are witnessing a massive nationwide attack against crime and criminal offenders. Policy-workers, government administrators, and the general citizenry have reached a consensus that *crime must be reduced.* The approach for resolving this social problem includes: goal-setting, planning, programs, research, and public involvement.

Goals   Over the past decades, numerous government commissions have struggled with the issues and challenges of crime. In nearly

1

every instance, their efforts resulted in short-lived hopes and on-the-shelf studies. Further, the commissions usually focused on only one component (police, courts, or corrections) of the criminal justice system (CJS). The President's Commission on Law Enforcement and the Administration of Justice (1967) brought within its purview all of the parts comprising the CJS. Additionally, it gave impetus to the National Advisory Commission on Criminal Justice Standards and Goals (1973) to: (1) recommend precise standards of improvement, (2) establish a working relationship with a fourth and needed partner—the community, and (3) promote the concept and use of crime prevention programs. In summary, each of the three CJS components and its newly acquired colleague were conceived as having alternative rather than singular strategies for crime reduction. While simplistic, the before-and-after can be viewed as follows:

The Old	The New
Police-Control (Apprehension)	Control and Prevention (Alternatives to arrest)
Courts-Control (Conviction)	Control and Prevention (Diversion)
Corrections-Control (Institutions)	Control and Prevention (Community based treatment)
Community-Control (Social)	Control and Prevention (Programs)

Planning   National, state, intra-state regions, and urban centers are receiving federal funds along with a requirement to build and implement CJS and community (CJS/C) plans for decreasing the threat (actual and perceived) and expense of crime to the public. The leader in this effort is the United States Department of Justice, Law Enforcement Assistance Administration (LEAA). Similarly, at state, regional, and urban levels of government, we now find planning bodies, whose challenge is to create a comprehensive blueprint which effectively organizes priorities and directs available resources to those who are in need of help.

Programs   The planning process involves the development of programs, and the programs are made up of specific projects, which in turn vie for scarce fiscal resources. (For example, a program may be to upgrade the training of CJS personnel, while a project within this program could be the appropriation of a sum of money to train corrections officers.) In some cases, CJS/C agencies are capable of fulfilling their objectives through the funds allocated to them from traditional sources. In other cases, we see CJS/C agencies that require external supplemental funds or technical assistance in order to reduce crime in their area of concern.

Research   It would appear that a large number of scientists, representing all of the various disciplines, began to turn their heads, minds, and capabilities in the direction of the problems confronting the CJS/C during the mid-60s. The political scientists started to examine the policy environment and political position of the CJS components in relation to other institutions. The communication engineers sought to resolve the technical problems associated with data transmission within and among police agencies. The clinical psychologists and psychiatrists focused their attention on the categorizing and placement of inmates into various rehabilitative programs. This list could be expanded ad infinitum. At this point it is significant to note that much of the experimentation and scientific inquiry deals with the identification of relevant crime prevention programs.

Public   As mentioned earlier, public or community involvement in
Involvement coping with the crime problem is now recognized by many as being not only helpful but also imperative. The so-called fourth partner is a most welcome and essential addition to a concerted drive toward crime reduction. Admittedly, however, this fourth dimension requires considerable development, coordination, and direction before sustained levels of success are evidenced. Then again, the CJS leaves much to be desired in terms of its internal transactions and overall goal accomplishments. In any event, it appears that the future will see the community playing an ever expanding and important role in dealing with criminal offenses.

Background

Until a few years ago, the theory or practice of crime prevention was rarely discussed, and even less frequently was it intentionally practiced in this nation. Paradoxically, the reforms being articulated in England by Sir Robert R. Peel in 1829 emphasized the fundamental significance of crime prevention; nevertheless, the goals of our CJS were formalized along the lines of *controlling criminal behavior*. The reasons for this condition are varied and are firmly rooted in our historical development. The Peelian reforms, while of interest to us, were not adopted in the United States to any significant extent. Our nation at that point in time was in transition from a recent revolutionary period to one of frontier exploration; thus, our national character was more congruent with the immediacy of control as compared to the longer term prevention. For those interested in the history of the police see the bibliographical references in the President's Commission on Law Enforcement and Administration of Justice, *Task Force Report: Police* (Washington, D.C.: U.S. Government Printing Office, 1967). Hence, we find our police more in agreement with the goal of apprehending offenders, the court more comfortable with providing swift justice to accused offenders, and corrections officials professing a fundamental mission of institutional control over those convicted. There are notable exceptions to these observations. Let us examine, for example, the police.

As a rule of thumb, a task analysis of the police officer's work will reveal that about 80 to 90 percent of his time is expended on matters other than crime control. Consequently, it seems reasonable to predict that from the time of his earliest predecessors to now, the police officer had time to, and probably did, conduct himself in such a fashion that he prevented crime. With the advent of police-community relations (PCR), we see rather sizable and well-defined crime prevention efforts. PCR eventually subsumed three related programmable areas: race relations, public information, and crime prevention. This author believes that the 1970s and 80s will result in the emergence of crime prevention *as a separate and prominent goal for all CJS components and the community as well.*

Definition

Attempting to draw a definitive line around crime prevention so as to make it easily discernible from other programs and projects in the CJS/C is a problem at this time. The related theory and its applications are just now being tested and validated. Nevertheless, a common understanding of what is meant by crime prevention seems necessary in order to provide at least a loose guideline for us to follow in this text. In its broadest sense . . .

> Crime prevention is the reduction or elimination of the *desire* and/or *opportunity* to commit a crime.

Thus, if upon examination the primary intent of a CJS/C program reflects this thinking, it should be labeled as preventive rather than controlling in nature.

The Delivery System: Criminal Justice and the Community

The major premises of this text are:

- To effectively reduce crime, crime prevention efforts must be included.
- To effectively *prevent* crime, crime prevention efforts must extend beyond the CJS to include the community.

In regard to criminal justice, the creation of a delivery system for preventing crime is one, if not *the*, principal challenge of the decade. The probabilities of enhancing crime prevention are quite favorable. Let us all hope that the trends, ideals, and proposed CJS standards of the late 60s and early 70s come to fruition within the near future.

The Chapters That Follow

The remainder of this section is comprised of two chapters. Chapter 1 presents an overview of crime prevention. It discusses the roles that the police, the CJS, and the community should adopt in order to abate crime. Chapter 2 describes the state-of-the-art in crime prevention. Recently promulgated CJS goals and standards will be covered. As a final comment pertaining to the entire book, an effort has been made to view crime prevention as it exists or should exist in the CJS/C. Thus, each component will be examined as to its *actual* and *potential* involvement. Some components will or will not, by their very nature, relate more readily to preventive measures (such as the police and the community). A careful attempt is made to present accurately and completely *each* component and its prevention role.

1

Crime Prevention: The Police, The Criminal Justice System, and The Community

Preview

There has been much confusion over what is, or what is not, *crime prevention*. Frequently, there is equivocalness between crime prevention and the concept of *crime control*. In combination, both serve as a means of reducing crime in our society. Significantly, we can now observe an established and growing concentration on the prevention as compared to the control of criminal events. This trend, in turn, has resulted in the criminal justice system (CJS) actively seeking assistance from external organizations and citizens. In essence, this trend is telling us that in order to effectively prevent crime, the CJS *and* the community must act in concert with one another.

An "integrated" system is one that has the capability for *efficient internal* and *effective external* transactions. Plainly the CJS leaves much to be desired in this regard, yet it is to be admired for functioning as well as it has been able to over the recent past. The rationale for such thinking originates in an appreciation of the innumerable political barriers and social issues with which the System has had to deal. In theory, and even in practice to a lesser extent, a somewhat dim promise is that the necessary improvements can be identified and operationalized. Optimistically, we can now see the so-called system integrators (planning, information, education/training, legislation, and prevention) that may well cement the functional requirements in such a fashion that the delivery of criminal justice services is enhanced.

An Introductory Comment

To draw a fine distinction between the concept of *crime prevention* and that of crime *control* is no small chore. Moreover, where do the ancillary concepts such as crime reduction, citizen participation, crime specific, defensive space, diversion, and so forth, fit in with prevention as compared to control? One is compelled to assess each individual project and program in order to ascertain if it is mainly preventive or control in nature. Basically, one should focus on the design and objectives of a project or program for such a determination. For our purposes, as mentioned earlier, a program such as crime prevention encompasses one or more *projects* intended to accomplish program goals. While this text will describe, and at times recommend, certain programs and projects, any attempt to list all of the so-called crime prevention projects would be both impossible and impractical. However, a concise list of prevention projects can be found in the publications of the federal government.[1]

Three presumptive statements should be offered at this point:

- The concept of preventing crime is increasing in importance in this country and should continue to do so well into the late 1970s.
- Crime prevention transcends the CJS to the extent that it includes public and private organizations not typically associated with the reduction of an opportunity or motivation to commit a criminal offense.
- This nation will indefinitely expend considerable effort and resources in the prevention of criminal activity.

In summary, there is sufficient evidence for agreement that while the CJS may be vague as to what is meant by crime prevention, it at the same time has a relatively high consensus as to its current and future import in our society.[2]

The remainder of this chapter further analyzes the concept of crime prevention, looks at the prevention of crime as it relates to the CJS and the community, and describes how the various CJS components can be interfaced in a more rational and effective manner.

The Concept of Crime Prevention

The idea of preventing crime is not new, though its acceptance has been slow. For example, the *Report of the President's Commission on Law Enforcement and the Administration of Justice* (February 1967) called for public involvement in such ways as: reporting offenses; taking the common sense precautions against crime recommended by law enforcers; becoming familiar with the problems of crime and the justice system; and by support for adequate finances to control crime. The *Report* continues: "Beyond this, controlling crime depends to a great degree on interactions between the community and the criminal justice system."

The same call came six years later from the *Report of The National Advisory Commission on Criminal Justice Standards and Goals* (January 1973). In the section on Community Crime Prevention, the *Report* concludes: "The local community is one of the nation's most underdeveloped and underutilized crime fighting resources. It is a resource that needs to be utilized by everyone concerned about the incidence of crime in his community."

Evidence exists that law enforcement agencies are currently becoming more aware that the public can and must help them to do a better job in preventing crime, that they are seeking such involvement, and that the public is becoming more ready to respond. This is the direction we must take ever more vigorously.[3]

Let us, on the one hand, view crime prevention as an integral and programmatic function of the CJS. Crime prevention and the administration of justice should be fundamental goals for the criminal justice system and its three major subsystems. On the other hand, "The final assumption is that crime prevention efforts include demonstrable benefits for institutions and agencies with other primary goals (schools, churches, recreational activities, and the like)."[4] At this point, therefore, one may correctly assume that crime prevention is an activity that occurs both within the CJS (police, courts, and corrections) as well as without its loosely defined parameters.

As an aside, we should be aware that the benchmark National Advisory Commission on Criminal Justice Standards and Goals proposes that there are four main linkages existing between the three criminal justice components: planning, information systems, training and education, and legislation. To these four we will add *prevention*. Prevention, indeed, not only serves as an internal bonding agent, but also serves as a most critical supersystem linkage. In other words, crime prevention is, or should be, of concern to the criminal justice system as well as to the organizations and people on its periphery. Briefly, then, while not unequivocally defined, the concern for and challenge of crime prevention pervades the fabric of our society and definitely is not the sole responsibility of the CJS! Therefore, it is critical that we come to the full realization that crime prevention roles are inherent in both the CJS and the community.

Police: Crime Prevention Role

> Every police agency should immediately establish programs that encourage members of the public to take an active role in preventing crime, that provide information leading to the arrest and conviction of criminal offenders, that facilitate the identification and recovery of stolen property, and that increase liaison with private industry in security efforts.*

The above statement strongly implies that *police* crime prevention ought to emphasize programs that involve the citizen in reducing the opportunity to commit criminal offense. During a moment of reflection, a long-time colleague of mine said "Mistakes: doctors bury them, the military classifies them, and the police arrest them."[5] In essence, my scholarly buddy was inferring with tongue in cheek that the police have a responsibility for crime prevention by seeing to it that its commission is made more difficult if not actually impossible. Such thinking subsequently could cause one to debate the not-so-simplistic issue of, "Should we endeavor to lock up our windows, and/or lock up the criminal?"

The National Advisory Commission went on to propose that all police agencies actively assist in the establishment of volunteer neighborhood security programs that involve the public in neighborhood crime prevention and reduction.[6] The police should supply the community with information and assistance regarding the techniques of avoiding victimization, and they should seek to inform neighborhoods of developing crime trends in that area. Also, the police should train neighborhood volunteers to telephone the police concerning suspicious situations, to identify themselves as volunteers, and to provide pertinent information. Participating volunteers should not be permitted to take enforcement action themselves, however. Police units should respond directly to the incident rather than to the reporting volunteer. If further information is needed from the volunteer, the police should contact him

---

* National Advisory Commission on Criminal Justice Standards and Goals, *Police* (Washington, D.C.: U.S. Government Printing Office, 1973), p. 66.

by telephone and, if an arrest results from the volunteer's information, the police should immediately call him. Finally, the police should acknowledge through personal contact, telephone call, or letter, every person who provides information.

Police agencies should establish or assist in programs that get businesses, industries, and the community involved in preventing and reducing commercial crimes. The police should seek the adoption of local ordinances establishing minimum security standards for all new construction and for existing commercial structures. Once regulated buildings are constructed, ordinances should be enforced through *inspection* by police or fire personnel. In a similar regard, the police should conduct security inspections of businesses and residences and recommend measures to avoid being victimized by crime. Larger police agencies should consider establishing specialized unit to provide jurisdiction-wide coordination of the agency's crime prevention programs; and such programs should be operationally *decentralized*.

Concrete examples of such programs as those alluded to will be depicted in later chapters. It is timely, however, to caution you (and in doing so remind myself) that not all crimes are preventable —nor can they ever be. Hence, we must establish certain tolerances for the type and number of crimes committed in our society. Crime prevention is not, therefore, a panacea or fail-safe device. It is a set of programs and techniques that make the commission of a crime either more difficult, or risky, or both to the perpetrator.

The Criminal Justice System: Crime Prevention Role

> Crime prevention and the provision of justice should be primary goals for the criminal justice system and its components.*

Crime prevention and crime control are interdependent, yet to some degree they are separate strategies intended to reduce crime. The concept and practice of criminal justice by our CJS is broadly discussed today. Typically, we view it as a set of agencies that have been given the formal responsibility of dealing with crime and criminal offenders: police and sheriffs' departments, judges, prosecutors and their staffs, defense attorneys, jails and

* Charles P. Smith, "Perception and Crime Prevention," *Crime Prevention Review,* 1 (January 1974), p. 32.

prisons, and probation and parole agencies. Many of us tend to view the CJS more concisely as being comprised of three subsystems: police, courts, and corrections. In doing so we err; for there are much wilder ramifications associated with the term CJS. To explain, many public and private agencies and citizens ought to be involved in reducing crime—the primary goal of criminal justice. These agencies and persons produce a significantly enlarged and uniquely modified system.

Since the term "system" is destined to be with us now and in the remainder of the text, let us digress at this time and examine in more detail the concept of a system. Human organizations are one form of a system (other examples of systems are biological, mechanical, communications, and work-flow). Until recently, CJS organizations have tended to be perceived as "closed." This propensity has caused a disregard of the differing CJS organizational environments. And agencies are to a large degree dependent on their environment. It has led also to an overconcentration on principles of internal organizational functioning, with consequent failure to develop and understand the processes of feedback which are essential to organizational success and more basically—to *survival.*[7] There is sufficient research and practical experience to make the following recommendations. First, an organization (police, courts, corrections) or group of organizations (CJS) should be conceived of as an *open* system, which means that it is in constant interaction with its environment, taking in raw materials, people, energy, and information, and transforming these into products and services that are exported into the environment.[8] Second, an organization(s) must be conceived of as a system with multiple purposes or functions that involve multiple interactions between the organization(s) and its environment. Consequently, many subsystem activities within the CJS should not be interpreted without looking at multiple interactions and functions. Third, the CJS consists of three major subsystems that are in constant interaction with one another. Instead of analyzing subsystem phenomena in terms of separate functions, it is becoming increasingly important for us to examine the functions of such subsystems, as they relate to the overall system. Fourth, because the subsystems are mutually dependent, changes in one subsystem are likely to affect the behavior of other subsystems. Fifth, a subsystem exists in a dynamic environment that consists of other systems, some larger, some smaller than the subsystem (organization). The environment places demands upon and simultaneously constrains the subsystem in various ways. The total functioning of a subsystem cannot be understood without explicit consideration of these environmental demands and constraints. Sixth, the multiple links between the CJS, its subsystems (internal), and its environment (external) make it difficult to specify clearly the boundaries of any given subsystem or system. Finally, for our purposes a system denotes a set of components (subsystems) that are interrelated by process and possess a functional goal(s) (e.g., reduction of crime) that provides a unity of mission.

Now, let us return to our discussion of the CJS and its broadened perspective. The National Advisory Commission, evidently, refers to the so-called traditional concept of the CJS as "CJS 1." In turn, the more modern view is classified "CJS 2." Because of the particular emphasis of this text and the emerging trends at this period in time, it appears more appropriate to refer to the expanded version of the CJS as CJS/C with the "C" indicating the community. However, it should be kept in mind that a state legislature, for example, becomes part of the expanded CJS when it considers and debates any proposed law that might affect, even indirectly, any area of criminal justice activities. Similarly, the executive agencies of the state, educational administrative units, welfare departments, youth service bureaus, recreation departments, and other public offices become a part of CJS/C in many of their decisions and actions. Community organizations, union offices, neighborhood action groups, and employers may also be important participants in the broader system.

The next section presents an overview of *community* crime prevention, after which we will return to the CJS/C and discuss the reasons for its deficiencies and means for the possible methods or processes for their rectification.

The Community: Crime Prevention Role

The Commission proposes that all Americans make a personal contribution to the reduction of crime, and that all Americans support the crime prevention efforts of their State and local governments. Key recommendations include:

- Increased citizen contribution to crime prevention by making homes and businesses more secure, by participating in police-community programs, and by working with youth.
- Expanded public and private employment opportunities and elimination of unnecessary restrictions on hiring of ex-offenders.
- Establishment of and citizen support for youth service

bureaus to improve the delivery of social services to young people.
- Provision of individualized treatment for drug offenders and abusers.
- Provision of statewide capability for overseeing and investigating financing of political campaigns.
- Establishment of a statewide investigation and prosecution capability to deal with corruption in government.*

The above quotation is a synthesis of recommended programs that the National Advisory Commission considered critical for mounting an effective community crime prevention strategy. We can see that the proposed activities span a large number of seemingly diverse social areas. Once combined, however, they provide an invaluable approach for attacking crime's *infrastructure*. To explain, many of us believe that crime can be more effectively prevented by focusing the citizens' attention on the underlying social conditions that cause criminal behavior: unemployment, inadequate education, lack of recreation, and poor social counseling and treatment.

At the same time, the community is adopting an alternative approach with hoped-for immediate outcomes. In essence, the community is deciding more often to privately employ their own security units. Today we can witness within the private sector a variety of security forces. They are either *contract forces,* providing security services for a fee, or *in-house forces,* not for hire, providing services exclusively for the business institution or individual employing them. Contract security agencies furnish one or more of the following personnel services: guard; roving patrol (on foot or in cars); armored-car escort; central station alarm; and various investigative functions, such as credit, insurance, and pre-employment background checks, and ·investigations in connection with civil and criminal court proceedings. Guard, patrol, and investigations in connection with alarm services are also provided by in-house forces. Both types of security personnel are utilized by a wide variety of consumers, including individual citizens, banks, retail establishments, insurance companies and other financial institutions, hospitals, industrial firms, educational institutions, apartment houses, and at recreational events. It should be noted that most private security personnel have no peace officer (government) powers.

* National Advisory Commission on Criminal Justice Standards and Goals, *A National Strategy to Reduce Crime* (Washington, D.C.: U.S. Government Printing Office, 1973), iii.

Table 1.1   A Taxonomy of private police forces and organizations

PURCHASED OR CONTRACT PRIVATE SECURITY SERVICES[a]

Guards and watchmen employed by detective agencies and protective-service establishments

Detectives, investigators, and undercover agents employed by detective agencies and protective-service establishments

Patrolmen employed in private patrol establishments

Guards employed in armored-car-service establishments

Guard respondents employed in central station alarm services establishments

IN-HOUSE OR PROPRIETARY PRIVATE SECURITY SERVICES

Guards and watchmen employed by industries, businesses, institutions, and individuals

Detectives, investigators, and undercover agents employed by industries, businesses, institutions, and individuals

[a] Each class of private security service can be subcategorized by type of client or user, e.g., by broad industry, business, and institutional categories.

Source: James S. Kakalik and Sorrel Wildhorn, *The Private Police Industry: Its Nature and Extent,* Vol. 2 (Washington, D.C.: U.S. Department of Justice, 1971), p. 3.

In many ways, the public and private sectors overlap. As one example, a small fraction of the privately employed security personnel are granted either full or limited public police powers by virtue of being deputized or commissioned by local police or state agencies. The powers of the special police generally may be exercised only while on duty at a specified geographic location, such as their employer's or client's property. A more detailed taxonomy of the various types of private security forces appears in Table 1.1. More will be said later about the private police. We should appreciate, in passing, that while the public police have received a great deal of attention and serious study; the private police have not. Nevertheless, of the nearly 800,000 public and private security personnel in the United States, only *half* are public police officers. Additionally, expenditures on public police (counting the costs of security devices as well as personnel) account for only roughly half of the $9 billion spent annually on both public and private security (criminal justice).

While everything from improving recreational opportunities to the staffing of a private security force has been mentioned so

far, there remains a single and most vital factor that tends to congeal all avenues of attack—an involved and aware citizenry that
concurs with the premise that crime prevention is not the sole
responsibility of the CJS, but includes private organizations with
other primary goals as well. Regardless of the social issue or involved governmental agency, there is a logical sequence of events
that must occur in order to achieve community crime prevention:

- Remove citizen apathy and replace it with a desire for
  action.
- Remove governmental separateness and replace it with
  mechanisms that encourage involvement.
- Remove administrative isolationism and replace it with a
  willingness to allow the clientele to participate in decisions
  that affect them.
- Remove centralized delivery systems and replace them
  with those that are decentralized.

A Coordinated Delivery System

The governmental commissions that have studied the criminal
justice process in recent years have begun to ask whether fragmentation should continue to be tolerated as a necessary by-
product of the separation of functions. They have sought to
re-define the criminal justice process as a composite of
agencies which, while necessarily independent at the decision-making level, can and must work closely together at the
administrative level. Under that view, the nation's criminal
justice apparatus must be converted at all levels of government from a diffuse group of agencies, each acting without
regard to the other, into a unified system which will permit
them to interact on a coordinated basis to achieve the common goal of crime control. The key word is "system," for the
Task Force Report on Law and Law Enforcement to the National Commission on the Causes and Prevention of Violence
has aptly described the present criminal justice process as a
"non-system" of criminal justice.*

Admittedly, both the CJS and the CJS/C are deficient in many
ways. Nonetheless, they have not—so far—totally failed. Indeed,
based on the internal operating constraints, inordinate external demands, and contradictory goals, it is a wonder that we can still

* Special Committee on Crime Prevention and Control, *New Perspectives
on Urban Crime* (Washington, D.C.: American Bar Association, 1972),
p. 13.

look to the CJS with a degree of credibility. Even with a modicum of success, the degree of controversy over criminal justice is rising, not diminishing. The causes of the controversy are varied, but most important is the widespread belief among citizens and professionals that the CJS is failing at an accelerated pace. There is ample evidence to substantiate or intensify such beliefs in our daily news media, research literature, and crime statistics. The contentiousness over criminal justice has also been heightened by repeated conflicts among the various components of the CJS. The genesis of the conflict is in the differing roles that police, courts, and corrections agencies seek to fulfill. The Science and Technology report of the President's Commission on Law Enforcement and Administration of Justice describes the problem appropriately:

Police, court, and corrections officials all share the objective of reducing crime. But each uses different, sometimes conflicting, methods and so focuses frequently on inconsistent subobjectives. The police role, for example, is focused on deterrence. Most modern correctional thinking, on the other hand, focuses on rehabilitation and argues that placing the offender back into society under a supervised community treatment program provides the best chance for his rehabilitation as a law-abiding citizen. But community treatment may involve some loss of deterrent effect, and the ready arrest of marginal offenders, intended to heighten deterrence, may by affixing a criminal label complicate rehabilitation. The latent conflicts between the parts may not be apparent from the viewpoint of either subsystem, but there is an obvious need to balance and rationalize them so as to achieve optimum overall effectiveness.[9]

Although the challenges of securing coordination among the various functions of the CJS are great, they are enormously greater within in the CJS/C. Unfortunately, many public agencies and private citizens refuse even to acknowledge that they have a responsibility for preventing crime. Making this problem more severe, many police, courts, and corrections agencies do not possess a conceptualized approach on how to develop the assistance of other public and private organizations.

The main axiom of this text is that no one part of the CJS or CJS/C can reduce crime by itself. Each component must be compatible with the other's activities and objectives. With this theme in mind, five intrasystem *integrators* are identified as possessing the requisite capability for unifying the CJS and building a functional CJS/C. Graphically, they can be expressed as:

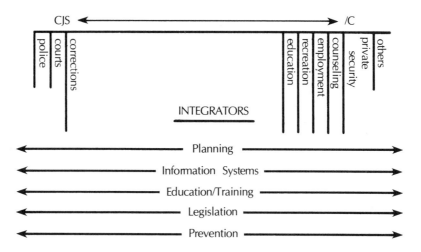

Each of the integrators are intended to serve as horizontal linkages which merge the CJS/C into a viable and effective delivery system for reducing crime. These integrators will receive more comprehensive coverage in subsequent chapters. For the present, one can envision each integrator as taking on some form of concrete organizational manifestation. To illustrate, CJS planning is currently conducted at the national (LEAA), state (State Planning Agencies), and regional (intrastate local planning boards) levels. The nation has developed a large-scale interactive computer-based information/telecommunications system that processes and transmits information and statistics on crime and criminals. In some jurisdictions the grade school through the college classroom serves as a forum for the development of knowledge about, interest in, and support of an improved CJS/C. Similarly, cross-functional in-service training of CJS agents is fostering an understanding of CJS subsystem roles and a desire to cooperate in the overall mission of the system. Legislative changes are being enacted that are designed to promote and facilitate mutually supportive transactions within the CJS/C, while simultaneously abating internal tensions among the components. Finally, we can currently see CJS/C programs, which include two or more components, being developed and implemented (e.g. police juvenile officers, juvenile probation officers, youth service agents, recreational specialists, and educators comprising a delinquency strike force). Hence, we have a basis for hope, but without action our hoping is not only useless, but also frustrating. In conclusion, it is essential that we first *hope* and then *act* to *prevent crime.*

Endnotes

1. National Advisory Commission on Criminal Justice Standards and Goals, *Community Crime Prevention* (Washington, D.C.: U.S. Government Printing Office, 1973), p. 362.

    See also the more comprehensive list of crime prevention projects contained in the document compiled by J. F. Murphy, Jr., *Crime Deterrence and Prevention* (Washington, D.C.: National Criminal Justice Reference Service, Law Enforcement Assistance Administration, 1974). Interestingly, this report contains annotated descriptions of 367 crime prevention projects. Finally, it is worthwhile to scan the following crime prevention sources mentioned in the *Crime Prevention Review,* (January, 1974), pp. 61–4.

    General Crime Prevention Literature
    - Block, Irvin *Violence in America*
    - *Controlling Crime in California: Report of the Governor's Select Committee on Law Enforcement Problems*
    - *Criminal Justice Agencies in California*
    - Emerson, Thomas I. *The Bill of Rights Today*
    - *Experiments in Police Improvement—A Progress Report*
    - *Fourth United Nations Congress on the Prevention of Crime and the Treatment of Offenders*
    - Frederick, Calvin J. and Lague, Louise *Dealing with the Crisis of Suicide*
    - *International Review of Criminal Policy*
    - Kaplan, John *Criminal Justice: Introductory Cases and Materials*
    - *Legislative Guide for Drafting State-Local Programs on Juvenile Delinquency*
    - Lewis, Joseph H. *Evaluation of Experiments in Policing: How Do You Begin?* (Four Cases)
    - Morris, Norval and Hawkins, Gordon *The Honest Politician's Guide to Crime Control*
    - *Policewomen on Patrol (Major Findings: First Reports, Volume I)*
    - Rice, Robert *The Challenge of Crime*
    - Sax, Joseph L. *Law and Justice*
    - *Search and Seizure: A Statement of the Current Principles and Their Application*
    - Stewart, Maxwell S. *When People Need Help*
    - Sutherland, Edwin H. *On Analyzing Crime*
    - *Toward a Political Definition of Juvenile Delinquency*

- Zimring, Franklin E. and Hawkins, Gordon *Deterrence: The Legal Threat in Crime Control*

Burglary and Building Security Literature
- Kingbury, Arthur A. *Introduction to Security and Crime Prevention Surveys*
- *National Survey on Library Security*
- *Residential Security*

Community Involvement Literature
- *Better Ways to Help Youth—Three Youth Service Systems*
- Brayer, Herbert O. and Cleary, Zella W. *Valuing in the Family: A Workshop for Parents*
- Carter, Robert M. *Diversion of Offenders*
- Casper, Jonathan D. *Criminal Justice: The Consumer's Perspective*
- *The Community and Criminal Justice: A Guide for Organizing Action*
- *Community Services Coordination in Elementary Schools—Bring the Systems Together*
- *Delinquency Prevention Reporter—Perspectives on Delinquency Prevention Strategy*
- *Delinquency Prevention Reporter—Children Needing Help*
- *Delinquency Prevention Reporter—Youth Involvement*
- *Delinquency Prevention Reporter—Youth Services*
- Hewitt, William H. and Newman, Charles L. *Police Community Relations: An Anthology and Bibliography*
- *Modernizing Criminal Justice Through Citizen Power*
- Norman, Sherman *The Youth Service Bureau: A Key to Delinquency Prevention*
- Olson, H. C. and Carpenter, J. B. *Survey of Techniques Used to Reduce Vandalism and Delinquency in Schools*
- *Planning Guidelines and Programs to Reduce Crime*
- *Volunteers Help Youth*

Drug Abuse Literature
- *ALFY—A National Alternatives Strategy*
- *Alternative to Drugs*
- Cohen, Pauline *How to Help the Alcoholic*
- *A Community Program Guide: Drug Abuse Prevention*
- *Drug Abuse Prevention Materials for Schools*
- Erskine, Helen *Alcohol and the Criminal Justice System: Challenge and Response*
- *Here's Help*
- Smith, David E., Bentel, David J., and Schwartz, Jerome L. *The Free Clinic: A Community Approach to Health Care and Drug Abuse*

Although the reading of the above subject titles may have consumed more than a few seconds, it served to underscore a point—considerable ambiguity surrounds the meaning of crime prevention (note that the term crime *control* occurred more than once).

2. As a case in point relative to the differences in the connotations of crime prevention, the author, while serving as a rookie police officer in a major metropolitan police department, decided to engage his seasoned partner in a discussion of preventing crime. The author initiated the conversation by relating that he felt, "If society eliminated the opportunity to commit a crime, a lot fewer crimes would occur." The senior officer retorted that, "Crime would best be prevented if we would eliminate the criminal." The discussion ended at that point.

3. Evelle J. Younger, "Crime Prevention Concepts," *Crime Prevention Review* 1 (January 1974), p. 65.

4. *Community Crime Prevention*, 3–4.

5. A twofold dilemma occurs wtih this quotation. First, I cannot claim it as my own for fear that he will accuse me of stealing ideas. Second, I cannot reveal his identity for a more practical apprehension—he said definitely not to, and he is bigger than I am.

6. National Advisory Commission on Criminal Justice Standards and Goals, *Police* (Washington, D.C.: U.S. Government Printing Office, 1973), p. 66.

7. Daniel Katz and Robert Kahn, *The Social Psychology of Organizations* (New York: John Wiley and Sons, 1967), p. 29.

8. The majority of this thinking is derived from Edgar H. Schein, *Organizational Psychology*, 2d ed. (Englewood Cliffs, N.J.: Prentice-Hall, Inc., 1970), pp. 115–6.

9. President's Commission on Law Enforcement and Administration of Justice, *Task Force Report: Science and Technology* (Washington, D.C.: U.S. Government Printing Office, 1967), p. 53.

2

A Strategy to Prevent Crime: Goals and Priorities

New Courses–Same Destination

Goals for Crime Reduction

*The Commission proposes as a goal for the American people a 50%
reduction in high-fear crimes by 1983. It further proposes that crime
reduction efforts be concentrated on five crimes. The goals for the
reduction of these crimes should be:*

- Homicide: Reduced by at least 25% by 1983.
- Forcible Rape: Reduced by at least 25% by 1983.
- Aggravated Assault: Reduced by at least 25% by 1983.
- Robbery: Reduced by at least 50% by 1983.
- Burglary: Reduced by at least 50% by 1983.

Priorities for Action

*The Commission proposes four areas for priority action in reducing the
five target-crimes:*

- *Juvenile Delinquency.* The highest attention must be
  given to preventing juvenile delinquency and to minimizing the involvement of young offenders in the juvenile and
  criminal justice system, and to reintegrating juvenile
  offenders into the community.
- *Delivery of Social Services.* Public and private service
  agencies should direct their actions to improve the delivery
  of all social services to citizens, particularly to groups that
  contribute higher than average proportions of their numbers to crime statistics.
- *Prompt Determination of Guilt or Innocence.* Delays in
  the adjudication and disposition of criminal cases must be
  greatly reduced.
- *Citizen Action.* Increased citizen participation in activities

to control crime in their community must be generated, with active encouragement and support by criminal justice agencies.*

Preview

Among the many social ills present in our society, we find that crime receives a high degree of public concern. Indeed, in our urban centers the concern has grown to the point of anxiety. Some people have become prisoners within their own homes. We find many citizens expending large sums of money on devices that harden both business and home alike against being a target of the criminal offender. Our sense of insecurity, whether founded or not, is being translated into action-oriented strategies that are intended to reduce crime.

As with the vast majority of corrective programs, they tend to cost something. Any endeavor to permanently reduce crime will be expensive. As a nation we are currently expending close to $9 billion per year on criminal justice activities. Moreover, this figure will, of necessity, show sharp increases in the years to come. While a monetary figure has been emphasized, one should not forget the more significant cost—that of marshalling a citizenry that is committed to making our streets and homes safer from crime.

The more prominent crime reduction goals are seen above; they were not selected at random or on a whim. The underlying reasons for establishing these five crimes are that they are most feared and most violent. In turn, five high priority activities designed to affect the crimes are recommended. Not expressed above is the concept of coping with the energy crisis which we are told will be with us and affect criminal justice functions well into the 1980s. Although the issue of crime prevention is not overt, certainly it will play a paramount part in the various activities that comprise a priority item and thus subsequently the attainment of the stated goals. Together the goals provide a broad strategy to reduce the threat of crime in our nation.

* National Advisory Commission on Criminal Justice Standards and Goals, *A National Strategy to Reduce Crime* (Washington, D.C.: U.S. Government Printing Office, 1973), p. iii.

Crime and The Fear of Crime

Crime is not a recent factor in American life. Administrators, politicians, scholars, and commissions have over a long period of time documented the growth and complexity of the crime problem in the United States—its causes, and its destructive effects on this society. The likelihood of damage to a person's property and well being, and the fear of unprovoked, unpredictable violence are omnipresent. Clearly the crime about which the nation is bestirred, the kind of crime that is accelerating, is crime against property; and it is often attended by violence—robberies, larcenies, assaults, and thefts of all kinds. This is not to say that Americans are indifferent to other types of criminal offenses. There is, and should be, concern over such white-collar crimes as tax fraud or price fixing, the corruption of public officials, such victimless crimes as gambling or prostitution, and the lawlessness of collective violence. (See Figure 2.1.) We are, it appears, most upset about, and feel immediately threatened by, crimes against person and property—crimes we (you and I) fear we might fall victim to.

> Urban crime has created an atmosphere of unparalleled fear among this nation's citizenry. Seventy percent of the American people feel that law and order has broken down. Almost 60 percent consider that the control of crime in the streets of urban America is the number one domestic issue facing this country. A 1969 survey taken in Baltimore indicated that between 30 and 43 percent of the people lived in fear of being the victim of a street crime in their own neighborhood. Sixty percent of the residents of Baltimore's high crime districts considered it likely that they would be victimized by a criminal in their own community.[1]

The crime rate continues to climb, although there are a few bright spots we can point to where it has not increased as rapidly as in the past, or a brief and unexplained dip has occurred. (See Figure 2.2.) However, we must remind ourselves on occasion that crime statistics are reported rates only. For a number of reasons, we often bear the impact of crime in private. Many of us feel that the police are powerless to do anything about crime; consequently, researchers estimate that the actual number of forcible rapes is some three and one-half times the number reported to the police, and the actual rates for robbery, aggravated assault, burglary, and grand larceny range from 50 to 300 percent more than the reported figures.[2]

As an aside, there are currently two methods for measuring national crime rates: the Uniform Crime Report (UCR), compiled

COST OF CRIME—

NEARLY $90 BILLION A YEAR

Estimates of economic impact of crime per year –

TOTAL TAKE BY ORGANIZED CRIME FROM ILLEGAL·GOODS	
	Gambling
	$30.0 BIL.
	Narcotics
	$5.2 BIL.
	Hijacked goods
	$1.5 bil.
$37.2 BIL.	Interest from loan sharking
	$0.5 BIL.

CRIMES AGAINST PROPERTY AND BUSINESS (excluding organizad crime)	Embezzlement, fraud, forgery	$7.0 BIL.
	"Kickbacks" paid by business	$5.0 BIL.
	Unreported business thefts	$5.0 BIL.
$21.3 BIL.	Robbery, burglary, theft, shoplifting	$3.0 BIL.
	Vandalism, arson	$1.3 BIL.

OTHER CRIMES	Homicides, assaults (loss of earnings, medical costs)	$3.0 BIL.
$9.5 BIL.	Drunken driving (wage loss, medical costs of victims, property damage)	$6.5 BIL.

LAW-ENFORCEMENT COSTS	Police (federal, State, local)	$8.6 BIL.
	Penal system	$3.2 BIL.
$14.6 BIL.	Court system	$2.8 BIL.

PRIVATE CRIME-FIGHTING COSTS (cost of services and equipment)

$6.0 BIL.

TOTAL CRIME EXPENSE $88.6 BIL.

Source: Estimates by USN & WR Economic Unit. based on data from Government and industry.

Figure 2.1 A high price tag that everybody pays, *Source:* "A High Price Tag That Everybody Pays," *U.S. News and World Report*, (December 16, 1974), p. 32.

24

annually by the FBI, and the national victimization survey, developed by LEAA. The UCR has a fundamental limitation of being based on reports from police departments. Thus it enumerates only those crimes known to the police. Victimization surveys, made since 1966 in various cities, report that at least half of all crimes against persons and property are not reported to the police. Moreover, there have been findings that some local law enforce-

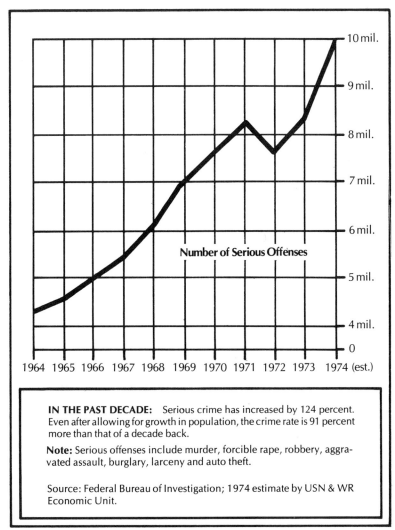

IN THE PAST DECADE: Serious crime has increased by 124 percent. Even after allowing for growth in population, the crime rate is 91 percent more than that of a decade back.

Note: Serious offenses include murder, forcible rape, robbery, aggravated assault, burglary, larceny and auto theft.

Source: Federal Bureau of Investigation; 1974 estimate by USN & WR Economic Unit.

Figure 2.2   Serious Crime: Speeding up again. *Source:* "The Losing Battle Against Crime In America," *U.S. News and World Report* (December 16, 1974), p. 31.

ment agencies have not recorded fully the extent of crimes that are reported by citizens, or have not accurately classified and defined reported offenses.[3] Consequently, the victimization survey is now believed by some practitioners to give a more precise estimate of the volume, type, and cost of crime than the UCR.

The growing threat of crime has caused more and more people to take concrete steps to protect themselves and their property. Testimony before the House Select Committee on Crime in July of 1969 sketched some manifestations of the public's reaction to fear of crime.[4]

- Nationally, private police outnumber public police by almost two to one.
- German shepherds have jumped in popularity on the American Kennel Club list from fourth to second.
- In Los Angeles, burglar alarm sales increased 40 to 60 percent in one year.
- In Seattle, a private security organization reported its business has increased 300 percent over a four-year period and 50 percent in the past year.
- Installation of security lighting increased nine-fold in three years in Dallas, Texas, with total costs estimated into the millions. Likewise, an Internal Revenue Service survey showed ammunition licenses increasing from 15,000 to 30,000 over the previous year.
- In Detroit, gun permits issued by police soared from 3,753 in 1964 to 16,167 in 1968.

This same testimony disclosed distressing behavioral changes as a result of increased fear about crime on the part of 1,545 residents of Baltimore who were surveyed in 1969 by Louis Harris Associates.

1. Fifty-five percent said they were keeping their house locked now, even when there were people at home.
2. Forty-seven percent said they were staying home in the evening.
3. Forty-five percent said they talked to callers through the door, rather than opening it.
4. Twenty-two percent said they watched out the window for suspicious strangers.
5. Forty-eight percent said they used the parks less in the evening for fear of crime.
6. Thirty-eight percent said they go out in the evening to eat or to a movie less often.

The Harris survey concluded that fear of crime is now producing in many American cities an epidemic of silent terror. No emotional or economic barometer is totally capable of measuring the fear of crime—but, one merely has to observe the rapid exodus from the cities, strangling businesses, and people mistrusting one another to realize that, regardless of the lack of a precise method to measure it, it is present! In conclusion, then, crime is with us; it has us frightened, and we seem more interested than ever before in mounting a counterattack. Significantly, a key feature of the counterattack includes the prevention of criminal behavior.

The Cost of Crime Reduction

Local governments continue to spend more than the federal and state governments combined for all criminal justice activities.*

While the *commission* of crime, the *reduction* of crime, and the *cost* of reducing crime are centered at the local government level, we can now see major federal and state efforts to assist them both directly and indirectly in coping with its adverse impacts on the citizens of this nation. Direct efforts are those programs and agencies such as the Federal Bureau of Investigation, Drug Enforcement Assistance Administration, state criminal investigation units, and the like. On an indirect basis, we find an infusion of funds to support state and local criminal justice planning, operational programs, and research projects. Briefly stated, federal and state governments have vastly expanded their commitment to reducing crime by direct intervention—and to sharing in its cost at the local level. The remainder of this section is devoted to an explication of dollar figures supporting this contention.

To start with, federal outlays for crime reduction more than doubled between the years of 1968 and 1971. By the end of fiscal year (FY) 1972, the amount spent on crime reduction programs more than tripled, reflecting the extent of the many and diverse crime reduction programs initiated and enlarged under the auspices of the federal government. It would appear that the magnitude of such doubling and tripling of fiscal allocations must eventually come to an end; however, it also seems reasonable to predict that yearly incremental increases in financial outlays to reduce crime certainly will be sustained during the 1970s.

* Law Enforcement Assistance Administration, *Expenditure and Employment Data for the Criminal Justice System: 1970–71* (Washington, D.C.: U.S. Government Printing Office, 1973), p. 1.

Federal outlays for crime reduction programs in FY 1971 totaled $1,348,204,000 which was more than was spent for those programs in FY 1970 ($856,916,000). In FY 1968, $530,643,000 was spent by the federal government, and in FY 1969, $658,353,000. (See Table 2.1 for finite expenditure data.) Of the FY 1972 expenditures, 36 percent was directed to assisting state and local governments, compared with 31 percent in FY 1971, and 21 percent in FY 1970.

A study completed in 1972 showed that almost $8.6 billion was spent on all forms of law enforcement and criminal justice in the United States in the 12 months ending June 30, 1970.[5] The survey covered expenditures of the federal, state, and local govern-

Table 2.1 Federal outlays for the reduction of crime by agency

[In thousands of dollars]

Agency	Outlays	
	Fiscal year 1971 actual	Fiscal year 1972 estimate
The Judiciary	$ 60,703	$ 76,132
Executive Office of the President	—	2,800
Office of Economic Opportunity	15,500	18,200
Department of Agriculture	4,511	4,665
Department of Commerce	800	1,100
Department of Health, Education, and Welfare	98,510	166,197
Department of Housing and Urban Development	17,228	26,450
Department of the Interior	22,916	25,104
Department of Justice	742,641	1,043,907
Department of Labor	14,373	32,700
Department of State	53,598	141,771
Department of Transportation	38,958	51,497
Department of the Treasury	167,894	228,592
Atomic Energy Commission	104	—
General Services Administration	38,513	43,551
National Aeronautics and Space Administration	1,342	987
Postal Service	32,654	39,054
Veterans Administration	37,560	66,034
Other independent agencies	399	255
Total Federal Outlays	$1,348,204	$1,968,996

Source: Office of Management and Budget (1972).

ments and reflected the full-time employment of almost 753,000 persons. The study showed that about $5 billion, or almost three-fifths of the total, was spent as follows: almost $1.2 billion for judicial activities; almost $442 billion for prosecution; $102 billion for indigent defense; $1.7 billion for corrections; and $50 million for other criminal justice agencies.

A more comprehensive and updated version of the above study was conducted in 1973.[6] It revealed that in 1970 local governments accounted for 63.0 percent of all direct criminal justice expenditure ($10,513 million), while state governments contributed 25.5 percent, and the federal government contributed 11.5 percent. (See Table 2.2.) However, when each activity is examined separately, the proportion accounted for by the different levels of government varies throughout the criminal justice system. Three of the activities—police protection, judicial and legal services, and prosecution—are supported mainly by local governments; the federal government is the principal supporter of indigent defense; while state governments are the largest supporters of correction and those activities included in the other criminal justice sector.

Proportions similar to those found for expenditure among the levels of government also hold for the employment situation. Table 2.3 shows that two-thirds of the total full-time equivalent criminal justice employees of all governments are employed by local governments. In general, the level of government which expends the largest percentage of the total expenditure for an activity also employs the greatest number of workers for that activity. The area of indigent defense is an exception to this pattern due to the extensive use of private counsel systems whereby fees are paid private counsel to defend indigent clients accused of crimes.

Goals for Crime Reduction

Our existing social problems and the costs associated with them necessitate a two pronged response. First, we should approach the crime problem with realistic optimism—realism in the sense that we should clearly understand its gravity and the level of effort required to successfully combat it; and optimism in that we should be firmly convinced of our ability to do so. Second, we should set definitive and attainable goals—definitive to the extent that the goals aim our resources toward the desired ends; and attainable in that, while challenging, they are capable of being accomplished within an established time-frame. I am asserting, therefore, that our nation can reduce the social and economic damage caused by

Table 2.2 Criminal justice expenditures, by type of expenditure and level of government, fiscal year 1972

[Dollar amounts in thousands]

Activity	Amount				Percent distribution		
	All governments	Federal Government	State governments	Local governments	Federal Government	State governments	Local governments
Total criminal justice system[a]	$11,721,194	$1,873,217	$3,341,507	$7,372,509	X	X	X
Direct expenditure	11,721,194	1,491,855	2,948,091	7,281,248	12.7	25.2	62.1
Intergovernmental expenditure	(a)	381,362	393,416	91,261	X	X	X
Police protection[a]	6,903,304	963,108	1,048,094	4,978,854	X	X	X
Direct expenditure	6,903,304	962,149	992,801	4,948,354	13.9	14.4	71.7
Intergovernmental expenditure	(a)	959	55,293	30,500	X	X	X
Judicial[a]	1,490,649	179,099	371,014	973,918	X	X	X
Direct expenditure	1,490,649	179,099	346,290	965,260	12.0	23.2	64.8
Intergovernmental expenditure	(a)	—	24,724	8,658	X	X	X
Legal services and prosecution[a]	580,381	107,071	127,879	350,150	X	X	X
Direct expenditure	580,381	107,071	124,959	348,351	18.5	21.5	60.0
Intergovernmental expenditure	(a)	—	2,920	1,799	X	X	X
Indigent defense[a]	167,630	80,237	25,571	63,573	X	X	X
Direct expenditure	167,630	80,237	23,963	63,430	47.9	14.3	37.8
Intergovernmental expenditure	(a)	—	1,608	143	X	X	X
Correction[a]	2,422,330	146,491	1,467,524	961,338	X	X	X
Direct expenditure	2,422,330	133,272	1,377,776	911,282	5.5	56.9	37.6
Intergovernmental expenditure	(a)	13,219	89,748	50,056	X	X	X
Other criminal justice[a]	156,900	397,211	301,425	44,676	X	X	X
Direct expenditure	156,900	30,027	82,302	44,571	19.1	52.5	28.4
Intergovernmental expenditure	(a)	367,184	219,123	105	X	X	X

[a] The total line for each sector, and for the total criminal justice system, excludes duplicative intergovernmental expenditure amounts. This was done to avoid the artificial inflation which would result if an intergovernmental expenditure amount for one government is tabulated and then counted again when the recipient government(s) ultimately expend(s) that amount. The intergovernmental expenditure lines are not totaled for the same reason.

Source: U.S. Department of Justice, Law Enforcement Assistance Administration. "Expenditure and Employment Data for the Criminal Justice System, 1971–72." January 1974, p. 11.

Source: Law Enforcement Assistance Administration, Sourcebook of Criminal Justice Statistics—1974 (Washington, D.C., U.S. Government Printing Office, 1975), p. 33.

Table 2.3 Percent of full-time equivalent employment in the criminal justice system by activity and level of government: October 1971

Level of government	Total	Police protection activities	Judicial activities	Prosecution activities	Indigent defense activities	Correction activities	Other activities
Total	100.0	100.0	100.0	100.0	100.0	100.0	100.0
Federal	9.0	10.7	6.9	14.2	1.5	4.0	26.0
State	23.9	13.1	18.5	20.5	28.1	58.9	51.3
Local	67.1	76.2	74.6	65.3	70.5	37.1	22.7

Source: Law Enforcement Assistance Adiminstration, *Expenditure and Employment Data for the Criminal Justice System: 1970–71* (Washington, D.C., U.S. Government Printing Office, 1972), p. 2.

all forms of crime.[7] It is also proposed that certain types of crimes threaten you and me and the very existence of a just and civilized society. It would seem that the rate of these crimes can be studied and controlled—they are the violent crimes of murder and non-negligent manslaughter, forcible rape, robbery, and aggravated assault and the property crime of burglary.

Why These
Crimes?

The five crimes cited above are particularly grave when perpetrated by one stranger on another.[8] In such instances, an extra dimension is present—fear. Thus, when these crimes are committed by strangers, they can be termed as "high-fear" crimes. However, violent "people" crimes and the "property" crime of burglary are equally as serious when committed by offenders known to the victim. (If I point a gun at you, or your brother, sister, wife, or husband does so, are you any less threatened?)

As we saw earlier, the National Advisory Commission proposed a two-level attack on these five crimes. First, the rate of "high-fear" (stranger-related) crimes should be cut in half by 1983. Second, regardless of whether the crime is committed by a relative, acquaintance, or stranger, the crime rates should be cut by 1983 as follows:

- Homicide (murder and nonnegligent manslaughter)—at least 25 percent.
- Forcible rape—at least 25 percent.
- Aggravated assault—at least 25 percent.
- Robbery—at least 50 percent.
- Burglary—at least 50 percent.

The Commission admits that the selection of these crimes and percentages of reduction will arouse the doubts of skeptics, but they submit that their proposed crime reduction goals are reasonable. They define what we can hope for, not necessarily what we can expect.

Why Set
Quantitative
Goals?

The use of numerical values gives a dimension to goal-setting that has been lacking in prior recommendations for reducing crime. Previously, government reports and political leaders have spoken in broad terms such as: crime should be controlled and reduced; administration of the criminal justice system should be improved; public expenditures on the system should be increased; Americans should redouble their efforts to eliminate the causes of crime, such as poverty, discrimination, urban blight, and disease;

planning should be improved; additional research should be undertaken; citizens should become more involved; and so forth. Regrettably, these broad statements do not easily translate into action. What, for example, does it mean to say that crime should be reduced? Which crimes? What is to be reduced—the rate, the actual number, the economic and social impact, or something else? How great a reduction is possible? How great a reduction is acceptable? How do state and local governments, criminal justice agencies, and citizens go about realizing these goals? And how is it possible to tell if a goal has been achieved?

These are not rhetorical questions. They have real implications in time, dollars, and lives. Goals are most helpful when they are measurable, when at the end of a specific period actual *achievements* can be compared with desired *achievements* and an assessment of the reasons for gaps can be made. For citizens, goals to reduce crime serve as a yardstick for measuring the effectiveness of criminal justice operations and other public service programs. For legislators, goals are guides to funding; for operating agencies, they provide a rationale for the allocation of men and equipment.

Priorities: Ranked Ordered Activities Intended to Achieve Goals

The five *high priority crimes* create a need for *high priority programs* that are capable of reducing them. Thus, five priorities for action are proposed:

- Preventing juvenile delinquency
- Improving delivery of social services
- Reducing delays in the criminal justice process
- Securing more citizen participation in the criminal justice system
- Minimizing the adverse impact of short-term crises (energy crisis, for example) on the criminal justice system.

These priorities are, or will be, more congruent with crime prevention as compared to crime control programs. More important, however, is that they hold for us a reasonable hope of accomplishing the goals expressed in the preceding section.

Priority: Preventing Juvenile Delinquency

The highest attention must be given to preventing juvenile delinquency, to minimizing the involvement of young offenders in the juvenile and criminal justice system, and to reintegrating them into the community. By 1983 the rate of delinquency cases coming before the courts involving offenses that would be crimes if committed by adults should be cut to half the 1973 rate.

We have numerical evidence that street crime is primarily a young person's caper. More than half the persons arrested for violent crime in 1971 were under 24 years of age, with one-fifth being under 18. For burglary, over half of the 1971 arrests involved youths under 18. Moreover, we have statistical data showing that the majority of ordinary crimes against person and property is committed by young people who have had *previous contact* with the CJS or juvenile justice system. Increased efforts must be made to intervene in this cycle of recidivism at the earliest possible point. One approach is to reduce the time involvement of the offender in the CJS. "Minimized involvement" is not a euphemism for the coddling of criminals. It merely means that we should use the means of controlling and supervising the criminal offender that will best serve to extricate him from the recidivism cycle and, at the same time, protect the community. Hard data purports that: the further and the longer an offender penetrates into the criminal justice process, the more difficult it becomes to divert him from the CJS in the future.

We tend to learn from those closest to us. Regrettably, prisons and jails for juveniles, first offenders, and hardened criminals have been found to be "schools of crime." Also, we tend to become what we are told or expect to be. The stigma of involvement with the CJS, even if only in the informal processes of juvenile justice, separates persons from lawful society and can make further training or employment difficult. A survey conducted in 1972 for the Department of Labor revealed that an arrest record served as an absolute bar to employment in almost 20 percent of the state and local agencies surveyed and was a definite consideration for not hiring in most of the remaining agencies.

The U.S. Department of Health, Education, and Welfare, which collects information on juvenile courts, estimates that about 40 percent of cases disposed of by courts, are cases of running away, truancy, and other offenses termed "status crimes" that would not be crimes if committed by an adult.[9] As indicated, these are referred to as juvenile status offenses. The remaining 60-odd percent of cases estimated to be disposed of by juvenile or family courts are nonstatus crimes (or those that would be crimes if committed by adults). It is the rate of these cases which the National Advisory Commission proposes to cut in half by 1983. We can hope, therefore, that in meeting this goal significant decreases in crime will occur. Further, preventing recidivism may prove less costly than dealing with delinquents under present methods. *To process a youth through the juvenile justice system and to keep* *him in a training school for a year costs almost $6,000.* Currently there is no reason for us to believe that the cost of a diversionary program would exceed this figure, since most such programs are not residential. In fact, we may find that diversion provides significant savings.

Minimizing a young person's involvement with the CJS does not mean eliminating the use of confinement for certain individuals. Until we can develop more effective and lasting means of "treatment," dangerous delinquents and offenders should be closely secured in order to protect society.

Priority: Improving Delivery of Social Services

Public agencies should improve the delivery of all social services to citizens, particularly to those groups that contribute higher than average proportions of their numbers to crime statistics.

We are confronted with irrefutable proof that crime occurs with greater frequency where poverty, illiteracy, and unemployment exist, and where medical, recreational, and mental health resources are deficient. When unemployment rates among our youth in poverty areas of central cities are well above the norm, crime is omnipresent. It is impossible for us not to draw conclusions about the interdependency between jobs and crime. Does anyone doubt that the effective and responsive delivery of public services dealing with our individual economic well-being will contribute to a reduction in crime?

Undoubtedly, a meaningful and lasting improvement of social services to the degree necessary to abate crime will take years and not a few months. Building career education programs into elementary and secondary school curricula, for example, cannot be accomplished in the next 2 or 3 years; but we must start now if our nation is to attain desired benefits at the end of 10 years or more. Likewise, our communities must accept and adjust to the diversity of drug abuse and alcohol problems, and the need for a variety of alternative treatment tactics. We must be willing to meet the costs of such treatment—not only because it will lessen crime, but also because effective treatment is fundamental to attacking an increasingly serious national health problem.

Priority: Reducing Delays in the Criminal Justice Process

Delays in the adjudication and disposition of cases must be greatly reduced and the period between arrest and trial must be reduced to the shortest possible time.

In recent years, backlogs and delays in our courts have been repeatedly exposed. Many courts in large cities and countries have professed delays of 300 to 1,000 days from arrest to trial and final disposition. Our legislatures, as well as judges, defense attorneys, and prosecutors, must assume some of the responsibility for this problem. Inordinate sluggishness in the criminal justice process corrodes law enforcement efforts and in turn creates a feeling of injustice in offender, victim, and citizen alike.

The harmful effects of judicial delays are significant. The number of defendants temporarily in jail and awaiting trial has reached dangerous proportions, and holding facilities are inadequate and overcrowded. The LEAA National Jail Census in 1970 revealed for us that 52 percent of the jail inmates were awaiting trial. Pretrial incarceration is costly to the individual, for it precludes his earning an income and, in fact, may cause him to lose his job. Extended incarceration caused by judicial delay is also costly to us as taxpayers, since pretrial detainees must be housed and supervised.

The pressures of heavy backlogs are linked to the controversial practice of *plea bargaining*. When confronted with an overwhelming caseload, we often find prosecutors seeking to avoid time-consuming trials by disposing of felony indictment (through negotiated guilty pleas) to less serious felonies or misdemeanors. Whether we view this situation from a rehabilitation, deterrence, or workload perspective, plea bargaining is a low visibility practice that can be gradually stopped if less burdensome court caseloads are achieved.

Expediting the CJS processes, however, will not reduce crime by itself; but, when we tie it to the more effective treatment alternatives and intelligent correctional decisions, it should have an advantageous result. Additional judges are urgently needed in many jurisdictions today. Yet, much can be done to improve our existing adjudicatory process by merely improving court management.

Priority:
Increasing
Citizen
Participation

Citizens should participate in activities to control crime in their community, and criminal justice agencies should actively encourage citizen participation.

Out of necessity, the CJS relies on citizen participation.[10] The majority of crimes do not come directly to the attention of our police; they are reported by you and me. After all, without the active cooperation of citizen jurors and witnesses, our judicial process cannot operate. Further, institutional education and training programs will not be helpful to the offender if he cannot find employment in the community when he is released. Moreover, our best-trained and equipped police agencies will continue to fail in combating crime if we do not take basic precautionary measures to protect ourselves by reducing our vulnerability to crime.

Some of us may have or are now organizing to form block crime prevention associations and court-watching groups, and to furnish volunteers to work in the CJS. One example of our concern is a nationwide program that began with the involvement of a few citizens in Royal Oak, Michigan. The Volunteers in Probation program grew from eight citizens in 1959 to an estimated quarter of a million people (nationwide) in 1972. The Royal Oak concept utilizes volunteers and professionals together. Statistics are indicating that volunteers and professionals, in combination, can provide probation services that are three times more effective than those furnished by a probation officer working alone.[11]

Our cooperation with *our* police has great potential, but is underdeveloped at the present. In 1970, 18 percent of the households in the United States adopted some form of home protection —special locks, lights, alarms, watchdogs, and/or weapons.[12] Cannot our police agencies perform a useful service by actively disseminating its crime prevention knowledge to citizens? It is not necessary to "sell" self-protection to most of us, certainly not to those of us who have been victimized. Nevertheless, in many jurisdictions, there is an absence of outreach programs for crime prevention.

All of our CJS agencies can do much in their operations to entice us to support their activities. This suggests, for example, that our police *can* process citizen complaints efficiently and courteously; that courts *can* minimize the time lost by jurors and witnesses; that corrections *can* operate its institutions to permit the community reasonable access to those incarcerated. *These are minimums.* Criminal justice agenies can do much more, if they earnestly attempt to: explain their role to you and me; and depict how we can participate in community crime prevention. But first, our criminal justice agencies *must understand* and *respect* us and the communities they serve.

Priority: Minimizing the Adverse Impact of The Energy Crisis on The Criminal Justice System

There is a lack of pertinent information on the many effects of a sudden energy shortage as it relates to criminal activities. Literature on causes of criminal activities cite the usual variables as being population density, ethnographic composition, unemployment, average income, law enforcement funding, and technology. Therefore, the probable effects of the energy reduction on criminal activity are the development of additional adverse environmental conditions such as: reduced lighting, transportation problems, petroleum-derived product unavailability, and increased unemployment. Hence, it is imperative that both short and long range studies be conducted to develop appropriate counter-measures.

In his celebrated book, *Future Shock,* Alvin Toffler strongly warns us to be prepared for rapid changes in our social and technological environment.[13] He refers to the future as invading our individual and organizational lives at a constantly accelerating pace. The energy crisis is clearly one case in point. Granted, there are a few—very few—sages who can say "I told you so" in regard to the global energy shortage. Yet, it is with us now and ostensibly *will be into the 1980s.* More pertinent to our interests, at this point, is the fact that any curtailment of energy will have an impact on the CJS/C; and, the impact looks to be considerably more adverse than helpful. This is the rationale for adding a fifth priority dealing with the consequences of limited energy supplies.

Steps have been taken to abate any injurious effects that the energy shortage may hold for the CJS/C. For one example, a new clearinghouse for information on crime related to the energy crisis has been established by the National Criminal Justice Reference Service under LEAA. As mentioned above, an immediate and extensive short and long range countermeasure study should be implemented.[14] Table 2.4 presents an overview of energy related problems and recommended areas of study.

A Moment of Reflection

In your judgment, are the recommended goals, the recommended priorities, and the concept of crime prevention compatible? If you think that they are, then there is *no* problem. But, if you believe that they are in juxtaposition (or worse, still contradictory to one another), then what?

Would you agree to some extent that the proposed goals are: (1) specific in terms of percentages and time-frame, and (2) grossly demanding of the existing police, court, and correction resources? Similarly, would you concur that to some extent the priorities are meaningful yet difficult to relate to the goals? Or for that matter, are you convinced that the reduction of forcible rape by 25 percent by 1983 is dependent on improving our CJS capability for: preventing juvenile delinquency, delivering mental health services, prompt determination of guilt or innocence, involving the citizenry in crime prevention, or adjusting to the energy (or other) problems? I am convinced of the validity of the interrelationship of the goals, the priorities, and crime prevention! What tends to bother me is that I have little empirical evidence for such a conclusion beyond the fact that it allows me to feel more intuitively

Table 2.4 Crime countermeasures necessitated by the energy crisis

Main Problem	Affected Phenomena	Criminal Justice System	Crime Environments	Recommended Studies
• Oil Shortage	• Lighting		• Public Facilities	• Minimal Illumination For Security
		• Law Enforcement	• Residences	• Public Facility Lighting Strategy
				• Harden Selected Public Facilities
				• Blackout Emergency Security
	• Transportation	• Courts	• Schools	• Crime Model For Deterring Change In Criminal Activities
	• Petroleum Products	• Corrections	• Commercial Areas	• Deter Organized Crime
	• Heating/Air Conditioning			• Public Facility Low Energy Alarm Systems
	• Unemployment		• Transportation Systems	• Law Enforcement Modifications

Source: California Crime Technological Research Foundation, (1974) Sacramento, California

comfortable in regard to my own, as well as others', individual safety from being the victim of a crime.

Endnotes

1. Special Committee on Crime Prevention and Control, *New Perspectives on Urban Crime* (Washington, D.C.: American Bar Association, 1972), p. 2.
2. For details on victimization studies see National Advisory Commission on Criminal Justice Standards and Goals, *Criminal Justice System* (Washington, D.C.: U.S. Government Printing Office, 1973), pp. 199–206.
3. The usefulness of officially reported crime statistics has been widely debated. Doubts have been expressed as to how accurately UCR data can show the extent of and changes in crime. After careful study, a task force of the Violence Commission concluded, "For individual acts of violence covered by national police statistics, limitations on the accuracy of the data are apparent." Such limitations affect understanding of the levels, trends, incidence, and severity of crime. Mulvihill and Tumin, *Crimes of Violence*, pp. 16–38.
4. As reported in the Special Committee on Crime Prevention and Control, *op cit.,* pp. 3–4.
5. Law Enforcement Assistance Administration, *Expenditure and Employment Data for the Criminal Justice System: 1969–70* (Washington, D.C.: U.S. Government Printing Office, 1972).
6. Law Enforcement Assistance Administration, *Expenditure and Employment Data for the Criminal Justice System: 1970–71* (Washington, D.C.: U.S. Government Printing Office, 1973).
7. The remainder of this and the subsequent section are drawn in part from the National Advisory Commission on Criminal Justice Standards and Goals, *A National Strategy to Reduce Crime* (Washington, D.C.: U.S. Government Printing Office, 1973), pp. 7–10.
8. Ibid. In making its judgment on goals for crime reduction, the National Advisory Commission considered in depth many factors. It is impossible to list all of the factors, although the Commission believes that among the most important are the following:
   * Characteristics of the target crimes
   * Socioeconomic changes
   * Changes in public attitudes
   * Public support for the criminal justice system
   * New methods of measuring progress.
9. A provocative policy statement on this subject is made by

the Board of Directors, National Council on Crime and Delinquency, "Jurisdiction Over Status Offenses Should Be Removed from the Juvenile Court: A Policy Statement," *Crime and Delinquency* 21 (April 1975), pp. 97–99.

10. One case in point is presented by Gary T. Marx and Dave Archer, "Citizen Involvement in the Law Enforcement Process,"*American Behavioral Scientist* 15 (September/October, 1971), pp. 52–72.

11. For details on the Royal Oak Project, see the National Advisory Commission on Criminal Justice Standards and Goals, *Report on Community Crime Prevention* (Washington, D.C.: U.S. Government Printing Office, 1973).

12. This data is contained in an unpublished survey conducted by Law Enforcement Assistance Administration in 1970.

13. Alvin Toffler, *Future Shock* (New York: Random House, 1970).

14. Two relevant documents on the energy crisis as it might pertain to the criminal justice system are: (1) Office of Criminal Justice Planning, Application for Grant to Office of Emergency Services, Title: *Fuel Curtailment Impact on Public Safety and Criminal Justice* January 10, 1974; and (2) Office of Science and Technology, State of California, *Energy Research and Development Program for California* January 9, 1974.

PART TWO

Police Crime Prevention

I am committed to the view that the basic function of the police is to help society maintain, in a democratic manner, the degree of order which is an indispensible condition of life in a complex society. This role includes the identification and apprehension of criminal offenders. It implies an ambiguous and broad role of human service which only the police can perform and which is vital to the health of our communities. It also implies a commitment to develop and implement programs that will prevent crime.

It is in this last responsibility that the police and our society have been particularly deficient.*

Mr. Cizanckas (Chief of Police, Menlo Park Police Department) finds measurable and growing concurrence over his above assertion. Fortunately, the International Association of Chiefs of Police (IACP) is an active participant in fostering such thinking. Significantly, the IACP has a select committee dedicated to the subject of crime prevention. Labeled as the Crime Prevention Committee, it: (1) investigates and studies all conditions and situations which induce and encourage crime, develop anti-social attitudes, foster civil disturbances, and generally contribute to juvenile delinquency, (2) considers and evaluates ongoing programs, (3) develops techniques and methods for the interchange of information and ideas relating to crime prevention between police agencies, (4) and reports to the IACP for dissemination to all pertinent agencies the information and recommendations relating to prac-

---

* Victor I. Cizanckas, "Perspectives on Crime Prevention," *Crime Prevention Review* 1 (October, 1973), p. 1.

tical crime prevention programs and legislation that will assist them in establishing effective programs within their jurisdictions.

In 1972 this committee expressed strong feelings concerning the involvement of the public in crime prevention. It was indicated that the much used word "involvement" has never been more important than it is today. The police are in need of people who will come forward and testify to what they have observed—people who recognize their obligation to report crimes and suspicious circumstances. This lack of witnesses is one of the most serious deterrents to successful prosecution. While we are constantly providing more money and more manpower to the law enforcement agencies, the legislative bodies do not furnish the real tools needed by the prosecution; mainly, how to get witnesses to testify to facts within their knowledge. The Committee decided to study this problem and make recommendations on the type of legislation that would solve the problem.

The Committee recently emphasized that the reporting of crimes is a problem not limited to individuals.* Two areas of major concern are the reluctance of schools and businesses to report crime to the police. School administrators in many instances feel that school problems (including many crimes) should be handled within the school without any outside assistance. Business must also assume a greater role in crime prevention. It is important that as much detail and identification as possible be obtained when reporting a crime; an active rather than a passive role of crime prevention must be undertaken by all segments of society. The shoplifting epidemic being experienced by the nation's retail outlets has forced the necessity of business/police cooperation into the spotlight. Many businesses still do not treat shoplifting as a crime and feel calling in the police will only be bad for business. Not only does shoplifting force higher prices, but also it can easily cause a business to fail. The programs in use to educate the public, and the need for police and private security forces to coordinate their efforts should be expanded to other jurisdictions. Finally, in 1972 the Crime Prevention Committee voiced their support for the use of paraprofessionals. Paraprofessionals in public work afford an opportunity for the police department to enlarge its role in the community by providing increased service to citizens while freeing sworn officers from tasks which, although important to the community, do not require professional attention. Such a program can

*An overview of the Committee's annual deliberations can be found in the *Police Yearbook* (Gaithersburg, Md.: International Association of Chiefs of Police).

also assist untrained men and women to become qualified for police service.

Part Two expands on these concepts. Chapter 3 deals with the crucial role that the police should assume in congealing crime prevention efforts. Next, Chapter 4 discusses what can be done to effectively elicit the support of the community in their own self-defense through assisting the police in preventing crime. Chapter 5 is devoted to a review of a particular mode for organizing crime prevention activities—team policing. Subsequently, Chapter 6 examines the significance and benefits of crime prevention planning. The planning process is looked upon as being comprised of three different types (environmental, internal, and tactical) and phases (program development, expected results, and estimated resources). Chapters 7 and 8 present a variety of crime prevention programs that range along a hardware-peopleware continuum, from one pole to the other. The programs are depicted in sufficient detail that they should be easily related to existing real-world work environments. Thus, in the main, Part Two begins with a conceptual and descriptive approach, and ends with a highly pragmatical and prescriptive format.

3

The Police Role

*History has left us a bewildering hodgepodge of contradictory roles
that the police are expected to perform. We may well ask, for example,
are the police to be concerned with peacekeeping or crimefighting?
The blind enforcers of the law or the discretionary agents of a benevo-
lent government? Social workers with guns or gunmen in social work?
Facilitators of social change or defenders of the "faith?" The enforcers
of the criminal law or society's legal trash bin? A social agency of last
resort after 5:00 P.M. or mere watchmen for business and industry?*

*Actually, the police are expected to do all those things and become
all things to all people, at once the confessor and the inquisitor, the
friend of all yet the armed nemesis of some. Supermen, not men, could
do all these things; but, the theory of supermen was practiced three
decades ago, and the civilized world is the less for it.*

*In sum, the public had developed such high expectations of its
police that those expectations moved beyond reality to something that
could be better described as faith. As the public came to have faith in
the police to do all things, the police came to have faith that they
could do all things; when disillusionment set in, the singers lost faith in
the song, in each other, and in themselves.*

*If we are to restore any semblance of faith in the police by the public
—and the police themselves—we must begin first by defining the
police role very carefully so that it does not distort reality. The
historical definition of the police role eventually achieved this regret-
table result by fostering the belief that police, because they were
present and visible twenty-four hours a day, could function as a gigantic
surrogate service agency to the community handling all the needs of
the people all of the time.*

*To establish credibility or faith in the police service requires that the
police role be delineated so that there are reasonable expectations
about what the police should do and can do.**

---

* Bernard L. Garmire, "The Police Role in an Urban Society," in *The Police
and the Community*, Robert F. Steadman, ed. (Baltimore, Md.: The Johns
Hopkins University Press, 1972), pp. 2–3.

Preview

Practitioner, policy-maker, and scholar alike are disturbed over the lack of clarity and inordinate conflict in the police role. There is considerable ambiguity over what the police ought to be doing, and what they are presently doing—crimefighting and peacekeeping—creates an intolerable state of tension for the role occupant. Currently, it appears that the only common thread holding the role together is the use of force. Effective crimefighting and peacekeeping require that actual or potential force is available and legitimately implementable by the police officer.

Any endeavor to define the police role must take into account that: (1) the police officer has broad decision-making powers, (2) the police are often expected to (and do) provide services that are atypical of the traditional concept of their role, (3) the police have a major influence on the CJS since they determine if a person will or will not enter into its processes, and (4) the police are daily the most visible representatives of our governmental system. Three fundamental steps are necessary in order for us to accurately identify, comprehend, and concur with the police role. First, the police chief and sheriff, in cooperation with appropriate governing bodies, must express clearly in written terms the parameters of their mission and the general methods by which it will be performed. Second, once defined, the police personnel must be instructed fully in both the expected objectives to be attained *and* the expected behavior deemed prudent for their accomplishment. Third, a massive program must be developed and maintained informing the public of: what they can reasonably expect of their police, what the police can reasonably expect of them, and what both parties can do to modify the mutual set of expectations.

Role Conflict: Built-in Antagonisms

Of the many problems plaguing the police, that of role definition should be placed at the top of a list of present challenges. The term "role" means a specific type of behavior that is to be expected from an individual who occupies a particular position. For example, we expect medical doctors to manifest dedication and empathy in curing our ills. Further, we expect members of the clergy to express a religious fervor over the dissemination of the "word." All of this is to say that once inserted into an organizational position, a person learns that he is expected to evidence a set of behaviors. Most positions, fortunately, contain congruent expectations; we do not expect the medical doctor simultaneously to behave in such a way that he attempts to heal us and bury us. The position of police officer, however, lacks congruency. In fact, there is considerable role ambiguity (and worse yet, role conflict) inherent in the position. First of all, there is the question, "What do you want me to do as a police officer?" The answer commonly has been, "Everything." Hence, the second question, " 'Everything' implies crimefighting and peacekeeping, *but* how can one be expected to fulfill two roles which, by their very nature, are antagonistic?"

One study described the problem of role clarification as follows:

> Recognition of how policemen actually spend their time points up that the policeman suffers from role conflict. He wants to function as a crime fighter, but does not. He is not trained or rewarded for being a peace keeper or community service agent. His quasi-judicial role is poorly differentiated. He works on the one hand in an autonomous situation on the street, but on the other hand is supposed to be highly responsive to a chain of command. All these issues engender role conflict in the policeman.[1]

In yet another study, the American Bar Association proposed a standard concerning the role of the police officer.

> The nature of police operations makes the patrolman a more important figure than is implied by his rank in the organization. He exercises broad discretion in a wide array of situations, each of which is potentially of great importance, under conditions that allow for little supervision and review. Even with the controls recommended in these standards, in the interest of developing a police profession as well as in the interest of improving the quality of police operations generally, the patrolman himself should understand the important and complex needs of policing in a free society and have a commitment to meeting those needs.[2]

Finally, Egon Bittner views this problem thusly:

> Because the idea that the police are basically a crimefighting agency has never been challenged in the past, no one has troubled to sort out the remaining priorities. Instead, the police have always been forced to justify activities that did not involve law enforcement in the direct sense of either linking them constructively to law enforcement or by defining them as nuisance demands for service. The dominance of this

view, especially in the minds of policemen, has two pernicious consequences. First, it leads to a tendency to view all sorts of problems as if they involved culpable offenses and to an excessive reliance on quasi-legal methods for handling them. The widespread use of arrests without intent to prosecute exemplifies this state of affairs. These cases do not involve errors in judgment about the applicability of a penal norm but deliberate pretense resorted to because more appropriate methods of handling problems have not been developed. Second, the view that crime control is the only serious, important, and necessary part of police work has deleterious effects on the morale of those police officers in the uniformed patrol who spend most of their time with other matters. No one, especially he who takes a positive interest in his work, likes being obliged to do things day-in and day-out that are disparaged by his colleagues. Moreover, the low evaluation of these duties leads to neglecting the development of skill and knowledge that are required to discharge them properly and efficiently.[3]

Dr. Bittner went on, however, to propose that there is a common bonding agent that links the two opposing roles together and consequently serves as justification for their coexistence within a single position.

Because only a small part of the activity of the police is dedicated to law enforcement, and because they deal with the majority of their problems without invoking the law, a broader definition of their role was proposed. After reviewing briefly what the public appears to expect of the police, the range of activities police actually engage in, and the theme that unifies all these activities, it was suggested that *the role of the police is best understood as a mechanism for the distribution of non-negotiably coercive force.*[4]

Role Clarification: Coping with Complexity

The police in the United States are not (or should not be) separate from the people.[5] Therefore, some alternative approaches for creating a productive relationship between the people and their police will be described.

To a police officer, public service is indeed more than an obscure concept. When we need help, it is to a police officer that we are most likely to turn. He responds—immediately (we hope)—without first ascertaining the status of the person in need.

Decision Makers   Our police officers are discretionary decision makers. A decision—whether to arrest, to make a referral, to seek prosecution, or to use force—has a profound impact on those of us the police officer serves. Most of these decisions are consummated within a few moments and within the context of the most serious social problems. Yet, we find that the police officer is just as accountable for these decisions as the judge or corrections official is for decisions he deliberates for months. Moreover, the function that the police officer performs in our society is a demanding one; he must understand clearly the complexity of social relationships to be effective.

The specific goals and priorities that our police establish, within the limits of their legislatively granted authority, are determined to a large extent by community interests. These interests are transmitted to our police through the community and the governing body of the jurisdiction in which the police operate. For example, elements of the community might seek increased patrols around schools, stricter enforcement of parking regulations in congested areas, or reduced enforcement activities against certain crimes. The priorities established by our police agencies in such cases are often affected more by the "influences" of those policed than by any other consideration. Our police officers are, therefore, accountable to us for their decisions.

Delegated Responsibility

Under our form of government, police power is exercised by the states and their political subdivisions in the formalization of laws and regulations concerning building and safety, zoning, health, noise and disturbance, disorderly conduct, and traffic regulations. Each state has developed a comprehensive criminal code defining crimes and providing punishments. In turn, the responsibility for the enforcement of these laws, has been delegated largely to our local governments.

Far too often we fail to differentiate between the various components of local government. When we become irate, we are simply concerned that we are not receiving a service to which we feel entitled. If we become bewildered by the obfuscation of government divisions, we turn to the one most familiar and most recognizable—the police. Because their service to us affects our respect for government in general and the police in particular, the police are expected to respond with as much help as possible, even if the matter is outside their purview.

Systemwide Processes

Through the identification and arrest of a suspected offender, our police activate the CJS. The individual's guilt or innocence is then determined in the courts. If the individual is found guilty, an attempt is made to rehabilitate him through a correctional process that may include probation, confinement, parole, or any combination of these. While each of the components of the CJS is organizationally separate, these components are functionally interdependent.

A very high percentage of police work is done in direct response to our complaints. This underlines the frequently overlooked fact that members of the public are an integral part of the CJS; in fact, the success of the System depends more on our participation than on any other single factor. Our police are the CJS component in closest contact with us; as a result, we often blame them for failures in other parts of the System. Additionally, our confidence in the CJS depends to a large extent on the trust that we have in our police. Our police, our CJS, and government in general could not control crime without the cooperation of a substantial portion of the people.

Supportive Relations!(?)

In most communities today the relationship between the police and the people is not entirely satisfactory. Frequently we do not notify the police of situations that require enforcement or preventive action. Often, we avoid involvement in averting or interfering with criminal conduct, and many people are suspicious of the police, the CJS, and the entire political process.

Following World War II, our police became increasingly isolated from the public. Reasons for this separation include urbanization, rapidly changing social conditions, greater demands for police services, increased motorized patrol, police efforts to professionalize, and reduced police contact with noncriminal elements of society. These factors, joined with the people's apathy, caused many police agencies to try to combat rising crime without actively involving the public in their efforts.

Due in large part to the widespread riots in the 60s, and the report of the President's Commission on Law Enforcement and Administration of Justice, many of our police agencies analyzed their role and made changes that culminated in enhanced community involvement in crime prevention. Police agencies throughout our nation have measurably improved their ability to cope with crime and disorder. They have also made great strides in responding to our demands for greater service involvement and responsiveness, and more than any other group, our police have advanced their ability to adjust to rapidly changing social conditions.

In attempting to reduce tension and improve their relationship with the public, police have adopted innovative programs. In some communities policemen wear blazers instead of the traditional military-type uniform, operate storefront offices, discuss local problems at neighborhood "coffee klatches," and engage in "rap sessions" with juveniles.

Nonetheless, the lack of both manpower and fiscal resources has caused delay or abandonment of many programs to improve police-community relations, and the police have had to assign higher priorities to the delivery of direct law enforcement services.

Program-matic Con-siderations   Attempts to involve us in crime prevention programs and improve police-community relations have often been met by an apathetic citizenry, on the one hand, and resistance within police agencies on the other. Middle managers and police officers, accustomed to taking public support for granted and dealing primarily with law violators, had little faith in nonenforcement programs. Many citizens, accustomed to relying upon the police to deal with crime, were slow to respond to public involvement programs. Fortunately, there are many successful programs, and community-police relations have improved.

A "program" can be defined as the planning, development, and implementation of specific solutions to identified problems. These solutions should take the form of organizational goals and objectives rather than specific activities. Where programs are constructed of specific activities rather than goals and objectives, implementation tends to be delegated to a specialized person or group as opposed to the employees as a group. Such programs tend to be unrelated to other agency efforts and are often, from the beginning, doomed to fail.

The success of a nonenforcement program is often determined by the number of citizens involved or by the absence of unfavorable incidents. Programs that do not produce results relative to their cost may still be difficult to discontinue. In these cases, administrators may be reluctant to admit failure or they may fear public criticism that the program was a facade. However, programs planned on a cost-effective basis with identified objectives, built-in methods for measuring effectiveness, and suggested alternatives in case of failure, have produced beneficial results.

The Police Function: Role Definition

Recommen-dation   Every police chief executive immediately should develop written policy, based on policies of the governing body that provides formal authority for the police function, and should set forth the objectives and priorities that will guide the agency's delivery of police services. Agency policy should articulate the role of the agency in the protection of constitutional guarantees, the enforcement of the law, and the provision of services necessary to reduce crime, to maintain public order, and to respond to the needs of the community.

1. Every police chief executive should acknowledge that the basic purpose of the police is the maintenance of public order and the control of conduct legislatively defined as criminal. The basic purpose may not limit the police role, but should be central to its full definition.

2. Every police chief executive should identify those crimes on which police resources will be concentrated. In the allocation of resources, those crimes that are most serious, stimulate the greatest fear, and cause the greatest economic losses should be afforded the highest priority.

3. Every police chief executive should recognize that some government services that are not essentially a police function are, under some circumstances, appropriately performed by the police. Such services include those provided in the interest of effective government or in response to established community needs. A chief executive:

   a. should determine if the service to be provided has a relationship to the objectives established by the police agency; if not, the chief executive should resist that service becoming a duty of the agency

   b. should determine the budgetary cost of the service

   c. should inform the public and its representatives of the projected effect that provision of the service by the police will have on the ability of the agency to continue the present level of enforcement services

   d. if the service must be provided by the police agency, it should be placed in perspective with all other agency services and it should be considered when establishing priorities for the delivery of all police services

   e. The service should be made a part of the agency's police role until such time as it is no longer necessary for the police agency to perform the service.

4. In connection with the preparation of their budgets, all police agencies should study and revise annually the objectives and priorities which have been established for the enforcement of laws and the delivery of services.

5. Every police agency should determine the scope and availability of other government services and public and private social services, and develop its ability to make effective referrals to those services.

Some General Considerations

Our police do not bear the exclusive responsibility for preserving a peaceful society; that responsibility is shared by each element of society—citizens, institutions, and government. However, because crime is an omnipresent threat to the order of all communities, our police exist to meet that threat and to reduce the fear of it.

The extent to which our society achieves public security through police action depends on the price that we are willing to pay. That price is measured, overtly, in tax levies and the establishment of punishable rules. For example, if we were willing to live in a totalitarian state, where the police had unlimited resources and authority, we *might* find our parks more safe to walk in but less enjoyable. Obviously, a balance must be created that permits sufficient freedom to enjoy what is secured by sacrificing unlimited freedom. That balance must be identified by the public if a supportive relationship with the police is to be achieved.

Defining the Police Role

The primary purpose of the police throughout America is crime prevention through law enforcement; however, enforcement priorities must be established locally for every agency. In certain cases, our police must provide nonenforcement services, and they have a responsibility to aid persons in need or to refer them to the proper agency for aid. Once established, an agency's police role should be put in writing so that police employees have a model, and in turn we have a standard by which to measure police performance. It is stressed that a definition of the police role should be central to all written policy. Further, the policies of our police must be based on the policy of the governing body that provides formal authority for the police function.

The Police and Their Authority

Patrolling officers are responsible for seeing and attempting to correct conditions that provide an opportunity for crime. In order to maintain the peace and to prevent crime, they question those behaving suspiciously, even if there may not be legal cause to make an arrest. These inquiries at times lead to arrests for outstanding warrants, possession of narcotics or concealed weapons, burglary, robbery, and other serious crimes. They also may lead to the recovery of stolen property. Furthermore, written reports of the contact may result in a subsequent arrest by placing the subject in the area of a reported crime and by furnishing descriptive data revealing his identification.

The actual effectiveness of police patrol as a crime deterrent is obscure.[6] Nonetheless, we assume that if patrols are conducted infrequently because of insufficient manpower, or if patrols are inadequately deployed, whatever deterrent effect they may have is reduced.

Our police are often requested to intervene in conflicts that, if unresolved, might result in crime. Such situations commonly include family, landlord-tenant, and businessman-customer disputes; control of unruly crowds; and quieting of loud parties. The legal authority for their intervention is based upon their power to arrest for disturbing the peace or for disorderly conduct. Their effectiveness in restoring peace, however, mainly rests on their acceptance by citizens as a neutral stabilizing influence, or on our belief that the police have more authority than they actually have. The recommendation that a husband leave home for the night, that a landlord allow the removal of a tenant's furniture, or that a stereo be turned down is based more upon common sense than legal authority. Mere police presence generally provides at least a temporary reduction in the possibility of crime.

Concern for the constitutional rights of accused persons processed by the police has tended to hide the fact that our police have an obligation to protect all of us in the free exercise of our rights. The police must provide safety for those exercising their constitutional rights to assemble, to speak freely, and to petition for redress of their grievances. Any definition of the police role must recognize that the Constitution imposes restrictions on the power of legislatures to prohibit protected conduct, and to some extent defines the limits of police authority in the enforcement of established laws.

Enforcement Priorities

Full enforcement of all laws is impossible. Furthermore, it is uncertain that full enforcement (if it were possible) would be consistent with either legislative intent or the desires of those for whose benefit laws are enacted. That our police exercise considerable discretion is well known, and that our police do not and cannot enforce all the laws all the time is implicit in a definition of the basic purpose of the police.

As a consequence, police executives must make the difficult determination of which reported crimes will be actively investigated and to what extent, and which unreported crimes will be sought out and to what degree. For example, a determination must be made as to whether a reported theft warrants the same investigative resources as a crime of violence. Our police must also assess the extent to which their resources should be used to suppress gambling, prostitution, and liquor law violations. The law provides only broad guidance. In their statutory form, laws define crimes; classify them as felonies or misdemeanors; and assess penalties for them. But the law does not provide a criterion to guide enforcement priorities, particularly at the community level.

In determining enforcement policies and priorities, our police agencies should direct primary attention to those crimes that stimulate the greatest fear and cause the greatest economic loss. Beyond that, our police agencies should be guided by the law, collective police experience, public needs and expectations, and the availability of resources. Since these are in a constant state of flux, the priorities should be re-examined at least once a year.

Determination of Service Priorities

The police role must be determined at the local level by the police chief or sheriff. He should state policy, assuring that the objectives, priorities, policies, and practices adopted by the agency are consistent with the law, the needs of local government, and the public. This policy will in turn guide the decision making of the police officers under his command.

While it may be appropriate in certain instances for our police agencies to perform a nonpolice function, such as providing ambulance service or collecting stray animals, it must be undertaken only after a full public examination of its effect on other more basic services provided by the agency. Consequently, when a proposal is made that a police agency provide a service not directly related to its essential purpose, the chief executive should decide whether provision of the service would serve indirectly to achieve agency objectives. If so, he should ascertain if the resources necessary might be used to a greater benefit by expanding existing programs or in some alternative program that achieves a similar objective. This is especially important because it can mean the difference between having a crime prevention program or not.

If the proposed service does not relate to the police agency's objectives, the chief executive should resist efforts to make it the agency's responsibility. In so doing, he should determine the budgetary cost of the service and the projected effect the provision of the service would have on the ability of the agency to continue its present level of service. He should then inform the public and legislative representatives of his findings and of any suggested alternatives. Subsequently, if it is legislatively determined that a police agency is to provide a service, it should become a specific budgetary item, and resources necessary for its delivery should be detailed.

Referrals

The nature of their duties often exposes police to deteriorating social, psychological, and economic conditions. They see people in need of help that is customarily provided by some other community agency. Prompt and effective assistance for those in need helps to build our trust in government. To the extent that the police facilitate the delivery of community services, they develop citizen support and their tasks are performed more easily and effectively.

A growing number of police agencies are undertaking a more direct role in seeking solutions to problems that are the concern of other departments of local government or of social support agencies. For example, the police in some cities and counties operate store-front offices or deploy community service officers to receive and channel complaints and requests for government or social services, and to serve as a means of communicating with the public. The extent to which police agencies engage in such referral services should be influenced by local conditions. However, the indirect effect of such programs upon the achievement of agency objectives should be weighed against the need for crime prevention services, and a balance should be struck to most effectively serve both needs. It would seem that as a minimum, every police agency telephone communications facility should be able to transfer calls for community service assistance to the proper agency, or to inform citizens how to contact the appropriate agency.

Again, every police chief executive immediately should develop written policy, based on policies of the governing body that provides formal authority for the police function, and should set forth the objectives and priorities that will guide the agency's delivery of police services. Agency policy should articulate the role of the agency in the protection of constitutional guarantees, the enforcement of the law, and the provision of services necessary to reduce crime, to maintain public order, and to respond to the needs of the community.

Police Understanding of Their Role: Self-Awareness

Recommen-
dation   Every police agency immediately should take steps to insure that every officer has an understanding of his role, and an awareness of the culture of the community in which he works.

1. The procedure for developing policy regarding the police role should involve officers of the basic rank, first line supervisors, and middle managers. Every police employee should receive written policy defining the police role.
2. Explicit instruction in the police role and community culture should be provided in all recruit and inservice training.

3. The philosophy behind the defined police role should be a part of all instruction and direction given to officers.

4. Middle managers and first line supervisors should receive training in the police role and thereafter continually reinforce those principles by example and by direction of those they supervise.

5. Methods of routinely evaluating individual officer performance should take into account all activities performed within the context of the defined role. Promotion and other incentives should be based on total performance within the defined role, rather than on any isolated aspect of that role.

Some General Considerations

A police officer's workday usually involves many varying contacts. His day can range from periods of calm to periods of intense pressure. At times he is forced to make decisions during conflict-laden situations. A police officer often sees some of us at our worst. It is inevitable that his personal concept of his role will be constructed largely from what he experiences during his daily encounters with the public. If he is not given an accurate understanding of what the police agency expects of him, he will be guided only by that personal concept of his role, which may be inconsistent with that of the agency.

The police officer's job is further complicated by the public's conflicting expectations of his role. Some people believe an officer should not merely enforce the law but should provide social services as well; others hold that efficient law enforcement is the crux of his role; and far too many have only a vague understanding of what the police role should be.

Every police executive must endeavor to identify the particular needs of the various *communities* within his jurisdiction and to reconcile those needs with the *law*, and with the policies and resources of *local government* and the police *agency*. The role agreed upon must then be instilled in each officer. It is not the individual officer's responsibility to reconcile the incompatible expectations of conflicting elements of society—it is the "boss's!"

Employee Participation in Role Definition

Officers must be convinced that the official concept of their role is valid. Now, especially, when employee groups representing officers are becoming more aggressive, basic changes will be resisted. The most effective and sensible way to overcome employee resistance to policy defining the police role is to enlist their cooperation at all levels. Their varied experience can contribute to making the policy realistic and acceptable. Moreover, an officer's self-respect is enhanced when he realizes that his superiors value his opinion. Finally, training can instill the realization that, by fulfilling their defined roles, they are serving the highest ideals of their profession.[7]

Training in the Police Role   Recently, our police agencies have vastly improved the quality of officer training. Regardless of substantial improvement in courses on police-community relations, ethics, and human relations, most training is not designed to communicate the abstract concepts of the police role and the nature of the community to be served.

The homogeneity of a community affects an officer's perception of his role. Middle class suburbs tend to have fewer internal conflicts regarding expectations of police service; consequently, those officers who work in the suburbs encounter conflict situations less often than those who work in the inner city. Further, police officers are recruited predominantly from the middle class; most of them have lived in a single neighborhood where they were not exposed to the varying lifestyles of the larger community they are expected to serve. A young person raised in a city's suburbs, for example, may not be prepared to deal with the culture of its inner city. What he was taught to regard as unacceptable behavior might be common practice in the area where he is assigned.

Hence, an understanding of the sociology of his community should be basic to a police officer's training. The relative complexity of such training depends on the differences in communities that will be policed. Techniques of teaching officers the nature of their community are similar to those of teaching interpersonal communications. Instruction in role identification, community awareness, and interpersonal relations should be combined.

There has been little research data accumulated regarding the effectiveness of this sort of training. Interestingly, the Kansas City, Missouri Police Department, after the establishment of a general education social science program for recruits that involved role identification and social awareness, found that a control group of sixty officers were the subject of twenty-one citizen complaints during their first six months of service, while only twelve complaints were made against the 154 officers who received specialized training.

Goal-Oriented Direction and the Officer's Role   An agency's objectives and priorities should be reinforced continually by illustrating the connection between principles and practices. Many of our police agencies publish general orders that promulgate procedures for specific activities. Frequently those orders include a statement of purpose or a brief introduction. All such orders, however, should state explicitly the particular objectives and priorities to which the activity is directed. Thus, activities become goal-oriented instead of merely task-oriented, and as a result officers become enlightened about the abstract concepts of their role.

The Training
of Leaders

The cooperation of management and supervision should be enlisted in teaching policemen their role. We should recognize, however, that some built-in human resistance to change exists in these upper ranks. Most large police agencies have special training for officers who are promoted into the supervisory rank, and many agencies have undertaken varying forms of management-development training. These programs are best used to teach the defined police role to the middle managers and first line supervisors, with precise instructions on how they are to reinforce those principles through their own actions.

Role
Adherence

The police role not only must be taught to our police officers, but incentives must be developed to encourage each officer to adopt that role. If a stronger service orientation is desired, an agency must assure their officers that service will be rewarded, not ridiculed. An officer who takes time to learn how to refer persons in need to the proper agency *deserves recognition as much as one who makes an arrest.* The degree of recognition should be determined by the priorities established within the police role. Therefore, there must be a means of evaluating compliance. Too often the police service measures performance solely by the number of arrests made, traffic citations issued, or radio calls answered. Such performance measures are replete with abuses. Any measurement must encompass all of the indicators that would reveal the level of role conformance. To summarize, again it is recommended that *every police agency immediately should take steps to insure that every officer has an understanding of his role and an awareness of the culture of the community where he works.*

Public Understanding of the Police Role:
External Awareness

Recommen-
dation

Every police agency immediately should establish programs to inform the public of the agency's defined police role. These programs should include, but not be limited to, the following:

1. Every police agency should arrange for at least an annual classroom presentation by a uniformed officer at every public and private elementary school within its jurisdiction.
   a. The content of the presentation should be tailored to the learning needs of the students; however, each presentation should include a basic description of the police role.
   b. Every agency should work through the school to develop a basic study unit to be presented by the teacher prior to the officer's arrival, and every officer assigned to a school visit should be provided with prepared subject matter to be reviewed prior to making his visit.
2. Every police agency with more than 400 employees should, dependent upon securing the cooperation of local school authorities, assign a full-time officer to each junior and senior high school in its jurisdiction.
   a. The officer's assignment should include teaching classes in the role of the police, and serving as a counselor. His assignment should not include law enforcement duties except as related to counseling.
   b. Course content should be developed in cooperation with the schools and should include discussion of the police role, juvenile laws, and enforcement policies and practices relating to juveniles.
3. Every police agency, where permitted by local conditions, should participate in the classes in government and civics offered in local evening adult schools and community colleges.
4. With agency resources, where available, or in cooperation with employee organizations or local civic groups, every police agency should develop or participate in youth programs including scouting and other athletic or camping activities.
   a. All such programs should be designed to provide officers and young people with the opportunity to become personally acquainted with each other.
   b. Every officer participating in youth programs should be provided with written material describing the objective of the program and its relationship to the police role.
5. Every police agency should accept invitations for officers to speak to business and civic organizations. Efforts should be made to provide speakers in response to every reasonable request and to coordinate the speaker's ability and background with the intended audience. Every opportunity should be taken to describe the police role and the agency's objectives and priorities.
6. Every police agency with more than 150 employees should publish a statement of the police role, the agency's objectives and priorities in filling that role, and the

agency's activities to implement its role. An annual report should be used for this purpose. In addition, periodic statistical reports on crime, arrests, and property loss due to crime should be disseminated to the public. These reports should include an evaluation of significant trends and other interpretations.

7. Every police agency should inquire into the availability of public service resources from advertising and communication organizations to assist in developing support for the agency and its programs.

8. Every police agency should hold an annual open house and should provide other tours of police facilities and demonstrations of police equipment and tactics when appropriate to create greater public awareness of the police role.

Some General Considerations   As part of the process of police-public communication, we need information about the nature of the police role in order to develop understanding. Our acceptance of activities that are an essential part of routine police duties will then be fostered. Indeed, most of us have a fair understanding of what the police do, but often we do not know why a particular police action was or was not taken.

Some police agencies hesitate to publicize their policies and practices in the belief that publicity might aid criminals or increase public criticism. This risk should be taken because misconceptions of the police role hinder the delivery of services. Many of us, for example, think more uniformed policemen are on duty at any given time than actually there are. Therefore, they are critical of the police if police response to a complaint, however minor, is delayed. Written policy defining the police role, priorities for the delivery of police services, and performance guidelines should be provided to all officers and made available to the public. Also, police executives should develop new means of informing us about the police function and our citizen role in controlling crime.

School as a Media   Most of our police agencies are now using public and private schools to increase understanding of their role. Many agencies cooperate with local schools in programs that encourage young people to accept the police officer as their friend rather than as a threat. Most programs have been concentrated in the lower grades where students are taught bicycle safety, and how to shun potential molesters.

Some departments recently have enlarged their programs to include upper grades and have expanded the scope of their presentations. Hence, as part of their public education programs, several police agencies currently assign officers full time to junior and senior high schools. These programs are of two basic types. School Resource Office programs, pioneered by the Cincinnati, Ohio, Police Department in 1967, assign officers to certain schools where they have both law enforcement and teaching duties. Officer Instructor programs, of the type developed by the Los Angeles Sheriff's Department and the Los Angeles Police Department, assign officers and deputies to selected schools where they have full faculty status and limited law enforcement duties. Both can be viewed as pre-delinquent or prevention in format. Similarly, the results of both programs have been most encouraging.

As mentioned, the Los Angeles Police Department's Police Role in Government program and the Los Angeles County Sheriff's Department's Student and the Law program have sworn personnel assigned to them on a full-time basis to teach in selected junior and senior high schools. The basic purpose of these programs is to teach students the role of the police in government and to minimize conflicts between students and the law through the development of greater understanding of its processes and enforcement.

Most police agencies that have adopted school programs require participating officers to dress in uniform. This requirement encourages students to identify with the police generally, and discourages the impression that participating officers are in a class apart from other officers of the police agency.

Criticism of these programs have at times been based on the assertion that police presence in an enforcement role inhibits the educational process. Because the programs are in line with the long term goal of crime prevention by encouraging student respect and understanding of the law, and the role of the police in its enforcement, these programs best concentrate on teaching and counseling duties. Participating officers should take enforcement action in appropriate cases, but such action should not be their primary responsibility.

Miscella-
neous
Media

First, in addition to school activities, many of our police agencies have found that scouting, athletic, and camping programs aid development of beneficial relationships between officers and the young people in their community. For example, the Salt Lake City, Utah, Police Department provides an extensive Public Safety Athletic Program for disadvantaged youths. The program, which is supported by private contributions, uses police officers as coaches and game officials in citywide basketball, soccer, volleyball, track, boxing, and softball leagues. A few critics claim that such programs should be conducted by recreation departments or that the benefit to police is limited. However, I am convinced that such programs are an effective force in crime prevention because they encourage our youth to view police as a positive influence and to better understand their own responsibilities.

Second, police agencies can reach a broad and receptive audience through local civic groups. Most business and service organizations have a need for speakers and an interest in law enforcement. Although most agencies, provide speakers on request from civic organizations, presentations frequently are limited to a review of outstanding programs or discussion of a single or pressing problem such as drug abuse. Police spokesmen should take advantage of the opportunity to discuss the role of the police in our society.

Third, police have information in their files that can contribute to the planning efforts of local government, social agencies, and other elements of the criminal justice system. In addition, the public needs information regarding crime, arrests, and property loss to evaluate the criminal justice system. Many agencies give out such information on a regular basis, and most contribute to the Federal Bureau of Investigation's *Uniform Crime Reports*. In turn, all police agencies should allocatè funds for a comprehensive annual report. If funds are not available in smaller agencies, information can be published in the local newspaper or it can be duplicated and distributed by other means. Finally, efforts should be expanded to isolate and develop data for long range planning both inside and outside the police service. Reliable police reports provide excellent material for persons studying the causes of crime, as well as data for enhancing police response to crime.

Fourth, an improved public image can be a beneficial by-product of successful public information programs. Who would argue that a convincing explanation of the role of the police, their policies, problems, and proposed solutions to the community is conducive to an improved public image? A few departments have undertaken advertising campaigns in an attempt to improve recruitment or to gain support for a particular program. Advertising agencies will often donate billboard space as a public service, and radio and television stations will give air time for spot announcements supporting the police. Further, many police agencies hold an annual open house and offer tours of police facilities to those who are interested. Some agencies permit citizens to accompany officers on patrol. Also, demonstrations of police equipment and tactics are often presented in association with tours or at public gatherings.

To repeat, in closing, *every police agency immediately should establish programs to inform the public of their defined role.*

Endnotes

1. Daniel Cruse and Jesse Rubin, *Determinants of Police Behavior: A Summary,* A study conducted for the Law Enforcement Assistance Administration (Washington, D.C.: U.S. Government Printing Office, 1973), p. 16, 17.
2. Special Committee on Standards for the Administration of Criminal Justice, *The Urban Police Function* (Washington, D.C.: American Bar Association, 1973), pp. 192–3.
3. Egon Bittner, *The Functions of the Police in Modern Society* (Chevy Chase, Md.: National Institute of Mental Health, 1970), p. 42.
4. Ibid., p. 46.
5. This section and those following are taken from Chapter 1 in the National Advisory Commission on Criminal Justice Standards and Goals, *Police* (Washington, D.C.: U.S. Government Printing Office, 1973).
6. A highly provocative experiment on the effectiveness of routine patrol was performed by the Kansas City Police Department. See *Kansas City: Patrol Experimentation* (Washington, D.C.: The Police Foundation, 1974). See also the following newsletter which describes a study of the preventive impact on crime of enhanced street lighting, International City Management Association, "Does Better Street Lighting Reduce Crime?" *Target* 4 (March 1975), p. 6.
7. An exhaustive social science study was recently conducted on the various *roles* of criminal justice personnel. In regard to police officer role training see Project STAR, *Police Officer Role Training* (Sacramenta, CA.: California Commission on Peace Officer Standards and Training, 1974).

4

Community Support

THOUSANDS EXPECTED AT ANTICRIME RALLY, ONLY 350 SHOW UP
Pleas for greater citizen involvement in fighting crime and supporting
law enforcement resounded through a nearly empty Los Angeles
Memorial Coliseum Sunday.

The occasion was what sponsors called a "public meeting" between
Los Angeles residents and county and city officials on the problem of
crime.

Police and sponsors late in the week expected 25,000 to 50,000
persons to attend. But under sunny blue skies Sunday, only a disap-
pointing 350 persons dotted the 92,000-seat stadium.*

Preview

The causes and concerns about crime in this nation
have been with us since our earliest beginnings. Moreover,
there is ample reason to believe that crime and the fear of
crime are increasing in magnitude and gravity. Those with
an *assigned* responsibility for meeting this challenge (CJS
components) are urgently turning to those who have a *basic*
responsibility for curtailing it (the community). In short, the
CJS is looking to the public for assistance. The police, more
specifically, are proactively encouraging public cooperation
in the abatement of both the frequency and personal threat
that crime poses to us. The individual, his residence, and
his place of occupation are being conceptualized as targets
—potential targets for criminal activity. In turn, programmatic steps are being taken by the police to significantly
reduce their vulnerability to criminal attack.

The axiom, "Reality is that which has real conse-

* Robert Rawitch, "Thousands Expected at Anticrime Rally, Only 350
Show Up," *Los Angeles Times* January 14, 1974, Part 1, 3.

quences," explicitly relates to the idea and act of crime. Whether we are in fact or in our own minds susceptible to criminal attack is academic. If we are fearful of being victimized, regardless of whether the fear is justified, our anxieties remain the same. Our perception of being a victim has a direct and interactive relationship with the actual probabilities of becoming so. Hence, the concept of believing that a certain phenomena exists, in fact, influences our attitudes and behavior irrespective of the validity of the belief. All of this is to say that we must pay careful attention to our *perceptions* of reality as well as that which actually exists. Our perception of crime, and our perception of the response of the CJS to it must be balanced with the *facts* of crime and the *facts* of the CJS. An assessment and understanding of perceptions in this case are of equal value as the measurement and comprehension of the realities. Significantly, a recent research study revealed through a sampling of public opinion that:

1. crime prevention should receive top priority by the CJS,
2. the public should be involved in crime prevention, and
3. perceptions exert a powerful influence on our society's reaction to crime and the CJS.

Activating Community Potential

Our crime problem is a fundamental social problem that can never be resolved by the CJS alone.[1] Crime is destined to distress our nation unless our citizens, you and I, assert greater responsibility. Attempts to improve relations between the general public and our police have been most successful when the two have combined and acted together in the pursuit of common goals. When the police officer who patrols a neighborhood confers with residents on crime problems in the area and they then jointly develop solutions to those problems, there is an opportunity to develop respect and understanding. More importantly, the probabilities of reducing crime are significantly enhanced.

Police operations stand to benefit from involving police officers in neighborhood programs on a semipermanent assignment basis. Police officers typically are quick to identify with their assigned area and the people in it. Most often they become more concerned with the solving of problems of that area as compared to rotating beats without a sustained responsibility for specific area crime problems. The following example is offered as evidence in support of this proposition.[2]

Investigating a robbery report in the barrio in Riverside, California, a police patrol car sighted some possible suspects: a group of Chicanos packed in a gaudily painted Chevy. One of the cops barked the usual command: "Everyone out with your hands in sight!" As the Chicanos emerged, the policeman's jaw dropped. Among the suspects was a fellow cop, Gerald Carroll, outfitted in jeans and dark glasses, his blond hair hidden under a knitted cap. Carroll hastily explained. He was living among the Chicanos as part of a program sponsored by the Riverside police department; he was just out for a ride with his new friends. Afterward Carroll described his feelings on being confronted by a cop: "My emotions were of fear, of apprehension, and of being at the other end of the stick."

That sort of perception is exactly the point of the department's course, an unusual program conceived by Riverside Police Chief R. Fred Ferguson and his staff. He has been worried by the persisting clashes and lack of cooperation between his cops and the 18,000 Mexican Americans who live in the city. The cops regard the high-crime area as enemy territory bristling with real and imagined dangers; the Chicanos view the police as alien, brutal oppressors who despise their way of life.

The get-to-know-the-barrio program starts with a forty-hour crash course in Chicano history and culture at Loma Linda University. The policemen learn about Mexican character, art, music, and food. They go to a town south of the border for two weeks to study Spanish. The live-in phase of the program is optional.[3] "It's not fair to mandate that kind of emotional experience," says Ferguson. Some fifty policemen have taken the Chicano course; eight have stayed with a family and several more volunteers are waiting their turn. "A lot of guys think they're going to be with someone who'll cut their throats," says Patrolman Mike Robitzer who was the first cop to live in. (He emerged from his three-day, two-night stint without a scratch.) Joining an eleven-member family with a father on welfare, he experienced a degree of cultural shock. He shared a drafty enclosed patio with a teenaged son. For his first breakfast he was offered "eggs and orange juice." He happily accepted until he noticed that the raw eggs were in the juice. With this came a bowl of brown soup. "What is that?" Robitzer gently inquired. The reply was, "Menudo," or tripe soup. Robitzer settled for coffee. Conversation did not come easily in the beginning, but eventually they made a breakthrough. Says Robitzer: "Somehow we managed to talk about everything from police brutality to life in Mexico."

In the course of their barrio sojourn, the police made some surprising cross-cultural discoveries. Women's liberation, for example, has not yet penetrated the barrio. The father remains the head of the household in all matters; he and the other males are even served their meals first. The women eat later.

Ferguson is not expecting dramatic overnight changes in police-Chicano relations, but already at least one potential explosion was defused by the live-in sessions. Shortly after his barrio stint, Carroll was arresting a Chicano who had attempted to rob a store. As usual, a jeering mob gathered and started heckling the patrolman. Then he recognized a youth he had met while living in the barrio. The two exchanged greetings; the crowd grew silent and slowly drifted away. "All of a sudden, the hostility was gone," recalls Carroll. He adds: "We all have these preconceived ideas. You see a car full of Chicanos with their long hair and their dress, and they look pretty bad. Now I'm a little more open-minded about what I do. A little more walk-around-in-my-moccasins type of thing."

In closing, there is much that we can do to reduce crime even without joint police-public programs. We can lock our doors and windows when we leave home. We can install better door and window locks and make a list of personal property serial numbers. We can notify our police if we see an unfamiliar person in a vacationing neighbor's backyard. We can, in these and other virtually effortless ways, protect ourselves and our neighbors against crime. Recognizing their constrained ability to cope with the causes of crime, police agencies across our nation are reassessing their role in crime prevention and are adopting a new role analogous to that performed by fire departments in fire prevention. Approximately 500 cities have enacted minimum building security ordinances, which are enforced in most cities by building inspectors during new construction and thereafter by operational police personnel. Police officers in these and other jurisdictions perform security inspections of businesses and residences upon request, and there is a growing consciousness and proof of the value of "site hardening" and other programs that impede if not eliminate the opportunity for victimization.

We now turn to a discussion of the *proposed* and *perceived* roles of the police in eliciting community support and putting community resources to work. Relatedly, subsequent chapters will concentrate on the opportunity and *its responsibility* for reducing the opportunity and tendency to commit criminal offenses.

The Prevention of Crime: Some Requirements of Our Police

Recommen-
dation
Every police agency should immediately establish programs that encourage members of the public to take an active role in preventing crime, that provide information leading to the arrest and conviction of criminal offenders, that facilitate the identification and recovery of stolen property, and that increase liaison with private industry in security efforts.

1. Every police agency should assist actively in the establishment of volunteer neighborhood security programs that involve the public in neighborhood crime prevention and reduction.
   a. The police agency should provide the community with information and assistance regarding means to avoid being victimized by crime, and they should make every effort to inform neighborhoods of developing crime trends that may affect their area.
   b. The police agency should instruct neighborhood volunteers to telephone the police concerning suspicious situations and to identify themselves as volunteers and provide necessary information.
   c. Participating volunteers should not take enforcement action themselves.
   d. Police units should respond directly to the incident rather than to the reporting volunteer.
   e. If further information is required from the volunteer, the police agency should contact him by telephone.
   f. If an arrest results from the volunteer's information, the police agency should immediately notify him by telephone.
   g. The police agency should acknowledge, through personal contact, telephone call, or letter, every person who provides information.
2. Every police agency should establish or assist programs that involve trade, business, industry, and community participation in preventing and reducing commercial crimes.
3. Every police agency should seek the enactment of local ordinances that establish minimum security standards for all new construction and for existing commercial structures. Once regulated buildings are constructed, ordinances should be enforced through inspection by operational police personnel.
4. Every police agency should conduct, upon request, security inspections of businesses and residences and recommend measures to avoid being victimized by crime.

5. Every police agency having more than seventy-five employees should establish a specialized unit to provide support services to and jurisdictionwide coordination of the agency's crime prevention programs; however such programs should be operationally decentralized whenever possible.

Some General Considerations

As noted earlier, crime prevention can be conceptualized in several ways, depending upon the type of criminal behavior to be prevented. It may, on the one hand, relate to the resolution of social, psychological, and economic conditions that stimulate a desire to commit crime. On the other hand, crime prevention may concern the elimination of the opportunity for crime through the presence of police patrols and "hardening the site" to the potential violator. Further, while final success or failure may well depend upon alleviating the conditions that provoke crime, the presently overburdened CJS may be relieved somewhat by placing impediments in the path of potential criminals. The following discussion centers on community-oriented efforts to impact crime.

Citizen Security Programs. In many of our cities, police agencies have involved, or have attempted to involve, the public in crime prevention efforts through neighborhood security and citizen watch programs. These programs are designed primarily to encourage citizens to report suspicious circumstances in their neighborhoods to the police.

The security procedures should be described for participating citizens in a pamphlet prepared by the agency so they will know what to do and expect if they provide information. Also, details of what kinds of information are helpful to the police should be included. It is important that police agencies immediately notify volunteers by telephone when an arrest results from their information. Additionally, agencies should acknowledge any person providing information through a letter, telephone call, or a visit.

Identification Programs. Many neighborhood security groups have adopted programs designed to identify personal property. Electronic marking tools can be used to mark personal property with either state driver's license numbers or social security numbers. Decals can be furnished for exterior windows to identify participants, and forms can be used for listing factory serial numbers of personal property. It should be mentioned that the use of social security numbers creates problems because the Social Security Administration cannot reveal the names the numbers identify. Using driver's license numbers, in turn, presents problems with people who don't have a license—and it presents the problem of an overload of inquiries in the information system.

Business, Trade, and Commercial Crime Prevention.   Crime reduction programs pertaining to business traditionally have consisted of warnings—once information is received or a trend is developed—to the specific businesses that may be in jeopardy. Police agencies quite often initiate chain-call warning systems operated by businessmen to alert others to shoplifters or bad check passers operating in the area. We should expect our police agencies to establish or assist community programs that supply crime prevention protection to business establishments. Written material that describes both the program and potential crime hazards should be prepared and distributed to commercial establishments. Further, every time a police officer visits a commercial establishment or meets a businessman, he should seek opportunities for offering crime prevention advice.

Minimum Security Regulations and Inspections.   A number of cities have enacted ordinances that require minimum security devices to prevent burglaries in buildings used for business. Such ordinances, which are generally made a part of the building code, permit the police to enforce their provisions through routine inspections. The building department usually inspects for compliance with the building code during construction; thereafter, the police and fire departments enforce compliance. Unfortunately, a lack of performance standards too often has hampered the effective enforcement of minimum security ordinances in the past. Questions such as how much pressure a one-inch dead bolt or burglary resistant glass will withstand must be resolved and ratings determined before these ordinances can became fully effective.

In some instances we find police crime prevention officers routinely advising burglarized businesses on security measures to avoid further occurrences. Further, they frequently conduct inspections of residences and businesses upon request. Programs such as these are within the capability of all police agencies, and are similarly an invaluable tactic for improving relations between the public and police. Interestingly, certain homeowners who participate in crime prevention programs may receive benefits beyond property security. As an example, insurance companies may lower homeowner insurance rates for persons who allow a security inspection of their residence by police officers and who comply with suggested security improvements.

In conclusion, crime prevention programs should be functionally decentralized. This is to say that inspections and enforcement should be performed by operational personnel who are familiar with the geographic area and its crime problems.

Perception and Crime Prevention

In 1974 Dr. Charles P. Smith interpreted research findings on perceptions (i.e., mental images) of the public and operational criminal justice personnel as they pertain to crime prevention. (The interpretation of these findings is Dr. Smith's and does not automatically reflect Project STAR.) His observations are based on Project STAR (Systems and Training Analysis of Requirements) which was created to provide: (1) a foundation for public protection, public service, and the administration of justice through improved public support, and (2) improved performance of front-line operational criminal justice positions who directly work with crime victims, witnesses, suspects, and offenders. These positions are the police officer prosecuting attorney, defense attorney, trial judge, caseworker, and correctional worker. Project STAR objectives included the identification of roles, tasks, and performance objectives for these critical positions and development of educational recommendations, training packages, and selection criteria for these positions based on field survey research. In addition, education programs for the public were developed and a technique for assessing the impact of social trends on the CJS has been established.

With its research design encompassing a mixture of survey research, observation, search of the literature, and expert opinion, Dr. Smith comments that Project STAR represents the most comprehensive effort to date to build an empirical foundation for desired criminal justice roles, tasks and performance objectives, and relevant education and training requirements.[4]

Project Findings on Perceptions   Project STAR research identifies for us the perceptions of the public and criminal justice personnel on various crime and criminal justice conditions, goals, issues, and situations. Perceptions on the situations included both the *desirability* of certain behavior in particular situations and the *probability* of it occurring in actuality. In surveys of representative samples of 937 members of the public and 1,266 operational criminal justice personnel completed in the spring of 1972, perceptions identified included the following:

Impact of Crime and the CJS.   Both the adult and teenage public cited crime and criminal justice issues most frequently when asked to spontaneously indicate the most pressing community problem. More specifically:

- 45 percent of the adults and 37 percent of the teenagers in the public opinion poll indicated that each had been a victim of a listed crime during the year preceding the survey; 95 percent of both groups related that each expected to be a victim of some crime in the future. Burglary, automobile offenses, robbery, and assault (in that order) were anticipated by adults and teenagers combined as the most likely crime to be perpetrated against them.
- 28 percent of the males and 42 percent of the females in the public opinion poll reported that they had recently stayed home because they thought it unsafe to go out. Greater fear for their safety was also expressed by persons in large urban centers, by the lower socio-economic classes, by blacks, and by the adults than by other related subgroups.
- Over 50 percent of the public respondents revealed that they had been interrogated by the police for one reason or another.
- 62 percent of the public respondents reported that they have been in a courtroom as a party in a case, a witness, a spectator, or a juror.
- 48 percent of the public respondents alleged that they personally know someone who has served time in a correctional institution.

The above perceptions provide conclusive evidence that the public in one state, and in all probability throughout our nation, are (1) deeply concerned and often fearful about crime, (2) more frequently victims of crime than criminal statistics reports, (3) generally expecting to be victims of serious personal and property crimes in the future, (4) more in contact with the CJS than would generally be expected, and (5) affected by crime differently, depending on sex, age, residence location, social class, and ethnic group.

Effectiveness and Performance of the CJS.   When asked to rank community issues and the job performance of public officials in

Table 4.1 Community issues

	Rank order of importance	Rank order of performance
Controlling pollution	1	9
Protecting against burglary and theft	2	3
Dealing with unemployment and poverty	3	8
Providing high quality public schools	4–5	2
Protecting against violence in the streets	4–5	1

dealing with these issues, adults in the public sample reported that crime rated high, and that the CJS was performing quite well (see table 4.1.) Additionally, from samples of the public and the operational criminal justice personnel, key criminal justice components were rank ordered according to overall effectiveness. Table 4.2 shows that the public felt that the police were thought to be the most effective in doing their jobs compared to other criminal justice components.

Goals. In specifying goals for criminal justice positions, a wide variety was detected among the different criminal justice components. Operational criminal justice personnel were asked to rank the four highest and four lowest goals for the CJS as a whole from a list of twenty-two alternatives. Analysis of the data (see

Table 4.2 Effectiveness

	Respondent Group	
	Public	Operational Personnel
Police	1	1
Judicial	2	2
Corrections	3	3

Table 4.3   Goals

Goal	Rank
Prevent Crime	1
Protect Life and Property	2
Rehabilitate Offenders	3
Assure Timely and Uniform Justice	4
Detect, Apprehend and Detain Suspected Offenders	19
Maintain Control of Offenders	20
Maintain Custody of Offenders	21
Provide Personal/Community Services of Noncriminal/ Nonemergency Nature	22

table 4.3) on goals suggests that: (1) even though criminal justice components have widely varying individual goals, common goals for the CJS can be established and followed, (2) prevention of crime should be the top priority for the CJS, (3) those activities consuming the majority of time expended by the CJS (e.g., apprehension, custody, and general public services) are a low priority even though each may contribute to the prevention of crime, and (4) more specific definition of the broad goals is required since many terms used in the goal statements mean different things to different people.

Values.   Table 4.4 depicts variations in mean scores to sets of questions related to four personal values as expressed by public and operational personnel. Five equals strong agreement, 1 equals strong disagreement. The perceptions on personal values indicated that, compared to the public, operational personnel were: (1) less

Table 4.4   Values

	Mean Score	
Value	Public (adults)	Operational personnel
Acceptance of Authority	3.9	3.5
Situational Ethics	2.8	2.6
Social Equality	3.5	3.1
Individualism	3.6	3.1

willing to accept authority, (2) less willing than the public to adapt to certain behavior due to the situation, (3) less willing to support social equality, and (4) less willing to recognize individuality.

Issues.   Table 4.5 shows the responses that were obtained in relation to several relevant police-community relations issues. It will be noted that the image of police street behavior was similarly positive among both respondent groups. However, the public did not feel as strongly as did operational personnel that police get citizens involved in police services or that police really know residents of the areas where they work. Nevertheless, both groups agreed that police encouraged citizens to get involved in local law enforcement much more than they themselves became familiar with local residents.

Responses to relevant sentencing and correctional issues are reflected in Table 4.6. The above findings indicated that, compared to operational personnel, the public is: (1) less critical of court leniency, (2) more supportive of alternatives to incarceration, (3) more supportive of the successful rehabilitative impact of prisons, and (4) more supportive of eliminating social stigmas or constraints

Table 4.5   Policy-community relations issues

| | Percentage of Agreement | |
Issue	Public (adults)	Operational personnel
Police officers on the street behave in a way that earns the confidence and support of the public	65%[12]	65%[12]
The police encourage people in the community to help them in providing law enforcement services	58%[13]	68%[15]
The police become personally familiar with residents of the neighborhoods they patrol	32%[14]	42%[16]

Table 4.6   Sentencing and correctional issues

	Percentage of Agreement	
Issue	Public (adults)	Operational personnel
Courts these days are too lenient in the sentences they pass on criminal lawbreakers	62%[17]	71%[19]
The crime problem would be reduced if fewer offenders were sent to prison and instead more of them reeducated and readjusted outside of prison	52%[18]	32%[19]
Too many people are being released from prison on parole before they are rehabilitated	69%[18]	77%[20]
Once a person convicted of a crime fulfills his sentence, he should be treated no differently from any other citizen	88%[17]	77%[21]

placed on offenders after completion of their sentence. Both groups concurred, however, that the courts were being too lenient, that too many people were being released from prison who are not rehabilitated, and that those who successfully complete their sentence should not suffer forever. Also, we can see that both groups were decidely lower in their support for incarceration alternatives than for other issues.

Situations.   From a total of 566 survey questions comparing the desirability and probability of occurrence for certain criminal justice personnel behavior in the specific situations, the following expectations concerning crime prevention were discovered:

• The adult citizens considered it *highly* desirable, yet only *fairly* probable, that criminal justice personnel take every opportunity to prevent the occurrence of crime. Operational personnel felt the same way, except that it was considered improbable that the prosecutor and defense attorney would use all of their crime prevention opportunities.

- Adult citizens thought that it was undesirable, yet probable, that police officers and prosecutors are lenient in enforcing laws which are frequently violated by the public; conversely, the adults felt that it was undesirable and improbable that judges would be lenient in these cases. Operational personnel thought it undesirable yet likely, that all three of these positions would be lenient in such a case.

- Both the adult members of the public and operational personnel thought it was *highly* desirable *and* probable that police officers deter crimes such as picking pockets, purse snatching, and auto thefts during gatherings involving large crowds.

- The adult citizens and operational personnel also agreed that it was undesirable, yet probable, that police officers attempt to stay invisible to trap violators of traffic regulations.

- Adult citizens thought it undesirable, yet probable, that defense attorneys were more concerned with obtaining the defendant's freedom than with seeing that justice was done. Operational personnel thought such behavior was undesirable and highly *probable*.

- Both adult members of the public and operational personnel considered it *highly* desirable and probable that caseworkers would recommend revocation of probation or parole when warranted.

Analysis of the above situations suggests that: (1) criminal justice personnel should use more opportunities to prevent crime, (2) criminal justice personnel should not be lenient in enforcing laws frequently violated by the public, (3) police officers should be visible in an effort to deter crime, (4) defense attorneys should not place client need over community need, and (5) individuals on probation or parole should not be permitted to remain in the community if they cannot meet appropriate behavioral standards.

Conclusions   Analysis of the Project STAR findings suggests the following conclusions:

1. Impact of Crime
   - The incidence of crime is *more frequent:* (1) than is generally estimated, (2) in certain types of crimes,

(3) in certain geographical areas, and (4) in relation to certain sexes, age groups, social classes, and ethnic groups.

- Fear of crime is *greater* than the incidence of crime.

2. Impact of the Criminal Justice System

- The public is more: (1) familiar with the criminal justice structure than is generally estimated, (2) supportive of the effectiveness of the criminal justice structure in crime prevention than might be expected, particularly in consideration of data on the impact of crime, and (3) supportive of other criminal justice components.

3. The public should be more involved in crime prevention.

4. The criminal justice system should be: (1) *less* lenient in law enforcement and case disposition, (2) *more* concerned with the successful rehabilitation of adjudicated offenders, and (3) *more* visible in efforts to prevent crime.

5. Goals and Objectives

- Criminal justice goals should be more clearly defined, including improved identification of specific crimes, objectives, and measures of achievement.

- The goals and objectives of CJS personnel should be congruent with those of the general public.

6. Resource Allocation

- Criminal justice resources should be allocated in relation to priorities concerning the impact of crime, the impact of the CJS, and the achievement of desired goals and objectives.

7. Impact of Values

- Personal values are likely to have considerable impact on the function of the CJS and the achievement of its goals.

8. Implementation of Crime Prevention Programs

- *The extent of crime is proportionate to the level of criminal behavior deemed unacceptable by a society, the amount of social control it is willing to accept, and the resources it is willing to commit.*

- Improved education and training of the public and operational criminal justice personnel on shared responsibility and techniques to achieve desired goals and objectives of crime prevention is required.

The above findings and conclusions vividly and convincingly depict a strong relationship between perceptions, crime, and criminal justice that consequently should be prudently considered in the development and implementation of crime prevention strategies.

Learning Exercises*

1.   Re-read the material on the Riverside experiment. Next, divide yourselves into groups of four to six individuals each. Assign one-half of the groups (P Groups) the responsibility for developing a positive argument along with advantages of motivating such a program. Assign the remaining one-half of the groups (N Groups) the responsibility for conceptualizing a negative argument along with the disadvantages of using such a program. Each group should take fifteen minutes to develop their particular argument. Then pair a P with an N group. Now debate your respective position for twenty minutes with one another. At the end of this period select one person from each pair to provide a four minute summation of the results of their interaction. (Be certain to stress points of consensus and lack of agreement.) Hence, if there were five P and five N groups there would be five, four minute presentations. This entire process should take approximately one hour.

2.   Divide your class into three groups. Those in Group One should develop in twenty minutes a questionnaire that will either elicit identical or similar data to that reported in Tables 4.1 and 4.2. Group Two, do the same with Tables 4.3 and 4.4. And, Group Three, handle Table 4.5 likewise. Each group then administers in ten minutes their questionnaire to all members of the class, including themselves. (As an alternative, you can administer the questionnaire to members of the general public and/or the criminal justice system.) Take fifteen minutes to process the data and prepare to present it in graphic form as a table or bar chart. Have one member from each group verbally summarize in five minutes your findings. Where appropriate compare them to those that were reported by Project STAR. This process can last from sixty minutes to many hours, depending on the size of your sample.

Endnotes

1.   This part of the chapter is drawn from Chapter 3 of the National Advisory Commission on Criminal Justice Standards and Goals,

---

* This chapter, as will most of the others subsequent to it, concludes with a set of learning exercises. Each exercise is designed to: enhance your understanding of the subject matter, and motivate you to evaluate more actively and carefully ongoing crime prevention programs. You will note that the majority of the exercises are small group in format and thus are intentionally structured to maximize interaction.

Police (Washington, D.C.: U.S. Government Printing Office, 1973), pp. 61–9.

2. This section originally appeared as a journal article by Charles P. Smith, "Perception and Crime Prevention," *Crime Prevention* 1 (January, 1974), pp. 26–32.

3. This example is based on an article entitled "Community Relations—Living In," *Time* 105 (April 21, 1975), pp. 33–34.

4. Beginning in May, 1971 and ending in late 1974, the 39-month Project STAR involved the Law Enforcement Assistance Administration; criminal justice planning agencies, operational agencies, and advisory councils in four states (California, Michigan, New Jersey, and Texas); the California Commission on Peace Officer Standards and Training; and the American Justice Institute. To date, the project has involved some 1,500 criminal justice agencies and 6,000 individuals from these agencies and the public in California.

5

Organizing for the Delivery of Crime Prevention Services

More flexible organizational arrangements should be substituted for the semimilitary, monolithic form of organization of the police agency. Police administrators should experiment with a variety of organizational schemes, including those calling for substantial decentralization of police operations, the development of varying degrees of expertise in police officers so that specialized skills can be brought to bear on selected problems, and the substantial use of various forms of civilian professional assistance at the staff level. *

Preview

There is a growing concern among our police agencies and the communities they serve to consider change. In the main, the change centers on making the police officer more responsive to our expressed need for crime prevention. This concern has surfaced in many projects besides those we see labeled as "team policing." Whether a specific community should adopt team policing, however, depends first on that community's goals, and second on that community's estimation of team policing's effectiveness within its own situation. Most of all, it depends on both the commitment and the available resources to manage a complex process of organizational and community change.

It is tempting to conclude that team policing has positive consequences for crime prevention, police morale, and productivity. The data are far too insufficient, however, to

*Special Committee on Standards for the Administration of Criminal Justice, *The Urban Police Function* (Washington, D.C.: American Bar Association, 1973), p. 227.

make such conclusions final. However, early findings strongly imply that team policing will improve the quality and quantity of service delivered. More important is the question many readers will have: should we try team policing in our police department? Most important of all is the question: how can we decide whether team policing makes sense? While admittedly simplistic, the answer is basically "yes" if it is approached with due caution, experimentation, and evaluation. Keeping in mind that team policing must be custom-fitted to the interests of the community, it most effectively acts as a vehicle for the improvement of reducing crime and in particular its prevention.

Team policing was originally conceived as a means to an end—a decentralized professional patrol. In none of the cities and counties that adopt team policing has it met with immediate and total success. This does not imply that it has failed, but only that where the commitment and expertise exists team policing can provide an opportunity for greater professionalism. Yes, as with any organizational change, certain barriers to change will emerge. The critical point here is not to lose sight of the goal—increased crime prevention through citizen involvement—while one eradicates the barriers. The obstacles experienced by team policing projects demonstrate the depth of the change they attempt, which cannot realistically succeed overnight. In all the team policing jurisdictions, there were three major reasons that team policing either failed or reached only partial success. These were: (1) resistance on the part of police middle management, (2) inadequate dispatching technology, and (3) poor role definition for the team policing patrol officers.

As mentioned earlier, evaluation data are just now being made available to those who are anxious to learn more about the benefits and problems associated with team policing. It is predicted, although from limited observations and intuition at this time, that team policing will be proven more successful than not.

Organizing for Action: No One Way Best

The police chief and sheriff are in a quandary. They are aware that corruption and the abuse of authority are constant dangers within their agency, that collective violence has occurred before in their city/county and may occur again, and that people are frightened and want visible evidence of a police presence that will reduce crime.[1] They also realize that, however much the city council/county board of supervisors may complain of rising crime rates, they are concerned about rising tax rates, and thus want the police agency to be operated as economically as possible. For all these reasons, the police administrator is influenced to organize and manage his department along tight, quasimilitary lines, with strict supervision of patrol officers, a strong command structure that can deploy effectively large numbers of police in emergency situations, powerful and mobile tactical forces that can saturate areas experiencing high crime rates, and close controls over costs, scheduling assignments, and discipline.

But the police administrator also is aware that his patrol officers exercise great discretion and thus can never be closely supervised, that much of their time is spent on noncriminal matters, that some parts of the community fear and distrust the police while other parts want closer contact with them, that massive displays of police power can sometimes aggravate tense situations, and that quasimilitary discipline can lower the morale and perhaps the effectiveness of many officers. For these reasons, he is influenced to organize and manage his department along highly decentralized lines, with considerable discretionary authority given to patrol officers and their sergeants, great attention given to the resolution of community disputes and the provision of social services, and little use of tactical forces.

Even if the chief or sheriff could be clear as to what he wants, he faces two important constraints on his freedom of action, one internal to the department and the other external to it. His officers, in all likelihood, will be accustomed to a particular routine of doing things and they will see any effort to change that as a threat, not only to their habits and expectations, but to their promotion prospects, assignments, and authority. Community groups, on the other hand, will be ambivalent as to what they want: some neighborhoods may welcome tough, vigorous policing as a way of keeping the streets safe and the "kids in their place," while others may prefer a police agency that is closely integrated with the community and perhaps even subject to its control. Ironically, it is likely that any given community will want both things at once—be tough and concerned, visible and invisible, enforcement-oriented and service-oriented. Thus, one can well understand why a variety of organizational designs in combination with a variety of managerial strategies currently exist in order to meet the multifarious expectations placed on our police agencies.

Because of differing expectations, it should be concluded that there is not any "one best way" to organize for the delivery of police services. On the contrary, there are many ways to organize a police agency. Further, the prime determinent of how an agency should structure and manage itself is what the clientele (the community) expects in the type and quality of services. Since this text (particularly Part Two) concentrates on police crime prevention, any discussion of organizing will obviously stress organizational systems that are effective in fulfilling this mission. For our purposes, let us refer to a police organization that is primarily arranged and directed toward preventing crime as one of *team policing*. Team policing is a police strategy—or a collection of somewhat similar police strategies—which some police chiefs and sheriffs believe may be a partial answer to the dilemma they face. Ideally, it combines the benefits of a substantial police presence in a neighborhood (placing the maximum number of officers on the street during times of largest need, and supervising so as to encourage the maximum use of information about the area and its citizens) with the advantages of a police style devoted to servicing complaints, helping citizens, and establishing good relations. Most fundamentally, it serves as a contemporary vehicle for the delivery of both crime prevention and control, with an emphasis on the former.

The remainder of this chapter, therefore, deals with team policing. The next two sections present a general background on organizational structure and management style, while the later sections are more specific in nature.

The Police Organization as an Open Participative Social System

The police organization conceptualized as an open participative social system acts as the point of departure for our forthcoming discussion.[2] All systems possess the following nine characteristics:[3]

1. *Input.* Open systems input various types of energy from their external environment.
2. *Processing.* Open systems process the energy available with an output.
3. *Output.* Open systems output products or services into the environment.
4. *Cyclic character.* The product or service output furnishes the source of energy for an input and thus the repetition of a cycle.

5. *Arresting of disorganization.* Social systems process and store energy in order to combat the natural trend toward disorganization.
6. *Information: input, processing, output, and feedback.* Information is handled much the same as energy. In fact, information can be considered a form of energy.
7. *The steady state.* Open systems seek to maintain a viable ratio between energy input and service output. This state is not to be confused with the status quo. A steady state allows for change by constantly adjusting the input and the output so as to achieve a healthy relationship between the two.
8. *Specialization.* Open systems move in the direction of specialization.
9. *Equifinality.* Open systems can reach the same final state from differing initial considerations and by a variety of paths.

In addition to these nine characteristics, all modern social organizations are comprised of the following five subsystems which enable the total system to accomplish its goals and to survive: (1) operations subsystems to get the work done, (2) maintenance subsystems to indoctrinate people and service the technology, (3) supportive subsystems for procurement and environmental relations, (4) adaptive subsystems concerned with organizational change, and (5) managerial subsystems for the direction, coordination, and control of the other subsystems.[4] Obviously, if we were to remold the present structure of a police organization according to the five subsystems, the results would be significant. It would be even more revolutionary when experienced in terms of its new processes—the *new* way of arranging its resources. Table 5.1 contains an explanation of the purpose, functions, and activities of each subsystem.

To the notion of the police organization being an "open" system, we now add one other idea—that of the police agency becoming an open and participative organizational structure. The latter idea denotes increased community involvement through greater decentralization of services. Robert Wood expresses this requirement and challenge as follows:

Our experience in urban administration suggests that one of the critical components in our new urban programs calls for a historical reversal in American administrative doctrine.

Specifically, the confrontation now posed is between the several versions of citizen participation that have been foundations in the federal government's urban strategy and the century-old effort in public administration to establish coherent executive structures manned by professionally compe-

Table 5–1. The subsystems of a police organization: their purposes, functions, and activities

Subsystem	Purpose	Function	Activity
1. Operations Patrol, traffic, investigation, jail, communications, etc.	Efficiency in field operations	Task accomplishment —processing of inputs within the organization	Division of labor: specialization and job standards
2. Maintenance Training Personnel	Maintenance of subsystems: their functions and activities	Mediating between organizational goals and personal needs, indoctrination, and servicing manmachine activities	Establishing operating procedures, training and equipment maintenance
3. Supportive Community relations	Environmental support for the organization	Exchange with environment to obtain social support	Building favorable image by contributing to the community and by influencing other social systems
4. Adaptive Planning and research	Planned organizational change	Intelligence gathering, research and development, and planning	Making recommendations for change and implementing planned change
5. Managerial Chief of police, staff and subsystem commanders	Control and direction	Resolving internal conflict, coordinating and directing subsystems coordinating external requirements and organizational resources and needs	Use of authority, adjudication of conflict, increasing of efficiency, adjusting to environmental changes, and restructuring the organization

Source: Paul M. Whisenand and R. Fred Ferguson, *The Managing of Police Organizations* (Englewood Cliffs, N.J.: Prentice-Hall, Inc., 1973). pp. 169–70.

tent managers. The satisfactory resolution in American political thought is the principal precondition for success in our urban programs. It is on this issue—between effective, purposeful, expert action, and widespread public participation—that I focus.[5]

With citizen participation there usually comes a heightened sense of representation on the one hand and a reduced apathy and resentment toward an organization on the other.

> But in that century of building professional bureaucracies and executive capacities for leadership, the need for new modes of representation designed to keep pace with new economic, social, and political developments did not arouse equal concern. Partly for this reason, and partly because the burgeoning of large-scale organizations in every area of life contributes to the sensation of individual helplessness, recent years have witnessed an upsurge of a sense of alienation on the part of many people, to a feeling that they as individuals cannot effectively register their own preferences on the decisions emanating from the organs of government. These people have begun to demand redress of the balance among the three values, with special attention to the deficiencies in representativeness.[6]

The movement for representativeness at this time centers primarily on administrative agencies such as the police. Since administrative agencies have grown dramatically in size, function, and authority—especially in the middle third of this century—this is not surprising. Chief executives, legislatures, and courts make more decisions of *sweeping* effect, but the agencies make a much greater number of decisions affecting individual citizens in *intimate* ways. In them resides the source of much present tension; in them, consequently, the resolutions are sought.

One type of recommendation for making administrative agencies more representative is traditional: to situate spokesmen for the interests affected in strategic positions within the organizations. Frequently, this means nothing more than filling vacancies on existing boards and commissions with appointees who enjoy the confidence of, or perhaps even were chosen by, those interests. In the case of the controversial police review boards, it involves inserting into administrative structures new bodies, dominated by ethnic minority groups or their friends, to survey and constrain antisocial behavior. Structurally, such plans do not require major changes in existing organizations, and their purposes could probably be met by movement of personnel at high organizational levels.

Unorthodox, but rapidly gaining acceptance, is the concept of a centralized governmental complaint bureau, with legal powers of investigation into citizen complaints against administrative agencies and into inequities and abuses. This is the office of "ombudsman." The most sweeping expression of *the dissatisfaction over lack of representativeness is the growing demand for extreme administrative decentralization, frequently coupled with insistence on local clientele domination of the decentralized organizations.* Prior manifestations of this movement have occurred in the antipoverty program and in education; it is now impacting the police.

The issue of citizen participation is a moral issue—the power-less should have a share of power. It is a legal issue—the right of participation is conferred by law in antipoverty, model cities, and other programs. And it is a practical issue—the poor and others of low influence now have enough political power to protect and expand their participatory role.

> In short, "decentralization of administration" is in the air everywhere. While it is sometimes defended on grounds of efficiency, *it is more truly justified in terms of effective popular participation in government*. Reformers of earlier generations succeeded in raising the level of expertise and professionalism in the bureaucracies, and to a lesser extent, in improving the capacity of chief executives to control the administrative arms of government. *Now, people are once again directing their attention to representativeness, and are seeking to elevate it to a more prominent place in the govern-mental political arena.*[7] (Italics added.)

The police department's response to the problem of partici-pation and decentralization is underway on a major scale. This response, moreover, is specifically intended to *enhance the prob-abilities of preventing crime.*

The Organization and Management of Team Policing

As mentioned earlier, although vague in its meaning to date, team policing is a sincere and major effort to better relate the police de-partment to the community. Team policing is different in each city and county where it has been implemented, but generally it has been an attempt to find a new balance between the presumed efficiency needs of police centralization and community needs for police decentralization in order to be more responsive to citizens.

The term "team policing" originated in Aberdeen, Scotland immediately after World War II. The Aberdeen project began as an effort to counteract the low morale and boredom of single officers patrolling quite streets. It allocated teams of five to ten men on foot and in cars to cover the city. The patrols were dis-tributed according to concentration of crimes and calls for service, with the teams moving to different parts of the city as the workload demanded. The monotony and loneliness of the patrolmen were relieved.

A second form of team policing, called "Unit Beat Policing," appeared in the town of Accrington in the County of Coventry, England, in 1966. Its stated purpose was to overcome a shortage of manpower by effectively utilizing the existing limited resources. Under the Coventry Unit Beat Policing system, constables were organized into teams which remained in one specific area. Although the constables working in the same area did not patrol as a team, they all fed information about their area to a central collator who was responsible for the exchange of knowledge about that area. By maximizing coordination and the exchange of information through the collator, fewer men could cover a wider territory than was previously possible.

The Aberdeen system was abandoned in 1963, but it had already been tried in Tucson, Arizona and a number of other small American cities. The Coventry form of team policing is still in practice and has been expanded to other police forces in England; it is the form most prevalent in the United States and is generally known as "neighborhood team policing." A third variant combines aspects of both the Aberdeen (manpower allocated according to workload) and Coventry (neighborhood-based) systems and was instituted in Richmond, California in 1968. To date a number of American cities have experimented with team policing in one way or another.

In theory, the patrol force is reorganized to include one or more quasiautonomous teams, with a joint purpose of improving police services to the community and increasing job satisfaction for the patrol officers. Usually the team is based in a particular neighborhood. Each team has responsibility for police services in its neighborhood and is intended to work as a unit in close contact with the community to prevent crime and maintain order. Essentially, team policing is a vast structural-functional change in local law enforcement. The impetus for team policing rests on the presently recognized ambiguous and transitory nature of the beat officer's relationship with his clientele. No clearly placed responsibility exists for the adequacy of police service in any particular neighborhood. Final accountability is placed only in the chief of police. This is because of the highly centralized command structure (common to all American police departments today) which is primarily organized around time shifts (e.g., 4:00 p.m. to midnight) and includes considerable emphasis on job specialization. Thus, when the beat officer comes upon a crime, he turns over investigation to a detective. If juveniles are involved, the juvenile specialists handle the case from that point. Traffic control activities, too, are handled by functional specialists.

Community-centered team policing attempts to change this

situation. This concept seeks transition from a centralized organization to a decentralized one where the beat officer has more
responsibility and the citizen has an improved means of participating. The officer will be involved in all police field functions.
These can be categorized into three types: *major crime functions*
(including the use of patrol strategies and tactics to prevent serious
crimes and disturbances, the collection of information on such
activities, and the endeavor to apprehend perpetrators); *traffic
functions* (including the control of pedestrian and vehicular movement, the investigation of accidents, and the alleviation of congestion when it arises); and *social service functions* (including the
pursuit of order and peacekeeping activities demanding use of
police advice and authority–control of minor disturbances, intervention in family crises, etc.—as well as activities where assistance
rather than authority is required, e.g., aid to injured and elderly
persons, and improvement of relations with the community).

The generalist-officer will have total responsibility for these
functions on his beat. Further modifications would be made on
the basis of such factors as community wishes, evaluation of functional and cost effectiveness of possible alternative agency (or
citizen) discharge of the function. To illustrate, thirty police officers and thirty community service officers, directed by a supervisor
and lower-level group leaders, might be the best team for a given
geographical area. One team model might provide that team
officers and leaders undergo a four-week training program designed to teach needed skills, including family crisis intervention
and investigative methods. Members will then be required to live
with a family in their beat neighborhood for a few days to learn
the values and norms of the local culture.

In addition to police officers and supervisors, a number of
integrative or supportive personnel will work on the team. Community service officers are one such possibility. They will attempt
to increase police responsiveness to neighborhood concerns and
will thus be responsible for handling many of the social service
tasks which now fall to the police and are of great importance to
the neighborhood. At the same time, they will work with individual team members in dealing with special problems where the
community service officer's experience would be beneficial. A
position of community coordinator might also be included. This
person will develop within the community an understanding of
what the police are doing, interpret policy to the community, and
most importantly assist the community in representing its concerns
and interests to the department. The community coordinator will
be a resident of the neighborhood hired to assist the community in

developing defensive security tactics, community concern, and community action.

Concisely, then, team policing is an endeavor to increase departmental decentralization in order to build an improved relationship between the police and the community for the prevention of crime. *In practice,* team policing has not always been able to accomplish these goals, although it seems to have come very close in some jurisdictions. In others, team policing has become an in-word, a public relations device. Still others have seen a measure of achievement, but it has been less than was anticipated by those who initiated the project. The reasons for inconclusive results are varied, but would include among others:

- team policing is embryonic and lacks ample testing by which it can achieve full maturation,
- team policing, like many other concepts and technologies, was oversold to begin with and unreasonable results were expected,
- team policing has been falsely used to denote organizational arrangements that were in fact not team policing,
- team policing structural-functional relationships were established without the appropriate managerial system to nurture and maintain it.

The last point deserves amplification. So often the central importance of managerial leadership receives only lip service. Are we not constantly voicing the need for professional and competent police management, while all the time in reality not paying for it, not promoting it, and not permitting it? The success or failure of team policing is inextricably linked to the skills and values of police management. Of the many proposed "modern" management styles (McGregor's Theory X and Theory Y, Likert's Systems 1–4, and so on), the one that seems to hold the greatest promise for facilitating the operationalizing of team policing is that referred to as participative management.[8]

To begin with, participative management has proven to be an effective vehicle for encouraging line employees to share directly in the making of decisions that impact them. This is not to say that management in any way abdicates its responsibility for directing the organization, but that police management should afford the employees an opportunity to express their opinions and thereby *perhaps* influence the judgments of the manager(s). Second, such a process most often results in a vastly superior decision in that more voices are heard than those few positioned at the top of the hierarchy. Third, an expanded involvement of those responsible for the carry-through means an increased commitment on their part for operational success. Four, the typical line-management schisms and adversity in all likelihood will be minimized. Finally, and of immeasurable importance, participative management affords an invaluable opportunity to apply social equity (justice as fairness) within the police organization.

Although the concept of social equity is not altogether foreign to contemporary public administration theory and practice, its ethical content has usually been loosely defined and its application has been restricted to the distribution of public benefits to recipients external to the distribution agencies. The importance of Rawls' theory of justice is that the concept of social equity derived from it has not only a clearly defined ethical content, but also it extends to the structure of and relationships within public organizations. Two principles fundamental to Rawls' argument imply a normative commitment to internal organizational democracy. *This commitment is not dependent on empirical evidence showing that democratic or participative management leads to utilitarian ends, such as higher productivity or higher commitment of organization members to pre-established organizational objectives.*[9] Briefly stated, then, we see that participative management seeks to make work as meaningful and as satisfying as is possible by fostering "social justice" within the confines of an organizational setting.[10]

Team Policing: Some General Considerations

To repeat, team policing is a contemporary police attempt to reduce isolation and involve community support in the prevention of crime.[11] Team policing can be administered in small or large amounts. Syracuse, N.Y., the first city to try team policing in the United States, uses teams of ten officers to patrol, investigate, and control crime. Team leaders have considerable discretion and authority. In Los Angeles, nine-member units have patrol responsibility; investigation remains separate, however. Dayton, Ohio, has an extremely advanced concept of team policing in operation.

As we discussed earlier, team policing essentially is assigning police responsibility for a certain area to a team of police officers. The more responsibility this team has, the greater the degree of team policing. For instance, team policing that has "investigative authority" is more complete than team policing that does not. Teams having the authority to tailor programs and procedures to the needs of their areas go even further. The underlying premise is that the team is able to learn about its neighborhood, its people, and its problems. Some may view it as an extension of the "cop on the beat" concept, brought up to date with more personnel and modern police services.

We should realize that team policing has certain inherent difficulties. To begin with, combining patrol and investigation personnel into teams can cause friction. Investigation personnel are usually higher paid and think of themselves as being farther up in the police hierarchy. Moreover, team policing requires tremendous individual initiative, responsibility, and competence. Many patrol officers are reluctant to exercise such authority. Additionally, there are some situations that require quick, military orders and obedience. How can this be reconciled with team member equality?

These are the problems that are being addressed and answered in ongoing programs. One definite benefit is that team policing concepts are rich in fresh thoughts; they stir police agencies to analyze many of the traditional assumptions about police procedures. Fortunately, we find that even when team policing is not adopted, examining other agency programs can prove beneficial to overall police thinking. Nevertheless, even where team policing has proven most beneficial, programs are to be considered experimental. Any agency evaluating team policing designs should plan carefully before going ahead. In doing so, larger agencies have the advantage of being able to test programs in certain precincts while carrying on traditional police work in others. Usually, smaller agencies have no such option; for the smaller agency, it is total or nothing.

We should not assume that the benefits of team policing, primarily greater police-public cooperation, are automatic. Team policing merely presents the opportunity for acquiring such benefits. It is up to the police officers to go out into the community and foster the desired cooperation. Police agencies must let the citizens know about their new program and what it hopes to achieve. Just as importantly, in agencies where a team policing experiment is being prepared, all police employees—not just those taking part—must understand and be encouraged to support the program.

There are no right and wrong procedures. Nonetheless, agencies committed to improving cooperation between the public and their police officers for the purpose of preventing crime can use team policing as a starting point to develop their own programs or to apply concepts of team policing in ways not yet envisioned.

Team Policing: Crime Problem Identification

Recommen-
dation
Every police agency should insure that patrolmen and members of the public are brought together to solve crime problems on a local basis. Police agencies with more than seventy-five personnel should immediately adopt a program to ensure joint participation in crime problem identification.

1. Every police agency should, consistent with local police needs and its internal organization, adopt geographic policing programs which ensure stability of assignment for individual officers who are operationally deployed.
2. Every patrol officer assigned to a geographic policing program should be responsible for the control of crime in his area and, consistent with agency priorities and policies and subject to normal approval, should be granted authority to determine the immediate means he will use in fulfilling that responsibility.
3. Every police agency should arrange for officers assigned to geographic policing programs to meet regularly with persons who live or work in their area to discuss the identification of crime problems and the cooperative development of solutions to these problems.
4. Every agency having more than seventy-five personnel should establish a specialized unit which provides support services, functional supervision, and administrative review and evaluation of the geographic policing program.

Some As-
sumptions
The importance of the community aspect of team policing was emphasized by Richard A. Myren, writing on "Decentralization and Citizen Participation in Criminal Justice Systems." He stated that three of the major assumptions common to all team policing programs in metropolitan areas were:

> ... That support of the citizens living and working in the many discrete neighborhoods of our metropolitan areas, which is absolutely necessary for successfully policing, can best be achieved by having a police subunit permanently assigned to each neighborhood; that the personnel of these subunits must get to know the peoples in the neighborhood through positive efforts to promote continuous dialog in both formal and informal settings; and that assistance to the people, both in handling their crime problems and in helping them to make contact with the proper agencies to handle the myriad other problems of big city living, is the best means of achieving respect for and support of police operations.[12]

In the early 1940s, many of our police agencies sought to increase efficiency and minimize corruption through motorized patrol and regular rotation of assignments. Regrettably, we found that the benefits of increased flexibility in responding to calls for services and reducing opportunities for corruption were accompanied by a reduction in police responsiveness to community needs. In our eyes, the police officers tended to become indistinguishable from one another; to the officer, the citizens in his patrol area became an amorphous crowd.

The possibility that long assignments may give rise to corruption is minimized by responsible supervision. Further, sophisticated inspection and control techniques will also do much to minimize police corruption. In whatever manner a police agency decides it should deploy its resources, stability of officer assignment and corresponding administrative and supervisory controls must be a part of the program.

Responsibility for the Assigned Area

Officers assigned to specific areas under geographic team policing programs should be given the responsibility for the control of crime within their area. This responsibility must be accompanied by commensurate authority; for, if the officers are truly to feel responsible for their areas, they must know that they can initiate action to deal with the police problems in their areas.

Many team policing programs have been tried as limited experiments only, and unassigned officers have furnished traditional services in other areas. Police agencies should perceive the potential for conflict in implementing geographic policing programs and should adjust to it by trying to make program success an *overall objective of the agency* and to include the greatest possible number of officers in the program.

Although officers assigned to geographic policing programs should be expected to define precise priorities and to have the authority to determine immediate action, that authority must be in conformance with jurisdictionwide policies and priorities as established by the police agency.

Neighborhood Meetings and Centralized Controls

I believe that the greatest success of geographic policing programs has come from the involvement of thousands of citizens in a direct effort to make their neighborhoods safer. The fact that thousands of persons are attending meetings across the country is clearly significant. The requirement that on-duty police officers attend meetings with residents and businessmen in the neighborhood where they work is common to all geographic policing programs. The man-hours required by public meetings pose problems if officers attend meetings while on duty, in that police operations are hampered because the officer is not available. Or if officers attend off duty, reimbursement in the form of compensatory time usually reduces available manpower in the future.

While all geographic policing programs should be decentralized as much as is possible, some level of centralized management control is required to eschew duplication of effort and to enhance program effectiveness. For example, we might find a centralized support unit preparing pamphlets, arranging for meeting locations, providing written policies and objectives of the program, and maintaining a continuing evaluation of the program. In turn, evaluation efforts might include attendance reports of residents at neighborhood meetings and surveys to ascertain if attendance is static or if new people are regularly attending. At the same time, the program's crime reduction figures should be constantly analyzed.

Selecting A Team Policing Plan

Recommen-
dation

Every police agency should examine the team policing concept to determine its value in increasing coordination of patrol and specialized functions within the agency. A team policing system should be adopted when research and testing indicate that such a system would enable the agency to use its resources more efficiently.

1. Every police agency should conduct research into the team policing concept to determine its value to the agency. This research should include:
    a. Evaluation of the structure and effectiveness of various forms of team policing applied by other agencies of comparable size and resources; and
    b. Assessment of the resources necessary to implement various team policing systems.
2. Every police agency should test and evaluate applicable forms of team policing prior to formal implementation. Testing should be conducted:
    a. To minimize disruption of ongoing agency operations; and
    b. To measure effectiveness in achieving predetermined objectives and goals.

*Team
Policing
Models*

Most of our police administrators appreciate the need for change in law enforcement in a changing society. Team policing has become one of the most popular forms of police reorganization. Practiced different ways in different agencies, it continues to receive considerable publicity. As indicated before, total team policing can be defined as: (1) combining all line operations of patrol traffic, and investigation into a single work group under one supervisor; (2) forming teams with a mixture of generalists and specialists; (3) permanently assigning the teams to geographic areas, and; (4) assigning the teams with responsibility for all police services within their respective areas. Most team policing programs have not taken this total approach.

*Testing a
Team
Policing
Model*

We find that most agencies that have tried team policing have tested the concept on a limited basis. Many of the systems that we can now see in operation have not been expanded to include the entire agency but continue in a small area that is conducive to limited testing and evaluation. Agencies that have attempted team policing innovations usually approach the subject from the standpoint of demonstrating that the innovation will work rather than trying to prove or disprove team policing through extensive experimentation.

The paramount objective of most agencies—the avoidance of disruption of ongoing operations—hampers true experimentation. Police agencies should conduct extensive research and plan comprehensive testing prior to formal implementation of agencywide team policing. For most medium-sized and large agencies, a limited test of a proposed team policing system can be accomplished by designating one geographic area as a test site. Smaller agencies with limited personnel may have to test the system agencywide.

In all cases, the research and planning phase must include program objectives and goals. It must foster the evaluation of the effectiveness of the program in reducing crime, increasing arrests, increasing the general level of service rendered to the community, and enhancing police-community cooperation.

Implementation of Team Policing

*Recommen-
dation*

Every police agency implementing team policing should ensure that the system effectively facilitates the agency's efforts to reduce crime, detect and apprehend criminal offenders, improve the quality of police services, and enhance police-community cooperation.

1. Every police agency should include its personnel in the team policing planning and implementation process. Personnel participation should be consistent with the degree of ultimate involvement in the team policing system.
2. Every police agency should provide preparatory and inservice training for all personnel involved in the team policing system. The objectives of the training program should be to acquaint all agency personnel with team policing policy, procedures, objectives, and goals, and to provide specific training according to the extent and nature of personnel involvement in the team policing effort.
3. Every police agency should develop programs to encourage community involvement in the agency's team policing system.

A Brief Backdrop   The team policing concept has been viewed by some as a return to a bygone year of police work exemplified by the friendly, well-known beat cop who helped us resolve the problems of urban life. In the late 1940s and early 1950s, however, reformers found this friendly officer on the foot beat to be corrupted by his familiarity with local residents, and he was found to be slow to respond to the scene of emergencies. In part to solve the latter problem, they put him in a radio car, and partly to solve the former problem, they transferred him so frequently that he would not have a chance to know people well enough to become corrupt.

The impersonal police officer created new problems for us. The President's Crime Commission and the President's Riot Commission both emphasized lack of community contact between the police and the citizens as a serious weakness in patrol operations. The Crime Commission, in fact, urged that patrol officers should be thought of as foot officers who use vehicles for transportation from one point to another. Many patrol officers resist the idea of getting out of their patrol cars to talk to residents; a few even view this activity as a degrading form of appeasement. The idea is also contrary to the tactical principle that the moving omnipresence of motorized patrol is required to provide adequate preventive patrol. Many of our police agencies endorse this axiom to the extent that irrelevant conversations with the public are discouraged by agency regulations. Current research on the effectiveness of preventive patrol, however, reports that any crimes prevented by passing patrol vehicles can be, and usually are, committed as soon as the police have left.

Police presence can only prevent street crime if the police are everywhere at once.   A more effective way to enhance the risk involved in committing a crime is to raise the probability of apprehension after the crime has been committed. Without information supplied by the community, apprehension is quite difficult. The best way to obtain information about a crime is for the police to talk to those who may have knowledge of the crime or the offender.

Once prevention and interception have failed, the only tool left to the police is investigation. But like prevention and interception, investigation requires our cooperation in apprehending the suspect and providing testimony in any subsequent court proceeding. In turn, team policing in any of its various forms is an attempt to strengthen cooperation and mutual coordination of effort between the police and its public in preventing crime and maintaining order.

Personnel Participation: The Key to Success or Failure   The lack of involvement of line-level police personnel in the planning and implementation of programs has been a basic defect in many team policing experiments. Involvement begins, as in most cases of organizational change, with a personal and continuing commitment on the part of the police chief executive. This does not mean that the idea must originate with the chief, or that he must personally direct all planning and implementation. However, the chief executive has to assume leadership by supporting the project and identifying himself with its implementation and long range operational aspects. The same is true of the agency's high ranking staff and command personnel. If support from all or some of these key personnel is withheld, we can predict that the project's chances for success are vastly reduced.

Middle management support has been absent from several team policing programs. The lack of this backing, in many cases, can be traced to top management failure to communicate to middle management the value of the team policing concept and middle management's role in making the concept work. We can avoid this situation through sufficient planning and implementation time to permit maximum participation by middle management.

Training for
Team
Policing

The implementation of a team policing system necessitates comprehensive training for police personnel at all ranks. With proper planning, there is great potential for obtaining needed support for the system by acquainting all agency personnel with its objectives, and with their roles in achieving those objectives. Hence, specific inservice training should be provided to all personnel regardless of their involvement in the team policing effort.

The training of team policing supervisors or team leaders must stress planning, directing, and coordinating the activities of team members. Team leaders should also be taught the techniques for teaching and training team members on an ongoing basis. The role of the team leader requires knowledge for maintaining liaison between the team and all other involved agency entities and community organizations. In turn, police officers assigned to teams should be trained in the theory of team dynamics and provided with information to enable them to function effectively as team members. Communications, conference leadership, and interpersonal relations training will assist team officers in their work with the community. At the same time, patrol, traffic, and investigative techniques and skills should also be covered.

Community
Involvement

One, if not *the* most, grave problem confronting police agencies today is isolation from the community. Several factors, including police organizational inflexibility and the attitudes of both the police and the public, have caused this isolation. Fortunately, team policing places the police officer in an environment that encourages cooperation with the public and thus tends to reduce isolation. As reviewed earlier, it brings the police organization down to the community level (or vice versa).

Thus, we can conclude that effective police-community cooperation is critical to the success of a team policing system. The public must be informed of the team policing concept, its objectives and goals; public assistance and participation must be solicited actively. This is to say, successful community involvement programs depend on our direct participation in the planning stages. Ongoing public commitment is encouraged by continually seeking citizen's opinions, ideas, and assistance in resolving problems of mutual concern.

Obstacles To Team Policing

In addition to the inevitable influence of individual leaders, police organizations can contribute three major barriers to team policing:

middle management, trial by peers, and dispatchers.[13] Let us examine each of these more closely.

Middle Manage-ment   By direction from the top, team policing offers increased powers to the bottom (patrol officers and sergeants) that had traditionally been exclusively reserved for the middle (lieutenants, captains, etc.). Thus, team policing is a form of decentralization which lessens the power of middle management. One way in which middle management limits the success of team policing can be by failing, as precinct or division commanders, to deal with problems arising out of team policing programs under their purview. One might reasonably anticipate the development between team leaders and officers of the next higher rank a problem apparently endemic to the team policing concept. It surfaced in England almost immediately where, despite the role definitions of inspectors as strategists and sergeants as tacticians, one Home Office study found that both ranks were confused and dissatisfied about their new roles.

Another, more overt way in which middle management can detract from the goals of team policing is by simple carping: sending out the message through informal channels of communication that this "senseless' team idea is a sham. Precinct commanders are also able to undermine the operational latitude of the team leader. By discouraging the team leader's initiative on day-to-day issues, middle management can defeat the program's goal of innovative team response to local conditions.

A third form of resistance by police middle management can be a candid expression to top management of disagreement about team policing issues. For example, one precinct commander complained to the police commissioner that by implication the "Beat Commander" system criticized the precinct commander's performance, implying that his managerial ability was insufficient to ensure adequate police service. Middle-management opposition is not unavoidable, however. If police middle management is brought into the planning process for decentralization, it is entirely possible that its cooperation and support for the new system will be won. A *participative* and consensual form of planning with all middle management can cultivate their support for plans which might otherwise be resisted. Most team programs have been perceived as giving more power to the bottom at the expense of the middle, a perception which has been the crux of middle management's opposition. However, it is possible for the power of each level to be expanded simultaneously with benefits for the entire organization. One goal of team policing is to expand the effectiveness of the police in the community: talking to more people, establishing more positive and informational relationships, apprehending more criminals, and providing more and better crime prevention services. This expanded role requires a new structure: the followers (patrol officers and sergeants) must do more leading of themselves, and the leaders (middle management) must lead in new and different ways. Police middle managers must analyze the new influx of information, plan for better manpower utilization in light of that information, and obtain more resources to support the expended role of their officers. If their function is viewed equally as *support* and control, middle management can gain power under team policing rather than lose it.

Trial by
Peers   It was found that in most of the cities studied, the larger patrol force—those not involved in the team project—objected to team policing. The opposition was strongest when the project split a precinct or a division. The first pilot teams formed new elites. The patrol officers had learned to accept the old elite forces (e.g., detectives) but they were not eager to accept new ones. There was also jealousy, in many instances stemming from the fact that the patrol officers first heard about the program through the news media—after the personnel had already been chosen. Not all patrol officers would have volunteered, but many would have liked to have had the chance to decide not to. When one is shut out of a newlyformed club, the natural response is to attack the club—and certain aspects of team programs were "clubby" and, superficially at least, elitist. For example, one team policing project invited resentment by flaunting their accomplishment of reducing the average time required to complete radio runs from forty minutes to twenty-seven. The freedom of team police officers in some cities produced irritation. In one case, the team was freed from roll calls. In another, the overtime pay available to the team was greatly resented by other patrol officers in an under-paid department.

Given all of these irritations, one might expect the outside patrol officers' field cooperation to be affected. With the exception of experimental projects (where the team had virtually seceded from the rest of the department), this did not happen. The team members were always backed up by nonteam cars. The opposition, however, was evidenced by strong vocal criticism and internal political maneuvers to keep the team idea from spreading.

Dispatchers   Another indirect team group, the radio dispatchers, can intentionally or inadvertantly hamper team policing. Quite often we find that the dispatcher is functioning under stressful conditions and he is not particularly concerned with neighborhood or team boundaries. He must be instructed that the neighborhood team should stay in its assigned geographical areas. At times the teams cannot do so, and when the team members find that the neighborhood concept is myth, many might conclude that the team project is a farce.

Sociologist Albert Reiss made an observation on the Chicago Police Department's dispatching system, which is probably valid in other large agencies:

> In Chicago in 1966, we observed that fewer than one-third of all criminal incidents were handled by beat cars in their own beat. . . . Many police administrators regard a patrolman's intelligence on a community to be of most importance in non-criminal matters, where an officer must exercise the greatest degree of discretion. However, despite this, officers in Chicago handled an even smaller proportion of all non-criminal incidents, arising from dispatches to their own beat, than criminal incidents . . . . Beat cars handled only one-third of all incidents, and one-fifth of all criminal incidents arising on their own beats.
>
> Based on these Chicago data, it appears conclusive that beat cars, whether dispatched or on routine preventive patrol, are more likely to handle incidents outside their own area than within it . . . . This problem may actually be due to the fact that beat cars are dispatched to handle incidents outside their beat. Once a car is dispatched to handle a call outside its beat, the probability of its handling outside calls increases, since, while that car is in service, any calls to its beat must be assigned to a car from a neighboring beat. Calls to that beat in turn must be handled by a neighboring car. The problem of such chain effects is a familiar one in systems analysis.[14]

Today's radio systems give little latitude for the kind of screening that once occurred when telephone complaints came in at the precinct switchboard and the sergeant held the less important calls or threw out the ones from known neighborhood cranks. Computerized dispatch systems treat almost all calls as being serious, and the widespread use of the "911" police telephone number has increased the volume enormously. Nevertheless, the dispatching difficulty is not insurmountable, and it is not universal. In the dispatching issue, small cities or self-contained units within a city/county have a clear advantage—the pressure is less and the boundaries are easier to maintain.

Team Policing: Evaluation

An evaluation of the success of team policing in producing the desired end can be done only if the concept itself is *fully* tested. But in many agencies, the team policing concept has never been fully developed and put into practice. Of the agencies which have evaluations, few of them included both of these issues.

Research vs. Action   The state-of-the-art in evaluation of social experiments is still very primitive, especially in police experiments.[15] Team policing has presented evaluators not only with problems of measuring such elusive data as the amount of real crime, but also with potential problems of conflict between research goals and action goals. Team policing, like many other institutional change efforts of the 1960s and 1970s, is usually conducted as a "demonstration project": one that demonstrates, on a limited scale, the hypothesized superiority of a new approach, prior to its adoption on a wider scale. In many instances, objectives were not clearly specified at the beginning and evaluation considerations played little or no part in design of the demonstrations. When evaluation is "tacked on" at the end, it can rarely prove either what happened or what may have caused what is thought to have happened (ex post facto research). Hence, we should not be surprised to learn that many evaluators of demonstration projects have taken the position that unless it is known precisely what a project has demonstrated (i.e., has it really prevented crime or improved response time?), then there can be no assurance that the innovation is in fact an improvement.

Local government agencies, however, usually take the view that they are mainly in business to deliver services and not to conduct research. The administrators, not the researchers, are in charge. They are legally and ethically bound to deliver the "best" service possible, regardless of research needs. Yet can we not also argue that the best way to provide the "best" services in a changing world is to allocate some resources on a regular basis to research, as all successful industries do, to try things out and, if they do not work as well as hoped for or conditions change, to try other methods or tactics and compare the results?

This research/action dilemma cannot be solved in principle, only in practice. A police chief or a sheriff who is committed to getting reliable data on how a project is working, and a researcher who is sensitive to the political, operational, and (even) psychological needs of a police agency, can together produce both research and action.

Methods and Measurements

Every team experiment studied by the Police Foundation had as one of its goals to improve crime control. Yet none of them included an evaluation component which could measure the amount of real crime in the team areas. Reported crime records have long been recognized to be undercounts of real crime. Increased citizen confidence in the police, another goal of team policing, could lead to more crimes being reported even though real crime may be decreasing. The only available means for measuring real crime are victimization surveys, and they are extremely expensive. Without victimization research, team policing experiments are not worth conducting as crime control experiments. In general, the evaluations are plagued by poorly specified objectives; poorly chosen (or no) control or comparison groups or areas; failure to gather baseline or "before" data; poorly designed data collection questionnaires; and weak quality control over interviewers. A crime control evaluation industry has only begun to emerge in the last two or three years as some of the 1968 Safe Streets Act money has been invested in it, and like any new industry, its products have many bugs.

The role of evaluation in police agencies, again, is to say more precisely what happened and why. The important point is that police administrators will have better information for decision-making if independent evaluators are present to give objective feedback. A subsequent chapter is devoted to the subject of performance, work measurement, and evaluation.

Evaluations and Decisions

Demonstration projects, by definition, are based on an assumption by the police executive that the project will work as the way to improve his organization, or that it is politically popular and likely to be relatively harmless. In the absence of any persuasive evidence to the contrary, a police executive is likely to feel the same way at the end of the demonstration, regardless of the findings of the evaluation. The decision about what action to take with team policing at the end of the demonstration period, like all highly visible governmental decisions, is political. The factors a chief must consider include opinions of the community, opinions of the political interest groups that support or attack his administration and performance, opinions of the interest groups within the department, and ideally (the most important factor) his judgment as to the effectiveness of the team policing as a means to accomplish certain goals for organizational change.

Police agencies have different histories and different conditions of such resources as leadership, community support, integrity, and initiative. While there are problems in all police agencies, there is a wide range of variables. There is no panacea for all of them. Team policing may not be appropriate for many communities even if results from other cities are highly favorable. But without valid information, there is no way to decide that issue on the facts, and evaluations are necessary to generate that information. *Clearly, communities that pay more attention to both the political and the methodological problems of evaluation will get better information about team policing and, thus, be in a position to make more sound decisions concerning the issue.*

Learning Exercises

1.   Early in the chapter, it was indicated that the police executive is confronted by two "constraints on his freedom of action." One was described as internal to the agency, while the second was viewed as external. Divide yourselves into groups of four to six members each. Each group is to separately brainstorm the internal and external constraints. Allow fifteen minutes for this process. Next, take ten minutes to select from each list the five most critical internal and external constraints. Then conceptualize a solution or partial remedy for each constraint. This phase should last twenty minutes. Finally, a member from each group is to present orally in two minutes the results of their deliberations to the entire class.

2.   Again divide yourselves into groups of four to six members each. Within thirty minutes develop three different team policing models. Assign priorities to the models according to which the group members feel to be the most effective. Then have a member of each group make a three-minute presentation to the entire class on the three models, emphasizing them in order of preference. (Be careful to note any models that appear to be either identical or very similar. Also, note those that are significantly different.)

Endnotes

1.   This thinking is supportive of that contained in the monograph by Lawrence W. Sherman, Cathrine H. Milton, and Thomas V. Kelly, *Team Policing* (Washington, D.C.: Police Foundation, 1973).

2. The majority of this section is drawn in part from Paul M. Whisenand and R. Fred Ferguson, *The Managing of Police Organizations* (Englewood Cliffs, N.J.: Prentice-Hall, Inc., 1973).

3. These common characteristics are drawn from Daniel Katz and Robert Kahn, *Social Psychology* (New York: John Wiley and Sons, 1967), pp. 19–26.

4. This typology of subsystems is suggested in Katz and Kahn, *Social Psychology,* pp. 39–44.

5. Robert C. Wood, "A Call for Return to the Community," *Public Management* 51 (July 1969), pp. 3–4.

6. Herbert Kaufman, "Administrative Decentralization and Political Power," *Public Administration Review* 29 (January/February, 1969), p. 4.

7. James L. Lundquist, "Citizen Participation: A New Kind of Management," *Public Management* 51 (July 1969), p. 9.

8. See Douglas McGregor, *The Human Side of Enterprise* (New York: McGraw-Hill, Inc. 1960) and Renis Likert, *Human Organization* (New York: McGraw-Hill, Inc., 1967).

9. For further explanation of this most exciting thinking see Michael Harmon, "Social Equity and Organizational Man: Motivation and Organizational Democrary," *Public Administration Review* 34 (January/February, 1974), pp. 11–17.

10. One of the most cogent arguments for social justice both within and without organizational settings is contained in the book by John Rawls, *A Theory of Justice* (Cambridge, Mass.: Harvard University Press, 1971).

11. This section and the two following it are excerpted from The National Advisory Commission on Criminal Justice Standards and Goals, *Police* (Washington, D.C.: U.S. Government Printing Office, 1973), pp. 154–61.

12. Richard A. Myren, "Decentralization and Citizen Participation in Criminal Justice Systems," *Public Administration Review* 32 (September/October, 1972), p. 721. Of parallel interest are the research findings reported by Roger Mansfield. In summary, the results of his study strongly suggested that the larger the size of an organization the more it is impelled to delegate authority and thus decentralize decision making. See "Bureaucracy and Centralization: An Examination of Organizational Structure" *Administrative Science Quarterly* 18 (December, 1973), pp. 477–88.

13. This section and the subsequent one are derived from the text by Sherman, Milton, and Kelly, *op. cit.,* pp. 91–103.

14. Albert Reiss, *The Police and the Public* (New Haven, Conn.: Yale University Press, 1971), pp. 98–99.

15. See Joseph H. Lewis, *Evaluation of Experiments in Policing: Where Do You Begin?* (Washington, D.C.: Police Foundation, 1972).

6

Police Crime Prevention Planning

The first major effort of the Federal Government to provide large-scale financial assistance for the prevention and reduction of crime at the state and city levels began with passage of the Omnibus Crime Control and Safe Streets Act of 1968 (P.L. 90–351). State Planning Agencies. All 55 jurisdictions funded by LEAA block grants have State Planning Agencies (SPAs), which are required by law to be established as the official recipient agency for federal funds on behalf of the state. The 55 jurisdictions consist of the 50 states and American Samoa, the District of Columbia, Guam, Puerto Rico, and the Virgin Islands. Comprehensive plans. Before it can receive its block action funds, each SPA must submit and obtain LEAA approval of a comprehensive plan for the reduction of crime.*

Preview

With the future invading our present at an ever increasing pace, it comes as little surprise to see many public agencies making plans to avoid the numerous dislocations and failures associated with a constantly changing environment. Crime prevention both now and over the coming years must be planned in order to enhance the probability of its reducing the incidence of crime.

Planning is, or it certainly should be, an integral part of the managerial process. Further, this process should encompass the concerns and judgments of others within the agency. Thus, while planning is natural activity within the

*Attorney General's First Annual Report: *Federal Law Enforcement and Criminal Justice Assistance Activities* (Washington, D.C.: U.S. Government Printing Office, 1972), p. 41.

overall managerial process, all members of the organization should participate in the formulation of plans and their program components.

The board process itself is actually composed of three interrelated forms of planning: environmental, internal, and tactical. The latter type of planning can be further divided into crime control and crime prevention planning. Basically, the process remains the same, only the intent differs in line with the proposed goals.

The very first step toward police planning is establishment by the agency to develop a process that will generate time-relevant plans. Second, planning, much like jogging, requires training and practice before it can be assessed as being effective in producing successful plans. Third, planning must be supported in terms of the organizational structure, skilled personnel, and necessary resources. Four, agency planning (this is especially critical in regard to crime prevention programs) must be coordinated with the plans of contiguous jurisdictions.

Finally, the planning process includes three major phases, two of which contain a set of more specific tasks. The phases are program development (tasks: goals, responsibilities, organization, scope, activities, and timing), expected results (tasks: measures of effectiveness and efficiency), and estimated resources.

The Avoidance of Future Shock

Modern society's growing awareness of the pending future has caused a variety of reactions not the least of which is a moderate form of collective paranoia. Alvin Toffler's best selling book *Future Shock*[1] urgently describes how the future is daily and at an ever accelerating pace invading our personal and organizational worlds. Further, concern over identifying, or better still controlling, the future has generated a new field or study that has been labelled "futuristics" or "futurology." A salient example of its application to the criminal justice system is seen in Project STAR.

The paramount finding of this study of long-range trends is that despite sustained improvements in American society, as measured by a large variety of economic, educational, and social indicators, growth in crime is highly probable in the rest of this century. Our continuing population growth (particularly in the young adult age group which commits the most serious crimes), urbanization, and poverty along with increasing economic affluence are the major factors that lead to this conclusion.[2]

Our nation, among others, is currently endeavoring to transform political/economic/social reaction and anxiety into proaction and confidence. It has been decided that a most essential vehicle for this transition is *planning*. For one, the CJS has placed a heavy reliance on systemwide and subsystem planning in order to prepare for tomorrow while coping with the challenges of today. Planning can be defined as a *dynamic process that involves a number of activities and methods for continuously generating plans that provide an organization with sustained renewal and change in terms of more effective goal accomplishment both now and in the future.*

This chapter emphasizes planning rather than the resultant plan. In other words, it is primarily devoted to the process—not the product. Few of us would challenge the idea that planning is central to the management of an organization. Ample evidence—theoretical and practical—is available to prove concretely just how vitally important planning is to the general success of an organization.

Of the many authorities who have offered witness to the significance of the planning process, Gardner is clearly an advocate. He writes:

> Every individual, organization, or society must mature, but much depends on how this maturing takes place. A society whose maturing consists simply of acquiring more firmly established ways of doing things is headed for the graveyard—even if it learns to do these things with greater and greater skill. In the ever-renewing society what matures is a system or framework within which continuous innovation, renewal, and rebirth can occur.[3]

Contained in the above statement is a partial reason or purpose for planning, "continuous innovation, renewal, and rebirth" of individuals and organizations—in this case, police organizations. We would add a second part to conform with the primary purpose of this text—the continuous innovation, renewal, and rebirth of individuals and *police organizations in order to more effectively coordinate their respective functions toward crime prevention.* Thus, crime prevention planning is a process that has as its fundamental product a *plan*. A plan intended to improve the CJS's capability to reduce the incidence of crime through its prevention.

During the eighteenth century, there were five generally accepted functions of management (planning, organizing, staffing, directing, and controlling), and it was at that time that several economists began to consider planning to be the most important. Laughlin gives the reasoning behind this:

> He who controls a large *capital* actively engaged in *production* can never remain at a standstill; he must be full of new ideas; he must have power to initiate new schemes for the extension of his market; he must have judgment to adopt new inventions, and yet not to be deceived as to their value and efficiency.[4]

The above quotation might be paraphrased to fit any particular organization. For example, substitute the words *public activity* for "capital," *law enforcement* for production and *service* for "market."

The Prussian General Carl von Clausewitz advocated this kind of thinking, since he stressed that careful planning was a necessity for the managing of a large organization, with the first requisite being to define one's goals.[5] Note the last term in the preceding sentence—*goals*. The General was quick to point out the interrelationship between planning and an organization's goals. He also asserted that all decisions must be based on probability, not on logical necessity, as was commonly believed at that time. Of course, his idea of probability was not as scientifically detailed as our current statistical probability, but the theory of trying to prepare best for what *might* happen is the same. Of all his pronouncements, perhaps Clausewitz's major contribution to management was that managers should accept uncertainty and act on the basis of thorough analysis and planning designed to minimize this uncertainty.

Our police are not alone in their recognized absence of a planning mechanism because, in general, most organizations engage in opportunistic decision making rather than in planning; rather than examine courses of action that will lead the way to the attainment of their goals (and in some cases identify new goals), they extemporize, handling each crisis as it emerges. Thus the challenge becomes all the more patent—our police need a process (planning) for generating, on a continual basis, *plans*.

The General Role of a Planner: Activities, Policy Formation, and Problems

To generate an individual and a collective climate conducive to cooperative participation, every police manager must perform several discernable roles. He must, for example, decide what the goals of his agency are, how they should be accomplished, when plans should be implemented, and how they relate to other components in the CJS. Making these decisions involves a conceptual look at needed future action—be it tomorrow or five years from now. It requires looking ahead, conceptualizing about the future, and planning today so as to adequately meet the future.

Obviously, planning is, in most instances, not a separate recognizable function; it is usually interlaced with other managerial activities. A police manager does not typically give a directive by mere impulse or reflex. On the contrary, even a casually written or oral communication about needed action may well involve some planning along with the message itself. To reemphasize, *every managerial act, mental or physical,* is linked to planning. Although we are able to conceptually separate planning for the purpose of theoretical discussion and analysis, we must remember that in practice it is neither a distinct nor a separable entity.

Let us now theoretically extricate the managerial planning function from the others to see how it is involved in the managing of a police agency. Planning, as a conceptually separate managerial role consists of looking ahead, "systematically" predicting, and anticipating probable future events and the actions needed to cope with them. Planning may involve nothing more than a simple plan for employee vacations in relation to the variations in the probable workload, or it may require the production of a plan of action to harden the targets against crime to minimize the impact of criminal activity eighteen months hence. Whatever the area of consideration, police managers during the performance of the planning function systematically should analyze the problem in light of probable future events and therefore make decisions *now* in order to deal more effectively with a constantly changing environment.

A *plan* (the output of planning) is a rational decision with regard to a course of action. The rational selection of a course of action, that is, the making of a rational plan, includes basically the same procedures as those of any rational decision. Most, and if possible all, of the courses of action must be identified, the consequences of each course must be predicted, and the courses having the preferred consequences must be selected. Hence the planning process is comprised of the following activities:

- Analysis of the situation (problem identification)
- Goal setting (desired future state of affairs)
- Design of courses of action (alternative approaches to goal attainment)

- Comparative evaluation of consequences (predicting the result of each alternative)
- Final selection of course of action (decision making)

It should be recognized that each of these activities is not only interrelated but also actually overlaps the others. All the activities can vary as to the type and the number of scientific tools employed. For example, an analysis of the situation might well include such scientific methods as operations research, mathematical modeling, survey research, and DELPHI and statistical inferences. The enormous data processing power of a computer can and should be used in support of these police agencies.

A basic problem for police agencies in urban America concerns their policy with respect to planning police agencies. Pointedly, once past a critical point in the accumulation of sufficient resources, they have grown at an unpredicted and an ever-accelerating pace. Through their development, services not available to our citizens a half century ago have become necessities for American society. Police services move in many directions: toward improving the physical security of life, toward maintaining justice, toward solving community social problems, and toward delivering general government services. The rapidity of societal and technological change, and the diversity of existing and potential police services, put a premium upon the anticipation and direction of these changes through systematic planning. "Any [police] organization which does not have a four-, or five-, or ten-year plan is risking destruction or a series of continuing crises in its operations."[6]

The planning process can be performed through two auxiliary or staff functions, one to develop specific alternative courses of action for anticipated changes in the environment, the other to gather predictive indicators about community changes and reactions to police programs. Both these functions are generally combined in a single staff group.

Once the policy questions have been answered affirmatively —that is, there will be in fact a planning process—still another question crops up. The police manager is confronted with a decision about the levels of detail and comprehensiveness that should be included in the plan(s). In this case, the manager must rely on the process itself to generate significant plans.

The planning process should be capable of handling various levels of complexity and scope. A plan that is overly narrow, or overly broad, frequently fails to meet its intended objectives. Of the two failings, inappropriate broadness is the more common.

Such grandiose but impractical plans are actually a *very* common phenomenon, particularly among managers entrusted with long-range planning. "Planners are notorious for designing master plans that call for absurdly unrealistic behavior on the part of other agents (such as massive expenditures on parks and nearly perfect law enforcement)."[7] Downs refers to this too broad approach as the *superman syndrome.*

All police managers engaging in crime prevention have some incentive for indulging in the superman syndrome. It is much easier to make theoretical assumptions about how others will behave than to negotiate with them and base plans on what they are likely to do in actuality. In theory, every police manager can assume that others will perform their functions and responsibilities in the way he himself regards as most efficient. The actual behavior of these people, however, will be heavily influenced by their own views of what is efficient as well as by self-interest. These elements are often difficult to foresee.

Superman planning is intellectually more satisfying than realistic planning. Unfettered by reality, crime prevention can develop far more original, daring, sweeping, and internally consistent visions of what should be done than if they actually have to deal with the disenchantment of conflicting interests in the real world. The superman plans produced by a solid agency far too often serve specific functions as targets or aspirations that are in fact unattainable (at least in the time proposed) but nevertheless provide utility to their beholders. For example, planning for preventive police patrol operations normally contains a statement in the plan that crime *will* decrease by a significant percentage. For the above reasons, superman planning is the great temptation of all managers faced by the immense complexities of attempting to develop appropriate maneuvers in policy space. The propensity to yield to this temptation is in direct proportion to the breadth of their operations and the absence of restraints forcing them to create realistic plans.

Planning for Crime Prevention Planning

Although the various managerial functions are interrelated and the police manager performs all at one time or another, any given phase of organizational activity must begin with planning. As mentioned earlier, planning is the process by which the police agency applies its resource to changing environmental forces and by which it achieves its goals. It is a highly dynamic function and must be carried out effectively so as to provide an integrated delivery system in which inputs (resources) are efficiently converted into outputs (services), and goals are attained (crime reduction).

Police planning is comprised of three levels of complexity. *Environmental* planning is the most basic, identifying the broad parameters (social, cultural, political, and legislative) within which the department must function. Further, the environmental plan explicates the goals that the agency is committed to accomplish. The second level is *internal organization* planning which specifies the organizational structure, procedures, policies, and functional relationships that the department utilizes to achieve both the environmental and tactical plans. In turn, *tactical* planning expresses the service demands, criminal justice relationships, agency-clientele relationships, and specific objectives that the department intends to achieve. Tactical planning for our purposes can be dichotomized into crime control and crime prevention.

While the programs and activities related to both crime control and prevention differ considerably in intent and style, the following planning model would apply to both. In this instance, let us view the proposed model as being one that perpetuates the prevention of crime. To start with and depending on the size and structure of the department, management first divides itself into a number of planning teams. Let us assume that there are three such teams: team policing (TP), sustaining activities (SA) or staff, and general management (GM). The GM team is the top team and provides overall coordination and direction for the others. In the main, the GM team concentrates on environmental planning. One or more of the members on the GM team is also included on one of the other teams. Thus, there is overlapping membership, which tends to facilitate coordination and communication. It is the task of the GM representative to aid the team members in organizing to acquire the skills necessary to create and maintain a planning process, and in supporting them in their attempts to implement the resultant plans. In essence, the GM team member serves as a stimulus linking agent to the other teams. The TP and SA teams contain a small number of middle managers, supervisors, and officers who represent the total divisional membership. Considerable rotation among the members ought to occur so that fresh ideas are constantly inserted into the process. The planning and research unit should be given the responsibility for facilitating, researching, developing, and implementing the ideas of the three teams. Thus, this unit acts as staff to the planning teams.

The planning teams are to be evaluated according to their output—*plans*. If the plan is viable, implemented, and evaluated as meeting specific crime prevention objectives, then one can assume that the processes being used by the teams are sound. Broadly speaking, the plans and the processes that they represent can be judged as follows:

- *Excellent*—rigorous logic is being applied and has resulted in a written description of a generalized plan and of specific action plans; they are widely understood and supported and have strongly influenced both effectiveness and development, as they are revised on a scheduled basis.

- *Average*—a strategic plan exists in that the character of the agency and the broad outlines of its probable growth are understood; it has not been evaluated against criteria of rigorous logic; there is no scheduled basis for plan review, though review of police operations and results does occur.

- *Unacceptable*—there is no plan to set the character or the direction of the agency; the department's operations are best pictured as evolving from tradition or as responses to community conditions in an opportunistic way.

Commitment to Planning

*Recommen-
dation*

Every police agency should develop planning processes which will anticipate short- and long-term problems and suggest alternative solutions to them. Policy should be written to guide all employees toward effective administrative and operational planning decisions. Every police agency should adopt procedures immediately to assure the planning competency of its personnel through the establishment of qualifications for selection and training.

1. Every police agency should establish written policy setting out specific goals and objectives of the planning effort, quantified and measurable where possible, including at least the following:
   a. To develop and suggest plans that will improve police service in furthering the goals of the agency;
   b. To review existing agency plans to ascertain their suitability, to determine any weaknesses, to update or devise improvement when needed, and to assure they are suitably recorded;
   c. To gather and organize into usable format information needed for agency planning.
2. Every police agency should stress the necessity for continual planning in all areas throughout the agency, to include at least:

a. Within administrative planning: long-range fiscal and management plans;
b. Within operational planning: specific operational, procedural, and tactical plans;
c. Extradepartmental plans; and
d. Research and development
3. Every police agency should establish written qualifications for employees assigned specifically to planning activities.
4. Every police agency should provide training necessary for all personnel to carry out their planning responsibilities.
5. If there are planning needs that cannot be satisfied by agency personnel, the police agency should satisfy these needs through an appropriate arrangement with another police agency, another governmental agency, or a private consultant.

The Requirement   Presently, extensive planning, administrative as well as operational, is one of the most critical needs of our police.[8] While few executives would disagree with this, we find even fewer who have taken positive steps to encourage or implement such planning. This failure implies to other police personnel that he considers planning to be unimportant, or that he is not interested in how they perform their work. The first tends to encourage the personnel to adopt the same attitude toward planning; the second, lowers morale and efficiency. Obviously, both detract from the effectiveness of agency operations. At the same time, when the police executive does take steps to establish a planning unit or to delegate planning responsibilities, problems can develop if he does not clearly delineate the relationship between the planning unit and other agency personnel. Far too often planning personnel feel removed from operations personnel, while operations personnel believe that they have been relieved of all planning duties.

The first step to rectify this situation should be the formulation and dissemination of a strong and unequivocal policy statement expressing commitment to planning and to positive change. Providing the necessary organizational structure and staff for planning should reinforce commitment; at the same time it prepares the agency to meet its needs. Further, the police chief/sheriff must establish the organizational structure and the staffing necessary to generate a full spectrum of effective planning for his agency. (When a product is primarily the result of an individual effort, its quality is usually limited to the qualifications, training, attitudes, and personality of that person—and police planning is no exception.)

*Broad
Goals and
Specific
Objectives
of Planning*

No police activity can be justified if it is not intended to further the goals of the agency, and planning is no exception. Furnishing assistance to the police executive in identifying and defining agency goals, and then developing plans to accomplish them is the crux of planning. Yesterday's plan usually has only historical value today; a continual, critical reevaluation of all existing plans is essential to the furthering of agency goals. Each plan, to be of the most value to agency personnel, must be formalized and made available to those concerned with its implementation.

The ultimate success of any plan lies in its degree of implementation. Indeed a good plan poorly executed is as ineffective as a poor plan. We can look at a plan as an insurance policy—it can remain on a shelf for years, and no one will know how well it will serve until the time arrives to use it. Each plan should include, therefore, preparation for its implementation. Also, each plan should endorse continuous planning throughout implementation in order to provide assistance in adapting the plan to existing conditions.

*Perpetual
Planning*

As mentioned above, agency policy on planning in addition to establishing the goals and objectives of the effort should stress that planning cannot be a one-time activity. On the contrary, it should be an ongoing activity that consistently guides the agency toward its goals and objectives. Adequate direction cannot be given to agency personnel if any phase of administrative planning —long-range, fiscal, or other management planning—is not kept current. Long-range planning is intended to furnish aid in establishing the scope and focus of agency goals, and in devising the means of accomplishing major projects of long duration. Long-range planning thus involves: (1) building upon past experience by gathering, organizing, and interpreting data; (2) forecasting future needs by analyzing public attitudes and values; (3) making predictions on the basis of current trends; and (4) offering ideas and suggestions for improvement through change. Many of the bases for long-range decisions are subject to changes, most of which are beyond the control of our police. An effective, continual, long-range planning program will facilitate the detection of these changes and corresponding modification of agency scope or focus. Let us suppose, for example, that an agency embarked on a long-range plan to establish a vice unit, and the state enacted legislation legalizing gambling; some modification of the plan would be necessary. Whether the plan should be abandoned or continued with an emphasis on regulation can be determined only with additional planning.

A continual fiscal planning program helps the police executive to determine the necessity for fiscal readjustments to meet contingencies, to reassess expenditure priorities to meet contingencies, to reevaluate expenditure priorities throughout the fiscal year, and to expedite budget preparation for the succeeding fiscal year. Other management planning also must be continual. The need for evaluation or reevaluation, for discontinuing or modifying the old or for implementing the new, and for supplementary data upon which to make planning decisions, does not arise at regular intervals or at predictable, prearranged times. The relaxation of an entrance requirement by a civil service commission, the increase in the minimum hours for a course required by the state's standards and training commission, and a court's decision regarding a disciplinary action could each be initiators of a need for planning in recruitment, training, and disciplinary procedures, respectively. Planning cannot satisfy these needs unless it is a continual program.

Because many police functions require action or assistance from persons or agencies outside the police agency (or are affected by them), police planning must be coordinated with them. This, of course, injects a major variable into the planning process, one that is in large measure beyond the authority of the police agency. To illustrate, the need for cooperative planning on a continual basis is apparent in jurisdictions with large college campuses (Madison, Wisconsin), large military installations (Oceanside, California), or large convention or amusement centers (Orlando, Florida).

Planning Competency Police agencies have a tendency to promote an individual or to give him a special assignment because of his proficiency as a police officer rather than because of his potential as a supervisor or specialist.[9] Hence, personnel are at times assigned to planning units for reasons other than their expertise in planning. Just as we have seen that the importance of planning in the police agency must be emphasized, so must the importance of the qualifications and training of the planner. To ensure the competency of personnel, our police agencies should determine the qualifications for such personnel, put them in writing, and establish procedures for the assessment of candidates for such assignments.

To begin with, planning is not a process that lends itself to close supervision, and most often the planner works independently. Therefore, he should be a self-starter and a diligent worker who needs only minimum supervision. Second, because of the subjective nature of his work, and because of the need for the concurrence of others, his work will be reviewed critically but constructively. He must be able to accept this without resentment.

For similar reasons, the planner should be able to work well with others of all ranks.

Third, the planner should be able to analyze information, recognize and understand relationships, and draw objective conclusions. At the same time, this individual should be capable of using imagination and creativity to conceive fresh solutions, to explore new alternatives, and to develop innovative ideas. Four, a planner must be able to articulate his plans by expressing himself clearly and concisely, both orally and in writing. Extensive correspondence to obtain information, both from individuals and by surveys, is essential; and the correspondents must understand precisely what information is needed. Initial drafts complete with recommended alternatives may be required for review and decision by command personnel. These too should be easily understood by readers.

The planner often needs to interview to obtain information. On occasion, he may need to make an oral presentation on behalf of a plan, and the adoption of his plan and its successful implementation might well depend upon his ability to verbally express himself. Finally, there is no need for all personnel in a planning capacity to be (or to have been) sworn personnel, but there is a need for every planner to possess a thorough understanding of the organization, its component parts and interrelationships, and the functions and responsibilities of each. Since the police agency is one part of the CJS, and many of its activities affect or are affected by each of the other components, the planner should be knowledgeable about them. He should know how the activities of one component affect the others; for without this knowledge he might find it difficult to recommend compatible procedures.

Training for Planning

To do their job effectively, all police employees must engage in planning to some extent. The type and degree of planning required of them will depend largely on their assignments and responsibilities. Unfortunately, not all employees are equally qualified to do so. Often an action is unsuccessful because an officer did not: understand the problem, determine specifically what he wanted to accomplish by the action, or consider alternatives. Incorporating into the recruit training program a course in basic planning techniques (and arranging comparable inservice courses for those past basic training) should be a step toward increasing effectiveness. Additionally, personnel assigned to specific planning responsibilities, even though they meet the agency's minimum qualifications for these positions, cannot be expected to perform effectively without appropriate advanced training. This training should include courses in planning methodology and research techniques; data collection and processing; determining criteria for evaluation; identifying problems, objectives, or alternatives; reducing risk in decision making; and activity scheduling, resource allocation, and program control.

We find that the majority of police agencies do not have the expertise to conduct the necessary advanced training. Educational intitutions are the most logical, and usually the most economical, source for this type of training on an ongoing basis, but where a new unit is being established, particularly if a group of police personnel are to be trained as a unit, consulting organizations may be in a better position to adapt the training to the specific needs of the police agency.

Planning
Resources A small police agency without a full-time planning capability can best obtain ongoing planning support from a larger agency. Similarly, a large agency with its own planning staff may need to arrange for occasional outside planning support and may acquire it from another police agency. Even the largest of agencies will require outside expertise at times. Our police agencies, regardless of their size, must not limit themselves to their own or other police agencies for needed expertise. Rather, they should consider such sources as government agencies, educational institutions, and private consultants. Plainly, no source should be overlooked.

Agency and Jurisdictional Planning

Recommen-
dation *Every police agency should immediately identify the types of planning necessary for effective operation, and should assign specific responsibility for research and development, and police agency and jurisdictional planning.*

1. Every police agency with seventy-five or more personnel should establish a unit staffed with at least one employee whose full-time responsibility will be intra-agency administrative planning and coordination of all planning activities for the agency.
   a. The size and composition of this planning unit should be proportionate to the size of the agency and the magnitude of the present and anticipated planning task.
   b. The employee in charge of the planning unit should have no more than one person in the chain of

command between him and the police chief executive.

2. Every police agency organized into subdivisions should delineate divisional planning responsibilities and should provide personnel accordingly.

   a. To the extent feasible, divisional planning should be a staff activity performed by the agency's central planning unit. If centralized planning for a division is not feasible, the agency should assign planning personnel to the division.

   b. The agency should assign a specialized section of the central planning unit or a separate specialized planning unit to specialized divisions or to divisions with specialized planning requirements.

   c. The agency should ensure coordination of all agency planning efforts.

3. Every police agency with fewer than seventy-five personnel should assign responsibility for administrative planning and coordination of all planning activities of the agency.

   a. If the magnitude of the agency's planning task justifies a full-time employee, one should be assigned; and

   b. If it does not, this task should be assigned to an employee with related duties.

4. Every police agency should assign responsibility for maintaining close interagency planning.

   a. Interagency planning should be engaged in by police agencies that are geographically close, that regularly operate concurrently within the same jurisdictional boundaries, that participate in a plan for mutual aid, or that logically should participate in any combined or regional police effort.

   b. Where regional police planning agencies exist, every police agency should assign responsibility for planning with those regional police planning agencies whose decisions might affect the assigning agency. This responsibility should include liaison with the established regional planning agency or other representative of the State Planning Agency.

5. Every police agency should participate in cooperative planning with all other governmental subdivisions of the jurisdiction when such planning can have an effect on crime, public safety, or efficient police operations.

   a. Every local governmental entity, in all matters of mutual interest, immediately should provide for police planning with that of other governmental subdivisions of the jurisdiction.

   b. Every police agency should assign responsibility for such planning immediately. This assignment should include at least the responsibility for joint planning, when applicable, with the local government administrative office, local government attorney's office, finance department, purchasing department, personnel department, civil service commission, fire department, department of public works, utilities department, building inspection unit, street or highway department, parks department, recreation department, planning unit, and health department.

Planning for Planning

Planning can be formal or informal, centralized or decentralized, structured or haphazard, painstakingly thought out or completed on the spur of the moment; whatever the form, planning occurs in every police agency. Obviously, the planning needs of each police agency are different. Clearly the large agency serving a densely populated urban area has different needs than the small agency serving a sparsely populated rural area. Moreover, the needs are not static.

When establishing operational plans, the police agency should research the activities of community groups and organizations whose activities might influence police operations. If possible, members of those groups should be involved in the planning of police service that may affect their activity. Included should be social groups, service clubs, civic and political organizations, educational institutions, professional or vocational associations, business groups and labor unions, and any others who might be appropriate. Therefore we can see that research and development is the foundation of progressive planning. Regrettably, the results of research and development are seldom shared by criminal justice agencies and, as a consequence, are often duplicated needlessly. A major step toward improving this situation was taken with the creation of the National Criminal Justice Reference Service (NCJRS) to meet the technical information needs of the CJS. The services provided without charge by the NCJRS are: (1) selective dissemination of information materials tailored to specific user needs; (2) selected distribution of hard copy documents; (3) selected topic digests; (4) current awareness materials; (5) document retrieval indexes; (6) a national criminal justice thesaurus; (7) search and retrieval services; and (8) references and referrals. The NCJRS will eventually have "on-line" capability that will allow access from remote terminals for interactive searchers. This shoud result in faster, more reliable access to existing documentation.

Staffing a Planning Unit

When the magnitude and complexity of an agency's planning needs justify it, the chief or sheriff should establish a unit staffed with at least one employee whose full-time responsibility is administrative planning and coordination of all planning activities of the agency. Many agencies will experience this need in the range of fifty to seventy-five sworn personnel. Indeed some agencies with fewer than fifty personnel have a planning unit. (Keep in mind that as with the creation of any organizational unit, whether line or staff, the magnitude and complexity of both present and projected tasks should be analyzed to assist in determining the size and composition of the unit.) Planning takes *time* and thus costs money. To understaff a unit will cause poor planning or result in a concentration on some aspects (usually the more overt or urgent short-range needs) while other planning, particularly long-range planning, will not be accomplished.

The planning unit should be staffed with those experienced and trained in administrative analysis, systems and data analysis, fiscal affairs, legislative analysis, and police operations. Where this is impractical, the agency should arrange for this expertise to come from without. Most of our larger agencies across the nation have found it advantageous to divide their planning process into such specialities as long-range planning, management services, operations analysis, fiscal affairs, grants, legislative analysis, and special projects. Functional specialization facilitates the provision of staff planning to all units in the agency.

The planning unit should be charged with coordinating the overall planning within the agency and assisting others in their planning efforts. Thus the planning staff must be aware of the planning that is being done in the agency and make certain that operational, administrative, and long-range plans are compatible. Further, they must see that there is a minimum of duplication of effort and that planning personnel are available to assist by providing data and expertise. Finally, it is best that the unit interfaces directly with the chief or a top level police manager.

Planning as it Relates to Organizational Size

Operational planning without divisionwide application, in turn, should be delegated to the commanders of smaller units. Further, operational planning without unitwide application should be even further delegated, some of it finally reaching the field supervisor and the officer in the field. The operational planning responsibilities for each level, therefore, from major division commander to field officer, should be articulated and documented through agency manuals, job descriptions, or agency orders.

To ensure a coordinated effort, administrative level staff planning should be performed by a centralized planning unit. If for any reason planning for a particular division cannot be effectively accomplished, personnel from the central unit are best assigned in a staff capacity within the division, preferably on an ad hoc basis until centralized planning is again feasible. Similarly, if a division (e.g., patrol) or a specialized police unit (e.g., juvenile) has unique planning requirements, the central planning unit should have the responsibility of assigning planning personnel to the division or unit for the duration of the special need.

Smaller police agencies should establish a planning unit based upon the same criteria used by their larger counterparts. The fact that a planning unit cannot be justified in some smaller agencies does not mean that planning can be de-emphasized. Instead the police chief should assign responsibility for administrative planning activities to the police managers of the agency (unless he performs these duties himself). In making the administrative planning assignment, the police chief has the same responsibility for providing training. Relatedly, some agencies have satisfactorily combined training and administrative planning assignments; others have combined planning and community relations. In any event, the assignment must not be delegated into obscurity.

Interagency Planning

Our nation's police system is a network of approximately 25,000 agencies, many with overlapping jurisdictional boundaries. There is an obvious need for interagency planning as a means to coordinate operational efforts; to avoid duplication of effort; to share common knowledge; and to devise more effective, more efficient, or more economical procedures and administrative arrangements.

Interagency planning is not new. Its history, however, has been primarily operational planning on an "as needed" or crisis basis. Hence, usually it was done to prepare for a specific and near-term event under circumstances which involved two or more agencies. Much has been done in the last decade to facilitate interagency planning. Police executives and sheriffs have recognized —and in some cases have been forced to acknowledge—the need to participate in planning for mutual aid, for interagency training programs, for consolidation or regionalization of certain functions, and for other programs of mutual benefit to their respective agencies. Local and national professional associations have played a major part in bringing city and county police personnel together to discuss mutual problems and promote interagency planning. Furthermore, the creation of local, regional, and state coordinating agencies by government has provided a more formal vehicle for interagency planning. Specifically, a result of the Law Enforcement Assistance Act of 1965 was the "encouragement" of each state to form a planning committee to coordinate crime control. The Omnibus Crime Control and Safe Streets Act of 1968 "required" each state to set up a State Planning Agency (SPA) to receive block grants from the Law Enforcement Assistance Administration and to disburse subgrants to local agencies.

In some SPAs and the regional planning agencies under them, the planners perform more coordinating than actual planning; they review plans and allocate, approve, or deny grants. The planner, the plan, or both may or may not be reflective of the needs of the community served. Problems usually considered impediments to effective planning at this level include a lack of expertise in persons serving as planners, insufficient participation by involved agencies, and failure to secure or even to seek agreement from the involved agencies. This is not to say that the SPAs and their regional counterparts have not carried out effective planning or that they have not provided valuable assistance. On the contrary, they are in line for commendations when one recognizes the tortuous political/economic environment within which they must attempt to plan.

In spite of the progress made in interagency planning, it is only a beginning—and much more interagency planning must be accomplished. It must be done horizontally, between cities or between counties; it must be done vertically, by city and county, or by county and state; and it must be done regionally. Every police agency should participate in this type of planning to increase the agency's effectiveness and efficiency and to contribute to the effectiveness and efficiency of the police system and the overall CJS.

Cooperative
Planning

Many activities of the police agency impact and are impacted by the activities of nonpolice agencies and subdivisions of our government. These activities may be either administrative or operational, they may or may not be public safety oriented, and they may be 24 hours a day or only between Monday and Friday from 8 A.M. to 5 P.M.; but many (in fact some would assert "most") are sufficiently interrelated with those of the police agency that they require some degree of cooperative planning.

Whether the administrative head of the government is appointed (a city manager or a county administrative officer) or elected (a major or chairman of a county commission), the police chief or sheriff executive must cooperate with that office. The many variances in governmental structure and approach throughout our nation generate different relationships between the administrative head of the government and the local law enforcement executive. We often find that the appointed administrator, particularly in strong manager-type governments, and occasionally the elected administrator, is in the chain of command between the police executive and the legislative body. The government administrator may have powers of review, recommendation, or even modification of police agency input to the legislative body. It is not uncommon for an elected "administrator" to have at least limited veto powers and thus control police agency input. Admittedly there is the same potential for conflict, but combined planning in areas of mutual responsibility can form the basis for unified direction.

The government's attorney (city attorney or county counsel, as distinct from district attorney or prosecuting attorney) is usually responsible for providing legal counsel to the legislative body and to major department heads, acting in civil suits, and drafting local ordinance legislation. Because civil suits sometimes involve the police as investigators or as parties to a suit, and because many local ordinances affect police activities, it is essential for the police to contribute early input through joint planning with the government attorney's office.

Other administrative subdivisions have duties that interrelate with those of the police agency. For instance, we can see that the police agency and the finance department have reciprocal concerns. It is important that the police agency conform to established accounting methods and that it provide information to the finance department. In turn, the finance department must provide expenditure account classifications and facilitate interfund transfers to the police agency. The police agency and the purchasing department also hold reciprocal interests. The police agency must comply with bidding regulations and furnish adequate requests for proposals, invitations to bid, and firm specifications. Again, the purchasing department must select vendors from whom service as well as price can be obtained, and must award bids in time to forestall delays in deliveries. Police, personnel, and civil service must coordinate recruitment, entrance requirements, promotions, and sometimes pay or fringe compensation. Planning concerns such reciprocal interests, and police participation in planning assures that police needs are presented and understood.

A number of civilian government subdivisions perform public safety or regulatory duties that often must be coordinated with police activities. Fire departments and government-operated rescue and ambulance units are directly involved in rendering aid. Fire prevention and building inspection units and certain health department units serve in a semi-investigative capacity, making routine or special inspections to ensure compliance with laws within their respective spheres of activity. When violations are detected, enforcement action is accomplished in many cases with the assistance of the police. Coordination between police and these units should be the result of joint planning.

Other governmental subdivisions such as the parks department, recreation department, and those controlling public facilities such as convention centers, are concerned with problems associated with large gatherings of people. These gatherings concern police too. Combined planning by the police and these departments should result in sound preparation for events and thus a reduction in the risks created by them.

Public works departments, utilities departments, and street or highway departments (departments involved in design, construction, and maintenance of public facilities) can contribute to the police effort in a number of ways. Much of the data on which city engineering is based are obtained and provided by the police. It is the same with the other departments; there are interrelated activities requiring joint planning. Additionally, we find that the government's planning department also contributes. A city or county master plan would not be complete without police input, nor would many smaller plans concerning city or county development. On the other hand, police planning can gain much from the planning department.

Regrettably, many local and state governments have no provision for joint planning between subdivisions. Admittedly, some department heads meet and confer regularly, thus providing general unity of direction. Also, representatives from two or more departments often will meet to plan for a specific event—but this is not enough. What is required is an established means for police planning in conjunction with other subdivisions. Every police executive should assign qualified personnel specific responsibility for combined planning with each subdivision of government that holds reciprocal interests with the police agency.

Crime Prevention Planning: Phases and Steps in the Development of a Plan

Fundamentally, a crime prevention plan should contain three major phases or sections: program, expected results, and estimated resources. When combined, the three phases and their respective steps will present a total view of the plan. While brief and essentially in outline format, the following serves as a guide for the construction of a plan. We began with a description of a program(s), since a plan consists of at least one, and usually more than one, program element.

Program   1. *Goals—Why*   This step should show, in terms of relating to the satisfaction of one or more specific client needs, the goals of the prevention plan and the specific objectives of each program component. In addition, reference should be made to the pertinent unit, bureau, and agency goals in order to show where the plan and each of its programs fits into the comprehensive plan of the agency. Schematically, it would appear as follows:

COMPREHENSIVE PLAN (Agency and Interagency)

Crime Prevention Plan (Agency)

Crime Prevention Programs (Intra-Agency)

2. *Responsibilities—Who*   Indicate the manager's name and title, and provide a statement of the responsibilities of each identifiable functional unit involved in fulfilling the goals listed in the plan and program objectives.

3. *Organization—How*   Express the relationships among functional units. Where appropriate, a chart can be used to depict how the various units are to arrange themselves so as to accomplish the plan.

4. *Scope—How much*   Indicate the volume of plan and program transactions. Examples could be the number of commercial business firms and managers visited in regard to anti-burglary techniques and devices; citizens involved in a ride-along program; presentations given to public groups on the topic of avoiding being the victim of a crime; students contacted while in school concerning the subject of an individual's rights and responsibilities in our society.

5. *Activities—What*   Provide brief statements of the involved tasks.

6. *Timing—When*   Describe both the requirements for turnaround and the seasonal or cyclical aspects of the program. That a ride-along program should be offered during periods of time when the probabilities of collective violence are low is a case in point.

7. *Location—Where*   Indicate whether the program is performed only in a single location or involves field officers. Is it strictly a specialized activity or are field activities required? As an example, should the patrol officer periodically visit students on the school grounds in his assigned area, or should a specialist provide such coverage to all schools within the jurisdictional boundaries?

8. *Interrelationships—With Whom*   The final section of the Program Description should indicate any interfaces or interrelationships with other intra- and inter-agency programs.

Expected Results

1. *Measures of Effectiveness*   Develop measures of effectiveness that relate achievements to stated objectives in terms of citizens' benefits. If possible, these should be quantitative. A method for systematically obtaining information as to citizen satisfaction with the programs is most desirable.
2. *Measures of Efficiency*   Quantitative standards should be developed to indicate program efficiency. Efficiency is concerned with productivity, unit cost, work measurement, and similar matters—it is concerned with how economically a job is done. (On the other hand, effectiveness, although concerned with efficiency, fundamentally addresses goals and objectives in getting the job done and whether accomplishment of the job has the desired impact on goals and objectives.)
3. *Targeted Milestones*   List the dates of any event that would constitute significant insights to the management plan, and the checkpoints for the program components. (This step is usually more appropriate for programs than for levels of effort.)

Estimated Resources

Provide a schedule of the estimated resource requirements for the plan and programs by type of expenditure. Plans should show total estimated cost as well as cost by year. Levels of effort require an estimate for the current year plus the following year (at least). The format for the Estimated Resources Phase should be developed jointly by the Crime Prevention Group and the Budget Group. In general, it should be as close to the budget proposal as is consistent with the purposes of the Crime Prevention Plan.

A Generalized Example of a Crime Prevention Plan

Let us now take a graphic look at the beginning of a plan development for a local government.[10] It will be seen that the plan is comprised of program components that are intended to reduce crime through its prevention and control. Also, one will observe that the federal government is providing both technical and monetary assistance during the *planning process* and *program implementation*. The following figures respectively depict:

Figure 6.1   Bar chart showing three-year timetable.
Figure 6.2   Relationship of LEAA Assistance Team and Police Agency Planning Unit.
Figure 6.3   Overview of three-year improvement program.
Figure 6.4   Organization of government agencies expected to participate.
Figure 6.5   Major program goals and suggested projects.

Activity	Calendar Years			Remarks
	1974	1975	1976	
1.0 Program design & development				
1.1 Selection of LEAA assistance team _____				
1.2 Coordination with local officials _____				Continuous activity
1.3 Problem diagnosis _____				30-day effort
1.4 Development of project work plans _____				60-day effort
1.5 Development of responsibility analysis papers _____				Continuous activity
2.0 Program implementation				
2.1 Selection of contractors & project staff _____				
2.2 Implementation of planned projects				
2.2.1 Projects for 1974 _____				Various grants awarded
2.2.2 Projects for 1975 _____				Various grants awarded
2.2.3 Projects for 1976 _____				Various grants awarded
2.3 Program review & modification				Continuous activity
3.0 Program evaluation				
3.1 Selection of evaluation contractor _____				
3.2 Selection, design & implementation of evaluation studies _____				Continuous activity

Figure 6.1 LEAA initiatives program: Proposed development plan for Police Agency X

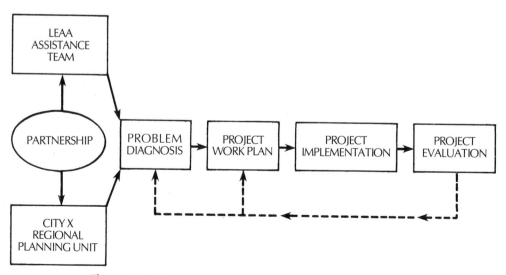

Figure 6.2 LEAA National priority program assistance team

133

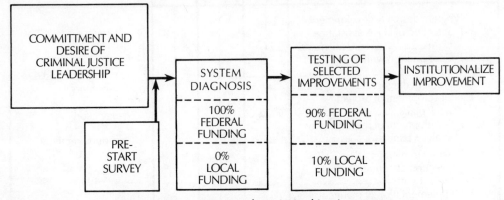

Figure 6.3 Improving the criminal justice system

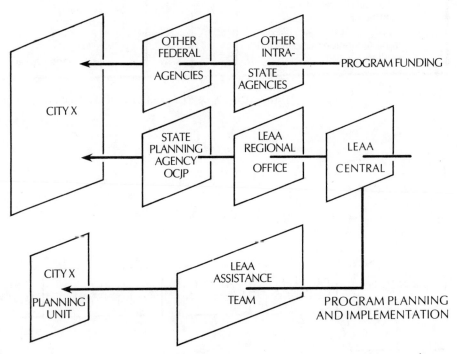

Figure 6.4 Organization and management: Police Agency X Project (proposed)

Figure 6.5 Crime prevention & control in Police Agency X: System-wide goals

Major Goals	Suggested Projects
I. Crime prevention	
A. Increase public awareness	• Multi-media programs • Local volunteer groups that publicize CJS efforts • CJS-sponsored crime prevention clinics
B. Reduce opportunities for crime	• General urban design and specific urban housing planning • Neighborhood crime control programs • "Operation identification" projects • Portable alarm systems • Rape and assault prevention programs
C. Alleviate social and economic conditions that promote crime	• General housing, education, health, and transportation programs • Police Youth Corps projects • CJS drug treatment referral programs • Employment assistance programs for disadvantaged youth • Vocational and educational training projects • "New pride" projects • Youth services bureau program • "Street academy" program for school dropouts
II. Crime control	
A. Reduce juvenile gang activities	• Juvenile gang intervention programs • Program to protect school staff, property, and students
B. Increase CJS coordination	• Probation-parole coordinator project • Programs to improve CJS data • Family crisis intervention training for CJS personnel • Courts, prosecutors, and police liaison project • Court diagnostic center for juvenile offenders • Youth neighborhood coordinator projects
C. Reduce obstacles to citizen support	• Courts' initiative program
D. Rehabilitate the victim	• Medical and psychological assistance • "Self-help" projects involving families and neighbors • Financial assistance programs • Organized counseling and referral services • Field assistance to victims
E. Reduce recidivism	• Coordinated juvenile work release projects • Civilian community service officer program • Community residential facility for youthful offenders • Community-based probation projects

Learning Exercises

1.   Divide the class into groups of four to six members each. Assign each group a crime prevention planning project. Some of the possible projects are: (1) burglary prevention, (2) robbery prevention, (3) school resource officer, (4) neighborhood watch, and (5) pre-delinquency youth counselling. The groups are to take thirty minutes to generate a plan for mounting their particular project. Next, each group is to present its plan orally in three minutes. Finally, for fifteen minutes, or more, the entire class should discuss the interrelationships of their various plans. (In your planning be certain to include goals, time-frames, resources needed, and projected costs.) The entire exercise can be conducted in sixty minutes.

2.   Again, in groups of four to six members secure a criminal justice plan from a police, courts, or corrections agency. Individually review the plan; then as a group examine it. Some questions to pose of one another are: "Is it relevant?" "Is it realistic?" "Is it overly limited?" "Is it overly comprehensive?" "Are there clear-cut goals?" In general compare it to the recommendations in this chapter. (This group phase of the exercise should consume no longer than forty minutes.) Lastly, each group should present orally in three minutes its critique of the plan. This exercise can be performed in sixty minutes or more.

Endnotes

1.   By far one of the most exciting books of this decade is Alvin Toffler's *Future Shock* (New York: Random House, 1970).
2.   Perry E. Rosove, *The Impact of Social Trends on Crime and Criminal Justice* (Sacramento, CA.: American Justice Institute —Project STAR 1973), p. 331.
3.   John W. Gardner, *Self-Renewal: The Individual and the Innovative Society* (New York: Harper & Row, Publishers, 1963), p. 5.
4.   J. Lawrence Laughlin, *The Elements of Political Economy* (New York: American Book Company, 1896), p. 223.
5.   An excellent discussion of the relationship between decision making and planning can be found in Amitai Etzioni, "Mixed Scanning—A Systems Approach," *Public Administration Review* 26 (January/February, 1969), pp. 3–15.
6. Daniel Katz and Robert L. Kahn, *The Social Psychology of*

Organizations (New York: John Wiley & Sons, Inc., 1966), p. 272.

7. Anthony Downs, *Inside Bureaucracy* (Boston: Little, Brown and Company, 1967), p. 218.

8. This section and the next are extracted from the National Advisory Commission on Criminal Justice Standards and Goals, *Police* (Washington, D.C.: U.S. Government Printing Office, 1973), pp. 117–28.

9. This phenomenon is clearly not unique to the police environment. Dr. Peter conceptualizes it as achieving one's highest level of incompetency. See Lawrence J. Peter and Raymond Hull, *The Peter Principle* (New York: William Morrow and Company, Inc., 1969).

10. In unmasking "Police Agency X" we discover that in the real world it is the City of Compton, California. In summary, in 1974 LEAA selected Compton as a target site for massive assistance under its National Priority Program. A recent text pertaining to the subject of this chapter is worthy of your attention. See Michael E. O'Neill, Ronald F. Bykowski, and Robert S. Blair, *Criminal Justice Planning: A Practical Approach* (San Jose, Ca.: Justice Systems Development, Inc., 1976).

7

Crime Prevention Programs: Hardware Emphases

Subjecting our crime prevention strategies to evaluative research will prove less comforting but, in the long run, more valuable. On some occasions, close analysis will show that the crime rate could have been expected to decrease even if no new treatment had been administered; in other situations, a steady rise in crime over a long period of time that can be attributed to factors such as an increase in the population at risk will indicate that, in the absence of a new treatment, the crime rate would probably have continued to increase. In some, but not all cases, evaluative research may be able to provide rough estimates of how much the rate would have increased or decreased in the absence of treatment and thus give us a baseline for testing the value of new treatments.

Providing a baseline, so that reliable determinations can be made about the degree of crime reduction attributable to particular counter-measures, is an absolute necessity in any but the most wasteful of crime-control policies. Without such a baseline, it may be assumed that some strategies reduce crime when in fact they do not. Then, too, the preventive effects of other programs may be underestimated because we fail to account for expected increases in crime. Even when counter-measures have some effect on crime, overestimating that effect by neglecting the possibility of natural decrease may provoke the use of programs that are not worth their cost—and, worse still, postpone the development of new and more effective strategies.*

Preview   Hardware oriented crime prevention strategies are omnipresent in contemporary criminal justice thought, if not in deed. Basically, such programs are structured in accordance

*Franklin E. Zimring, *Perspectives On Deterrance* (Washington, D.C.: U.S. Government Printing Office, 1971), p. 16.

with reducing our threat of being victimized—or at least reducing the impact of the victimization. In any event, and in this case, hardware crime prevention programs encompass the use of physical devices and concepts to reduce crime.

Physical planning is of paramount consideration today in our attack on crime. The police most certainly, and perhaps in some instances other criminal justice agencies, should be involved in decisions that affect the general configuration of the community. Many crimes could be avoided, if not totally precluded, if only the police were allowed to input their judgments in the physical planning of the community in which they serve. The identification of property is yet another example of a hardware emphasis. Most simply, it means the marking of one's property in order to better identify it, and make it more difficult to "fence." In turn, bicycle security programs utilize a form of marking (licensing) in order to reduce the opportunity and motivation to steal. Finally, the most pervasive of all major crimes—burglary—has come under carefully deliberated programs of prevention which include public education; improved security, preventive patrol, and investigation; and curtailing the receiver market.

The reader is strongly cautioned *not* to infer that the crime prevention programs described in this and the following chapter exhaust all possibilities;[1] for, this field is in such a rapid state of development and transition that refinements of existing programs, or relevant innovations create a need to constantly be alert to "a better way." Furthermore, any meaningful understanding of the costs and benefits of the crime prevention programs necessitates an indepth exploration of the various elements comprising the program. Finally, it is to be noted, that the dichotomization of crime prevention programs into hardware vis-a-vis software is based on intuition, if not bias, rather than a precise criterion for doing so.[2] Thus one will find that all of the programs have, to a greater or lesser degree, hardware and peopleware dimensions.

This chapter examines four hardware oriented crime prevention programs. Each should be assessed in the light of Dr. Zimring's recommendation that, "prevention strategies to evaluate research will prove less comforting but, in the long run, more valuable."[3] We will review, in turn, the following: (1) physical planning, (2) operations identification, (3) bicycle security, and (4) crime-specific/burglary prevention. The last subject area will be given considerable amplification, in that burglaries are accelerating in the frequency of occurrence and as a general threat to our personal security.

Physical Planning

Prior to undertaking implementation of any program aimed at crime reduction through physical planning, a varied number of issues must be acknowledged and resolved.[4] Only after such resolution will a program yield the desired positive results.[5]

Cause and Effect Relationship Between Crime and Physical Planning

The basic laws of physics have proven that for every effect there is an identifiable cause. Therefore, if the prevalence of crime is the effect, then no one can argue that physical planning is not a major contributing cause. Having identified the role of physical planning, it is encumbent upon all components of the CJS and all other contributing disciplines to accept their responsibility in assisting in the perception of the anti-social "effects" caused by the overall planning process. Note the following standard proposed by the National Advisory Commission on Criminal Justice Standards and Goals.

STANDARD 5.5—*Police-Community Physical Planning*
Every police agency should participate with local planning agencies and organizations, public and private, in community physical planning that affects the rate or nature of crime or the fear of crime.

1. Every government entity should seek police participation with public and private agencies and organizations involved in community physical planning within the jurisdiction.
2. Every police agency should assist in planning with public and private organizations involved in police-related community physical planning. This assistance should at least include planning involving:
   a. Industrial area development
   b. Business and commercial area development
   c. Residential area development, both low rise and high rise
   d. Government or health facility complex development

     e.   Open area development, both park and other recreation

     f.   Redevelopment projects such as urban renewal, and

     g.   Building requirements (target hardening), both residential and commercial.[6]

Does it make any difference what valid police procedures are used to reduce crime if the power structure within a city, state, or nation refuses to acknowledge its responsibilities concerning crime prevention? Our police can do little without the cooperation of those who, by virtue of their authority, can pass laws, establish standards, provide materials, education, and financial assistance to reduce the opportunity which a law breaker may find to commit a crime. Both crime itself and the prevention of crime rest with the citizens, society, and the authorities, and the police are only tools for assisting in combating and preventing crime.

Therefore, the accurate answer, or one of the most prevalent solutions that has been made available to us today within the CJS, is crime prevention through community planning. Crime prevention can be built into almost every aspect of community planning. Unfortunately, it is too often ignored because of the fragmentation or compartmentalization of municipal, county, and state agencies. Crime, historically and with only a few exceptions during recent years, is looked upon as the exclusive province of the police department and not the concern of those in charge of education, housing, urban renewal, health, welfare, or streets and highways. Both the police themselves and other governmental agencies are guilty of this type of fragmentation and individualism.

Inter-disciplinary Under-standing

Law enforcement has long recognized that inadequate and improper design of communities has had a substantial effect on its service requirements to the community. Conversely, the service capabilities of any law enforcement agency will affect its community's ability to grow, revitalize, or to provide necessary and desirable services. It becomes quite apparent that no individual discipline can effectively function without an understanding of its effects on the total service spectrum. Effective planning requires the ability of each discipline to "walk in the other man's shoes."

Efforts in building parks within a community will be self-defeating if their location and design do not allow for the provision of adequate security and protection. Park development, for example, if it is to become an asset to a community, must include the mutual understanding of the interrelated effects of disciplines such as parks, recreation, traffic engineering, schools, utilities, transportation, law enforcement, and planning.

Inter-
disciplinary
Coordination

Mutual understanding is only a part of what is necessary to the establishment of totally coordinated planning. A mere understanding of the relationship of one unit to another does not ensure a coordinated planning process. Specific efforts are required in order to develop a method or system that will guarantee, rather than randomly provide, the necessary coordination of applicable disciplines in all phases of planning. The development and establishing of a coordinated process or system must also take into account various factors such as community size, organizational structure, manpower availability and capabilities, political attitude, new growth versus urban renewal, etc. Therefore, cities and counties must evaluate their own goals, objectives, and resources, and develop the best method of coordination in planning and decision making.

As mentioned in the preceding chapter, planning can and should encompass almost the entire spectrum of governmental agencies, especially local and county government. For instance, our police should be aware of public transportation developments insofar as they may relate to crime at terminals or on public transit conveyances. Divisions within public works departments should adopt building design and lighting provisions that minimize crime hazards. Parks and recreation departments need advice on the location, lighting, and supervision of playgrounds and recreation areas and the grouping and scheduling of recreational activities. Planning and development should include zone controls, which influence population movements and demands for police services. In turn, building and safety departments should take action to abate nuisances, hazards, and abandoned buildings and lots. Our streets and highway departments should continuously oversee street lighting, driveway requirements, traffic flow, the adequacy of off-street parking, and parking lot regulations.

Role of
Educational
Process

Due to the far reaching scope and impact of this concept, it has been found that individuals within or entering different disciplines often lack the necessary education, training, and skills to meet the demands of this new responsibility. Therefore, the provision of additional training for individuals currently involved is extremely necessary, and it is critical that future participants receive the required training and education prior to assuming an operational role in their chosen field.

Education and training in all disciplines relevant to municipal problems should undertake to develop data on comprehensive physical planning and to provide continuing research. Additionally, efforts should be designed within training and education to develop guidelines and to provide a catalyst for sound comprehensive systems and methods. The above responsibilities apply equally to formal education courses in a college or university, to police academy or inservice training, and to specialized or advanced study in any relevant discipline.

Legislative Impact   Improving American cities by crime prevention through physical planning is extremely complex, and due to the necessary involvement of different disciplines, agencies, and the private sector, legislative bodies must acknowledge and accept their area of positive action to the various operational components in meeting their goals and objectives.

The First Step is the Administrator's   Included within a public manager's role of ensuring the delivery of services to the community is the obligation to foster efforts (take-the-first-step) designed to provide the needed systems and methods for crime prevention through physical planning. If our local government ever hopes to provide a measurable degree of safety and quality, now and not tomorrow is the time to take the first step. Leadership is essential.

Implementation: Essential Design Factors for Law Enforcement   Police agencies, along with other agency representatives, should formulate a set of guidelines or criteria for evaluation of such projects. The criteria can and should include accessibility of buildings to patrol units, proper traffic flow and off-street parking provisions, lighting requirements, location and regulation of cul-de-sacs, playgrounds, common greens, fences, and security entrances. Internally, police departments can develop broad range liaison with other governmental units through the expansion or creation of community planning units headed by officers or civilians skilled in disciplinary planning.

For example, one city has held frequent meetings with the city planning department, American Institute of Architects, Association and Institute of Planners, Public Works Association, Association of Public Utilities, and others. During their discussions, certain items were brought to their attention depicting how their respective roles and responsibilities could assist in crime prevention (e.g., removing that important causative factor to crime—the opportunity). Many of the representatives of these groups said they had previously been unaware of these causative factors related to crime problems. The following are samples of specific design concerns which local law enforcement agencies should consider:

1. Setbacks of Buildings
   a. Front
   b. Sideyard
   c. Rear
2. Wall Construction (interior and exterior)
   a. Industrial
   b. Commercial
   c. Residential
3. Doors (setbacks and security)
   a. Industrial
   b. Commercial
   c. Residential
      (1) garages
      (2) carports
      (3) sliding glass
4. Windows and Skylights
   a. Setbacks
   b. Heights (from ground)
   c. Show and Display
   d. Type
      (1) frame
      (2) pane
5. Stairs (stairwells and staircasings)
6. Balconies
7. Utility Boxes
8. Fences, Walls, Hedges, and Screens
   a. Setbacks
   b. Heights
   c. Louvers
9. Parking
   a. Public
   b. Private
10. Lighting
    a. Industrial
    b. Commercial
    c. Residential
11. Streets, Sidewalks, and Walkways
    a. Location
    b. Slopes
    c. Curvature
    d. Grades
    e. Block Lengths
12. Alleys
    a. Blind
    b. Through

13. Visibility of Valuables
    a. People
    b. Safes
    c. Cash Registers
    d. Personal Property
14. Signs
    a. Street Signs and Signals
    b. Traffic Signs and Signals
    c. Advertising Signs
15. Accessibility (approach, entrance, and exit)
    a. Pedestrian
    b. Vehicle
    c. Services
    d. Residential
    e. Commercial
    f. Industrial
16. Public Utilities and Easements
    a. Gas
    b. Water
    c. Telephone
    d. Electrical
17. Public Areas and Facilities
    a. Public Restrooms
    b. Parks
    c. Bus Stop Shelters
    d. Playgrounds
    e. Recreation Halls
    f. Other
18. Street Trees and Shrubbery
    a. Type
    b. Height

Cost Effec-
tiveness
One of the first questions asked when employing crime prevention through the physical planning processes, as cited above, is whether such efforts are cost effective, both to the public and to the private development sectors. Admittedly, such measures usually involve additional costs at implementation, but from a *long-range perspective, the costs are often recovered in savings of services*. At the same time, not all desired changes involve additional costs.

Let us return to the above mentioned city. First, a developer submitted a plan for the construction of thirty-four single family detached dwellings. The review of the plan by the police agency revealed that a large number of the homes would be backing up to a flood control channel which bordered on one edge of a high school campus. Recognizing that such a design would increase the possibility and probability of burglaries, an alternative design was sought to provide a greater degree of security by lessening the opportunity and desirability factors for committing a burglary. Through discussions with the developers, they were able to invert the original design, thereby providing a residential street between the flood control channel and the residences. This action relieved the problem foreseen by the police department and involved absolutely no additional costs to the developer. Second, a neighborhood park across the street from a high school campus had a history of greater than average amounts of vandalism, crimes, and other police service requirements. This site was thoroughly studied to determine what changes could have been made at the design phase (from the police's input) that could have reduced or eliminated the resulting costs and service requirements. The study revealed the following: the costs to improve the park at time of implementation have been exceeded by the costs for vandalism and above average service requirements.

An additional major implication of this example is that the costs for vandalism and above average service requirements will continue, due to the original design, thereby further reinforcing the justification for preventive design. This case illustrates that in some instances preventive design can not only pay for itself, but can in fact produce substantial cost savings over an extended period of time.

Operation Identification

Operation Identification (ID) is most basically a programmatic attempt to encourage and assist the public in marking their property with a serial number. Such a program is intended to: (1) prevent burglaries by advertising to potential burglars the fact that all major items in the house or commercial establishment have been inscribed with a traceable serial number; (2) deter conversion of stolen property from burglars to fences by showing the fences that the property can be easily identified and traced; (3) aid in the apprehension of burglars and possessors of stolen property by providing an easy method for identifying stolen property in their possession; (4) assist in the return of located stolen property to the legal owners. Preliminary results from existing efforts strongly indicate that these objectives are being met by Operation IDs.

Implemen-tation   The program should be directed by sworn personnel; however, the actual inscribing of property may be done by paraprofessionals. One possible implementation procedure is to establish target areas within the jurisdiction. Residents of these areas should be notified of the impending visits by inscribers in advance. This notification should include the date and time of the visit, a detailed explanation of Operation ID, and a request that all property be laid out for inscribing. As the property is being inscribed, the inscriber should recommend that the merchant or resident list on a provided form all items inscribed. Permanently affixed serial numbers should also be recorded. These records should not be kept by the law enforcement agency; rather, they should be retained and updated by the property owner. This list should be stored in a secure place such as a safe deposit box. If a burglary should occur, the list would then be given to the reporting officers.

Until such time as a set of national identifying numbers may become available, a recommended identifier is the property owner's driver's license number. This should be preceded by alphabetic letters that designate the state. It is *not* recommended that local identifying numbers be used. Should the property be found in another jurisdiction, there would be no way to trace ownership. Driver's license numbers can, in most instances, easily be traced through statewide computer-based information systems. In addition to inscribing the number in an easily seen location, the number should also be inscribed in one or more covert areas on the item.

Items having a permanently affixed serial number should also be engraved. Extreme care must be taken not to damage any property. Items that should be marked are those that a thief would be most likely to steal: television sets, radio, stereos, cameras, binoculars, appliances, power tools, tool boxes, typewriters, tape decks, office machinery, watches, and some types of jewelry.

Another method of implementation is to have burglary reporting officers ask burglary victims if they wish to sponsor neighborhood meetings. If so, a crime prevention officer can give a presentation on Operation ID, residential security checks, and neighborhood alert programs. These neighbors may wish to share a department-provided inscriber among themselves. In any event, extra pens should be available from the law enforcement agency for any resident who may not be in the target area or who may have purchased items since the initial inscribing session. The police agency should be responsible for coordinating the use of the inscribers.

As legal ownership of an item of property is transferred, a single diagonal line should be drawn through the driver's license number. It should run from the upper right corner to the lower left corner. The old number should *not* be obliterated. The new owner's license number should then be placed next to the old number.

Residences and commercial establishments of citizens participating in Operation ID should have small notices informing passers-by that items located within have been inscribed for ready identification by law enforcement agencies. These notices should be posted near potential points of entry for burglars.

Two possible problems are associated with Operation ID. First, if the law enforcement agency relies entirely upon unsolicited requests for inscribing, the program will not achieve anything near the potential impact. Second, after all appropriate items in a house or business have been initially inscribed, owners may neglect to inscribe subsequently purchased items. The following exhibits provide model forms which may be adopted for actual use.

Bicycle Security

The frequency of bicycle thefts has grown at an alarming rate, and associated with the increasing number of thefts is the cost to the victim. Ironically, we seem more, rather than less, dependent on the bicycle for transportation in our urbanized society. There are many reasons for this, but the main point is that bicycles are expensive and important to us. Therefore, they have become the target of the criminal element in this nation.

To begin with, a bicycle security program should be designed to: (1) prevent the occurrence of bicycle thefts; (2) raise the apprehension rate of bicycle thieves; and (3) increase the rate of bicycles recovered and returned to their legal owners.

Implementation

The local legislative body should pass an ordinance requiring all bicycles owned by residents of that jurisdiction to be licensed. The licensing period should be for more than one year and less than five years. If a licensing fee is to be charged, it should be low enough not to discourage voluntary compliance, and funds generated from fees might be used to defray costs of the program or they might be earmarked for construction or marking of bicycle lanes.

Sworn and nonsworn personnel can be designated to perform the registration and licensing of bicycles. Logical candidates would be local police, fire, and recreational personnel, as they are located at convenient points throughout the jurisdiction. The nature of

Dear Citizen:

The _____ Department is attempting to reduce crime in the City/County through the implementation of a crime prevention program called "Operation Identification." The purpose of this program is to discourage thefts and burglaries by recording the serial numbers or engraving your driver's license number on portable items such as tools, radios, appliances, television sets, cameras, and so forth.

A special decal, prominently displayed on front and back windows, should discourage burglary by serving notice that the items in the house have been marked and recorded. If marked items are subsequently stolen, the chance of recovery by a police agency would be materially increased, and the property could then be returned to the owner.

A member of our department will be in your neighborhood on _____ between _____ and _____. If you wish to participate in this program, please have those articles you wish engraved readily available.

Our primary purpose is to prevent crime. However, crime prevention is everybody's business, and we need your support.

Sincerely yours,

(Signed)

_____ (Agency Head)

_____ (Title)

Figure 7.1   Letter to citizen about Operation Identification.

Figure 7.2   Warning sticker for Operation Identification

Protect your home against intrusion by burglars and prowlers!

Burglary is a problem, but to avoid it happening to you, a number of things should be done! Whenever you leave your residence to spend an evening at the movies, or take off for a weekend of fun in the sun, housebreakers can and will move in if they're *certain* you've left. Burglars spend their *daylight* hours canvassing neighborhoods, looking for uncut lawns and overstuffed mailboxes. They spend their *evening* hours looking for darkened houses—or lights that are left on too long. You can help your police department reduce burglaries in your city. Please read the other side and also enjoy both security and peace of mind with the knowledge that your home is protected.

Protect your home!

When making plans for an evening, weekend or extended vacation it will be reassuring to return to a normally-lighted home with a sense of well-being and security after following these tips the Burglary Prevention Committee has suggested:

1. Lock all doors and windows.
2. Arrange lamps and radios/TV in various parts of your home to be connected to Time-All automatic timers for use at customary hours to create a "lived in" appearance to the outside world.
3. Leave shades and blinds in normal positions.
4. Make sure that *no* deliveries of any kind (mail, newspaper, milk, etc.) will be made in your absence.
5. Arrange to have the lawn mowed or snow shoveled in its respective season.
6. Store valuables in a safe deposit vault.
7. Close the garage door. (A garage can have a particularly abandoned look.)
8. Alert the police and a close neighbor for unusual activity in your absence.
9. Arrange automatically-timed outdoor lighting for burglary prevention.
10. Refrain from notifying the newspapers of your whereabouts until your return.

BURGLARY PREVENTION COMMITTEE

TRIBUNE TOWERS, 435 N. MICHIGAN AVE., SUITE 2118, CHICAGO, ILL. 60611

Personal property record

Name:_____

Automobiles, Motorcycles, Scooters, Bicycles, etc.

MAKE	COLOR	LIC. NO.	SERIAL NO.

Guns

MAKE	CALIBER	SERIAL NO.

Small electrical appliances (radios, stereos, tape recorders, etc.)

DESCRIPTION	SERIAL NO.

Major electrical appliances, (TV, mixer, refrigerator, washer, etc.)

DESCRIPTION	SERIAL NO.

Cameras, Binoculars, Sporting Goods, Watches, etc.

DESCRIPTION	SERIAL NO.

Power tools & Miscellaneous equipment

DESCRIPTION	SERIAL NO.

Credit Cards

COMPANY	SERIAL NO.

IMPORTANT
Engrave Driver's License Number on all un-numbered valuable items.

Figure 7.3 Protection of personal property

their work provides times when they could perform the minimal amount of work required. As bicycles are presented for licensing, they should be inspected for existing frame numbers. If they exist and are readable, they can serve as the identifying number. If they do not exist, the licenser should stamp an identifying number on the crank hanger (area on the frame to which the pedals are attached). This number should be prefaced with the local law enforcement agency's identifier. If the frame number has been obliterated, it is recommended that the matter be referred to the local law enforcement agency to determine if there has been a criminal violation.

After the bicycle has been registered, a bright, highly visible sticker that is difficult to remove or re-use should be placed upon it. At this time literature should also be given to the owner explaining activities he should perform to reduce the likelihood of his bicycle being stolen. This would include a discussion of the need for locking his bicycle and a description of adequate chains and locks. The local jurisdiction may wish to supplement this with other material relating to safe riding.

The next step is to have regular patrol officers on the alert for bicycles not displaying the licensing tag. Once observed, the rider should be encouraged to license his bicycle. The last step is to provide each licensing station with lists of already-licensed bicycles. This should be updated *at least* monthly (preferably weekly or biweekly). Larger jurisdictions may have to provide this information in the form of computer printouts. This listing allows licensers to determine quickly if the bicycle has previously been licensed. If it has been, the matter should be investigated to determine whether the bicycle is in the possession of its rightful owner. Another possible approach is to enact a local ordinance requiring shopping centers, recreational facilities, schools, governmental agencies, etc., to provide stationary bicycle parking racks. These racks should be designed to provide secure anchoring spots for heavy-duty chains and locks. Consideration should also be given to regulating the resale of bicycles.

There are three potential pitfalls associated with the above program. First, if the licensing fees are set too high, there will be reluctance to participate. Second, unless patrol officers make it a regular part of their duties to look for bicycle licenses, the entire program will quickly degenerate. Third, if the community is not fully informed, the citizens may feel this to be an unnecessary enforcement effort.

The following exhibit presents a pamphlet that may be found useful by those interested in mounting a bicycle security program.

YOUR BICYCLE
Safety and Security

Los Angeles
SHERIFF'S DEPA

Figure 7.4

BICYCLE SECURITY

LAST YEAR OVER 60,000 BICYCLES WERE STOLEN IN LOS ANGELES COUNTY

PROTECT YOUR BIKE ! ! !

1.   You don't leave your car unlocked, so treat your bicycle the same way. Use an approved chain and padlock whenever you are not on the seat! Lock it to the garage — with a 3/8" x 6" eye screw fastened into a stud. The eye screw should be at least 3 feet above the floor, because this makes using a pry bar much more difficult.

Whenever you lock your bike in a public place, chain it to a secure rack or stanchion through the frame and a wheel. Keep the chain as high above the ground as the bike will allow. This reduces the leverage for a pry bar or bolt cutter attack.

2. *MINIMUM STANDARD FOR APPROVED CHAIN:*

Must be of at least 9/32" hardened steel alloy. The link must be of continuous welded construction. Lighter chain or chain with open links simply will not withstand bolt cutting attacks. Don't give your bicycle away. Using anything less will invite its theft. of your bike.

3. PADLOCKS: There are many padlocks on the market from which to choose. Do not be guilty of economizing on a padlock that will not give you the protection you need. The most common assault on a padlock is with a large bolt cutter or pry bar. The following description, which you can take to the locksmith or hardware store, is the *minimum standard* for an exterior padlock:

    . Hardened steel, 9/32" shackle. (Naturally, heavier shackles offer additional security.)

    . Double locking mechanism–heel and toe.

    . Five-pin tumbler.

    . A key retaining feature, whenever possible. This prevents your removing the key until you have locked the padlock.

4. Register your bicycle with your local law enforcement agency.

5. Record the serial number of your bicycle and keep it in a safe place.

A BICYCLE SAFETY TEST FOR YOU

NAME _____ DATE _____

INSTRUCTIONS: Read each question carefully and check the right answer.

EXAMPLE: Do bicycles have two wheels? | Yes ✓ | No |

1. Shall a bicycle rider obey traffic signals? | Yes | No |
2. Shall a bicycle rider obey stop signs? | Yes | No |
3. Shall a bicycle rider use the arm signals? | Yes | No |
4. Do you signal for a left turn by holding the left hand and arm straight up? | Yes | No |
5. Shall a bicycle be equipped with a headlight and a red tail light or reflector when ridden at night? | Yes | No |
6. Should you wear light colored clothing when riding at night? | Yes | No |
7. Shall a bicycle be ridden on the left hand side of the street facing traffic? | Yes | No |
8. When riding bicycles in groups should you ride single file? | Yes | No |
9. Shall a bicycle be ridden near the right hand edge of the road? | Yes | No |
10. If you can skid your rear wheel on loose dirt, but not on the pavement, are your brakes good enough? | Yes | No |
11. Are loose handlebars dangerous? | Yes | No |
12. Is it safe for two people to ride on a bicycle which is equipped with only one seat? | Yes | No |
13. Is it necessary to have brakes on a bicycle? | Yes | No |
14. Does a good bicycle rider weave in and out between parked cars?
15. Is it safe for experienced riders to take both hands off the handlebars?
16. Should you dismount and walk across streets with heavy traffic?
17. Should a bicycle be locked when it is parked?
18. Is a horn or a bell necessary on a bicycle?
19. Should your bicycle be licensed?
20. Is it alright to pass a car at an intersection if it is waiting for a red light?

Yes 3, Yes 4, No 5, Yes 6, Yes 7, No 8, Yes 9, Yes , Yes 12, No 13, Yes 14, No 15, No 16, Yes 17, Yes 9, Yes 20, No

SAFETY RULES YOU SHOULD KNOW AND FOLLOW

1. Keep your bicycle in good mechanical condition (tires, chain, brakes, etc.)

2. Obey all traffic rules and signs—always give proper hand signals.

3. Walk your bike across busy intersections.

4. Always ride with the traffic—as close as possible to the right side of the road.

5. Be sure the roadway is clear before entering.

6. Always ride single file and watch for opening car doors.

7. Most bicycles are built to carry one person—YOU! and you alone.

8. If you must ride your bike at night be sure your headlight and rear reflector are in good working order.

9. Select the safest route to your destination and use it. Avoid busy streets and intersections.

10. Yield right of way to pedestrians.

BE SURE YOU USE THESE HAND SIGNALS WHEN YOU CHANGE DIRECTIONS

STOP
Left arm straight down for slowing and stopping

LEFT
Left arm straight out for left turns

RIGHT
Left arm straight up for right turns

Crime Specific: Burglary

> We can reasonably hope that very few of our citizens will be the victims of rape, robbery, or murder, but the one crime that *is* very apt to strike any of us is burglary. *Evelle J. Younger,* Attorney General, State of California (1971).

Information Require- ments

Before developing and implementing a burglary abatement program, police agencies must acquire detailed information about the dimensions of the local burglary situation.[7] While much of the needed data exists within the agency (i.e., burglary reports and arrest records), it is often not in a format that lends itself to interpretation. Planning a program is a difficult and time consuming task, but unless the agency produces a specific and thorough plan, the program in all likelihood will not generate the desired results. The prerequisites for an effective burglary abatement program are to:

- *know* the local community
- *know* the local burglary problem
- *know* the local offenders
- *know* the local resources and constraints.

The kind of information needed, possible sources, and planning application are presented in the remaining sections of this chapter.

Know the Community.   Knowledge of the community should include an accurate understanding of the physical, social, economic, and demographic environment. Burglary is a crime against property; hence, its targets are homes, businesses, and other physical facilities that make up the community. To protect these targets, it is essential to learn what they are in terms of types, numbers, locations, security conditions, occupancy patterns, and visibility to patrol. It is also essential that the agency know something of the people who live and work in the community, so that the burglary abatement program can be custom-fitted to meet their needs and expectations and thus maximize the level of community support. Fortunately, much of the community information that is required can be acquired from local city or county planning departments, Chambers of Commerce, civic organizations, and from U.S. Census Bureau reports. Data is best aggregated at the census tract level to foster precise analysis. Some of the more significant data elements germane to the socio-economic and demographic conditions in a

Table 7.1 Significant data elements

Data	Use
Total population of the target area	Calculating burglary rates per 1,000 population
Total population by sex and age	Identifying areas with large groups of potential offenders
Non-English speaking persons by native language	Preparing public education materials
Median education levels	Selecting and preparing public education materials
Median household incomes	Recommending security improvements
Housing units by types	Calculating residential burglary rate per 1,000 targets by type
Median value of homes	Recommending security improvements
Median rental cost	Recommending security improvements
Commercial facilities by type	Calculating commercial burglary rates per 1,000 targets

community are presented in Table 7.1. Additionally, this table suggests applications of the data for planning burglary abatement programs.

Know the Burglary Problem.   Specific knowledge of the local burglary picture is essential for planning and operating a burglary abatement program. Whether pin-maps or computers are used, it remains essential to identify the overall magnitude and the unique patterns of burglary that are occurring in the community. Of special concern are patterns with exceptionally high numbers of burglaries, or those with consistent patterns in terms of time of day, method of entry, or type of property taken. To this end, a list of data elements taken from burglary reports is presented below. In many of our communities, this information is already being collected and is thus available for planning burglary reduction efforts.

- *Date of occurrence.* Record the day, month, and year of the burglary when known. Record the beginning date when the exact date is unknown.
- *Day of week.* Record the exact day (Monday, Tuesday, etc.) when known. Record weekday, or weekend, when exact day is unknown. Record "unknown" only when absolutely necessary.
- *Time of occurrence.* Record the exact time when known. Record morning, afternoon, or night, when a range of

time is given. Record "unknown" only when absolutely
necessary.

- *Location of occurrence.* Record beat, reporting district, census tract, and exact location.
- *Category of premise.* Record residence, business, or other category.
- *Specific type of premise.* Record the type of the premise, such as single family, theater, apartment, etc.
- *Occupancy Status.* Record whether or not anyone was on the premise.
- *Point of entry.* Record where entry was made into the facility, such as door or window.
- *Instrument used to gain entry.* Record the kind of instrument used, such as screwdriver, etc.
- *How entry was made.* Record what was done to get inside the facility, such as used passkey, smashed window, etc.
- *Type of property taken.* Record the type of items taken, such as money, sound equipment, etc.
- *Dollar amount taken.* Record the total reported dollar loss for all items taken.
- *Street lights.* For nighttime burglaries, record the existence or nonexistence of street lights.
- *Point of entry lighting.* For nighttime burglaries, record the existence or nonexistence of entry lights.
- *Visibility at point of entry.* Record whether or not the point of entry is visible to patrolling police units.
- *Alarm systems.* Record the existence or nonexistence of an alarm system.
- *Status of alarm.* Record whether the alarm operated or not, and whether it was defeated.
- *How incident was detected.* Record how the burglary was detected, such as by neighbor, police, alarm, victim, etc.
- *When detected.* Record as: in progress, same day, next day, etc.
- *Property identification.* Record whether or not the items taken had identifying numbers or markings.

Know the Burglars and Receivers.   Data pertaining to individuals and groups that are known or suspected burglary offenders or receivers of stolen property should be collected and analyzed. This effort should pool the information available from various sources such as crime files, arrest reports, field interrogation reports, informer reports, and other intelligence sources. Suspect files should include the following types of information on individuals:

- names and nicknames
- residence address
- business, work, or school address
- sex
- age
- race
- physical description
- prior arrest date, charge, and disposition
- current status—parole, probation, bail, etc.
- names of associates and gangs
- vehicles used—license and description
- summary of prior MO information

Know the Resources and Constraints.   A burglary reduction campaign naturally requires a certain commitment of personnel, physical resources, and time. Special skills, materials, and equipment are needed, and are limited by the usual financial and operational constraints. The policies and priorities of the agency best determine the amount and quality of manpower and other resources that can be mounted for the burglary program, since the needed resources normally are drawn from existing patrol, investigation, intelligence, crime analysis, and community relations staffs.

Staffing and Training Considerations

A burglary reduction project requires assertive leadership to successfully compete for the manpower, equipment, services, and public support that such an effort requires. Additionally, the project manager must be able to operate effectively within his department and with other public and private agencies, as well as with the general public. Further, the project staff should be comprised of individuals with high motivation and with specialized skills in patrol, security, investigation, intelligence, public relations, and analysis. It is to be noted that traditionally there has not been much status attached to the "burglary detail." The work is often considered dull and unproductive when compared to other areas of police work. A crime-specific program helps to overcome any motivational problems by offering special recognition and broader responsibilities to the assigned personnel.

Crime-specific agencies should conduct a training program

for members of the burglary reduction team. The purposes of such a training program are to[8]:

(1) familiarize team members with the objectives and procedures of the program
(2) to unify and standardize team operations
(3) prepare team members to perform residential and commercial security inspections
(4) provide patrol and investigative personnel with current procedures and techniques.

The training programs should consist of academic sessions, tours and visits, and on-the-job training activities. Training time should be approximately two weeks for the teams. Listed below are the major areas that are to be covered:

- program goals and objectives
- project organization and administration
- overall plan and schedule for accomplishing objectives
- special reporting requirements
- target area demographic and burglary problem descriptions
- presentations by alarm and lock companies
- procedures for performing security inspections of residential areas
- procedures for performing security inspections for business/commercial areas
- fire regulations concerning lock and other security measures
- building department codes, and other city or county agencies' responsibilities pertaining to security measures
- tours of the target area
- crime scene investigative activities
- interview and interrogation procedures
- arrest and search procedures
- suspect investigation and handling
- collection and use of physical evidence and latent prints
- undercover surveillance and investigation techniques
- systems available to support investigations and analysis
- known suspects
- use of criminal records
- community relations aspect of the program
- interactions with the district attorney, courts, parole and probation.

Six Crime-Specific Programs: Summary and Findings

The remainder of this section presents the results of six crime-specific programs. It will be noted that while each program has a different emphasis, the overall mission remains—hardening the target (you, and your home, your business, etc.) against the probability of being burglarized.

Crime-Specific Burglary: Public Involvement   A public information effort is a critical feature of a burglary abatement program. Initial publicity and, in turn, our support can be achieved with minimal effort; however, careful planning is necessary to sustain public interest and to achieve direct action. Crime-specific police agencies will find it advantageous to pool their resources and efforts for a joint public relations campaign that attracts statewide and national publicity, while still providing quality publicity materials for local application by the individual agencies. Direct measures of public involvement in burglary reduction as a result of the public relations activity include:

- improved use of existing security features
- installation and use of improved security features
- improved citizen reporting of burglaries.

See Table 7.2 for a list of public education/involvement techniques.

Crime-Specific Burglary: Security   The results of existing security portions of burglary abatement programs indicate the need for substantial improvement in the security features of both residential and commercial buildings in the areas of: (1) point of entry visibility, (2) security hardware, (3) street and entry lighting, and (4) alarms in commercial establishments. In California, each of six participating agencies used a variety of approaches for encouraging the public to increase the physical and psychological barriers between potential burglars and their perceived needs. The highlights of the security effort are as follows:[8]

- 29,657 residential and 11,772 commercial security inspections were performed and contributed to a better knowledge of security weaknesses for both the community and the law enforcement agencies
- security displays and fixed and mobile security centers

Table 7.2 Public involvement/education

PROJECT ACTIVITY	Los Angeles Police Dept.	Los Angeles County Sheriff	Oakland Police Dept.	Orange County Sheriff	San Diego Police Dept.	San Francisco Police Dept.	COMMENTS
INFORMATION DISTRIBUTION ACTIVITIES							
1. Pamplets and Literature	x	x	x	x	x	x	All projects distributed thousands of items, many printed in Spanish.
2. News Releases to the Press	x	x	x	x	x	x	Press publicity was extensive in all projects.
3. TV and Radio Coverage	x	x	x	x	x	x	While Oakland and San Francisco received project coverage, there was no specific plan or emphasis on utilizing this in their projects.
4. Public Speeches and Talks	x	x	x	x	x	x	This activity received considerable attention by all projects. Project members presented the program to almost all commercial, residential and other community groups.
5. Public Information Centers	x	x		x	x		Los Angeles Police and Sheriff's Depts. each established store front centers. San Diego and Orange Depts. used temporary security centers in shopping centers.

Table 7.2 (continued)

PROJECT ACTIVITY	Los Angeles Police Dept.	Los Angeles County Sheriff	Oakland Police Dept.	Orange County Sheriff	San Diego Police Dept.	San Francisco Police Dept.	COMMENTS
6. Signs, Posters, Decals, Buttons	x	x	x	x	x	x	All projects displayed and distributed these materials.
7. Special Public Events	x		x	x		x	Activities included: • Team-up Fair • Burglary Prevention Week/Month • Home Show • County Fair • Appliance Show
COMMUNITY ORGANIZATION ACTIVITIES							
1. Block or Neighborhood Citizen Groups	x		x				Organized to support law enforcement.
2. Home Owner Associations	x			x	x		Existing home owner associations were briefed and urged to actively participate in the home security portion of the program.
3. Merchant Association	x	x	x	x	x	x	All projects briefed and urged business associations to actively support the business security portion of the program.

Table 7.2 (continued)

PROJECT ACTIVITY	Los Angeles Police Dept.	Los Angeles County Sheriff	Oakland Police Dept.	Orange County Sheriff	San Diego Police Dept.	San Francisco Police Dept.	COMMENTS
4. Insurance Underwriters	x	x	x	x	x	x	Each project had discussions or correspondence with insurance groups concerning rate reductions for residential and business facilities which implement recommended security changes.
5. Civic Clubs	x	x	x	x	x	x	All projects provided speakers to civic clubs.
6. School Programs	x			x	x	x	These projects gave presentations on security to existing school organizations such as PTA, Advisory Council and Student Groups.
7. Church Programs						x	Letters were mailed to churches offering speakers but met with very little success.
8. Citizen Recognition and Reward Programs	x						Citizens who made substantial contributions in terms of support or by supplying information leading to an arrest were presented letters of appreciation.

were successfully used to attract interest and to demonstrate recommended security devices

- fixed security centers were successful during the initial
  months of the program, but their usefulness declined after
  the heavy promotion/advertising program abated
- promotion of insurance reductions was tried without
  success as an incentive for owners to improve the security
  of existing facilities
- promotion of building security ordinances was seen as the
  most effective and least expensive means for gradually
  upgrading residential and commercial security in new and
  existing facilities.

The analysis of the 7,763 burglary reports that were written
during the Crime-Specific Program shows that the major weaknesses of all types of structures are: (1) doors and windows, (2)
poor point of entry visibility, (3) poor point of entry lighting, and
(4) inadequate alarm systems.

The extent of physical security weaknesses in all types of
facilities is such that little or no force is required for burglars to
make most entries. Of particular concern to security planners are
those cases where visibility of the entry place could be easily increased to provide more deterrence to potential offenders. Table
7.3 presents a typology of burglary profiles. For specific techniques
of enhancing physical security see Table 7.4.

*Crime-
Specific
Burglary:
Improved
Preventive
Patrol*

The preventive patrol techniques for a burglary abatement
program should be designed to help deter burglaries in general,
but more specifically they should be planned to decrease the percentage of burglaries occurring where entry is made at a point
observable to patrol. Changes in patrol techniques should also be
expected to increase the detections of burglaries by patrol personnel, and to increase the percentages of on-the-scene
apprehensions.

Patrol planners need to deploy the available manpower in
proportion to the changing patterns and times of the burglary
experience in the area. The information needed for planning must
come from a continuous analysis of the community's burglary experience, while the necessary flexibility in scheduling can be
achieved through: (1) creation and use of unassigned tactical patrol
teams, (2) use of overtime, (3) a change to team policing, or (4)
overlap scheduling of patrol shifts or watches.

Preventative patrol tactics should emphasize improved suspect surveillance rather than building surveillance. This approach

Table 7.3 Typical MO burglary profile

MO Descriptors	"Hot Prowl" or "Cat Burglar"	Youthful Opportunist	Smash and Grab	Most Common Residential	Most Common Commercial	Most Common Other Businesses
Type Premises	Single family homes/small apartment buildings	Homes and apartments, including garages	Small commercial/retail stores	Single family homes	Small retail stores	Offices
Location	Less dense residential areas	On routes to/from school	Mixed residential and commercial areas	All residential areas	Frequently near freeway access	Individual office structure and small complexes
Occupancy Status	Occupied	Unoccupied	Unoccupied	Unoccupied	Unoccupied	Unoccupied
Point/Method of Entry	Unlocked window	Unlocked doors	Display window smashed	Door or window (no force or minor force)	Door or window (forced entry)	Door or window (forced entry)
Tools Used	None	None	Thrown brick or rock	Lock defeating or pry	Impact cutting and forcing tools	Impact cutting and forcing tools
Items Taken	Cash, jewelry, small items	Small sound equipment, sporting goods, cash	Anything on display	TV, sound equipment, sporting goods	Cash, merchandise, business machine	Business machines
Time	Any night—12:PM to 5:AM	Weekday—12:Noon to 5:PM	Weekday—9:AM to 6:PM	Weekday—9:AM to 6:PM	Weekend night—10:PM to 7:AM	Weekend night—10:PM to 7:AM
Property Damage	Removed window screen	May vandalize	Window	Minor or none	Point of entry, may attack safe	Point of entry

Table 7.4 Improved security

PROJECT ACTIVITY	Los Angeles Police Dept.	Los Angeles County Sheriff	Oakland Police Dept.	Orange County Sheriff	San Diego Police Dept.	San Francisco Police Dept.	COMMENTS
INSPECTION PROGRAMS							
1. Residential Inspections 2. Commercial Inspections	X	X	X	X	X		Many approaches were used such as: • Door-to-door solicitation by Police Reserves or Scouts • Telephone solicitation • Letter solicitation • Presentations to community associations and organizations • Mobile security centers • Store front centers • Block groups • Home Alert groups • Manned booths in shopping centers, fairs, shows and public buildings.
3. Post Burglary Security Inspections	X	X	X	X	X		The Oakland project placed heavy emphasis on this approach by having trained civilian security inspectors perform security inspections on all burglarized facilities. Other projects had officers provide security recommendations at the time the burglary report was taken. Perform security inspection.

165

Table 7.4 (continued)

PROJECT ACTIVITY	Los Angeles Police Dept.	Los Angeles County Sheriff	Oakland Police Dept.	Orange County Sheriff	San Diego Police Dept.	San Francisco Police Dept.	COMMENTS
4. Follow-up Inspections	x	x	x	x	x		Projects conducted mail and on-site follow-up program to determine how many persons had complied totally or partially with the security recommendations provided by the agency.
PROVIDE SECURITY SERVICES							
1. Evaluate and recommend specific hardware, devices and services	x	x	x	x	x	x	No testing. Recommendations based on available information.
2. Display security hardware and devices	x	x	x	x	x	x	All projects displayed security items by using large display boards for static display centers and personnel kits for door-to-door inspections.
3. Provide installation support and/or tools		x					Limited to special need cases.
4. Promote insurance reductions for secured facilities	x				x		Contacts were made with insurance organizations for this purpose.

Table 7.4 (continued)

PROJECT ACTIVITY	Los Angeles Police Dept.	Los Angeles County Sheriff	Oakland Police Dept.	Orange County Sheriff	San Diego Police Dept.	San Francisco Police Dept.	COMMENTS
5. Promote security ordinances/ legislation	x	x	x	x	x		All projects participated in the development and promotion of community security ordinances.
6. Promote improved street lighting	x	x	x	x	x	x	Projects had discussions with local electric and power companies and city officials concerning activities to improve street lighting in the target areas.

requires that patrol units be supplied with current descriptions of the groups and individuals who are most likely to commit burglaries, their known habits, and techniques.

Preventative patrol routes should be random in order to make pre-planning as difficult as possible for potential burglars. For the same reason, a mix of marked and unmarked cars, bicycles, motor scooters, and foot patrols should be employed by patrol at irregular intervals.

In order to determine the effectiveness of preventative patrol techniques tried in the Crime-Specific Program, the following elements of information were selected for analysis from the 7,763 burglary reports received:

- entry points visible to patrol units
- burglary detections by patrol units
- offender apprehensions by patrol units.

Specific techniques for improving preventive patrol are contained in Table 7.5.

Crime-Specific Burglary: Improved Investigation
Burglary investigation techniques and procedures should be changed to improve the clearance and arrest rates, and increase the complaint filing and conviction rates for burglaries. In order to accomplish those objectives, investigators need to: (1) increase the effective manpower available to perform more detailed investigations by spending more time per case, (2) improve the quality and completeness of burglary and suspect information, and (3) provide rapid and easy access to all relevant information which can help the investigator. Additionally, detective or investigator bureaus should consider developing a formal approach for determining the amount of time to allocate for each investigation based on the initial crime report. This approach requires that the agency determine which elements of information about a burglary are needed to warrant further investigation of the incident.

When clearance, arrest, and complaint filing rates rose during the Crime-Specific Program, the agencies attributed most of the improvement to additional manpower support for their burglary investigation efforts. The following investigative techniques and procedures were tried with the following reported results:

- use of patrol personnel to support investigation improved patrol morale and provided more manpower for investigation activities
- investigative techniques changed little, but improved re-

Table 7.5   Improved Patrol Preventive

PROJECT ACTIVITY	Los Angeles Police Dept.	Los Angeles County Sheriff	Oakland Police Dept.	Orange County Sheriff	San Diego Police Dept.	San Francisco Police Dept.	COMMENTS
MODIFIED PREVENTATIVE PATROL ACTIVITY							
1. Target area Saturation	x	x	x	x	x	x	All projects used this technique to suppress burglaries in areas experiencing an increase in burglaries.
2. Dynamic Scheduling	x	x	x	x	x	x	All projects augmented or adjusted patrol schedules based on day-to-day project experiences.
3. Tandem or Team Patrol	x		x	x			In this approach a minimum of two cars are used to perform area surveillance.
4. Bicycle Patrol	x	x			x		Some projects provided bicycles to patrolmen to use in certain sections in the target area.
5. Helicopter Patrol						x	This project uses helicopter patrol to support surveillance activities in areas not readily accessible to units in patrol cars.
6. Foot Patrol	x	x		x	x		This technique was used in conjunction with stakeout activities.

Table 7.5 (continued)

PROJECT ACTIVITY	Los Angeles Police Dept.	Los Angeles County Sheriff	Oakland Police Dept.	Orange County Sheriff	San Diego Police Dept.	San Francisco Police Dept.	COMMENTS
SPECIAL SURVEILLANCE ACTIVITIES							
1. Routine "Bird-Dog" Surveillance	x	x		x	x	x	Projects developed "most wanted" list of known burglary suspects and made an effort to remain aware of their crime related activities.
2. Special Undercover Activity	x	x	x	x	x	x	All projects utilized this technique against known or suspected burglaries.
3. Target Stakeouts	x	x	x	x	x	x	Target stakeouts were used when information was obtained either manually or by computer that identified a burglary pattern. The pattern had to be well identified including sufficient M.O. information to call for a stakeout.
4. Receiver Stakeouts	x	x	x	x	x	x	All projects included stakeouts of people and places suspected of receiving or selling stolen property.

Table 7.5 (continued)

PROJECT ACTIVITY	Los Angeles Police Dept.	Los Angeles County Sheriff	Oakland Police Dept.	Orange County Sheriff	San Diego Police Dept.	San Francisco Police Dept.	COMMENTS
5. Truancy Patrol	x	x		x	x		Projects attempted to provide additional surveillance around school grounds. This activity was based on experience which indicated that burglaries occur more frequently around schools.
6. Increased Field Interrogations	x	x	x	x	x	x	All projects emphasized importance of field interrogations of persons involved in suspicious activities in the target areas.

porting, and more investigation time per case improved
results

- closer work with district attorney, courts, parole, and
  probation probably contributed to improved complaint
  filing rates on those persons who were arrested.

In order to determine the effectiveness of the investigation
techniques tried in the burglary abatement program, the following
elements of information were selected for analysis from the 7,763
burglary reports and 1,078 offender reports received:

- case clearance status
- police disposition of arrested offenders.

Techniques pertinent to implementing this particular crime-
specific emphasis are depicted in Table 7.6.

Crime-
Specific
Burglary:
Reducing
the Receiver
Market

There is a ready market for stolen property in all types of
communities. Traditionally, law enforcement agencies have concentrated their efforts to reduce the market on pawn shops and
professional fences. However, it now appears that these two groups
may play a relatively minor role in the total distribution of stolen
merchandise. Used appliance and business machine dealers, rental
agencies, garage sales, swap meets, and direct sales to the public
appear to be the major outlets for the property stolen in burglaries.

A thorough analysis of the distribution of stolen property is
needed, and can only be accomplished if property identification
is improved sufficiently to permit better tracking. More undercover
activities are also needed to establish the connections between
burglars, receivers, and the buying public.

Public education campaigns to discourage citizens from supporting the market for stolen property should help decrease the
market, but have not yet been adequately tested. See Table 7.7 for
specific techniques relative to this particular program.

Learning Exercises

1. Divide the class into four research teams. Each team is to be
assigned one of the four hardware oriented crime prevention
topics covered in this chapter (physical planning, operations identification, bicycle safety, and crime-specific burglary). Next, each
team is to visit (four hours) a different police agency to learn of

Table 7.6 Improved investigation

PROJECT ACTIVITY	Los Angeles Police Dept.	Los Angeles County Sheriff	Oakland Police Dept.	Orange County Sheriff	San Diego Police Dept.	San Francisco Police Dept.	COMMENTS
STAFFING CHANGES							
1. Use of Patrol Personnel for Investigative Support	x			x	x	x	Patrol personnel conducted on-the-scene investigation.
2. Use of Investigative Aids			x				Non-sworn aids were used to handle much of the routine paper work, thus permitting investigators more time for direct investigation activities.
3. Team Approaches	x	x	x	x			Investigation teams composed of two or more investigators were used.
4. Special Staff Training	x	x	x	x	x	x	All projects devoted an average of 6 hours to specialized and refresher training for their investigative staffs.
TECHNIQUE CHANGES							
1. Use of Computer-based M.O. Profiles	x			x			Computer-based system containing Part I and II crime report data was used to retrieve information on crime reports containing similar MO information.

Table 7.6 (continued)

PROJECT ACTIVITY	Los Angeles Police Dept.	Los Angeles County Sheriff	Oakland Police Dept.	Orange County Sheriff	San Diego Police Dept.	San Francisco Police Dept.	COMMENTS
2. Use of Computer-based Suspect Files	x			x			Computer-based systems containing descriptions and modus operandi of arrested persons was used to retrieve persons matching the description and M.O. on the burglary report.
3. Use of Computer-based Pawn and Property Files	x				x		Computer-based systems containing information from pawn slips (person and property descriptions) and from burglary property reports (description of the property) were used to assist investigators working burglary cases.
4. Undercover Operations	x	x	x	x	x	x	This activity included: • Stakeouts of suspected receivers • Stakeouts of "stash" points • Undercover sales and buys • Surveillance of known burglars

Table 7.6 (continued)

PROJECT ACTIVITY	Los Angeles Police Dept.	Los Angeles County Sheriff	Oakland Police Dept.	Orange County Sheriff	San Diego Police Dept.	San Francisco Police Dept.	COMMENTS
SUSPECT HANDLING CHANGES							
1. Closer work with D.A. and Courts	x	x	x	x	x	x	All projects made efforts to work more closely with district attorneys to improve the filing rate on burglary arrests and the chances for convictions on the cases.
2. Case-Linking through MO Comparison	x	x	x	x	x	x	All projects (using computer or manual) made efforts to link arrested suspects with previously reported burglaries having the same suspect or vehicle descriptions and MO traits.
3. Increased Emphasis on Latent Print Checks	x	x	x	x	x	x	All projects placed additional emphasis on capturing suspect prints at the scene of the burglary.
4. Increased use of "Lie Detector"		x					Used to encourage arrested suspects to admit to other burglaries.
5. Closer Work with Deputy District Attorneys	x	x	x	x	x	x	To develop working agreement on acceptable support for case filings.

Table 7.7 Decreasing the receiver market

PROJECT ACTIVITY	Los Angeles Police Dept.	Los Angeles County Sheriff	Oakland Police Dept.	Orange County Sheriff	San Diego Police Dept.	San Francisco Police Dept.	COMMENTS
DECREASING THE RECEIVER MARKET							
1. Sponsor Property "ID" Program	x	x	x	x	x	x	All projects encouraged residents to mark their property by working with existing community organizations. Inscribing tools were made available to the public.
2. Increased Pawn Shop Surveillance		x	x	x	x	x	All projects concentrated on decreasing the receiver market for stolen property by frequent checks on locations where stolen property may appear.
3. Used Appliance Dealer Checks	x	x	x	x	x	x	
4. Appliance Rental Dealer Checks				x	x	x	
5. Garage and Swap Meet Checks				x	x		
6. Published Stolen Property Lists	x						This was done through Block Group Captains.
7. Published Business Machine ID Guide					x		This document published for field officers and investigators is used to locate serial and other identification numbers on the most commonly stolen business machines.

their effort on the assigned topic. Where a program does not exist, the team is to present verbally to the appropriate person (e.g., chief, lieutenant, sergeant) a preliminary plan for doing so. If a program is in existence, then the team is to assess its results. At the conclusion of the field visits, each team is to present orally (five to ten minutes) its findings.

2.   On an individual basis, develop a brief one to two page paper retracing your steps taken today. Relate in each instance, how *you* could have, or someone else (an institution) could have enhanced the security of your property. For example, you rode a bicycle to work or school and had to park it in an unsecured area. Verbally present in three minutes your experiences and recommended improvements. Do not fail to mention those situations where you detected that security measures had been taken.

Endnotes

1. Mainly, the programs constituting this, and the following, chapter were discussed in the government research documents *Selected Crime Prevention Programs in California* (Sacramento, Calif.: California Council on Criminal Justice, 1973).
2. The term "software" should be interpreted to encompass, and at times stress, the human element. "Peopleware" may well be the more germane term.
3. Franklin E. Zimring, *Perspectives On Deterrence* (Washington, D.C.: U.S. Government Printing Office, 1971), p. 16.
4. The majority of the thinking expressed in this section is drawn from John Fabbri, "Crime Prevention Through Physical Planning," *Crime Prevention Review* 1 (April 1974), pp. 1–6.
5. An outstanding text on this subject is written by Oscar Newman, *Defensible Space* (New York: Macmillan and Co., 1972).
6. National Advisory Commission on Criminal Justice Standards and Goals, *Police* (Washington, D.C.: U.S. Government Printing Office, 1973), p. 129.
7. This section is excerpted from the monograph *Crime-Specific Burglary Prevention Handbook*, (Sacramento, Calif.: Office of Criminal Justice Planning, 1974).
8. Ibid.

8

Crime Prevention Programs: Peopleware

Tiger Prevention

Another barrier to the revision of crime-control strategies is the official belief in a number of "tiger prevention" programs. Tiger prevention takes its name from the story of the gentleman who was going about the streets of Manhattan, snapping his fingers and moaning loudly, when he was intercepted by a police officer. Their conversation follows:

> **P.O.:** What are you doing?
> **Gtlm.:** Keeping tigers away.
> **P.O.:** Why, that's crazy. There isn't a wild tiger within five thousand miles of New York City!
> **Gtlm.:** Well then, I must be doing it right!

Other factors, of course, account for the absence of tigers in New York City, but as long as the gentleman continues to snap his fingers, he won't know that. And if the method of prevention were any less ridiculous, it would be difficult for observers to conclude for certain that his countermeasure, which is, after all, designed to prevent tigers, is not the reason why the number of wild tigers is low.*

Preview
One may consider it problematical as to which type of crime prevention activity—peopleware or hardware—is more useful. It seems reasonable to view both as being in-

*Franklin E. Zimring, *Perspectives On Deterrence* (Washington, D.C.: U.S. Government Printing Office, 1971), pp. 16–17.

178

terrelated, in fact interdependent, as far as achieving desired results. Nevertheless, peopleware would appear to have an edge in basic import; for it is people (citizens) who opt in favor or not of installing anticrime hardware devices. And it is people who will or will not maintain and use them. Thus the focus of this chapter is—crime prevention via the citizen.

The number of people oriented crime prevention programs that could be described herein is vast. Six have been selected as exemplifying typical police-citizen efforts. Depending on the situation and one's own personal bias, they may be ranked high, medium, or low in potential benefits to the community. First, the creation of a crime prevention unit provides a focal point of energy and direction for police-community prevention programs. Second, the neighborhood watch program seeks to organize people for the augmentation of their own personal security. Third, vacation inspections are intended to instruct residents in protecting their property while absent. Four, the community radio watch is somewhat analogous to the neighborhood watch in that the citizens are being alerted to possible intruders. Five, bunco preventer activities are designed to minimize the risk of being bilked out of one's property through deceit. Six, and finally, family crisis intervention techniques are discussed as they may prevent civil matters from becoming criminal in nature. Succinctly, the effective management of interpersonal crisis may preclude future police action in terms of a criminal offense.

Keep in mind that the preceding chapter included a direct and clear-cut warning that crime prevention activities should be carefully inspected and adjudged as to their costs and benefits.[1] If wisely designed, implemented, and supported, the following programs are not in danger of being assessed as "tiger prevention." Indeed, it is in peopleware as compared to hardware that an enduring hope for crime prevention resides. In this section we will cover: (1) crime prevention units, (2) neighborhood watch programs, (3) vacation inspections, (4) community radio watches, (5) bunco preventions, and (6) family crisis intervention tactics. The latter subject will be presented in more detail than the others because of its pervasiveness and inherent proclivity to expand beyond a civil to a criminal situation.

Crime Prevention Units

Many police agencies are currently undertaking at least limited crime prevention programs. These most often take the form of public speaking available on request, marking pens available for citizen use, or pamphlet distribution. Unfortunately, relatively few departments implement multiple programs designed to achieve before-the-fact prevention. What is lacking is a unit within the agency that can initiate and coordinate a varied selection of crime prevention programs. Officers should be assigned to new programs that can often be run with only minimal costs; they would then be available to work with community groups to implement combined approaches to crime prevention. Their continuing assignment should provide the momentum necessary for the continuation of these programs.[2] This is not to say that this unit is to have sole responsibility for all crime prevention activities. Conversely, each officer in the department should assume portions of this effort as a regular part of his duties. The crime prevention unit should inform other officers of ways in which they can help prevent crimes; consequently, it becomes the officers' responsibility to carry out those suggestions.

The success or failure of a crime prevention unit is inextricably dependent on top administrative leadership. Program directors should be exposed to specialized crime prevention training. It is recommended that program administrators consider having key officers attend either the National Crime Prevention Institute, Louisville, Kentucky, or the Crime Prevention Program conducted by the California Commission on Peace Officers Standards and Goals.[3]

The unit's efforts should involve assisting citizens to implement joint approaches to before-the-fact crime prevention. This may involve working with individuals, neighborhood groups, business associations, civic clubs, etc. As programs are started, the unit is responsible for maintaining community interest. Officers should remember that citizens who volunteer their time are doing just that—volunteering. It is unreasonable to expect that interested citizens will have the time to do the staff work necessary to continue such programs. Members of the unit should constantly focus on involving more citizens and developing new approaches. The majority of their tasks will involve implementing the programs described in this and the preceding chapter. Manpower requirements will, of course, vary depending upon such things as: (1) size of police agency, (2) community population, (3) nature and extent of crime problem, and (4) geography.

Administrators should be aware that crime prevention efforts can be successful only with complete agency support. Liaison should be maintained with the department's statistical units. Also, close liaison should be established with the patrol division. It is necessary that the beat officers be aware of the objectives and activities of the unit. One final point, if the units are evaluated only on a short-term basis, their true impact will not be measured. The results must be evaluated, however, on a long-term basis.

Neighborhood Watch Programs

The main goals of a neighborhood watch (or alert) program are: (1) to increase the cooperation between citizen and law enforcement in protecting their own and their neighbors' property, (2) to prevent the occurrence of crimes against persons and property in participating neighborhoods, and (3) to increase the apprehension rate for crimes against persons and property in participating neighborhoods.

Crime prevention officers should encourage residents to participate in such programs. This encouragement may be done by general advertising, random selection of homes, contacts through service groups, or contacts with crime victims. As soon as the program is explained to the selected citizen, he should be instructed to invite all of his neighbors to an evening meeting. The suggested lead time for this meeting is one to two weeks. At the time of the meeting the selected resident should again give a brief statement of the purpose for the meeting and then introduce the department's representative. This representative may be a crime prevention officer. If the department is operating a team-patrol plan, the representative can be the officer assigned to that neighborhood. If that is the preference, he should receive inservice training from the crime prevention officer.

Once he is introduced, the officer shoud deliver a prepared presentation covering the following areas: the nature and extent of crime, the roles of police and citizens in preventing crime, and general and specific crime prevention techniques. At this time the emphasis should be placed upon mutual reliance for the observation and reporting of unusual activities. Follow-up meetings should be held at least once every other month. At this time there can be a discussion of new crime techniques and crime trends surrounding that neighborhood. Other programs, such as "Operation Identification" and "Residential Security Inspection," could be explained and promoted. Residents may also wish to inform their neighbors of their vacation schedules at this time. As new residents move into the neighborhood, they should be invited to participate so that the program will become an ongoing activity.

As with any social endeavor, we can expect problems; two, in particular, loom rather large. First, the general apathy of the public may be difficult to overcome. Second, unless the department keeps its level of interest in the project high, public interest will not be maintained. The following paragraphs describe a case in point.[4] Finally, you will find a brochure that seeks to stimulate neighborhood watch programs. Hence, let us now examine Oakland's "Home Alert" program.

In the late 60s, a group of citizens had reported to the Oakland Police Department (OPD) that their neighborhood was being plagued with malicious acts: home burglaries and thefts from automobiles. They expressed their frustration and requested assistance to combat the crime problems. OPD officers met with approximately twenty families residing in the neighborhood and, together, the citizens and the police established the first Home Alert group in Oakland. The objective of the group was: protection through participation and cooperation, with each member of the group agreeing to observe and report to his neighbors and to the police any suspicious acts occurring in the neighborhood area.

The first Home Alert group was a success and crime in that particular neighborhood was significantly reduced. It became apparent that if such a crime prevention program could benefit a small group of concerned citizens, it could also benefit other citizens willing to assume responsibility for the safety of their neighbors. With that concept in mind, a Citizens' Crime Prevention Committee began work to establish more Home Alert groups. Within a short period of time, seventy-three groups had been formed.

The experience with the first Home Alert groups had made it apparent that many citizens were concerned about crime conditions in their neighborhoods and were anxious to learn what they could do to protect themselves and others. It was for these reasons that a determination was made to develop the new "Police-Community Cooperation Project" around a much expanded Home Alert concept. "Operation Crime Stop" and the initial Home Alert effort had made it clear that three requirements had to be met before the "Police-Community Cooperation Project" could be implemented. First, it would be necessary to establish a staff which could devote its full attention to the project and which could coordinate its activities with the administrators of the police department, the members of the Citizens' Crime Prevention Committee, and individual citizens involved in various aspects of the program. Second, a formalized structure which would accommodate and support the community-wide growth of citizen prevention activities would be needed. Finally, it would be imperative to develop and produce a great wealth of crime prevention literature and visual aids for dissemination to citizens.

The first step taken to implement the expanded Home Alert concept was to bring citizens together in mass meetings for the purpose of explaining the program and to gain their participation as Home Alert members. The president of the Citizens' Crime Prevention Committee mailed letters of invitation to every household in one neighborhood after another until eventually the entire community had been covered. At the mass meetings, police officers and members of the committee discussed neighborhood crime problems, the Home Alert concept, and the citizen's role in crime prevention. Individuals were asked to volunteer as Home Alert group members and, where needed, as group leaders and district directors.

The mass meetings were successful and, within a few weeks, 200 Home Alert groups were active in Oakland. A monthly newsletter was developed to keep Home Alert members informed concerning crime conditions in the city and in each of the fifty-five districts. The newsletters were prepared by crime analysis officers and were distributed by hand and by mail to all program participants. Each newsletter addressed specific crime problems and offered advice concerning measures which could be taken to prevent those offenses. Nontechnical language was used in the letters and only practical, easily implemented crime prevention methods were discussed.

The Home Alert Program began to receive attention in metropolitan and neighborhood newspapers and television stations broadcast special news features about it. An eight-page brochure describing the Home Alert effort was mailed to more than 107,000 households in Oakland, and police officers distributed crime prevention pamphlets through display racks, civic and social organizations, churches and schools. As word of the Home Alert Program spread, more and more citizens came forward to join in the crime prevention effort. The number of Home Alert groups grew rapidly and, within six months time, more than 1,000 groups were active in Oakland.

The goal of the "Police-Community Cooperation Project" and, specifically, the Home Alert Program, was to reduce crime in Oakland by developing in citizens the awareness that they have a responsibility for preventing crime, that they can meet that responsibility by working with the police to effect measures to harden the targets of criminal attack, and that each citizen has a responsibility for the safety and protection of other persons. Now, after many years of operation, the question must be asked, "Has Home Alert worked; has it been worth the effort?" The answer to that question appears to be "yes."

Serious crime in Oakland increased steadily from one year to the next during the 1960s and the efforts of the department to curtail the spiraling crime rate had not had sufficient favorable impact. In terms of crime, 1968 had been a disastrous year, with an alarming 52 percent increase in Index offenses; but particularly distressing was the fact that crimes of stealth—crime over which the police can assert little direct influence—increased phenomenally.

Serious crimes continued to increase in 1969, but at a decelerated pace, reflecting perhaps the efforts of the police department to field every available officer and some limited success of the early Home Alert and "Operation Crime Stop" programs. Finally, in 1970, the upward spiral of serious offenses was broken and the year ended with 7.4 percent fewer Index offenses than had been reported in 1969. Particularly gratifying was the fact that residential burglary—the prime target of Home Alert—decreased nearly 2 percent, the first reduction in that offense to be recorded in more than a decade.

Today, nearly 1,200 Home Alert groups are functioning in Oakland and the program has had its impact in virtually every neighborhood of the city. Because Home Alert is a citywide program, it has not been possible to evaluate the project in terms of control and program areas, and any attempt to assess the success of the program must be made in terms of the overall crime rate in Oakland. The precise impact that Home Alert has had on criminal activity in Oakland may never be known, but it clearly has had some influence. The OPD and the Citizens' Crime Prevention Committee will continue their commitment to Home Alert and the program will continue to serve as the nucleus of new and expanded community-based crime prevention efforts.

Vacation Premise Inspections

The prime purposes of vacation premise inspections are: (1) to identify prime burglary targets, (2) to deter burglaries by checks of vacant residences, and (3) to increase the burglary clearance rates by decreasing the time between offense and detection. Most basi-

Figure 8.1

cally, the program is intended to encourage citizens to inform the local law enforcement agency whenever they are leaving on vacation. Such encouragement can be transmitted through general advertising, presentations at civic groups, literature left at travel agencies, etc. As people call in to report their vacation plans, a summary of appropriate security measures should be related to them. This would include such things as stopping mail, newspaper, and milk deliveries, using a light timer, asking neighbors to watch for suspicious circumstances, and so forth. The actual checks can be performed by paraprofessionals. In the event any of these personnel come upon a burglary in process, it would be their responsibility to notify regular patrol units. Exhibit 8.2 depicts a vacation house check guide and a form letter.

Community Radio Watches

The principal objectives of a community radio watch crime prevention program are twofold: (1) to prevent the occurrence of crimes and incidents by increasing the eyes and ears of law enforcement, and (2) to assist the response capability to community safety needs. In this instance, operators of two-way radios within the jurisdiction should be contacted. One can do this by obtaining a list of "ham" operators from the Federal Communications Commission; by contacting companies and government agencies known to use these radios; by placing notices in retail establishments selling this type of equipment; and by general advertising. After explaining the program to them, these citizens should be asked to participate. If they concur, the police officer should carefully define the type of participation. Two dimensions are especially important. First, the officer should explain what kinds of incidents are to be reported. (Overly enthused citizens could easily flood the department with reports of minor problems.) Circumstances to be reported should in every instance include all crimes of violence, serious property crimes, fires, and injury accidents. Some police agencies may wish to include such things as generally suspicious acts and unusual occurrences, e.g., faulty traffic lights, fallen trees, etc.

When one of these incidents is observed, the citizen should radio into the agency with a brief description of the event and the specific location. It is *crucial* that, with usual criminal acts, the citizens be instructed to end their involvement at this point. It should be stressed that the police agency is, in most instances, primarily responsible for the apprehension of suspects. Relatedly,

VACATION HOUSE CHECK FORM

NAME: _____

ADDRESS: _____

RECEIVED BY: _____

TELEPHONE: _____

DATE/TIME: _____

HOUSE CHECK TO BEGIN: _____

DATE OF RETURN: _____

RESPONSIBLE PERSON/ADDRESS/TEL: _____

Yes	No		Yes	No	
		Pool in yard?			Newspaper stopped?
		Pets in yard?			Mail stopped?
		Rear yard locked?			Gardener/maid on property?
		Any broken windows/screens?	▨	▨	Day/
▨	▨	Where/			Anyone to be on property?
		Cars in garage/driveway?	▨	▨	Name/
▨	▨	License #	▨	▨	
		Misc.			Lights on inside?
▨	▨		▨	▨	Time/

ADDITIONAL INFORMATION: _____

_____

(OFFICERS' CHECKS)

Date	Time	Off.	Remarks

Figure 8.2

Figure 8.2 (continued)

(POLICE DEPARTMENT LETTERHEAD)

Dear _____ :

This is to inform you that your name has been taken off our house check list. We hope that upon your return you found everything in order, but if not, please contact us immediately. Due to the increasing number of families on our house check list and insufficient manpower, we were unable to check your home every day, but we did check your home as often as possible.

In the future, if you are again leaving for an extended period, do not hesitate to phone us for this service.

Assuring you of our cooperation at all times.

Very truly yours,

(Signed)

_____ (Name)

_____ (Title)

for this program to be effective, the police effort must not conclude with the agreements by citizens to participate. Unless one's interest is maintained, this participation will decrease. The most efficient method for maintaining interest is to distribute monthly newsletters to all participants. This newsletter should include descriptions of cases wherein "Radio Alert" information was of use. Citizens whose information was exceptionally helpful can be given personal certificates of appreciation by the police agency. If the agency feels it would be beneficial, a crime prevention officer can conduct bimonthly meetings with the participating citizens in order to inform them of past progress and new crime trends.

Certain problems are to be anticipated in this programmatic effort. They are: (1) unless citizens are completely instructed, they may report too many minor infractions, and (2) unless citizens are adequately informed, they may become overinvolved and actually interfere with police duties.

Bunco Prevention

The purpose of this program is to prevent the occurrence of financial institution bunco. In terms of implementation, all financial institution customers who make cash withdrawals of $250 or more should be given information describing common bunco operations. It is hoped that, if the withdrawal is being made for the purpose of forwarding cash to a "confidence" man, this information will alert the citizen to the "scam." The information sheets should, of course, be printed in English, and—where appropriate—other languages. The next two exhibits portray materials now in use.

Family Crisis Intervention

One of the most hazardous assignments police officers face is dealing with family quarrels and disturbances. In 1972, 13 percent of all policeman killed in the line of duty died while responding to disturbance complaints. Twenty-seven percent of the assaults on police officers occurred in the same setting. The risk is even greater for the participants in these quarrels. Of all murders reported in 1972, 24.3 percent occurred between family members, 7.1 percent during "lovers' quarrels," and 41.2 percent as the result of other arguments. The vast majority of all aggravated assaults involve relatives, neighbors, or acquaintances.

Despite these dangers, techniques for dealing with such crises are rarely included in police recruit and inservice training programs. Research, however, indicates that police trained in crisis intervention are less likely to be injured or assaulted when handling fights and disturbances. Some researchers believe well-trained officers also serve to reduce homicide and assault rates.

From a broader perspective, this sophisticated training technique changes the police function in concrete and positive ways. Success is measured in terms of police ability to solve disputes rather than piling up felony arrests. As the police begin to view themselves as skilled conflict managers who are capable of defusing potentially explosive situations, beneficial effects are felt throughout the department. Successful intervention in family disputes also can be economical in terms of eliminating the time and expense involved in bringing a case to court.

The Sweet-Talk Crimes:
Credit Card Fraud
Bad Check Passing
Confidence Games

Always get identification from people using a credit card or writing you a check.

Este folleto en español sobre prevención de fráudes con tarjetas de crédito, chéques y otros lo pueden obtener, llamando al: 273-3068 o 273-3827

The Confidence Game—the only way to win is to stop it

"Confidence men" are among the most inventive and persuasive criminals—it's a shame they don't put their ingenuity to honest use. Their stock in trade is tricking people into making cash withdrawals from bank accounts. They may represent themselves as bank security officers attempting to stop an embezzler, or promise to share a large "find" of money with you if you'll put up a "good faith" deposit. Sometimes they offer merchandise at ridiculously low prices, then take your cash payment and skip town without delivering the goods.

Whatever the scheme, when a stranger offers you a deal that sounds "too good to be true," chances are it probably is. Before you give your hard-earned money to anyone, it's wise to invest a dime in a call to the Oakland Police.

They've heard just about every get-rich-quick scheme there is, and can see to it that swindlers get what's coming to them—while you keep what's rightfully yours.

Your credit cards are valuable— to you, and to criminals

The credit card: honored at department stores, discount houses, gas stations, restaurants—almost anywhere. To you, it's as good as cash. To a criminal, it's better than cash.

The thief who steals your credit card has committed an "open end" theft—he can use your card to obtain money and goods until he is caught. Many credit card thieves call their victims and pretend to be honest citizens who have found a "lost wallet." They assure the owner of the credit cards that the lost cards will be mailed back to him, thus getting additional time to charge purchases to an unreported stolen credit card.

Credit card thieves figure they've got one week to use a stolen credit card safely. If they've stolen a bank credit card their usual first step is to attempt to borrow the maximum amount of cash that can be loaned on the card. After that, they charge merchandise, and often pawn it for more cash. Frequently, the credit card thief's final trick is to buy airline tickets with the stolen card, then resell them at the airport for half price. Often these criminals save the last ticket for themselves, and wing off to Hawaii, Puerto Rico, or the Bahamas—on someone else's good credit. There's even a black market for stolen credit cards—they're often sold for as much as $100 to $150.

Who pays when a thief uses your credit?

That depends. A new federal law says a credit card holder cannot be liable for more than $50 in fraudulent charges per credit card—*provided the credit card issuer is notified within a reasonable time*. What is a reasonable time? The law doesn't say—but the Oakland Police recommend that you notify the credit card issuer *immediately*—first by telephone, then in writing, with a telegram or registered letter. Then, call the Oakland Police to report the theft and its circumstances. It's also wise to notify your insurance company—many homeowner's policies cover losses from fraudulent credit card use.

How you can curb credit card crimes

The basic rule is careful and sensible use of your credit cards. If you follow these suggestions, you'll be making it harder for criminals to take advantage of your good credit:

- Keep credit cards on your person when you're traveling—don't leave them in a jacket hanging in a public place, or in a locker or hotel room.
- Don't carry more credit cards than you need.
- Keep a record of all your credit card numbers so you can report stolen cards by number.
- Never keep credit cards in your car.
- Destroy unwanted credit cards by cutting.
- Never lend a credit card to anyone.
- Report credit card loss or theft *immediately*.

Using your credit card

More and more merchants are requesting identification from credit card users—and it's a good idea. Don't be offended if you're asked for identification along with your credit card—it's for your protection. When you use a credit card, be sure you get a copy of the invoice—unscrupulous merchants or clerks can alter the invoice after you leave the store, and charge you with more than the amount of purchase. Finally, be sure your card is returned after each purchase.

Look for the following on checks:

1. *Printed name, address and telephone number of the maker. (Check this against the maker's driver's license)*
2. *Date (post-dated checks aren't criminal matters—checking the date is your only protection)*
3. *Amount*
4. *Maker's signature (compare spelling with printed name)*
5. *Bank account number*

Exercise extreme caution before honoring a bank counter check or out-of-town check.

Checks aren't money until the bank honors them

Bad check passers and confidence artists are a special breed: while other criminals usually do their work when no one is around, these operators base their hope for success on face-to-face meetings with their victims.

"Paperhangers"—writers of bad checks—prey on merchants or individuals selling automobiles or other goods through classified advertising. They exchange a worthless check for whatever merchandise they want —and frequently write the check for more than the amount of purchase to obtain cash as well as merchandise. There are a number of steps you can take to see that a check is in order, but it is wise to remember that until a check clears the bank, it is just paper. If you don't know the writer of a check, observe extreme caution and limit the amounts of checks you accept to small sums.

Figure 8.3

190

Are You About To Be Swindled?

¡No Sea Estafado!

Are You About To Be Swindled?

IS THIS BANK WITHDRAWAL BECAUSE:

. . . You were contacted by a man representing himself of a "Bank Investigator" or "FBI Agent?" Has he asked you to withdraw money from your bank to help in the investigation of an internal bank theft?

. . . you witnessed the finding of a large amount of money: Were you asked to withdraw your money to be held as an act of "good faith?"

IF SO, THIS MAY BE A SWINDLE! PLEASE CONTACT THE SAN JOSE POLICE DEPARTMENT IMMEDIATELY.

ATENCIÓN:

¡¡NO SE CREA!! ¡¡NO SAQUE SU DINERO!!
¡¡NO SÉA VÍCTIMA DE UN ROBO!!
¿Va usted a sacar dinero del banco por las siguientes razones?

PORQUE . . . .
Se ha aproximadó un extraño a usted pidiéndoe que saque su dinero del banco? ¡Alerta! ¡Mucho cuidado! Si eso sucede, usted está en peligro de ser defraudado. Por ningún motivo saque el dinero, especialmente si alguien se halló mucho dinero o un extraño con mucho dinero le contó una tragedia.

MUCHO CUIDADO . . . .
Usted va a ser víctima de un ROBO (Estafa) por individuos expertos en los ROBOS LLAMADOS juegos de confianza.

¡¡NO SE CREA!! ¡¡NO SAQUE SU DINERO!!
¡¡NO SEA VÍCTIMA DE UN ROBO!!
COMUNÍQUESE CON EL DEPARTMENTO DE POLICÍA INMEDIATAMENTE!

IF YOU SUSPECT YOU ARE ABOUT TO BE SWINDLED OR ARE A VICTIM OF A SWINDLE, CALL . . . .

SAN JOSE POLICE DEPARTMENT
297-3565

SI TIENE ALGUNA SOSPECHA O SI ES VÍCTIMA DE UN ESTAFO . . . .

LLAME AL DEPARTAMENTO DE POLICÍA
297-3565

SAN JOSE POLICE DEPARTMENT
201 W. MISSION STREET
SAN JOSE, CALIFORNIA 95110
LEAA FUNDED

Figure 8.4

In order to explain the importance of the term "family crisis intervention," two areas of human behavior which relate to this police function will be discussed. They are interpersonal conflict management and crisis intervention theory and practice.

Crisis Inter-
vention:
Theory and
Practice[5]

During the past three decades crisis intervention has occupied an increasingly important place in mental health applications. Lindemann, an early contributor to crisis theory, posited that early skillful and authoritative intervention in critical personal events could forestall the possibly more serious, long-term consequence of such events.[6] But intervention approaches based upon this theory posed an enormous challenge to mental health institutional practices. Long accustomed to operating by requiring people to "come in" for help, professionals were, and continue to be, hard put to develop methods of intervening when people are more susceptible to being influenced by others. A variety of efforts has been made by institutions to achieve some outreach capability, including twenty-four hour walk-in clinics, telephone hot lines, mobile crisis units, and local storefront clinics. These methods, intended to reduce the time interval between the crisis event and "laying on the hands," have brought to light some inherent flaws. For one thing, crisis services were usually secondary to the more central concerns of the mental health enterprise, namely diagnosis, treatment, and training. Crisis intervention as a preventive strategy received little more than peripheral attention. Early efforts to deliver crisis services brought other difficulties to the surface as well. Often, the use of the service was determined by the prior knowledge or experience of the person in crisis, that is, by his recognition of need for the service or even by his knowledge of the service's existence. More importantly, perhaps, the methods employed rarely reached those who by virtue of lack of education or improverished circumstances were unlikely to recognize their need and to reach out for help at the time of crisis.

Those who have worked with the crisis concept have emphasized the importance of the *earliness* of the intervention in taking advantage of the openness of the person in crisis. However, the speed with which intervention can be accomplished is strongly influenced by how predictable the crisis was. As McGee has suggested, crises fall on a continuum of predictability.[7] There are those that can be seen coming, so to speak. They range from the normal developmental crisis to such events as a new job, a school examination, or elective surgery. And then there are those crises precipitated by wholly unforeseen events such as natural disasters, serious accidents, or crimes.

Let us now consider the importance of authority. The perceived power of the care-giver has always been a secret weapon of the helping system. This phenomenon of power is even more important in the management of people in crisis—particularly those under the impact of a sudden, arbitrary, and unanticipated crisis. The crisis has a chaotic effect; coping mechanisms are severely taxed and a sense of helplessness ensues. In a sense, the individual is, to a lesser or greater extent, so reduced in his ability to cope that his behavior may be regarded as regressed. Either actively or passively, he seeks help or direction. And, those in the environment who are perceived as powerful are apt to be seen as the source of order and stability in an otherwise suddenly chaotic world.

Recognizing the significance of authority provides a context for answering the question about how it is possible to plan for prompt intervention in all crises. Clearly it is not possible to plan for the sudden, unpredictable and arbitrary stressful event. But it is possible to enlist the participation of an existing service delivery system whose domain is crisis, whose mode is immediacy and whose very essence is authority. These three attributes are all essential for effective crisis intervention. The irony is that they should be absolutely unique to an agency not usually identified as part of the helping system . . . the police.[8] *These factors, when taken together, attest to the unique potentials of the police as a primary crisis intervention resource.*

The following list typifies the kind of events that lend themselves to skillful crisis intervention as a preventive strategy by police officers:

- crime victimization
- natural disaster
- notification. (A frequent police activity with little recognition by laymen, this involves informing the family or next of kin of the death or injury of a family member.)
- accidents. (Ranging from vehicular homicides to falling objects, these events differ somewhat from the "disaster syndrome" in that the chaos is personal and exists in an otherwise ordered and intact environment.)
- psychotic reactions
- suicides and attempted suicides

Even a cursory examination of these crises communicates the unique potentials for crisis intervention in the police service delivery system. Further, it is suggested that the kind of immediacy in time and place that can be achieved by the police cannot be achieved by any other element in the helping system.

Inter-
personal
Conflict
Management

The management of interpersonal conflict is probably the most time-consuming aspect of the police agency function. One researcher monitored eighty-two consecutive hours of telephone calls to the Syracuse (N.Y.) Police Department and found that almost twenty percent of them were for disputes and fights in public and private places and among family members, neighbors, and total strangers.[9] The police departments of Dallas (Texas), Kansas City (Mo.), New York (N.Y.), and Cambridge (Mass.) report similarly high percentages of time allocated to interpersonal conflict. He concluded that although the "apprehension of law breakers may stand in the public mind as the crux of police work, most of a policeman's day is spent in more 'mundane' matters such as . . . acting as an outside mediator in situations of conflict."[10]

The word *mundane*, in this connection, has interesting connotations. For one thing it is a reflection of the police officer's denigration of an onerous function. For another, it projects the television and detective-novel inspired fantasy of what it is that occupies priority in police work. However, the incredibly complex role of mediation is anything but mundane and the consequences of incompetent third party intervention are very serious; it can and often does contribute to violence rather than to pacification. *A significant percentage of those police officers killed and injured in the line of duty were involved at the time in efforts to manage a human conflict.*

The usual role of a police officer is one which leads naturally to his or her becoming involved as a third party in interpersonal conflicts. This function is one which can neither be readily delegated nor ignored.

A recent study demonstrated that the performance of policemen trained in conflict management improved significantly as measured by traditional police criteria.[11] Furthermore, a general sense of security in a community is not only the product of a lower crime rate. There is mounting evidence that we feel secure when we are convinced that government is responsive to our needs. The police officer is both the most visible and the most immediately available extension of governmental authority. As a crucial service which communicates responsiveness, conflict management goes far toward generating a sense of security for us.

Many of these observations result from a number of years spent directing action research programs that have sought, among other things, to test the feasibility of training police for third party intervention in interpersonal conflict.[12] During the course of these studies in New York City, for example, it was possible to collect data on more than 1,500 cases of police management of conflicts among people. However, it should be noted that because of the nature of the original study involving family conflicts and the nature of the subsequent study's setting (low income housing projects), most of the data relate to family disputes. Nevertheless, it seems useful for us to touch briefly upon some of the findings.

Since training was a critical variable in these studies, a number of methods were used to assess training effects. Most striking was the finding that police officers can learn and practice relevant interpersonal skills to affect their performance as conflict managers. Moreover, the evaluation suggested that the changes in police behavior necessary for effective third party performance do not require a corresponding change in the attitudes and beliefs of the police officer. Additionally, the behavioral changes observed were related to the nature of the training. The training methods which were used can be labeled "affective" and "experiential" methods.

What does an "affective" and "experiential" training program consist of? Most of the course content focuses upon behavior within an actual social situation. The methods employed range from specifically prepared police social science information (communicated in a context which encourages discussion) to real life simulations and videotape role plays. A short period of intensive classroom training is followed by a period of field training, and the major thrust of the training is to encourage the kind of self-criticism which permits the practitioner to learn from his mistakes. Regularly scheduled case conferences are used which permit the officers to continue the process of learning as they practice in the field.

It seems useful to take a closer look at the kinds of changes experiential training methods brought about in the officers in the studies. The following are among the training effects noted: 1) the officers were better able to regard both parties in conflict as contributing to the situation rather than to see the dispute as the responsibility of one "crazy person;" 2) the officers were able to maintain objectivity in the way they behaved as well as in the way they perceived the conflict; 3) the response toward the police of those in conflict was positive; 4) there was little evidence of the need to employ force; 5) there was an absence of injuries to officers; and 6) the officers more frequently employed techniques other than arrest and/or court referral.

Studies to date have confirmed the President's Commission finding that in most disputes "often the parties really want (the officers) only to 'do something' that will settle things" rather than make an arrest.[13] It appears that when there is a conflict we want an objective, skillful and benign authority who can successfully negotiate, mediate, or arbitrate a constructive outcome. The passions of the moment require a "here and now" legally sanctioned intervention which no other agency of the helping system is capable of delivering.

We have only skimmed the surface phenomena in third party intervention. We are aware that much of a policeman's behavior results from a mix of understanding, insight, knowledge, and intuition. But exactly what is the full range of approaches used by officers in dealing with disputes? In order to learn the answer to that question and others, we must build bridges between the practitioner in the field and the researcher in the laboratory. A recently designed approach which is worthy of examination is a strategy suggested by R. E. Walton.[14] The model proposes an active and intimate collaboration between police practitioners in the field and university based social scientists. The suggested collaboration results in an instrument for knowledge-building for the police system and for social science as well. The opportunities for studying aspects of human aggression in an actual social situation are limitless.

For society to encourage excellence of police performance in conflict management is one way of removing the stigma which we place on conflict in human relations. As Deutsch recently said, ". . . the issue is not how to eliminate or prevent conflict but rather how to make it productive or at least how to prevent it from being destructive."[15] In providing a clear sanction for the police to deliver this much needed third party intervention service, we are acknowledging that conflict is not only a realistic and inevitable part of relationships between people, but can also present us with inherently constructive opportunities. In addition, by legitimating a human need whose traditional closet status has been so costly in terms of human life and social disorder, we are expressing our concern for and respect of the individuals in need.

Models of Implementation   The implementation of any idea requires a construct which contains all of the important elements of the concept and which can serve as the means for achieving the desired goal. Given the general structure of police organizations, three models will be discussed; the choice of a specific model, however, will depend upon the nature of each situation.

Generalist-Specialist Model.   This was the model used in the original family crisis demonstration projects. In essence, a selected group of general patrol officers processed all family disturbance calls in a specified area. The officers operated in uniform and on all tours of duty; when not engaged in the management of a family disturbance, they provided general patrol services in an assigned sector. This model has the following advantages:

- Professional identity of the officer is preserved. In the eyes of his colleagues and of the public, the officer charged with family crisis responsibilities is still a "real cop."
- In a large organization, it appears to be an efficient way of delivering a needed service without sacrificing general uniformed patrol coverage.
- It has implications for other generalist-specialist roles (e.g., youth, rescue, etc.) in which each officer has a specialized area of expertise. It avoids the need for each patrolman to be all things to all people.
- It enhances the morale of patrolmen in that their area of special expertise is respected by both their colleagues and the public.

Generalist Model.   An alternate model, more suitable to small organizations, is for all patrol personnel to be given training in family crisis theory and practice. The advantages of this model are:

- It is suitable for small organizations that turn out too few men to have the luxury of a generalist-specialist on each tour.
- It ensures involvement of all personnel in acquiring special knowledge.
- While the quality of service delivered will show greater variance than it would with selected generalist-specialists, it will tend to maximize the impact on the department itself and on the public.
- It reinforces family crisis as the ongoing responsibility of *all* patrol personnel.

Specialist Model.   In studying police operations and theory, it seems that this may be the least desirable model. The following disadvantages should be carefully weighed before proceeding with this model:

- This is the model through which organizational ambivalence is most apt to be expressed. The delivery of the service becomes the exclusive responsibility of the specialist and satisfies only the policy decision with no reference to the more encompassing responsibilities of the agency.

- It tends to develop two status levels within the organization; those who do "real" police work and those who do social work.
- It is initially destructive to morale and thus destructive to the function of the specialist. The specialist feels divorced from his co-workers and confused in his identity as a police officer if his functions are limited to a single dimension of service.

Training   Preparing police officers to deliver a *highly complex* human service requires *unusual training* for specific skills. In fact, it requires a type of training that is a blend of that which is traditional in police work and that which is inherent in fields dealing exclusively with human services. Hence, different training models must be analyzed.

Intensive Training.   In police agencies the usual means of preparing personnel with specific skills is to put them through a concise and intensive training program. The methods of instruction are usually of a "how to" nature, largely by lecture augmented by audiovisual aids. At the conclusion of the training experience, the patrol officer returns to the field.

Field Training.   Usually unsystematic, fragmented, and methodologically "iffy," field training ranges from the roll call exercise to informal "rap" sessions. It is this form of training that breeds the greatest cynicism, since it comes across as "lip service" or perfunctory. This approach is likely to communicate organizational ambivalence about the training itself.

Combined Intensive and Field Training.   This model, if properly conceived and applied, holds the greatest promise for human service functions. The intensive training must be skillfully planned to be congruent with the ultimate objectives of the program. But even more important, the intensive training should be regarded as orientative rather than conclusive. Naturally, the methods employed in that training should also set the tone and prepare the officer for the kind of methods to be used in the field. At the conclusion of the brief intensive and orientative training, it is essential that there be follow-up in the field. It is here that the bulk of training occurs, in the human service professions—that is, in "learning-by-doing."

Relation-
ship with
other
Agencies

An essential ingredient in making family crisis intervention a successful strategy is the establishment of cooperative relationships between the police and other agencies of the "helping system." Yet, given the fact that many of these agencies are already taxed, it would be dysfunctional to develop unreasonable expectations of their capabilities. Additionally, it should be noted that because a police officer is involved in a crisis when emotions are at their height, and is judged as someone with authority, he may be in the best position to produce a favorable result. Because of this, a competent police officer may be preferable to a community agency. There will be cases, however, which require services beyond the ability of the officer. In those instances, resources should be available.

A few final words are appropriate with respect to police family crisis intervention. This chapter has only briefly mentioned some of the issues relevant to the implementation of such a program by police agencies. The questions of social regulation and public security are inseparable from the day-to-day management of complex human problems. Our police are the most immediate representatives of a governmental authority, and if we are to cooperate in the process of crime prevention we must trust the police. Such trust is engendered by the *competent delivery of those human services* that occupy so much of a police officer's time.

Learning Exercises

1. Divide the class into groups of six to eight people each. Each group is to evaluate and modify one of the proposed "peopleware" projects: (1) neighborhood watch, (2) vacation premise inspection, (3) community radio watch, or (4) bunco prevention. Generate both a "hand-out", and a strategy for its dissemination and usage (allow thirty-five minutes). Finally, each group should present its project orally to the entire class (allow four minutes per presentation). The entire process should last fifty minutes.

2. Divide the class into teams of four members each. Two members of each team are to role play two police officers called to the scene of a family crisis. The other two members of the team are to role play a husband and wife engaged in a heated dispute. Take ten minutes to develop your "game plan." Next act out your scenario in front of another team of four who are to serve as evaluators. The objective of the officers is to resolve the argument. After

fifteen minutes, the two teams reverse positions with the first becoming the judges and the second acting out their respective roles. Finally, the teams should discuss before the class their general impressions of the behavior that seemed most helpful or harmful on the part of the conflict resolvers (police officers). The time-frame for this exercise is sixty minutes.

Endnotes

1. Review again, footnotes one and two in the preceding chapter.
2. This author experienced heated, but meaningful debate while delivering a lecture to a group of police officials at the National FBI Academy in November, 1973. Concisely, I asserted that all police community relations programs should be disbanded at once. In turn, I proposed that they be replaced by crime prevention efforts.
3. It is to be noted that most of the crime-specific programs are similarly crime prevention in orientation. For example, the "Crime-Specific Seminar: Burglary" provided by the Center for Criminal Justice, California State University, Long Beach concentrates on training· officers in the prevention of burglaries.
4. This case example is taken in part from George T. Hart, "Home Alert: Crime Prevention Through Police-Citizen Cooperation," *Crime Prevention* 1 (July 1974), pp. 20–24.
5. This section is excerpted from the monograph written by Morton Bard, *Family Crisis Intervention: From Concept to Implementation* (Washington, D.C.: U.S. Government Printing Office, 1973).
6. E. Lindemann "Symptomatology and Management of Acute Grief," *American Journal of Psychiatry* 25 (July 1944), p. 213.
7. T. F. McGee, "Some Basic Considerations in Crisis Intervention," *Community Mental Health Journal,* 4 (May 1968), p. 319. Additionally, see David Lewit, "Social Psychology and Crime Control," *Journal of Social Issues* 31 (Winter 1975), pp. 193–210.
8. I. Janis, *Psychological Stress* (New York: John Wiley and Sons, 1958).
9. E. Cumming, *Systems of Social Regulation* (New York: Atherton Press, 1968).
10. Ibid., p. 170.
11. J. Zacker and M. Bard, "Effect of Conflict Management Training on Police Performance," *Journal of Applied Psychology* 58 (July 1973), p. 202.

12. M. Bard, J. Zacker, and E. Rutter, *Police Family Crisis Intervention and Conflict Management: An Action Research Analysis* (Washington, D.C.: U.S. Government Printing Office, 1972).

13. J. S. Campbell, J. R. Sakid, and D. P. Stang, *Law and Order Reconsidered: Report of the National Commission on the Cause and Prevention of Violence* (New York: Bantam Books, 1970), p. 291.

14. R. E. Walton, *Interpersonal Peacemaking: Confrontations and Third Party Consultation* (Reading, Mass.: Addison-Wesley, 1969).

15. M. Deutsch, "Toward An Understanding of Conflict," *International Journal of Group Tensions* 1 (January 1971), p. 42.

PART THREE

Criminal Justice
Crime Prevention

Some of the problems of the criminal justice system could be eased if we could grasp a common analytical pattern. The system is very unique as an organization. Many of its component parts are very independent, and should remain so. The system sits right on top of the separation of powers doctrine, like a city on an earthquake fault. It lacks the easy-to-understand monetary measure of success or failure of business organization. Frequently authority to function within some aspect of the system is given to people for reasons other than an ability to manage a complicated and important enterprise.

If we look at our system from a viewpoint which is somewhat different than our usual stand, we may see things differently and more constructively. When we start our thinking in terms of existing institutions we may put our minds to readjusting the turns and bottlenecks of the assembly line, rather than asking a more original question such as: "Do we really want an assembly line?" Or a judge may spend much time developing better sentencing procedures and probation reports and never realize that the probation to which he refers defendants is nothing more than a paper myth.

It is my thesis that if we can recognize a common purpose for the system, and a common analytical way of relating that purpose to our more specific roles within the system, we can develop the means of making our system effective. We need not sacrifice independence in order to move in the same direction. The key elements are a way of thinking and much communication.*

The three chapters in Part Three focus on the criminal justice system, and two of its three subsystems. Chapter 9 concentrates on

---

* Edmund J. Leach, Jr., "A Plan for Meaningful Justice," *Crime Prevention Review* 2 (October, 1974), p. 37.

203

the issue of "systematizing" the system. Three major linkages for doing so are identified and reviewed: (1) planning, (2) information flow, and (3) education and training. Legislation and prevention are discussed later. Next, the role of the courts and corrections is inspected as they pertain to crime prevention. Chapter 10 focuses on the courts as a vehicle for enhancing the prevention of crime. The general theme of the chapter is "reform." Finally, Chapter 11 dwells on correctional programs as they do or do not influence the prevention of crime. Controversy, confusion, and change form a threefold challenge to the corrections subsystem—the challenge to play a more meaningful role in the control of crime. It will be seen that the concept of "diversion" is paramount within the chapter.

In general, then, Part Three is a conglomeration of subject areas. The underlying *theme* remains, however, congealing the criminal justice system through the forging of improved subsystem linkages and internal reforms. The underlying *goal* remains improving the capability of the system and its component subsystems to prevent (before-the-commission) crime.

9

Unifying the System of Criminal Justice

The police arrest an individual and arraign him in court. The prosecutor will decide whether or not to prosecute the case. If there is a trial, the presiding judge is most likely from a county or state court system. If the individual is convicted, he will probably be assigned to a state correctional institution.

However, no mechanism exists in the cities, counties, or states for coordinating this system, and its component parts do not relate at all well. In fact, there is an unfortunate tendency for each part to blame its problems on the others. The police tend to blame the courts; the police are critical of Supreme Court decisions; judges will frequently find fault with the police for their repeated failure to bring "good" cases to court, cases for which they have the proper amount of evidence. Judges also criticize police failure to testify well enough to support a conviction.

Given the present fragmentation of authority, cooperation will not come easily or in a rush. Fragmentation of the criminal justice system by governmental unit sets several hurdles in the path of a program of coordinated crime control. We know that the criminal justice system can be better systematized. How this can be done and who should assume the initiative and leadership are the difficult questions to which we lack definite answers.*

Preview

A few prefer to use the phrase "nonsystem of criminal justice" when discussing the CJS. Unfortunately, to a large

---

*Patrick V. Murphy, "The Criminal Justice System in Crises," in *Police and Law Enforcement: 1972* ed. by James T. Curran, Austin Fowler, and Richard H. Ward (New York: AMS Press, Inc., 1973), p. 27.

degree their perception of the CJS as being a nonsystem is accurate. The factiousness among the operating parts of the CJS is most distressing in that they are so heavily dependent on one another for both their singular and combined success. In turn, five integrative processes have been identified which can function to coalesce the component parts of the CJS into an effective vehicle for the delivery of services. This chapter examines three of these five parts: planning, information systems, and education/training.

First, planning, which encompasses more than a single criminal justice agency and more than a single criminal justice component and is extended into the community, provides an invaluable vehicle for fusing the cognizant units and subsystems into an effective system. Currently, the federal government is assisting state and local jurisdictions in developing comprehensive plans that define and assign priorities to their problems. The incentive for doing so is considerable since action grants are awarded to the states for their own needs and subsequent allocations are made as well to regional units within their boundaries. Moreover, it is mandatory that the resultant plans are, in fact, comprehensive and thus include the CJS and the community.

Second, it is recognized that meaningful and reliable CJS planning requires updated and accessible data from which accurate planning decisions can be made. Because crime and criminals are not confined to a single geographical area, the needed data must be collected, processed, stored, and accessed by many CJS users. Hence the requirement for computer-driven criminal justice *information* systems. Nothing else so vividly illustrates the need for viable linkages among CJS components than the plan and exchange of information within the system.

Third, criminal justice education/training curricula are being re-conceptualized and re-structured to instruct students and trainees in theories and practices that are universal within the CJS. To an awareness of the roles of the various components is being added an understanding and appreciation for their mutually supportive characteristics. Thus far CJS education/training programs have been primarily career oriented. Today practitioners and educators are collaborating to build a more relevant program for merging the CJS components, and extending CJS interactions in order to create a more meaningful and supportive interface with its surrounding environment—the community. Consequently, we have now arrived at a point of full realization that the success or failure of the CJS inextricably depends on its relationship or nonrelationship to its community; thus the concept of CJS/C was proposed. The key integrative processes for creating "systemic fusion" and hence operationally effective CJS/C were: planning, information systems, education/training, legislation, and prevention. The first process, that of planning, is examined in both a generic sense and with a police bias in Chapter 6. This chapter discusses planning as it pertains to the CJS/C. The fourth process, while vital, will be left for others to discuss. The last process, prevention, is the predominant theme of the book. Therefore, the following sections are devoted to an explication of the first three integrative processes. Please keep in mind while perusing the subsequent material that the CJS/C is in urgent need of improving its internal subsystem interactions so as to be more effective and efficient in the delivery of its services—and there are five main vehicles for doing so.

Pursuing A System of Criminal Justice

"Fragmented," "divided," "splintered," and "decentralized" are the adjectives most commonly used to describe the American CJS.[1] The sheer number of independent agencies is the most viable evidence of fragmentation. According to a 1970 survey, there are 46,197 public agencies in the criminal justice system that are administered at the state or local government level in towns of more than 1,000 population. Most states have hundreds of criminal justice agencies. For example, in Wisconsin, a medium-sized state whose criminal justice structure is typical of other states, there are 1,075 separate criminal justice agencies. These include 458 law enforcement agencies, 221 courts, 197 prosecution offices, five defenders' offices, 98 adult and juvenile corrections departments, 72 probation offices, and 24 other criminal justice related agencies.

Words such as fragmented and divided, however, suggest not only demarcations in authority but also differences in states-of-mind, and not only in geographical distances but also distances in philosophy and outlook. Relatedly, we find a recent study of conflict in which police, courts, and corrections personnel within a large urban CJS were asked what problems were caused for them by other criminal justice agencies. A sample of the responses exposes a variety of perspectives:

- *Criticisms of law enforcement:* "Police are disrespectful and tend to harass parolees." "Most of them believe in a police state and if one doesn't agree with their values, etc., they classify that person as the enemy."
- *Criticisms of the public defender:* "Excessive use of technical legal points to free an obviously guilty person." "Often times this agency will attempt to stall a case by using questionable techniques in court."
- *Criticisms of city and district attorneys:* "Tend to overcharge by filing too many charges of greater severity than offense calls for." "Go it alone attitude—entire division created for juvenile justice work with no discussion or involvement of probation people."
- *Criticisms of municipal and superior courts:* "The sentences have little or no relation to the crimes charged." "Entirely too many cases dismissed due to minor technicalities."
- *Criticisms of departments of corrections and probation:* "They take a soft approach to criminals." "Have no real rehabilitation—send problems back to the community."

The above statements should not be surprising. Criminal justice agencies are highly dependent upon one another (or should be). What particular law enforcement, courts, and corrections agencies do in handling offenders and processing information affects all the others. In addition, crime is an emotional issue. Its causes and solutions are the basis of profound disagreement among police, courts, and correctional personnel. Consensus among CJS professionals can seldom be obtained on basic questions such as:

- Which crime problems should receive greater criminal justice attention? Which ones should receive less?
- Which criminal offenses should be removed from the books? Which ones should be added?
- Which arrestees should be diverted before trial? Which ones should not?
- Which offenders should be channeled into community-based corrections? Which ones should not?
- Which aspects of the criminal justice process need to be improved immediately? Which ones can afford deferred action?

Lack of consensus on answers to these basic questions presents criminal justice with its most difficult dilemma. If criminal justice professionals cannot reach a consensus on what to do about crime and criminals, it is unreasonable to expect the public and politicians to do so. The most lasting problems facing the CJS are not technical or financial—they are *political*. The consequences of lack of professional agreement are deadlock, inaction, and obfuscation in making public policy. With regard to the three concerns common to the total CJS (criminal justice planning, criminal justice information systems, and criminal justice education), major recommendations of late call for:

- Development by states of a general system of multiyear criminal justice planning
- Establishment of criminal justice coordinating councils by all major cities and counties
- Creation by each state of an organizational structure for coordinating the development of criminal justice information systems
- Establishment by each state of a Security and Privacy Council to oversee security and privacy of information contained in criminal justice information systems
- Establishment of strict security and privacy procedures to protect the integrity of criminal history files
- Establishment by agencies of higher education of criminal justice systems curricula and programs to prepare persons to work in the criminal justice system.

Action in each of these areas can bring enhanced concensus on common goals and priorities. Another byproduct should be more meaningful daily relations among police officers, judges, defense attorneys, prosecutors, and corrections officers. To summarize, the areas of planning, information systems, and education are decision centers at which the various components of the CJS come together.

Criminal Justice Planning

Assume you are taking part in a community decision where $250,000 in additional funds has been made available for crime prevention purposes. How should this money be spent? What does it buy? In an urban city or county it will probably pay for ten policemen for one year, including salaries, uniforms, training, equipment, overhead, and fringe benefits. The same money would pay for eight new prosecutors along with their necessary support services. It might also buy three months of special training in prerelease centers for each of 120 offenders, or secure an entire year of noninstitutional aftercare for seventy people in the system. Also, the same money might greatly aid narcotics treatment centers, or maintain for one year two or three youth services bureaus that provide help for delinquent and troubled youth. With such diverse alternatives as these, is it any wonder that it is exceedingly difficult for executives, budget chiefs, and legislators to select alternatives? Fortunately, the decision-making process can be made more rational by improved planning techniques. The following recommendations are made:

- Multiyear planning in each state, taking into account all available federal, state, and local resources
- Metropolitan area coordinating councils to plan across county and city boundaries
- Expanded membership from noncriminal justice sources on criminal justice planning councils
- Formalized exchanges of ideas and personnel between planning and operating agencies.

State Planning Under the Law Enforcement Assistance Program

In the last decade, there has been a tendency toward establishing a network of institutions that will define appropriate goals and crime control strategies for state and local criminal justice activities. The Omnibus Crime Control and Safe Streets Act of 1968 requires that each state applying for federal law enforcement assistance funds create a State Criminal Justice Planning Agency (SPA) and develop an annual state comprehensive plan. Upon approval of the comprehensive plan by the Law Enforcement Assistance Administration, a "block action" grant is awarded. These grants are termed block action because they are awarded as a lump sum rather than on a categorical program-by-program basis, and because they provide direct support to state and local police, courts, corrections, and other criminal justice programs. Smaller "block planning" grants also are awarded to support the planning and administration of grants by the SPAs and to support whatever regional planning councils the SPAs establish.

The states have been receiving planning and action grants in increasingly large amounts. In 1969, $43.65 million was made available to the states.[2] In 1972, this figure had increased to $497.44 million in planning and action grants.[3] Nonetheless, criminal justice is still an activity funded primarily through state and local sources.[4] The federal block grant contribution is far less than 10 percent of combined state and local criminal justice expenditures, which in 1971 totaled $9,302.23 million.

Interestingly, the funds received from the federal government under the Safe Streets Act may be far less significant in the long run than the stimulus the act provided to criminal justice planning. *For the first time, state governments possess a staff arm for examining criminal justice problems from a systemwide perspective.* Moreover, in a number of states, SPAs are becoming useful instruments for policy analysis and comprehensive reform.

The role of SPAs as conduits for federal funds has received the most attention in the press and in Congress. Confronted with the need of supplying operating agencies with the resources to deal with crime in the late 1960s and early 1970s, many SPAs became preoccupied with funding. Concurrently, due to a variety of intergovernmental problems in the first three years of the Safe Streets Act program, SPAs experienced great difficulty in disbursing their action grants to state and local police, courts, corrections, and other criminal justice agencies. Data released in the early 70s indicate time lags in some instances of more than a year between congressional appropriation and SPA disbursement of funds. At the end of fiscal year 1972, for example, 10.2 percent and 47.9 percent of the block action funds appropriated during fiscal years 1970 and 1971, respectively, still had not been disbursed.[5] As a consequence, the SPAs were attacked by critics of the Safe Streets Act program for disbursing funds too slowly. They also were criticized for not establishing adequate fiscal controls for the awarding of subgrants. Specific instances of mismanagement of funds by SPAs led to congressional charges of inefficiency and waste. In more than one SPA, fiscal control personnel replaced planners, as executive directors acted to ensure the financial integrity of their programs.

As attention to the funding role of the SPAs increased, the concept of total CJS planning was given a low priority both by LEAA (which required plans for Safe Streets funds) and by the states that produced them. Within guidelines furnished by LEAA, SPAs generated weighty and lengthy volumes that often had questionable informational value for the executive, legislator, administrator, technician, or concerned citizen. A major deficiency of most plans to date is their inability to tackle the question of state and local agency priorities for reducing crime. We find that states have only now begun to define their crime problems and make decisions about the patterns of criminal activity in their jurisdictions. Relatedly, a survey of the 1972 plans showed:

- Four states did not cite any crime statistics in their plans.
- Only nineteen states cited data on the nature and extent of juvenile delinquency. These data usually were based on either police arrests or referrals to juvenile court.
- Many states did not cite common criminal justice performance statistics that relate to crime control, e.g., apprehension rates, recidivism rates, and court processing rates.

A second deficiency in the plans is that they generally attempt only to specify what use will be made of the funds available from LEAA and other federal sources. In its 1972 planning grant application to LEAA, the Wisconsin Council on Criminal Justice succinctly stated the problem:

> A reality that the Safe Streets planning concept does not take into account . . . is that Safe Streets funds represent only a small fraction of local government moneys available for law enforcement improvement. Regional plans (and state plans) cannot be realistic until the improvement strategy takes into account revenue for law enforcement improvement from all sources inclusive of local and state moneys.

If criminal justice planning is to have full impact upon the system, the scope of planning should be broadened to include the entire budgetary picture for criminal justice at the state and local levels. To this end, it is *recommended that SPAs develop a general system of multiyear planning that takes into account all funds directed to control activities within the state.* This system should include all sources of federal funds as well as state general and capital funds; state subsidy funds to local governments; local government funds; and private donations, endowments, and contributions. Under a prolonged planning process, therefore, proposed statewide changes in CJS programs would be analyzed and set forth by SPAs for governors, legislators, budget directors, agency heads, local officials, and the public. Priority problems calling for significant changes in state policy would receive special staff attention. Also, consideration of funding sources would not be limited to Safe Streets money.

Such a planning process would have several advantages. To begin with, a reliable comprehensive multiyear plan for criminal justice would make planning, programing, and budgeting more visible. It would encourage much needed question-asking by legislators and the press. It would provide a statement of crime-oriented goals and standards for which the public could hold elected leaders accountable. A multiyear plan would provide a baseline for budget and appropriations decisions.

Metropolitan and Regional Planning   The systemwide perspective that our SPAs can furnish at the state level must be extended to the local level as well. Large cities and counties in most states now are receiving direct planning money either from the state or from regional planning councils. A movement toward local criminal justice coordination councils (CJCCs) has taken place in large metropolitan areas, a main objective of which is to plan and coordinate local criminal justice activities. Many CJCCs receive Safe Streets assistance. By the early 1970s, thirty-three out of fifty of the nation's largest cities had CJCCs. (Keep in mind that CJCCs are creations of local government.) They may derive formal authority from a resolution or ordinance adopted by the city council and/or county board of supervisors, or from an executive order by the mayor and/or the county chief executive. On the other hand, CJCCs may function informally at the will of the mayor and/or the county chief executive and by the agreement of the various participating agencies.[6] CJCCs are to be regarded as more than mere funnels of Safe Streets funds. With broad-based representation of various elements of the CJS and competent staffs, they can suggest and plan for programs that have little to do with federal funding.

The twofold purpose of CJCCs is to: (1) coordinate local criminal justice planning efforts, and (2) serve as a staff for local authorities. Recently, in New York City, for example, the local jail was overcrowded. The CJCC analyzed the costs and benefits of various alternatives including construction of a new facility, release-on-recognizance projects, diversion projects, and speed-up of court processing. The research done by the CJCC and the consideration given to this research by the mayor and city council were critical in making an accurate decision on how to resolve the problem. Additionally, CJCCs may assume such responsibilities as reviewing and planning for Safe Streets funds from the state and the federal government; and as with any local agency, they are subject to statewide regulations and legislation.

CJCCs are no longer experimental institutions, but essential parts of the CJS. It is *recommended that all major cities and counties establish criminal justice coordinating councils under the leadership of local chief executives.* To this end, metropolitan cities and counties should be convinced to consolidate CJS *planning* and CJS *operations.* Indeed, in metropolitan areas with populations of more than 250,000, a criminal justice planning office should be established to support public executives and the CJCC in developing relevant priorities and meaningful programs.

Representation in the Planning Process

Criminal justice planning must extend beyond the usual police, courts, and corrections processes. Crime prevention requires representation and participation by persons other than criminal justice practitioners. Thus, we find that it is important to have the involvement of locally elected officials, non-criminal justice public agencies, labor unions, business associations, and citizen groups. Moreover, the participation of minority members on planning agency supervisory boards and councils is critical. Boards that wish to target efforts on urban street crime cannot afford noninvolvement or, for that matter, token involvement of minority populations. It is interesting that many boards of SPAs now reflect a non-criminal justice emphasis. (A 1971 internal LEAA survey indicated that twenty-two states had more than one-third of their board membership from non-criminal justice sources.)

The concept of participation should obviously be extended to operating CJS agencies. It would be nonproductive to establish a superstructure of state and local criminal justice planners if police departments, prosecutors, public defender's offices, courts, and corrections systems do not share in the planning process. Sound planning begins from the ground up. As a consequence, setting goals and priorities, developing programs, and defining performance measures are to be developed in the greatest detail at the agency level. To this end, in most states, law enforcement, courts, and corrections agencies are encouraged by the SPA to submit their needs and priorities for the state plan.

To avoid being isolated from concerns of other parts of the CJS, operating agencies and planning agencies are engaging in temporary staff exchanges. Exchanged personnel contribute to the expansion of new ideas and innovation throughout the system. Thus it is *recommended that criminal justice planning agencies request direct written communications from operating agencies to assist them in defining the jurisdiction's objectives, needs, problems, and priorities. Temporary exchanges of personnel between criminal justice planning agencies and operating agencies should be accomplished on a routine basis.* This standard is neither radical nor unique. Planning is so basic an activity that a person who is not aware of the chaos of a large urban CJS would scarcely think it needs to be mentioned. Unfortunately, it must be. In our nation a monolithic CJS is unthinkable. The judiciary is staunchly independent; federal, state, and local legislators, and other elected officials zealously guard their independence as well. If the imbalances and conflicts of the present system are to be minimized, a comprehensive and participatory planning effort of the type described in this chapter is essential.

Criminal Justice Information Systems

Organizing our nation's criminal justice information system (CJIS) into a useful body of knowledge has been discussed for decades—

but with little consequence. Recently, however, the urgency of the nation's crime problem *and* the availability of electronic data processing equipment have made the integration of state and national CJISs possible. Along with many other disciplines, criminal justice has been experiencing an "information explosion" since the late 1960s. Its characteristics are constantly increasing demands for more capability in gathering, processing, and transmitting information, and constantly increasing information needs. No one would doubt that the more frequent use of the computer and other automated technologies is a national CJIS trend. In 1968, according to LEAA, there were just ten states in the United States with automated criminal justice information systems at the state level. By 1972, forty-seven states had an operational automated CJIS serving at least one component of the system.

The uses of information and computers vary from jury selection to police manpower allocation to correctional program placement. A recent survey of states by LEAA identified thirty-nine different police functions, twenty-three different court functions, and thirteen different corrections functions performed by automated CJISs in one or more states or cities (see Table 9.1).

Criminal justice agencies, like most public and private agencies, are enormous consumers of information. As the pace and complexity of change in the CJS accelerates, police, courts, and corrections agencies will naturally seek more and more information and an ever yet faster response in its delivery. To avoid duplication of effort and to facilitate effective collection and proper dissemination of information during this period of hurried expansion, it is recommended that:

- state offices coordinate development of information systems
- high priority be given to development of computerized criminal history (CCH) and offender-based transaction statistics (OBTS) systems
- each state establish a "Security and Privacy Council" to prevent improper use of information.

Develop-
ment of
CJISs

Decisions must be finalized as to which CJISs should be afforded the highest priority; choosing the right jurisdictional level at which to apply and use the developing CJISs technology is an equally critical decision. Local, state, and federal agencies currently are spending considerable moneys for the hardware. Unfortunately, money is being wasted and the human resources, technical talents, and equipment available for development of a CJIS are being diffused in many redundant efforts.

Table 9.1   Criminal justice functions performed by
automated information systems

POLICE FUNCTION	COURTS FUNCTION	CORRECTIONS FUNCTION
Activity Reporting	Administration/Finance	Administration/Finance
Administration/Finance	Assignment—Attorneys	Corrections Personnel
Alphabetic Index	Assignment—Courtroom	Inmate Accounting
Arrests	Assignment—Judges	Inmate Records
Command and Control	Calendaring/Scheduling	Menu Planning
Communications—Message Switching	Case Control	Performance Evaluation
	Case Disposition Reports	Physical Goods Inventory
Communications—On-Line Inquiry	Citation Control	Planning
	Courts Personnel	Prison Industries
Communications—Other	Criminal History	Prisoner Behavior Models
Computer-Assisted Dispatch	Defendant Control	Rehabilitation
Crime Lab	Docketing	Research/Statistics
Crime Trend Analysis	Evidence Control	Trust Fund Accounting
Criminal Associates	Fines, Collateral, Bail	
Criminal History	Jury Management	
Evidence Control	Juvenile Records	
Field Contact Reporting	Probation Control	
Fingerprint Processing	Process Service Control	
Juvenile Index	Research/Statistics	
Licensing/Registration	Simulation/Modeling	
Missing Persons	Summons Control	
Modus Operandi	Warrant Control	
Narcotics Control	Witness Control	
Organized Crime		
Performance Evaluation		
Planning		
Police Personnel		
Research Statistics		
Resource/Allocation		
Simulation/Modeling		
Stolen Licenses		
Stolen Property—Guns		
Stolen Property—Vehicles		
Stolen Property—Other		
Subjects-in-Process		
Training		
Uniform Crime Reporting		
Vehicle Maintenance		
Warrants/Wanted Persons		
White Collar Crime		
Work Load Analysis		

Source: United States Department of Justice, LEAA, *Computer Summaries from the Directory of Automated Criminal Justice Information Systems* (1973), pp. 35, 45, 53.

Ironically, the availability of federal funds has contributed to the diffusion of effort. Most state criminal justice planning agencies have been faced with decisions on a project-by-project basis where all projects appear to be reasonable and no setting of priorities is possible. As funding expands, the demand increases. Nearly every state is in the position of having a multitude of CJISs which cannot be integrated into a single network. The price of neglected CJIS planning is often high; millions of dollars are spent by state and local governments without obtaining the necessary information in its most usable form. Hence, it is *recommended that each state create an organizational structure for coordinating the development of CJISs.* Such a structure should: (1) prepare a master plan for the development of an integrated network of CJISs; (2) provide technical assistance and training to all jurisdictions in data collection methods, system development, and related areas; and (3) arrange for audit and inspection of state and local information systems.

The most important principle of system integration is that identical records should not be contained within two separate repositories unless there are strongly overriding considerations of total system efficiency. In practice, this means that there should not be, for example, criminal histories stored at the local level unless the state is temporarily unable to provide this service. In a time of automated information technology, duplicate systems are usually unnecessary and wasteful.

Criminal Histories and Offender-Based Transaction Statistics

The computerized criminal history (CCH) record is a major thread in tying the criminal justice system together. It shows, as no other document or record does, the actions of the total system on individuals. It describes the official actions of police agencies, judicial and supportive agencies, and all correctional components. As such, it acts as a baseline for crime prevention programs.

The uses of CCHs are varied. A police detective may use a CCH to indicate whether a suspect is likely to have committed the crime under investigation and also the suspect's possible whereabouts. A district attorney may find an arrestee's CCH invaluable in making recommendations on the question of bail and its amount. Most judges who face the choice of placing a convicted defendant on probation or sending him to prison realize that a CCH is vital to intelligent sentencing. It is significant to note here that the various records can be analyzed relative to the formalizing of crime prevention projects.

Closely allied to the need for CCH data on a given offender

is the need for aggregate data on offenders processed through the system, namely, offender-based transaction statistics (OBTS). OBTS data have come to be thought of as "derivative" from individual CCHs since many data elements are the same. Statistics on what happens to offenders at each significant step in the criminal justice process can provide answers to questions such as these:

- What percentage of those arrested are prosecuted?
- What percentage of those prosecuted are acquitted or dismissed?
- What is the average length of time between arrest and final disposition?
- What percentage of arrestees wait more than one year before the final disposition of their case?
- What percentage of offenders in institutions and community-based corrections programs are rearrested and reconvicted upon release?
- What areas ought to be emphasized in order to prevent crime?

The evaluation of whether a part of the CJS is meeting its basic objectives must have its roots in the statistics describing the passage of offenders through the system. Without OBTS data, planners and legislators frequently find themselves relying on the vague grounds of good intentions and the often erroneous assumptions. Regardless of the need for particular statistical data derived from individual criminal histories, most CJISs find it difficult to produce, rapidly and easily, complete criminal history information. Local police department files are still the most important sources of criminal history information. Known as "rap sheets," summary criminal history records are maintained by police and are shared commonly with other criminal justice agencies. In most jurisdictions there is no readily available substitute for rap sheets; indeed they are central to the functioning of CJSs. Nevertheless, there are major difficulties in relying exclusively on local information. Rap sheets frequently are not complete; followup on the disposition of the offender after he has been arrested frequently is spotty. Offenders may be arrested for offenses in other cities and counties without the arrests ever showing up on the records of the original jurisdiction—and offenders are highly mobile.[7]

In most localities criminal history information is in manual files, impeding fast retrieval. However, police conducting investigations and judges setting bail cannot permit long delays. Retention of criminal history data in many files makes the compilation of OBTS on a sustained basis all but impossible. The need for states to become repositories for criminal history information is clear; this requirement coincides with other needs that demand state-wide attention, such as on-line files on wanted persons, stolen autos, and other identifiable stolen items. Therefore, it is *recommended that all state CJISs provide CCH files and collection and storage of additional data elements to permit collection of OBTS.*

Privacy: A Paramount Issue

The permanent storage, rapid retrieval, and national coverage of a computer-based CJIS could well deprive us of our "right to privacy"—our right to be free from unwarranted intrusion in our affairs. The problem in establishing a CJIS is to determine who should have access to the files or computer terminals, who should be eligible to receive information from these files, and under what circumstances. For these reasons, the collection and dissemination of criminal history information and other criminal justice information should be carefully controlled. Hence, it is *recommended that each state adopt legislation to establish a "Security and Privacy Council" which is vested with sufficient authority to adopt and administer security and privacy standards for criminal justice information systems.*

Criminal justice files contain information that may be useful to a wide range of agencies outside the CJS; for background investigations of potential employees of public agencies and private firms, for determining eligibility for occupational licenses, for credit evaluation, and for general public information supplied by news media. Thus, the potential damage to privacy is increased when the information in criminal justice files in inaccurate, incomplete, misleading, and unnecessarily disseminated to persons outside the CJS. *In view of the sensitivity and content of criminal history files, it is recommended that strict security and privacy procedures be established to insure that there be no dissemination outside the government.*

Credit bureaus, news media, employers, employment agencies, and other seekers of information should be denied access to criminal histories. Although items in a criminal history file are for the most part matters of public record, the government should not compile the items and turn the composite over to persons outside of government. This recommendation may appear to be an exception in freedom of information laws and practices, but the protection of individual privacy should be of paramount concern in this instance. Additionally, files should be reviewed periodically to eliminate inaccurate, incomplete, misleading, unverified, and unverifiable information. Individuals should be accorded the right to inspect their criminal history files and to challenge the validity of inaccurate or misleading entries. Also, information that, because of its age, is no longer a reliable guide to the subject's present attitudes or behavior should be purged from the files.

Legislation should be enacted to constrain questions about arrests on applications for public and private employment, and licenses. (See Chapter 12 for a further discussion of removing employment barriers resulting from arrests and convictions.) Few of us would doubt the necessity for the CJS to be aware of community conditions and potential criminal activity. Controversy occurs, however, on what information should be gathered, how it should be obtained, and who should have access to it. The threat to individual rights from unrestricted intelligence operations is omnipresent in our society. Leaks can and do occur. Details that should be strictly private unfortunately become public news. Reputations can be destroyed and careers ruined. Consequently, the retention of demonstrably inaccurate and unnecessary intelligence information must be avoided systematically. To this end, in no instance should criminal history files be linked with intelligence files. To minimize the threat to privacy, criminal history files must contain only information concerning formal contacts with the CJS such as arrest, charge, and release information. *Unproven allegations, rumors of illicit associations, and subjective opinions have no place in criminal history files.*

To conclude, developing adequate CJISs to safeguard basic human rights is not a police problem or a problem of the courts or a corrections problem—it is a criminal justice problem! Issues surrounding such areas as CCH exchanges, OBTS, and privacy and security requirements must be decided on a multi-agency basis. Finally, crime prevention programs rely on information. The *quality* of crime prevention programs relies on the *quality* of information. Invaluable data for planning and evaluation can be derived from CJISs, but unless strong and strict regulations are enforced on the questions of the "need and right to know," CJISs are destined to suffer criticism and curtailment. In turn, crime prevention programs will be deprived of much needed information.

Criminal Justice Education

Higher education in criminal justice has been stimulated by a number of reinforcing trends in recent years: increasing monetary support for criminal justice education through LEAA, increasing emphasis on career preparation in higher education, and rising salary scales which make criminal justice more attractive as a career. As an indication of the rapid advances that have been made, in 1972, 515 institutions of higher education offered full-time degree programs in criminal justice, as compared to only sixty-five a decade earlier.[8]

A characteristic of contemporary higher education in criminal justice is reflective of the CJS itself. Its roots lie in a number of different disciplines and fields: law, criminology, sociology, public administration, political science, physical sciences, and psychology. As a result, the present educational program does not provide common approaches to the problems of crime and justice that in turn divide the system. For example, legal education historically has deemphasized criminal justice. In many law schools one course in criminal law is sufficient for graduation. Outside of law schools, most professionally oriented higher education programs have concentrated on the police, neglecting a core curriculum that could apply equally to police, courts, and corrections agencies (although this is changing). Law enforcement programs have focused on training-type courses that can be more effectively provided outside of universities and colleges. Some colleges and universities, for example, have courses in such areas as officer's notebook procedures, first aid, defensive tactics, and weapons instruction. (Again, this phenomenon is being reduced.) Only a few institutions of higher education offer useful graduate programs in criminal justice to middle and upper management personnel who wish to upgrade their professional skills. College catalogs have scarcely acknowledged the emerging discipline of criminal justice planning in their course offerings, in spite of the serious need for skilled planners in the hundreds of jurisdictions throughout the country.

By failing to deal with criminal justice in a holistic sense, many institutions of higher education have neglected an opportunity to help in the integration of a frequently fractionated and unnecessarily competitive system. Hence, it is *recommended that CJS curricula and programs be established by agencies of higher education to congeal the body of knowledge in law enforcement, criminology, social science, criminal law, public administration, and corrections, thereby better serving as a basis for preparing persons to work in the CJS.*

Possible models for criminal justice education programs are presently available from the community college to the graduate level. In California, statewide core curricula have been developed for criminal justice education in the community college system. Additionally, the State University of New York, and California State

University, Long Beach, have pioneered the development of graduate curricula in criminal justice. Classes in subjects of common interest to police, courts, and corrections personnel, such as the prevention and control of crime and the administration of justice, reflect the systemwide perspective of such schools.

One of the reasons that criminal justice education is in such a disorganized state is that practitioners and academicians have not jointly specified what role higher education is to play in career development. A national survey of law enforcement programs by LEAA found that most curriculum development has proceeded independent of systematic analysis of the roles police, courts, and corrections personnel are expected to perform. This condition is being addressed through the efforts of Academy of Criminal Justice Sciences and other such associations of criminal justice educators. Further, the National Criminal Justice Educational Consortium, formed in November 1973, is dedicated to the strengthening of graduate programs in criminal justice and building a framework for cooperation and exchange of knowledge among affiliated institutions.

Moreover, it is vital that criminal justice education programs be developed with the active contribution of practitioners. If criminal justice education is to be effective, practitioners must understand the purpose of new programs and education must be familiar with the everyday concerns of practitioners. State planning agencies, standards and training councils, criminal justice agencies, and agencies of higher education should participate in the formation of academically relevant programs. Finally, we should realize that education alone cannot mold behavior, but when combined with an exposure to different values in the criminal justice system and the community, it can be an important catalyst for meaningful change.

A Concluding Remark

"The most enduring problems facing the CJS are not technical or financial, they are political/administrative." No one agency alone has been given the societal responsibility of reducing crime. Questions of major policy in criminal justice require agreement among police, courts, corrections, and other public and private agencies. Criminal justice planning, criminal justice information systems, and criminal justice education present avenues for reaching agreement and integration. Planning agency supervisory boards and college classrooms are forums where various parts of the CJS and the noncriminal justice community may come together to discuss particular concerns and ultimate objectives. Criminal justice information systems that are centrally planned and organized can provide data urgently needed in defining the problems of the criminal justice process. The concepts reviewed in this chapter obviously will take time to implement; their impact will not easily be measured by immediate decreases in crime. Yet they provide for a more effective approach to crime control and crime prevention.

Learning Exercises

1.   Divide the class into groups of four to six individuals each. Each group is to return to the question posed at the beginning of the section on criminal justice planning, "Assume you are taking part in a . . . ." Answer the query as to which of the various alternatives should be funded. Additionally, indicate what data sources you were in need of to make your decision (take forty-five minutes to complete this process). Finally, each group will make a three-minute presentation to the class on its selected alternative—including the rationale. The total time for this exercise is approximately sixty minutes.

2.   Again, divide into groups of four to six people. Develop an academically sound yet job-related curriculum for a four-year college degree in criminal justice. Brainstorm the subjects that should be included in such an offering. Attempt to anticipate "job related" job requirements in the next ten years (allow forty-five minutes to design the curriculum). Then, each group is to describe in three minutes their conceptualized set of classes. The overall exercise should take sixty minutes.

Endnotes

1.   The remaining portion of this chapter is derived from the National Advisory Commission on Criminal Justice Standards and Goals, *A National Strategy To Reduce Crime* (Washington, D.C.: U.S. Government Printing Office, 1973), pp. 41–63.
2.   Law Enforcement Assistance Administration, *Criminal Justice Agencies in Wisconsin* (1972), pp. 1, 10.
3.   Ibid.
4.   Bureau of the Census and LEAA.

5. Ibid.
6. National League of Cities and United States Conference of Mayors, *Criminal Justice Coordinating Councils* (1971), p. 3.
7. New York State Identification and Intelligence System, *System Development Plan* (1967), p. 58. The technology and social issues surrounding criminal justice information systems is in constant and rapid flux. In particular, the documents from Search Group, Inc. will be helpful. Two documents produced by this organization are *OBSCIS: Offender-Based State Corrections Information System* (Sacramento, Ca.: Search Group, Inc., 1975); and *Standards for Security and Privacy of Criminal Justice Information·* (1975).
8. International Association of Chiefs of Police, *1972–73 Directory of Law Enforcement and Criminal Justice Education* (1972), p. 2. Additionally, see Larry Hoover, *Police Educational Characteristics and Curricula* (Washington, D.C.: U. S. Government Printing Office, 1975); and Calvin J. Swank, "Criminal Justice Education: The Dilemma of Articulation," *Journal of Criminal Justice*, 3 (Fall 1975), pp. 217–222.

10

The Role of the Courts in Crime Prevention

Such ritualism and extreme emphasis on pattern maintenance are likely to occur whenever the norms dominate the other elements of any social system. But they do not help in achieving the objectives for which the system was established. It is typical of ritualistic organizations that the stronger the opposition they encounter the more they rely on traditional procedures. Instead of developing new policies better suited to goal attainment—or modifying old ones to the same end—they can think of nothing but preserving their orderly operations. Hence the system of justice may soon have to decide whether it is better to preserve the arrest/conviction/punishment model or to formulate new models hopefully more proficient in crime control and prevention. In view of the prevalence of diversions from the traditional model, it might seem that this decision has already been made. But the diversionary model has not been officially acknowledged, nor is it receiving the attention it deserves in the current movement towards judicial reform.*

Preview

Not unlike other components of the CJS, the courts in this nation are confronted with problems that seriously impede their effectiveness. We look upon our courts as a mechanism for delivering justice. More recently, however, we find the court system being viewed as an integral part of the expansive attempt by the CJS to reduce crime. As a consequence, it is the premise of this chapter that the role of the court systems should encompass (in addition to the traditional role of administering justice) a responsibility for

*Clarence Schrag, *Crime and Justice: American Style* (Washington, D.C.: National Institute of Mental Health, 1971), p. 186.

225

controlling and preventing crime. Programs that are designed, therefore, to improve the management and operation of the court system can be deemed pertinent to this newer challenge.

The subject of court improvement or reform can be divided into three areas of need. First, there is the need for increasing the speed and efficiency of the judicial machinery. Included in this category are the processes of screening, diversion, negotiated pleas, litigated cases, sentencing, and—as a unique problem—juvenile justice. Second, there is a need to enhance the professional standards of judges, prosecutors, defense attorneys, and court administrators. Finally, there is a general need to reorganize the structural relationships and functional activities of the courts. Specifically, the lower courts should be unified and some cases handled administratively; court/community relations must be improved; and computers introduced in support of legal research and court scheduling.

In conclusion, then, this chapter is devoted to an analysis of court problems in conjunction with suggested reforms that will serve in general to improve the CJS, and more specifically to assist the court system in the prevention of crime.

Introduction

In line with other components of the CJS, the role of the court in reducing crime is becoming more and more controversial. Most basically, the court system in the United States has serious problems. There are too many defendants for the existing system to handle them effectively and efficiently. Delays are growing; workloads are increasing. The entire court system is underfinanced. These problems have repeatedly come to the attention of the general public. Citizens—as victims, witnesses, defendants, or jurors—experience delay, inconvenience, and confusion. These personal experiences contribute to an undercurrent of popular dissatisfaction that is diminishing the public's respect for the American court system. In spite of this chronic concern, however, the court system has remained reluctant to change, particularly in its structure and processes. There are many reasons for this—primarily the *local character* of court organization, the *independent status* of the judiciary, and the *conservative nature* of traditional judicial responsibilities.

Fortunately, developments in the past few years suggest that this institutional rigidity is ending. A new sense of urgency has stimulated a number of attempts to improve the criminal justice performance of the courts. Reform is in the air, yet the multitude of ameliorative projects has not solved the problems underlying the inadequate performance by courts in its attack on crime.[1] Any improvement, however small, is destined to assist in controlling and *preventing* crime.

One such improvement that stands to play a major part in improving the ability of the courts to cope with crime is the augmentation of administrative or extrajudicial machinery in order to accelerate the movement of cases through the court system. Briefly, this means circumventing the full trial procedure whenever appropriate. But, the extensive use of extrajudicial procedures generates a twofold danger: false economy and speed may occur; and individual and public interests may be abused. Still, the potential advantages are far too attractive not to be evaluated carefully. If properly designed and applied, a swift and fair court system can prevent crime. This leads us to the underlying rationale for this chapter: the certainty of equal and expeditious justice for all will have a favorable impact on the prevention of criminal offenses. (Figure 10.1 depicts a paradigm of rapid movement through the court system.)

In order to better prevent the severity and incidence of crime, the National Advisory Commission on Criminal Justice Standards and Goals,[2] recommended that there be greater use of the extrajudicial process; *and* the visibility of discretionary decisions should be raised and reviewed.[3] In explication of the latter point, where possible and desirable, the visibility of extrajudicial processing of criminal defendants should be raised by insisting that rules for such decision making be formulated, written down, and publicized. Also, the reasons for making particular decisions should be revealed and recorded. If this is done, the substance of discretionary decisions and the process by which they are made will become more apparent. This will stimulate an assessment of the general operation of the administrative process, not only by outsiders (judges) but most importantly by the participants themselves, such as prosecutors. Many citizens are urging that in some specific circumstances the responsibility for court decisions be identified and legitimated in nonjudicial agencies, that rules for the making of such decisions be formalized and publicized, that the agencies be given discretion for the making of such rules and for their application to particular cases, that the reasons for particular decisions be articulated, and that the extrajudicial processes function fairly and efficiently. To sum up, then, enhanced use of extra-

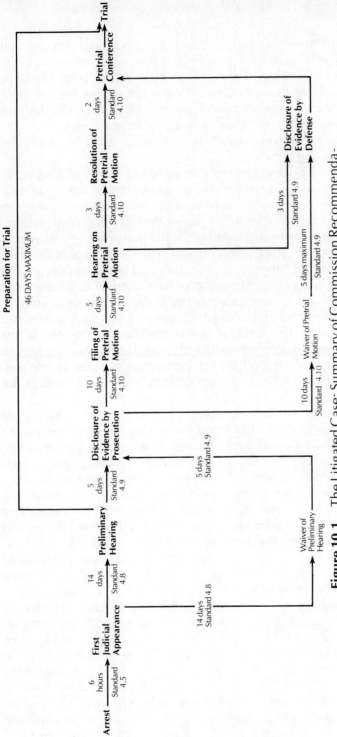

Figure 10.1 The Litigated Case: Summary of Commission Recommendations for Steps to Achieve Trial in a Felony Case Within 60 Days of Arrest *

In some felony cases, the Commission recommends that a summons or citation be issued in lieu of arrest. In such instances, there would be no first judicial appearance and the Commission calls for a preliminary hearing within 14 days of the issuance of citation or summons.

In felony cases in which there is a grand jury indictment, the Commission recommends that no preliminary hearing be held. The time limits and steps shown as following the preliminary hearing become applicable upon apprehension of the indicted individual or service of a summons following indictment.

*Source: National Advisory Commission on Criminal Justice Standards and Goals, Courts (Washington, D.C.: U.S. Government Printing Office, 1973) pp. xx, xxi.

228

judicial processes can promote efficiency and flexibility. Moreover, raising the visibility of decisions made within this process engenders fairness.

System Interaction

As mentioned earlier, the interaction among the three subsystems of the CJS is complex and frequently plagued with internal conflicts. One reason, among many, for such tension is due to viewing the common task of processing accused persons from different perspectives (police, courts, and corrections). Concisely, two different points of contention occur because of the differing perspectives. First, many of the *informal* aspects of court processing are areas of "interface" concern. To illustrate, *screening*—the cessation of prosecution—often is resented by the the police as unjustifiably negating their efforts. It also has implications for corrections because screening an individual out of the system eliminates the opportunity for correctional agencies to provide their services. Much of the same is true of *diversion* (motivating of an accused to participate in a noncriminal, rehabilitative program by suspending or dismissing formal proceedings). Police may view such action as unreasonable leniency. In turn, correctional agencies may resent prosecutors, courts, and defense attorneys seeking to pressure a person into participating in a program they feel is inappropriate for him. Further, the *plea bargaining* process—or the negotiation of pleas of guilty—is one of the most serious interface problems. Police tend to view the result of such bargains as unjustifiable leniency, brought about by a prosecutor's permissiveness or his inefficiency in not being able to try all cases brought to him by the police. Correctional officials, on the other hand, may feel that plea bargaining reinforces an offender's belief that he can manipulate the CJS, thus minimizing his motivation to participate in correctional programs.

Second, the formal trial of criminal cases also poses interface difficulties. For example, *delay* in processing cases is a source of irritation to police because they see offenders with pending trials free and engaged in further illegal acts. During the trial itself, police officers often must participate in or be present for what they think are useless procedures. When rules are applied that further some interest other than the determination of guilt, police officers may think the system is being diverted from its appropriate course. Correctional officials may resent the delay that formal processing often causes. The technicalities of litigation, such as plea negotiations may discourage an offender from endeavoring to modify his behavior by supporting his belief that he can "scam" the system. Both police and corrections officials also may feel that justice is prevented because of inappropriate defense tactics or an injudicious judge.

On the other hand, correctional tasks may be made more difficult by the resentment of a convicted offender who believes that he did not receive proper defense representation at his trial. Additionally, the *review* process has similar characteristics. Delay during appeal often means that institutionalization is delayed and the offender is at times given the opportunity to commit other crimes. Correctional officials may think that an offender who spends effort and time pursuing means of rescinding his conviction is discouraged from facing the requirement to develop new patterns of behavior and therefore is less susceptible to rehabilitation programs.

The Courts and Crime Prevention: A Basic Assumption

It is plausible to hold that the prevention of crime can be improved if the courts remedy their current dysfunctions. It is this underlying assumption that provides the rationale for the remainder of this chapter, which is divided into three parts discussing (1) the means for increasing the movement and efficiency in processing subjects through the system; (2) better selection, training, and utilization of judges, prosecutors, and defense attorneys; and (3) augmentation of support related functions.

Accelerating the Process

Any description of proposed changes in the role and operations of the courts requires some discussion of the formal procedural mechanisms. Although indirectly, the initial step begins with an *arrest*. Typically, a police officer completes this step independent of the court. Yet, in reality, much of what the officer does is determined by the court (e.g., search and seizure rules). Second, the suspect is brought before the judges of a *lower court*. Usually the defendant is informed of the charge(s) against him, apprised of his constitutional rights, and legal counsel is secured. Depending on the gravity of the alleged offense, a decision of guilt or innocence is made, or the case is referred to a higher court. Third, if the defendant is transferred to a higher court, then a formal *criminal charge* is filed by the prosecutor (in some cases, grand jury action may be involved). Fourth, the defendant is *arraigned*—whereby the judge requests that he state his plea to the charge. Fifth, if the plea is "not guilty" then the full adversary process becomes activated, starting with a *trial* by jury or court. Sixth, if the defendant is acquitted the process is terminated, if he is found guilty then he is *sentenced*. Finally, the defendant may *appeal* the decision or act on a "collateral attack" (constitutional issue).

Keep in mind that this formal process rarely occurs in a strict sense. In the vast majority of cases *the processing is replete with extrajudicial procedures that are more in line with negotiation and agreement rather than adversary arguments* before an independent decision maker. In regard to expediting the processing of criminal cases in the courts,[4] the following sections cover: screening, diversion, negotiated pleas, litigated cases, sentencing, and trial court review.

Screening   In general, screening means the removal of a person from the CJS. A police officer screens when he makes an investigatory stop and decides not to arrest the subject. Similarly, a jury screens when it decides to acquit a defendant. But here the term will be used in a more limited way. *Screening is the discretionary decision to stop, prior to trial or plea, all formal proceedings against a person who has become involved in the CJS.* Screening must be distinguished from diversion. Diversion involves a decision to encourage an individual to participate in some specific program or activity by express or implied threat of further formal criminal prosecution.

Screening has two objectives. One is to stop proceedings against persons when further action ultimately would be nonproductive because of insufficient evidence to obtain or sustain a conviction. The second objective is to screen according to the probability that a conviction might be obtained. In contemporary practice, this often implies an allocation of resources. If prosecutors have more important cases that demand their attention, other cases may be screened out regardless of the availability of evidence to convict. This aspect of screening is viewed by many as being harmful, in that, defendants at times are screened out of the CJS when both the evidence and the resources to obtain convictions exist. In these cases, the decision to screen reflects a determination that pursuing formal proceedings would not best serve the dual objectives of the CJS: reducing criminal activity and extending fairness to defendants.

The problems with current screening practices arise because of the "low visibility" of the power exercised by the prosecutor. The screening decision is a vital one for several reasons. Our society wants to have appropriate individuals screened out of the criminal justice process. Those charged with criminal offenses have an interest in the equity and reasonable administration of screening. Because screening is a low visibility process, however, there is a danger that these interests will not always be manifested. This problem is an administrative one; screening is a discretionary decision, and judicial participation in it should be minimal. What is needed is the development of criteria and procedures within police agencies and prosecutors' offices—on an administrative level—to furnish sufficient assurance of just and proper screening. The discretion to screen should be structured via the promulgation of specific criteria. Thus, it is recommended that:

- Certain accused persons should be screened out of the CJS
- Written guidelines should be formulated for the making of the screening decisions.

Diversion   The term diversion means the suspending, before conviction, of formal criminal proceedings against a person on the condition (or assumption) that he will do something productive in return. Action taken after conviction is not diversion, because at that point the criminal prosecution already has been permitted to proceed to its conclusion—the determination of criminal guilt.

Diversion may occur at many points as a case progresses through the CJS. A police officer who assumes custody of an intoxicated person is diverting him when he releases him to the custody of his family or a detoxification center. A prosecutor who holds formal charges in abeyance while the defendant participates in psychiatric treatment diverts. But in all situations, diversion involves a discretionary decision on the part of an official of the CJS that there is a better way to deal with the particular defendant than to prosecute him. As a consequence, diversion programs tend to fall into two categories. In one, the defendant is diverted into a program run by agencies of the CJS. In the other, the accused is directed into a program outside of the CJS.

A major benefit of diversion programs is that, like screening, they permit adjustment for possible overcriminalization. Legislatures have not been able to prescribe in criminal statutes exactly which individuals should—and which should not—be subjected to the formal imposition of criminal liability. The difficulties that courts and legislatures have experienced in formulating a satisfactory insanity defense is indicative of this. Hence, diversion enlarges and makes more *effective* use of the resources for dealing with offenders.[5]

Under existing circumstances, diversion facilitates the disposition of offenders that would be difficult or impossible as sentencing alternatives. Because of its informality and flexibility, diversion also is apt to encompass more programs than could be made available as sentencing alternatives. Moreover, it permits use of these programs sooner than if they were sentencing alternatives. Regardless of the efforts made to expedite the process, requiring conviction before referral to such programs would delay significantly an offender's entry into them. However, diversion also inheres certain disadvantages to those charged with criminal offenses—and therefore, its use should be carefully and comprehensively assessed. (1) Diversion programs must not impair unjustifiably the deterrent impact of criminal punishment. (2) Offenders must be carefully selected for division to assure that diversion will provide protection against future criminal acts. (3) Defendants whose guilt the prosecution cannot establish must not be caused to participate in diversion programs by the threat of formal proceedings.

If diversion is to be successful and to gain public support, it must be developed carefully and with full recognition of the need to have effective programs *before* displacing traditional methods of dealing with offenders.

- When feasible, divert into noncriminal justice programs before trial.
- Develop a checklist for diversion decisions.

Negotiated   In many courts, more than 90 percent of criminal convictions
Plea   are not obtained by the verdict of a jury or the decision of a judge. Rather, they are the result of the defendant's plea of guilty. Such a plea functions not only as an admission of guilt but also as a surrender of the entire array of constitutional rights that exist to protect a criminal defendant against unjustified conviction (including the right to remain silent, the right to confront witnesses against him, the right to trial by jury, and the right to be proven guilty beyond a reasonable doubt). However, a system that encourages the waiver of such fundamental rights is defensible only if it deals with the person waiving those rights.

Those pleas that are the result of agreements or plea bargains —are of several types. One consists of a plea to a lesser or different charge, in which we find the defendant trading his right to require the prosecution to prove guilt at a trial for a less serious charge.

In practical terms, the trial judge's sentencing discretion could be affected in several ways by such a change in the charge. The offense to which the defendant pleads guilty may have a lower maximum penalty; the defendant thereby assures himself that his sentence cannot be longer than a given period.

Another type of plea involves bargains between the prosecution and the defendant which may not include a change in the charge. The prosecution may, for example, agree to recommend a sentence to the judge in return for the plea. This recommendation typically is not formally binding on the judge, but under local practice the trial judge routinely may follow such recommendations. In these cases, the defendant trades his trial rights for the guarantee by the prosecution to attempt to influence the sentence by means of a recommendation.

The plea bargaining process has been attacked from many directions. Critics assert that plea bargaining endangers several interests, namely, those of the defendant, of court processing, and of society. First, in some cases, plea negotiation raises the danger that innocent persons will be convicted of criminal offenses. Underlying many plea negotiations is the understanding—or threat —that if the defendant goes to trial and is convicted, he will be dealt with more harshly than he would be if he pleaded guilty. Second, plea bargaining often occurs concurrently with the processing of the case through the routine steps. When a bargain is derived, the case is merely removed from the court system. Unfortunately, as critics of plea bargaining assert, the bargain is often entered at the last minute—sometimes on the morning of the trial —which causes difficulties in the efficient scheduling of cases. Third, critics of plea bargaining have stated that because the prosecutor must give something in return for the defendant's agreement to plead guilty, the usual result of plea bargaining is that defendants are not dealt with as severely as might otherwise be the case. Thus plea bargaining results, in fact or in appearance, in leniency which reduces the deterrent impact of the law. It is, therefore, recommended that:

- plea negotiation be prohibited in all courts
- documentation must exist in the court records indicating the basis for a negotiated guilty plea and the reason for its acceptance
- written policies governing plea negotiations be formulated
- a time limit be established after which plea negotiations may no longer be conducted
- service of counsel be provided *before* plea negotiations

- proper conduct be assured by prosecutors in obtaining guilty pleas
- all guilty pleas and negotiations be reviewed
- a plea of guilty not be considered when determining sentence.

Litigated
Cases

Although most criminal prosecutions do not involve the adversary determination of guilt or innocence that occurs at the formal trial of a criminal case, the trial process yet remains of vital importance to the CJS. Whether or not a defendant decides to invoke his right to trial, he still has an interest in the trial process because it represents to him a legal option guaranteed by the Constitution of the United States.

In regard to litigated cases, the fundamental concern is with delays in formal processing of criminal defendants throughout the court system. Pretrial delay is the major concern; it is not uncommon for ten to twelve months to elapse between the apprehension of an alleged offender and his trial. Further delays in the actual trial process are common. Jury selection, early adjournments of court during routine trials, and preparation of instructions are some of the causes for an extended time frame. Our interest in expedited processing has several facets. Insofar as the apprehension and punishment of offenders has a deterrent effect upon the offenders themselves and others, it is reasonable to expect that the more closely the punishment follows the crime, the greater the degree of deterrence. In addition, prompt processing serves society's interest in inhibiting those who have committed criminal offenses. Prompt processing of defendants also has indirect benefits to society as a whole; it abates the tensions upon defendants and eases the task of pretrial detention. It is difficult to comprehend the frustration over an offender's susceptibility to correctional measures. Clearly, rapid processing would enhance community confidence in the CJS.

Corrective measures include the following:

- assuring that the period from arrest to trial does not exceed sixty days in felonies and thirty days in misdemeanors,
- maximizing use of citations or summons in lieu of arrest,
- eliminating preliminary hearings in misdemeanor proceedings,
- adopting policies governing use and function of grand juries,
- presenting arrested persons before a judicial officer within six hours after arrest,

- eliminating private bail bond agencies; utilizing a wide range of pretrial release programs, including release on recognizance,
- adopting provisions to apprehend rapidly and deal severely with persons who violate release conditions,
- holding preliminary hearings within two weeks after arrest; eliminating formal arraignment,
- broadening pretrial discovery by both prosecution and defense,
- filing all motions within fifteen days after preliminary hearing or indictment; hearing motions within five days,
- establishing criteria for assigning cases to the trial docket,
- Limiting granting of continuances,
- assuring that only judges examine jurors; limiting the number of peremptory challenges,
- adopting policies limiting number of jurors to fewer than twelve but more than six in all but the most serious cases,
- restricting evidence, testimony, and argument to that which is relevant to the issue of innocence or guilt; utilizing full trial days.

Sentencing

For a defendant convicted of a criminal act, sentencing becomes the most crucial part of the court process. The options available to the sentencing power range substantially from leniency to imposition of the maximum penalty permitted by law. For the defendant, these alternatives may well mean the difference between a five or fifteen year prison sentence.

Sentencing determines both whether correctional agencies will receive an individual, and the conditions under which these agencies will receive him. Thus a defendant may be sentenced to imprisonment or to probation; in the latter situation, correctional authorities do not have the ability to apply full-time institutionalization as a technique for treating the offender.

Sentencing also affects the correctional process in a more implicit way. The degree to which a defendant considers his sentence equitable strongly influences his willingness to participate in correctional programs. Moreover, certain sentencing practices give correctional officials authority to detain an offender until his chances of successful reintegration into the community are at a maximum; other sentencing practices may require earlier release or detention beyond that point.

Sentencing directly has an impact on security in the community in that it affects the ability of correctional agencies to change the behavior of convicted offenders. It also may help prevent crimes by persons other than the offender who is being sentenced. This may result from deterrence (the creation of a psychological threat of swift and certain punishment) or through more complex means such as reinforcing social norms by the use of penalties. Further, the legitimate interests of the offender himself are affected by sentencing. A convicted offender is entitled to equal treatment, and uneven sentencing practices can endanger that right. While criminal punishment is an appropriate way of preventing crime, a convicted offender obviously should not be punished beyond the extent that is useful or justified. *Unnecessarily harsh sentences are to be avoided, as are unjustifiably lenient ones.* In summary, it is recommended that a policy be adopted stipulating that all sentencing be performed by the trial judge.

Trial Court Review

Because being convicted of a crime places a serious stigma on a person in our society, there is a widely held view that determining guilt and fixing punishment should not be left to a single trial court. The interests of both society and the defendant are served by providing another tribunal to review the trial court proceedings thereby ensuring that no prejudicial error was committed and that justice prevailed. Review also supplies a means for the ongoing development of legal doctrine in the common law fashion, as well as a way of ensuring the equitable administration of justice throughout the jurisdiction. "Review" is the final stage in the judicial process of determining guilt and fixing sentence.

Regrettably, the review stage, similar to many other aspects of the criminal process, is in trouble. In the past, appeals were taken only in a minority of cases, and collateral attacks on convictions were relatively few. However, the opposite is occurring; in some jurisdictions more than 90 percent of all convictions are appealed, and collateral attack is almost routine in state and federal courts. But courts are coping with appeals under procedures that have changed little in the past hundred years. The process is very slow. It is apparent that both state and federal courts are being hampered by existing procedures. Even now, the increase in workload is making it increasingly tough for appellate courts to give to substantial legal issues the careful and scholarly consideration so necessary to the development of a coherent body of case law.

At the state level, the review process may have as many as eleven steps, some of which actually can be replicated. While not every case proceeds through each of these steps, they are all potentially available, and it is not atypical for a defendant to pursue at least four or five. They are:

1. new trial motion filed in court where conviction imposed,
2. appeal to state intermediate appellate court (in states where there is no intermediate appellate court this step would not be available),
3. appeal to state supreme court,
4. petition to U.S. Supreme Court to review state court decision on appeal,
5. postconviction proceeding in state trial court,
6. appeal of postconviction proceeding to state intermediate court,
7. appeal to state supreme court,
8. petition to U.S. Supreme Court to review state court decision on appeal from postconviction proceeding,
9. habeas corpus petition in federal district court,
10. appeal to U.S. Court of Appeals, and
11. petition to U.S. Supreme Court to review courts of appeals decision on habeas corpus petition.

The actual operations and interplay of review proceedings are more complex than this listing suggests.

It is apparent that what is needed is not merely an effort to accelerate the existing review machinery; rather, it is presently necessary to consider a restructuring of the entire process of review. Thus, it is recommended that there should be a single, unified review preceeding in which all arguable defects in the trial proceeding can be examined and settled finally, subject only to narrowly defined exceptional circumstances where there are compelling reasons to provide for a further review. A unified reviewing court would combine into one proceeding all issues that are now litigated on new trial motions, direct appeals, and postconviction proceedings. The new trial motion would be abolished, and the traditional distinction between direct appeal and collateral attack also would be abandoned.

The reviewing court would have the authority to review not only the legality of all proceedings leading to the conviction and all matters that may now be asserted on new trial motions, but also errors and defects not apparent on the trial record and even potential errors that were not asserted as such at the trial. Essential to this expanded review is the creation of a full-time professional staff charged with the responsibility for ferreting out all arguable issues in the case, whether or not they are asserted by the defendant and his attorney. The staff would monitor each case to ensure timely compliance with the reviewing court's rules, and the reviewing court would be permitted to vary the process of its review according to the nature of the case and the substantiality of the issues involved. The following recommendations are related to the concept of a reviewing court. There should be:

- provision of opportunity to every convicted person for one full and fair review,
- provision of a full-time professional staff of lawyers in the reviewing court,
- assurance that review procedures are flexible and tailored to each case,
- established time limits for review proceedings,
- specified exceptional circumstances that warrant additional review,
- assurance that reviewing courts do not readjudicate claims already adjudicated on the merits by a court of competent jurisdiction,
- assurance that determinations of fact by either a trial or reviewing court are conclusive absent a constitutional violation undermining the factfinding process,
- assurance that claims are not adjudicated in further reviews which were not asserted at trial or which were disclaimed at trial by the defendant,
- assurance that a reviewing court always states the reasons for its decision; limitation of publication to significant cases.

Juvenile Justice   Juvenile offenders pose special problems and raise special hopes to the CJS.[6] While their past actions have shown that they are a danger to the community and to themselves, the youth of juvenile offenders creates a reluctance to use adult procedures in dealing with them. Moreover, in dealing with a juvenile offender, the CJS has an opportunity to intervene at or near the beginning of what is potentially a long-term pattern of criminal behavior.

The structures of our juvenile court systems differ widely. In some jurisdictions, for example, the juvenile court is a separate court—or a distinct division of a trial court with a broader jurisdiction—and hears only juvenile cases. Judges of these courts do not divide their efforts between juvenile and adult cases, and they therefore have an opportunity to develop expertise in juvenile matters. In other jurisdictions, however, courts hearing juvenile matters have other judicial duties; often the probate court is given jurisdiction over juvenile matters. Hence we find judges on these courts focusing less of their attention and efforts on juvenile matters, and they have less opportunity to develop specialized skills. Despite the variations, our juvenile courts possess five unique characteristics. In part, these create the special problems that juvenile courts pose in the court system's role in the attack on crime. The five common distinctive features we see in a juvenile court system can be categorized as dealing with philosophy, jurisdiction, procedure, screening, and disposition alternatives.

Philosophy.   While today's juvenile court personnel have in the main abandoned the past expectations of early reformers, it is still true that the juvenile courts are heavily imbued with a rehabilitative orientation. Less emphasis is given to the punishing of particular offenders in order to deter others, or on frightening particular offenders into avoiding future offenses. Indeed, emphasis is placed on social and behavioral methods to change the offenders' motivation to commit a crime.

Jurisdiction.   The finite boundaries and in-depth jurisdiction of juvenile courts also make them different. There jurisdiction generally is limited to individuals under a specific age (ranging from sixteen to twenty-one). However, authority over these juveniles is much broader than the corresponding authority of courts over adult members of the community. Juvenile courts ordinarily may assume control over a juvenile—take jurisdiction over him—if he has committed an act which would constitute a crime if committed by an adult. In addition, the juvenile court may assume control of a juvenile even though his actions, if committed by an adult, would not authorize a court of general criminal jurisdiction to exercise any control over the adult. (Truancy and running away are primary examples.)

Procedure.   Juvenile courts have used a more flexible procedure than their counterparts in the adult criminal justice system. This has meant that many of the procedural devices used in the adult process to guard against conviction of an innocent defendant have not been utilized in juvenile court. Since a juvenile court's proceeding results in treatment rather than punishment, the stringent procedural safeguards against unjustified punishment have been considered unnecessary. Interestingly, the difference in procedure —as well as the desire to set apart the juvenile system from the adult system—has resulted in the development of specialized terminology for the juvenile court system. The document upon which proceedings are brought does not charge delinquency, neglect, or dependency; it alleges it. The document is not an indictment on information, but a petition. The court, in determining whether the juvenile who is the subject of a petition is in fact delinquent, neglected, or dependent does not convict; it adjudicates. The process of deciding what to do with a delinquent, neglected or dependent juvenile is not sentencing; it is disposition.

Screening and Intake. Juvenile courts have had a relatively organized process for determining which individuals would be brought before the court on a petition alleging delinquency, dependency, or neglect. This initial screening function usually has been performed by an intake unit, consisting of caseworkers functioning as a court-attached agency. The court, then, has control and supervision over the intake unit. In many systems, the intake unit performs functions other than screening, such as conducting diversion programs which involve informal supervision over juveniles who have not been made the subject of formal court petitions.

Dispositional Alternatives. The juvenile court has had available a broader range of dispositional alternatives than has its counterpart in the adult system. This also is based on the difference in philosophy. Since the object of the proceeding is treatment, access to a broad range of potential treatment programs is essential.

The juvenile courts have come under attack in recent years, and much of the criticism has been of the failure of juvenile courts to adopt all of the procedural safeguards afforded a defendant in an adult criminal prosecution. In part, this criticism has been based on the conclusion that the difference in philosophy between the adult courts and the juvenile courts has not been carried into practice, and that for all practical purposes being adjudicated for a delinquent is no different from being convicted of a crime. The criticism also has been based on the view that even if there is a difference between the juvenile system and the adult system, this does not justify relaxing safeguards against unjustified state exertion of power over individuals.

Reform. Needed improvements in delivering juvenile justice can be dichotomized: jurisdictional and procedural. The former is concerned with the breadth of jurisdiction over juveniles, the authority within the jurisdiction to hear such cases, and the court's relationship to other agencies. The latter focuses on procedures used during the formal hearing, as well as the methods by which the decision is made to detain a juvenile prior to the formal hearing itself. The following recommendations underpin changes pertaining to these two areas.

- Place jurisdiction over juveniles in a family court, which should be a division of the general trial court.

- Place responsibility in an intake unit of the family court for decisions concerning filing of petitions and placement in detention or diversion programs.
- Place authority in the family court to transfer certain delinquency cases to the trial court of general jurisdiction.
- Separate adjudicatory hearings from dispositional hearings; assure that hearings have all the protections of adult criminal trials.
- Assure that dispositional hearing proceedings are similar to those followed in sentencing adult offenders.

Improved Professional Standards

The quality of those primary decision makers in the judicial process is in need of enhancement. Included in this select group are judges, prosecutors, defense attorneys, and court administrators. Each of these named participants in the judicial process is discussed below in terms of higher professional qualifications.

Judges   Because judges exercise tremendous discretionary power, and since trial judges function without any kind of direct supervision and perform their work alone rather than with collegues, the quality of judicial personnel is more important than the quality of the participants in many other professions. It is recognized that many factors have a bearing upon the quality of judicial personnel: salary and retirement, benefits, prestige, the nature of the judicial business, satisfactions derived from the position, opportunities to participate in creative change, independence, and security. Perhaps the most crucial factor in determining the quality of judicial personnel is the method of judicial selection. In regard to the means of selection, the traditional election of judges is being sharply questioned as to its effectiveness. The criticism is threefold: (1) it has failed to encourage the ablest persons to seek or accept judicial posts, (2) popular election of judges provides an incentive for judges to decide cases in a popular manner, and (3) the elective system places the crucial matter of selection in a context in which the electorate is least likely to be informed on the merits of the candidates.

Notwithstanding the deficiencies in the selection process, other features of the court system contribute to the poor quality of judicial personnel. The low level of compensation is one factor. The length of the term for which the judge is selected—his tenure —is another contributor to the difficulty of obtaining and retaining highly capable judicial officers. As a consequence, the following corrective measures are suggested.

- Select judges on the basis of merit qualifications.
- Establish mandatory retirement for all judges at age 65.
- Base salaries and benefits of state judges on the federal model.
- Subject judges to discipline or removal for cause by a judicial conduct commission.
- Create and maintain a comprehensive program of continuing judicial education.

Prosecutors   Based on the previous section, one can quickly see that the prosecutor occupies a critical position in the CJS. It is the prosecutor who must focus the power of the state on those who defy its prohibitions. He must argue to the bench and jury that the sanctions of the law need to be applied.

The prosecutor must be a full-time, skilled professional of high personal integrity. He must have an adequate supporting staff and facilities. The office of prosecutor combines legal, administrative, and judicial functions that require experienced, professional personnel and a rational and efficient organizational structure. Regrettably, the personnel policies, size, and organization of many prosecutors' offices do not permit an effective response to the complex demands of the CJS. The majority of the nation's 2,700 prosecutors serve in small offices with one or two assistants. Frequently, the prosecutor and his assistants are part-time officials who find it necessary to engage in outside law practices. The recommended improvements cited below are thus designed to promote the development of professional prosecutors' offices that will have the personnel, resources, and direction to perform their duties effectively. Selection of the legal staff should be made on the basis of professional competence rather than political affiliation. And in order to attract and keep qualified attorneys, salary levels and working conditions should be made comparable to those in private law firms.

- Assure that prosecutors are full-time skilled professionals, authorized to serve a minimum term of four years, and that they are compensated adequately.
- Select and retain assistant prosecutors on the basis of legal ability; assure that they serve full-time and are compensated adequately.
- Provide prosecutors with supporting staff and facilities comparable to that of similarly sized private law firms.

- Establish a state-level entity to provide support to local prosecutors.
- Utilize education programs to assure the highest professional competence.
- Establish file control and statistical systems in prosecutors' offices.
- Assure that each prosecutor develops written office policies and practices.
- Assure that prosecutors have an active role in crime investigation, with adequate investigative staff and subpoena powers.
- Assure that prosecutors maintain relationships with other criminal justice agencies.

Defense Attorneys   The focus here will be on public representation (as compared to private defense counsel) for two reasons: (1) public representation is a statistically significant part of overall defense services, and (2) confidence in the adequacy of public representation has been shaken. Further, the right to counsel is not confined to trial. Publicly provided lawyers now are involved in the investigatory stages of a criminal case, in appeals, and to some extent in collateral attacks upon conviction, and procedures within the correctional process such as parole decisions. Not only has the need for representation of the defendant increased, but also the legal tasks involved in this representation have become more complex. Hence, there is a fourfold need to: (1) provide more professional staff resources, supporting resources and staff, and education; (2) ensure that lawyers provided at public expense are experienced and well-educated; (3) involve the entire bar in the provision of public defense services, and to keep the provision of defense services from becoming the realm of a limited clique of practitioners, whether in a public defender's office or a private capacity; and (4) deal with the special problems raised by the provision of public defense services. The following recommendations serve to fulfill these needs.

- Make available public representation to eligible defendants at all stages in all criminal proceedings.
- Assure that any individual provided public representation pay any portion of the cost he can assume without undue hardship.
- Enable all applicants for defender services to apply directly to the public defender or appointing authority for representation.
- Make counsel available to corrections inmates, indigent

parolees, and indigent probationers on matters relevant to their status.

- Establish a full-time public defender organization and assigned counsel system involving the private bar in every jurisdiction.
- Assure that defender services are consistent with local needs and that they are financed by the state.
- Assure that public defenders are full-time professionals and adequately compensated.
- Assure that public defenders are nominated by a selection board and appointed by the governor of the state.
- Keep free from political pressures the duties of public defenders.
- Base upon merit, hiring, retention, and promotion policies for public defender staff attorneys.
- Assure that salaries for public defender staff attorneys are comparable to those of associate attorneys in local private law firms.
- Assure that the caseload of a public defender office is not excessive.
- Assure that the public defender is sensitive to the problems of his client community.
- Provide public defender offices with adequate supportive services and personnel.
- Vest responsibility in the public defender for maintaining a panel of private attorneys for defense work.
- Provide systematic and comprehensive training to public defenders and assigned counsel.

Court Administrators   Court administration (the management of the business of a court or court system) clearly is a matter of top priority in any re-examination of court processing of criminal defendants.[7] The primary mission of court administration is to relieve judges of some of their administrative functions, and to assist them in performing those they retain. The professional managers engaged in court administration are usually called court administrators, although in some jurisdictions they are called court executive officers, administrative officers, administrative assistants, or administrative directors. A court administrator can serve a single trial court, the judicial system of an entire state, or some intermediate or regional grouping of courts.

A recent survey of court administrators found that general administration or office management was cited by 47 percent of state court administrators as their major duty (most also listed this as their most time consuming duty). Other responsibilities reported by state court administrators included fiscal and budgetary matters, project planning and programs, calendaring, case assignment, payroll planning and programs, payroll administration, drafting of legislation, drafting of rules, and liaison duties with bar associations, citizen groups, and legislatures.[8] Trial court administrators reported performing such duties as caseload evaluation; office and general administration; and handling local rules, docketing, project planning and programs, and budget and fiscal matters. All reported collecting statistics and providing an analysis of them for the court; many reported allocating space and equipment and managing nonjudicial personnel. Duties most seldom reported were assigning judges, analysis of calendaring, evaluating judges' performance, and evaluating hours of court. All of the court administrators interviewed indicated that they met with the judges frequently. Finally, when queried about needed improvements, those interviewed indicated in order of frequency:

1. State Court Administrators
   - Advancing unification,
   - Advancing centralization,
   - Advancing reorganization,
   - Reducing backlog and delay,
   - Improving statistics,
   - Improving caseload analysis through implementation of automatic data processing,
   - Improving coordination, and
   - Advancing judicial independence.
2. Trial Court Administrators
   - Relieving judges of administrative chores,
   - Implementing data processing,
   - Improving personnel system, and
   - Speeding dockets and disposition.

The suggested improvements cited below are intended to create the desired results.

- Establish policies for the administration of the state's courts.
- Vest in a presiding judge ultimate local administrative judicial authority in each trial jurisdiction.
- Assure that local and regional trial courts have a full-time court administrator.
- Assure that ultimate responsibility for the management and flow of cases rests with the judges of the trial court.

- Establish coordinating councils to survey court administration practices in the state.
- Establish a forum for interchange between court personnel and the community.

Functional Reorganization and Support

This section addresses three subject areas that at first glance may seem unrelated. In one way they are, in that one can be accomplished without directly including the other. However, in another and more important way, when assessed as a composite package designed to reorganize structural and functional arrangements in order to promote improved court operations, one can see their interrelatedness. We begin by discussing the lower courts, then moving on to court-community relations, and ending with the use of computers by the courts.

Lower Courts   Lower courts, which process minor criminal offenses, ordinance violations, and infractions, are known by a variety of titles, including justice courts, district courts, city courts, police courts, magistrate courts, municipal courts, and county courts. These courts perform essentially the same functions: they hear cases involving traffic offenses, petit larceny, prostitution, drunkenness, and violations of city and county ordinances. Often they serve other limited functions such as hearing certain civil cases, conducting inquests, and holding initial appearances, bail hearings, and preliminary hearings in felony prosecutions.

There is state organization, administration, and financing of lower courts in only a few states. In most, the lower courts are operated by county and city governments. Traditional limits of venue and jurisdiction restrict each lower court to hearing cases arising in its own locale. In most cases, there is no coordination of lower courts within the same state, which severely hampers their efficiency.

Only recently has the importance of these courts been appreciated. There are an estimated 15,000 to 20,000 lower court judges; there are slightly more than 4,000 general jurisdiction judges. The lower courts handle about 90 percent of all criminal prosecutions in the nation. Thus, the courts that are lower, minor, and inferior (in nomenclature, financing, facilities, rehabilitative resources, and quality of personnel) conduct the overwhelming majority of all criminal trials and sentencings. These courts, moreover, are important qualitatively as well as quantitatively. Typically, they deal with defendants who have little or no criminal history. Often the offenders are young, and their antisocial behavior has not progressed beyond the seriousness of misdemeanors. Even when the offender is older, a first offense often is charged or later is reduced to a misdemeanor. Consequently, lower courts can intervene at what may be the beginning of a pattern of increasingly serious criminal behavior, and they can help prevent the development of long-term criminal careers.

The lower courts of most states share three problems. The first is their position on the bottom rung of the judicial ladder, which results in *neglect* by those forces that should be scrutinizing and aiding the level of court performance—bar associations, the state supreme court, the press, government agencies, and citizen groups. The second problem is the overwhelming volume and often minor nature of the caseload. The third problem is the trial *de novo* system which, in turn, precludes effective review and monitoring of the work and decisions of the lower courts by appellate tribunals, and enables judges of the lower courts, unlike their general jurisdiction judicial counterparts, to operate with improper procedures and under erroneous assumptions of the substantive law.

There are two suggested approaches to these problems.

- Assure that state courts are unified courts of record, financed by the state, administered on a statewide basis, and presided over by full-time judges admitted to the practice of law.
- Dispose administratively of all traffic cases except certain serious offenses.

Court-
Community
Relations

Courts must operate in a context that subjects them to public scrutiny, and consequently court-community relations inevitably become important. The quality of these relations has critical influence upon courts' ability to perform their function effectively. A law-abiding atmosphere is fostered by public respect for the court process. Such attitudes correspondingly suffer when public scrutiny results in public dissatisfaction. The perception the community has of the court system also may have a direct impact on court processes, as when it affects the willingness of members of the community to appear as witnesses, serve as jurors, or support efforts to provide courts with adequate resources. Court-community relations cannot—and must not—be avoided. Favorable court-community relations cannot be accomplished without a vigorous and well-planned program to ensure that courts deserve to be perceived favorably by the public and that they *in fact* are.

There are several areas of serious deficiency in present court-community relations. The first involves the facilities provided for court functions. While adequate facilities are obviously necessary for effective mechanical court operation, they also affect the court's relationship to the community. Clearly, witnesses and jurors, as well as the interested public observers, can form a low opinion of the court based on inadequate facilities. A second problem area involves the lack of information resources within the courthouse. Third, there is a paucity of public information and education concerning the role of courts in the criminal justice process. Finally, the methods and procedures by which witnesses are used are often filled with frustration. Witnesses are often required to make appearances that serve no function. Police officers, for example, sometimes are required to attend a defendant's initial appearance, although they serve no function at this proceeding. Also, frequently witnesses either are not compensated for time spent testifying and traveling, or are compensated inadequately.

The recommendations that follow are directed at correcting these deficiencies. The community should:

- provide adequate physical facilities for court processing of criminal defendants,
- provide information concerning court processes to the public and to participants in the criminal justice system,
- coordinate responsibility among the court, news media, the public, and the bar for providing information to the public about the courts,
- assure that court personnel are representative of the community served by the court,
- assure that judges and court personnel participate in criminal justice planning activities,
- call witnesses only when necessary; make use of telephone alert; assure that witness compensation is realistic and equitable.

Computers and Electronic Data Processing

Among the major problems of court processing of criminal defendants is the increasing amount of information that must be considered in court administration as well as the large number of statutes, court decisions, and other sources that must be considered in processing each case. Both forms of data potentially are subject to computer-aided methods of data management that would help alleviate the problems they present. But computer-aided court administration and legal research have not kept pace with data processing developments in general.

While interest in the computer's potential in court administration and legal research began at least twenty years ago, it has been the advances made since 1960 that make widespread application feasible. Given the limits of current techniques, however, *court administration* at present is more amenable to computerization than is *legal research*.

The failure of the computer in automated legal research relates to the differences between the language of law and the language of computers. The contents of a computer data storage bank—the opinions, decisions, citations, texts, and articles—are encoded from English. Working with a well-equipped data bank, a researcher who specifies "torts" as a key word may get thousands of references to review. This inability to define exactly what one needs in terms that a computer can understand is a major failing in automated legal research.

Court administration, on the other hand, does not suffer as seriously from inadequacies of the data base that must be used. Court scheduling and case monitoring by their very nature lend themselves to computerization.[9] While the automation of legal research is important, the present potential of the computer looms much larger in supporting the management and operations of the courts.

There are two main recommendations offered in connection with the above concerns:

- utilize computer services consistent with the needs and caseload of the courts,
- employ automated legal research services on an experimental basis.

Learning Exercises

1. Invite, as guest lecturers, a prosecuting attorney and public defender to address the class on their respective roles in the CJS. Ask that they describe their daily routine in the court processes. Be certain that they cover the subject of plea bargaining—its advantages and disadvantages. Allow enough time for interaction between your group and the two attorneys.

2. Divide the class into groups of four to six people each. The various groups are to visit different courts. Carefully observe the human dynamics that occur within the courtroom. Make summary notes and deliver to the entire class a three minute presentation on each group's observations and impressions.

Endnotes

1. Many examples can be pointed to regarding court reform. For one see the *Report of the Special Judicial Reform Committee* (Los Angeles, Ca.: Special Committee on Judicial Reform, Los Angeles Superior Court, 1971).
2. This chapter is both a synthesis of an existing report along with a salting of personal judgments by the author. Fundamentally, the material is elicited from the National Advisory Commission on Criminal Justice Standards and Goals, *Courts* (Washington, D.C.: U.S. Government Printing Office, 1973). The subject matter was altered and supplemented, where appropriate, to emphasize the concepts and practices associated with crime prevention. As mentioned in the body of the text, the courts, although perhaps not to the same degree, share a responsibility with other components of the CJS for *preventing* crime as well as administering justice to those brought into its purview.
3. The American Bar Association also promulgated (1972) a set of standards pertaining to the criminal justice system. Strong emphasis was given to the court and related processes. The titles in the series are:

    Appellate Review of Sentences
    Criminal Appeals
    Discovery & Procedure Before Trial
    Electronic Surveillance
    Fair Trial & Free Press
    Function of Trial Judge
    Joinder & Severance
    Pleas of Guilty
    Post-Conviction Remedies
    Pretrial Release
    Probation
    Prosecution & Defense Functions
    Providing Defense Services
    Sentencing Alternatives and Procedures
    Speedy Trial
    Trial by Jury
    Urban Police Function

4. For those interested in a more comprehensive discussion of court delays see the monograph *Reducing Court Delay* (Washington, D.C.: U.S. Government Printing Office, 1973); and *Prosecutor Management Information System (PROMIS): An Exemplary Project* (Washington, D.C.: U.S. Government Printing Office, 1974).
5. An expanded discussion of diversion can be found in the text by Raymond T. Nimmer, *Diversion: The Search for Alternative Forms of Prosecution* (Chicago, Ill.: American Bar Association, 1974).

6. A case in point can be found in an article by Jean Sutton which proposes that the parents of alleged dependent and/or neglected juveniles are entitled to legal counsel. See "Parent's Right to Counsel in Dependency and Neglect Proceedings," *Indiana Law Journal*, 49 (May, 1973), pp. 99–112. See also *Community-Based Adolescent Diversion Project: An Exemplary Project* (Washington, D.C.: U.S. Government Printing Office, 1975).

7. A more comprehensive treatment of this subject is presented by Ernest C. Friesen, Edward C. Gallas, and Nesta M. Gallas, *Managing the Courts* (New York: Bobbs-Merrill, Co., 1971). Also see Robert W. Gillespie, "An Analysis of the Allocation of Judicial Resources: The Illinois Experience," *Journal of Criminal Justice*, 3 (Fall 1975), pp. 207–216.

8. The details on this particular section are most interesting, in that, a considerable amount of sample survey information is presented in graphic form on the role and responsibilities. See the National Advisory Commission, *op cit.,* pp. 171–75.

9. One of many such systems is described in a monograph. *Data Processing at District of Columbia Superior Court* (White Plains, N.Y.: International Business Machines Corporation, 1974.) See also *SJIS: State Judicial Information Systems* (Sacramento, Ca.: Search Group, Inc. 1975).

11

The Role of Corrections in Crime Prevention

The history of imprisonment in the United States reveals a trend toward emphasis on treatment and away from punishment. The view which is now formally expressed by most prison leaders is that the prison should make every possible effort to treat prisoners, within the framework of a system of security. It is observed that practically all prisoners return to free society sooner or later and that the use of punitive methods alone does not produce the desired information. Consequently it is emphasized that nonpunitive methods should be used. At the same time, the prison system is organized in such a way that it impedes the efforts at treatment. As a result, treatment programs are often described in official statements of prison policy although they do not exist in fact. It is now becoming popular for prison workers and inmates alike to argue that imprisonment does not rehabilitate and that the paper efforts at rehabilitation ought to be abandoned. The prevailing conflict between punitive and treatment policies in prisons is a reflection of the more general conflicting societal reactions to crime.*

Preview

Controversy, confusion, and change appear to be the three "Cs" confronting our correctional system today. Some would accurately relate that the three are not only present now, but have been with us since the very inception of a correctional system in this nation. There is now a philosophical debate linked to somewhat questionable research on whether the assignment of resources should be weighed in favor of institutional as opposed to community-based correctional programs. Both are now being assessed in light

*Edwin H. Sutherland and Donald R. Cressey, *Criminology*, 9th edition (New York: J. B. Lippincott, Co., 1974), pp. 496–497.

of their *ability* to rehabilitate and reintegrate offenders, prevent and control crime, and protect society. Further, both are currently being *analyzed* for those procedures, programs and administrative activities that tend to differentiate one from the other in terms of cost-effectiveness.

Procedurally speaking, we are confronted with: dealing with the rights of the offenders; proper use of diversion; prudent pretrial release and detention decisions; individualized sentencing; and a proven classificatory system for judging offenders. In regard to correctional programs, there is great interest in: maximizing the use of community-based programs; improving juvenile intake and detention; clarifying the role of local institutions; making probation more effective; curtailing the use of major institutions; and modifying the parole function. Finally, in an "administrative vein," there is a need to: improve organizational arrangements and management capabilities; enhance the quality of personnel; develop better research data and information systems; and make the statutes and rules pertaining to corrections at once more equitable and relevant.

The General Setting for Corrections

The demand for immediate and massive change in our correctional system is great and is continuing to grow.[1] This demand is generated from other components of the CJS, correctional personnel, prisoners, elected officials, and concerned citizens. Prison riots and the overall failure of the system to "correct" criminal offenders have been the primary stimuli of this demand. In turn, the scramble to redress the identified problems has caused a schism among those responsible for improving the results of the correctional system. Basically, the conflict centers on the use of *institutions* as opposed to *community-based* correctional programs.

At one end of the spectrum, some argue that it is essential to abate the use of institutions. Much can be done to eliminate the worst effects of the institution—its crippling idleness, anonymous brutality, and destructive impact. However, the point remains that the failure of major institutions to reduce crime is incontestable. Recidivism rates are continually high. At the other extreme, the pragmatist admits that institutions do succeed in punishing, but they do not deter. They protect the community, but that protection is only temporary. They relieve the community of responsibility by removing the offender, but they make successful reintegration into the community unlikely. They change the committed offender, but the change is more likely to be negative than positive. Regardless of one's position in this running debate, it is unanimously held that a dramatic realignment of correctional methods is called for.[2] In all probability, as is the case in most polar differences, bits and pieces of both extremes will be amalgamated into a multifaceted attack on the problem at hand. Hopefully, the mix of "walls" and "reintegrative" tactics will culminate in a strategy that proves viable and just.

As with the preceding chapter, it is best that we establish from the beginning the relationship of corrections to prevention. Thus, it is axiomatically held that corrections must seek ways to become more attuned to its role of reducing criminal behavior. Changing corrections' role from one of merely housing society's rejects to one of sharing responsibility for their reintegration requires a major commitment on the part of correctional personnel and the rest of the CJS. Behind these clear imperatives lies the achievable principle of a much greater selectivity and sophistication in the use of correctional methods. These great powers should be reserved for either *preventing* or controlling persons who seriously threaten others. The CJS should become the agency of last resort for social problems. And, the institution should be the last resort for correctional problems.

Corrections alone cannot solve the diverse problems of crime and delinquency confronting America, but it can make a much more significant contribution to that task. Correctional planning and programs must be closely related to the crime reduction planning and programs of police and courts. Corrections' goals must be defined realistically and pursued with determination by the allocation of sufficient resources to accomplish them.

Correctional   Clearly, the penal sanctions imposed on convicted offenders
Goals   serve a multiplicity of purposes, of which *rehabilitation* is only one.[3] Additionally, crime and delinquency can be looked upon as symptoms of failure and disorganization in the community as well as in the offender himself. He has had too little contact with the positive forces that develop law-abiding conduct—among them good schools, gainful employment, adequate housing, and rewarding leisure-time activities. So a fundamental objective of corrections must be to secure for the offender contacts, experiences, and opportunities that provide a means and a stimulus for pursuing a lawful style of living in the community. Thus, both the

offender and the community become the focus of correctional activity. With this thrust, *reintegration* of the offender into the community comes to the fore as a major purpose of corrections.

Further, there is no doubt that corrections can contribute more than it does to the *prevention and control* of crime, and this is clearly one of its purposes. What is done in corrections may reduce recidivism. To the extent that recidivist crime is a substantial proportion of all crime, corrections should be able to reduce crime. A swift and effective CJS, respectful of due process and containing a firm and humane corrections component, may provide useful preventives to crime. Through these mechanisms, corrections can contribute to the overall objective of crime reduction. This is an entirely worthy objective if it can be achieved without sacrificing other important human values to which this society is dedicated. Finally, society is protected by housing, even though temporarily, those who tend to gravely threaten others. In summary, then, the correctional system should work toward: rehabilitation, reintegration, crime prevention and control, and human protection.

Converting *Obstacles* *into* *Challenges*   A substantial obstacle (challenge) to development of effective corrections lies in its *relationship* to police and courts, the other subsystems of the CJS. Corrections inherits any inefficiency, inequity, and improper discrimination that may have occurred in any earlier step of the criminal justice process. Its clients come to it from the other subsystems; it is the consistent heir to their defects. As a result, it is unrealistic to believe that the tensions and misunderstandings among the components of the CJS will quickly disappear. There are—and will continue to be—unavoidable conflicts of view. The police officer who must subdue an offender by force will never see him in the same light as the correctional officer who must win him with reason. The courts, which must retain their independence in order to oversee the practices of both police and corrections, are unlikely to be seen by either as a totally sympathetic partner.

On the other hand, the governmental institutions designed to control and prevent crime are closely and irrevocably interrelated, whether they function cooperatively or at cross-purposes. The success of each component in its specific function depends on the actions of the other two. Most areas of disagreement are the result of inadequate understanding, both of the need for cooperation and of the existing interrelationships. The extent to which this misunderstanding can be minimized will determine in large measure the future course of our efforts against crime.

One more challenge to reforming the CJS is the range and

variety of governmental authorities—federal, state, and local—that are responsible for it. This fragmentation complicates police planning, impedes development of expeditious court processes, and divides responsibility for convicted offenders among a multiplicity of overlapping but barely intercommunicating agencies. The organizational structure of the CJS was well suited to the frontier society in which it was implanted. It has survived in a complex, mobile, urban society for which it is grossly unsuited.

Further, the correctional administrator (and for the present purposes the sentencing judge as well) is the servant of a CJS quite remarkable in its lack of restraint. Historically, the criminal law has been used not only in an effort to protect citizens but also to coerce men to private virtue. Criminal law overreaches itself far too frequently. This overuse of the law is a major challenge to development of a rational and effective correctional system. Related to this point, the pervasive *overemphasis on custody* that remains in corrections creates more problems than it solves.[4] Our institutions are so large that often their operational needs take precedence over the needs of the people they hold.

Reform and rejuvenation costs money, and any such movement cannot be achieved without substantially increased government *funds* being allocated to the CJS and without a larger portion of the total funds being allocated to corrections. Correctional changes, especially those that are community-based, typically meet with *public resistance*. Plainly, community-based correctional programs require community support. Finally, the *lack of adequate data* about crime and delinquency, the consequences of sentencing practices, and the outcome of correctional programs is a major obstacle to planning for better community protection.

To reiterate, a more effective correctional system will lead to the improved prevention of crime. The considerations for bringing about this desired state-of-affairs are three in number: procedural, programmatic, and structural/functional.

Procedural Considerations

This section covers the five procedural subjects: rights of offenders, diversion, pretrial release and detention, sentencing, and classification of offenders.

Rights of Offenders   Until recently, an offender as a matter of law was deemed upon conviction to have forfeited virtually all rights and to have retained only such rights as were expressly granted to him by statute or correctional authority.[5] The belief was common that virtually anything could be done with an offender in the name of "correction," or in some instances "punishment," short of extreme physical abuse. He was protected only by the restraint and responsibility of correctional administrators and their staff. The courts are currently applying constitutional standards to corrections. Albeit far from complete, the magnitude and pace of change within corrections as the result of judicial decrees is remarkable. The correctional system is being subjected not only to law but also to public scrutiny. The courts have thus provided not only redress for offenders but also an opportunity for meaningful correctional reform.

With the increased willingness of the courts to consider offenders' complaints came a new attitude toward offenders' rights. As first enunciated in *Coffin* v. *Reichard,* 143 F.2d. 443 (6th Cir. 1944), courts are more readily accepting the premise that "[a] prisoner retains all the rights of an ordinary citizen except those expressly or by necessary implication taken from him by law." To implement such a rule, courts have found that where necessity is claimed as justification for limiting some right, the burden of proof (of the necessity) should be borne by the correctional authority. Administrative convenience is no longer to be accepted as sufficient justification for deprivation of rights. Additionally, correctional administrators are subjected to due process standards which require that agencies and programs be administered with clearly enunciated policies and established fair procedures for the resolution of grievances.

Following are recommended actions, designed to protect substantive legal rights. These recommendations may be implemented by statute, judicial decision, or administrative regulation. The emphasis is on a framework to define the rights of offenders who are subject to correctional control, consistent with concepts of fundamental legal rights, sound correctional practice, and humane treatment of offenders.

- Guarantee offenders' access to courts.
- Guarantee offenders' access to legal assistance.
- Guarantee offenders' access to legal materials.
- Protect offenders from personal abuse.
- Guarantee healthful surroundings for inmates.
- Guarantee adequate medical care for inmates.
- Regulate institutional search and seizure.
- Assure nondiscriminatory treatment of offenders.
- Guarantee rehabilitation programs for offenders.

- Legislate safeguards for retention and restoration of rights.
- Establish rules of inmate conduct.
- Establish uniform disciplinary procedures.
- Adopt procedures for change of inmate status.
- Establish offenders' grievance procedures.
- Guarantee free expression and association to offenders.
- Guarantee offenders' freedom of religious beliefs and practices.
- Guarantee offenders' communication with the public.
- Establish redress procedures for violations of offenders' rights.

Diversion

Diversion has been used informally and unofficially at all stages of the criminal justice process since its inception, but without being clearly identified and labelled.[6] The term diversion refers to formally acknowledged and organized efforts to utilize alternatives to initial or continued processing into the justice system. To qualify as diversion, such efforts must be undertaken prior to adjudication and after a legally proscribed action has occurred. In terms of process, diversion implies halting or suspending formal criminal or juvenile justice proceedings against a person who has violated a statute, in favor of processing through a noncriminal disposition or means. Diversion is differentiated from prevention in that the latter refers to efforts to avoid or prevent behavior in violation of statute, while diversion concerns efforts after a legally proscribed action has occurred.

It would seem that the positive argument for diversion is that it gives society the opportunity to consider the possibility of adjusting existing resources to programs that presage greater success in stimulating correctional reform and social restoration of offenders. Given the choice between expanding the capacities of police, courts, and institutions to the extent that they could accommodate the present and projected rates of criminal activity and the opportunity to establish diversion programs with public funds, the economics of the matter clearly favor a social policy decision for diversion. Keep in mind that diversion is an opportunity, and *not* a solution! If it is seen exclusively as a solution, diversion programs, like their correctional predecessors, will fail. To develop a system that utilizes diversion in a planned and constructive fashion, there must be a radical overhaul in the nature and character of some of today's most cherished social institutions. Commitment to diversion is in turn a commitment to the principle of change.

There are three main points at which diversion may occur:

prior to police contact, prior to official police processing, and prior to official court processing. Analysis of each of these potential points of diversion yields three basic models in terms of responsibility for diversion: community-based diversion programs, police-based diversion programs, and court-based diversion programs. Each of these models usually is cross-functional and involves the others. Community-based efforts are school related as are youth service systems and bureaus (the former is the linking of existing cognizant agencies, while the latter is a separate agency). Police-based programs include family crisis intervention, police-youth service bureaus, and referral to non-CJS agencies. Court-based diversion programs encompass civil commitments, pretrial interventions, and extra-agency pretrial interventions (use of funds to provide employment).

Because of the variety of diversionary methods, it is essential that the community obtain reliable information concerning their effectiveness in crime control. Information is needed regarding diversion's impact on the justice system, the role diversion plays in crime prevention, and the relative rates of success on cases diverted from the system at different stages. Such information is not now available, nor will it be available until records are kept on diversion as well as on cases that are processed officially.

Perhaps the single greatest contribution that diversion can make during the next decade is to make society more conscious and sensitive to the deficiencies of the justice system, and hence to force radical changes within the system so that appropriate offenders are successfully diverted while others are provided with programs within the system that offer social restoration instead of criminal contamination. Consequently, it is strongly recommended that: formal diversion programs be implemented.

Pretrial Release and Detention

Pretrial detention today lacks an advocate in both the administration and the reform of the criminal justice process.[7] It lies in between conflicting values and concerns—the right to bail, the risk of flight, the presumption of innocence, the safety of the community. The decision-making process is factionalized among a wide array of individuals and institutions. The management of jails and the treatment of unconvicted prisoners are the responsibility of a sheriff or correctional warden. The composition of the pretrial detainee population, and the terms and timing of their release flow from the decisions of the police, the judge, the bondsman, the prosecutor, and the defense lawyer. The laws and rules that determine the flexibility or rigidity of the pretrial process are made by legislators, courts, and political leaders. The fragmentation of responsibilities contributing to pretrial detention makes the plight of pretrial detainees worse than that of convicted prisoners. Coordinated efforts to redress the balance are required.

There are those who would contend that no other component of the CJS is as logical a choice as corrections for dealing with persons who are detained awaiting trial. Law enforcement agencies are ill-equipped to do so. The courts should not be burdened with additional administrative responsibilities. However, the experience of correctional administrators as middlemen in dealing with imprisoned persons on one hand and with the legal system on the other could become a dynamic tool for pretrial change. In the past few years, corrections in some areas has moved toward taking over or consolidating the local detention facilities in which sentenced misdemeanants and persons awaiting trial are housed. In the process, corrections has been gaining both a critical stake in maintaining, and a major opportunity for reforming, the pretrial criminal process. The profession that traditionally has concentrated its skills on the security, punishment, and correction of convicts has begun to enter a new field.

Three goals for pretrial reform can be isolated. First, detention and other restrictions on liberty should be minimized to an extent consistent with the public interest. As noted in the previous chapter, incarceration as a criminal sanction is widely overused. While confinement is necessary for the small percentage of offenders who are dangerous, it has all too often been considered the standard response to crime. Second, the treatment of persons awaiting trial should be consistent with the presumption of innocence. Third, the time prior to trial should be a constructive period in the life of the accused rather than one of idleness. Many persons awaiting trial require or could utilize assistance that only the state can provide, e.g., they may be suffering difficulties relating to alcohol, drugs, or physical or mental problems or defects.

The problems of excessive detention are caused or compounded by a number of widely acknowledged institutional defects in the system of pretrail justice. These include:

- excessive reliance on money bail,
- fear of crime while on bail,
- substantial trial delays,
- abridgement of detainees' rights,
- overuse of the criminal sanctions,
- haste to build large new jails for pretrial detention.

Improvements in the pretrial process range from field or station citations in lieu of arrest, to release on own recognizance, to state-supported 10 percent cash bonds. As a consequence, it is suggested that the following actions be taken.

- Develop a comprehensive pretrial process improvement plan.
- Engage in comprehensive planning before building detention facilities.
- Formulate procedures for use of summons, citation, and arrest warrants.
- Develop alternatives to pretrial detention.
- Develop procedures for pretrial release and detention.
- Legislate authority over pretrial detainees.
- Develop pretrial procedures governing allegedly incompetent defendants.
- Protect the rights of pretrial detainees.
- Establish rehabilitation programs for pretrial detainees.
- Develop procedures to expedite trials.

Under the formal model of the criminal justice process, the sentencing court makes the critical decision on sentencing criminal offenders.[8] In practice, a wide variety of other officers, institutions, and forces impinge upon or influence the sentencing judge's discretion. The police decision to arrest can have sentencing ramifications. Strategies to divert offenders from the formal criminal process preclude direct judicial participation.

It is being recognized increasingly that the decision to detain an offender prior to trial may have a direct influence on the nature and extent of the sentence eventually imposed. As noted in Chapter 4, pretrial detention appears to be closely correlated not only with confinement as the eventual disposition but also with the length of incarceration imposed by the court.

Under sentencing structures in which the court imposes an indeterminate sentence, correctional administrators often determine, to a greater extent than the court, the actual sentence to be served. When a court imposes a sentence of confinement, the parole board will decide the length of time actually served in confinement. Once parole is granted, the board's policy regarding revocations and recommitments for violation will determine whether the offender remains in the community.

Many of the suggestions in this section require consideration by the appropriate legislature. Three aspects of sentencing are particularly dependent on legislation: (1) articulation of the goals of the sentencing process; (2) authorization of a variety of sentencing alternatives; and (3) articulation of the general criteria to be used in determining sentence. The suggestions that follow are divided into those that address the substance of sentencing and those that would regulate sentencing procedures.

- Establish judicial sentencing of defendants.
- Establish sentencing practices for nondangerous offenders.
- Establish sentencing practices for serious offenders.
- Establish sentencing procedures governing probation.
- Establish criteria for fines.
- Adopt policies governing multiple sentences.
- Disallow mitigation of sentence based on guilty plea.
- Allow credit against sentence for time served.
- Authorize continuing court jurisdiction over sentenced offenders.
- Require judicial visits to correctional facilities.
- Conduct sentencing councils, institutes, and reviews.
- Conduct statewide sentencing institutes.
- Create sentencing councils for judges.
- Require content-specified presentence reports.
- Restrict preadjudication disclosure of presentence reports.
- Disclose presentence reports to defense and prosecution.
- Guarantee defendants' rights at sentencing hearings.
- Impose sentence according to sentencing hearing evidence.

Classification of Offenders   Most correctional classification schemes in use today are referred to as classification systems for treatment purposes, but even a cursory analysis of these schemes and the ways in which they are used reveals that they would more properly be called classification systems for management purposes.[9] This judgment does not imply that classification for management purposes is undesirable. In fact, that may be the only useful system today, given the current state of knowledge about crime and offenders. It is important, however, that corrections begin to acknowledge the bases and purposes of classification systems that are in use. Further, that the classification scheme be designed to: (1) accommodate offenders' needs rather than administrative routine, (2) involve the offender in analyzing his own problems, (3) instill objectivity in assignment decisions, and (4) provide sufficient time with each offender in order to acquire the necessary information for the assignment.

Organizationally, the classification system can be used to link administration, staff, and offender with a program providing planned experiences for the offender. These experiences must reinforce each other to move the client toward a planned program objective. This feat is not possible unless there is a basic theoretical plan that can be translated into program strategies and communicated in language common to all persons involved with the offender. Essentially, classification should ensure a more effective pooling of relevant knowledge about the offender and the development of a more efficient method by which all important decisions and activities affecting him may be coordinated. Ideally, it should provide offenders with a means for changing themselves rather than subjecting them, under coercion, to so-called "treatment."

Classification procedures generally are carried out through one of four organizational arrangements: classification units within an existing institution; classification committees; reception-diagnosis centers; and community classification teams. The first organizational alternative involves classification clinic reception units in the institutions to which offenders are committed. The second organizational arrangement is the institutional classification committee, which studies individual case records and collectively makes judgments as to the disposition of inmates in the institution (the committee is comprised of both professionals within and without the institutional setting). In the third method of operation, all offenders are committed to a central receiving institution for study, classification, and recommendations for training and "treatment" programs, and determination of the institution to which the individual should be assigned. The process presupposes a plan and theory of classification consistent throughout the system. Such an approach places a major responsibility for collecting diagnostic information on one facility, thereby requiring a high degree of specialization. Finally, with development of a realistic classification system to be used throughout the correctional system, the classification function can involve a much wider range of personnel and resources than previously supposed. For instance, a classification team consisting of parole and probation officers might collect the social history, while local practitioners could provide necessary medical and psychiatric examinations. State and local institution personnel, in cooperation with the other members of the community classification team, in turn would review the appropriate correctional programs available to meet the offender's needs.

Offender typologies represent an important method of

integrating and increasing knowledge in the correctional field. Ultimately, typological approaches will flourish in relationship to their fruitfulness in producing improved management, differential programming, and schemes for crime prevention. In the last analysis, a good classification system is one that enables a correctional agency to utilize its limited manpower to maximize its impact on offenders. The following recommendations are intended to serve this end:

- develop a comprehensive classification system,
- establish classification policies for correctional institutions,
- establish community classification teams.

Programmatic Considerations

The six major program areas are community-based corrections, juvenile intake and detention, local institutions, probation, major institutions, and parole.

Community-Based Corrections
There is a growing belief among CJS professionals and aware citizens that community-based corrections (CBC) is the most promising means of accomplishing the changes in offender behavior that the public expects, and in fact now demands, of corrections.[10] Further, it is recognized by many that the institution model for corrections has not been successful in curbing potential crime; but at least it exists with its physical plant and its identified processes of reception, classification, assignment, custody, work, academic and vocational training, religion, and recreation. The substitute models are talked about and occasionally are used. CBC is not well organized, planned, or programmed. This task is the challenge of the future. CBC programs embrace any activity in the community directly addressed to the offender and aimed at helping him to become a law-abiding citizen. Such a program may be under official or private auspices. It may be administered by a correctional agency directly or by a noncorrectional service. It may be provided on direct referral from a correction agency or on referral from another element of the criminal justice system (police or courts). It may call for changing the offender through some combination of services, for controlling him by surveillance, or for reintegrating him into the community by placing him in a social situation in which he can satisfy his requirements without law violation.

CBC programs may embrace any one or any combination of these processes. It is emphasized, however, that the use of control and surveillance is basic to a sound community corrections system. Both policy makers and the public must understand that the elimination of incarceration does not eliminate control.

The underlying rationale for CBC can be divided into five interrelated parts:

1. enhanced humanitarianism,
2. increased probability of restoring the offender to a proper position in society,
3. improved cost-effectiveness,
4. lessening the injurious impact of the prision setting on the offender, and
5. greater prevention of further criminal activity.

Correctional agencies must provide the *public,* pertinent *social service agencies,* and *school systems* with a continuous flow of information concerning issues and alternatives involved in implementing correctional programs, so that citizens may participate intelligently in making the major decisions. For example, a major difficulty in instituting various types of CBC treatment centers is refusal by the community to have centers located in its territory. Such resistance will not be overcome immediately, but involvement of many citizens can be expected to bring success eventually.

Diversion, probation, and parole—the major community alternatives—and the use of community resources and services that should characterize these programs, are discussed in more detail in other sections of this chapter. The wide variety of community *alternatives to confinement* can be seen in the following list of CBC programs:

- *Nonresidential Programs.* Structured correctional programs, which supervise a substantial part of an offender's day but do not include "live-in" requirements, are another community-based necessity. The clients are persons who need more intensive services than probation usually can offer, yet are not in need of institutionalization.

- *Foster and Group Homes.* Foster homes, also extensively used to meet child dependency needs (in the case of a group home six to ten young people may be involved), are operated under a range of administrative arrangements, public and private, state and local, court and correctional.

- *The Community Correctional Center.* This is a relatively open institution located in the neighborhood and using community resources to provide most or all of the services required by offenders. The degree of openness varies with offender types, and use of services varies with availability and offender needs. Such institutions are used for multiple purposes—detention, service delivery, holding, and pre-release.

The program activities that we considered above are designed to act as alternatives to the use of the penal institution. Those described below serve as logical extensions to the institutional environment.

- *Work Release.* This practice permits selected inmates to work for pay outside the institution, returning each night.
- *Family Visits.* As the term implies, this program seeks to bring the family to the inmate. It can vary from a few hours to conjugal visits.
- *Educational Programs.* The programs range from vocational to university offerings within the prison.
- *Ethnic Programs.* Through ethnic support between one group in the prison and another without, means assistance in the reintegration of inmates into their chosen communities.
- *Prerelease Programs.* In cities, small living units are organized, usually in leased quarters, to which individuals can be transferred for the final months of their sentence as part of preparation for release. Special orientation programs and employment assistance are provided, with gradually increasing opportunities to exercise decision making. The purpose is to phase inmates into community life under supervision, with assistance as needed.
- *Short-Term Return of Parolees.* Related closely to prerelease planning is the recent development of programs permitting the short-term return of parolees who have made a mistake that could be cause for parole revocation and return to the prison. Frequently, prerelease facilities are used for this function.

In due regard for the above thinking and programmatic activity, it is suggested that the correctional system . . .

- develop a range of community-based alternatives to institutionalization,
- insure correctional cooperation with community agencies,
- seek public involvement in corrections, and
- establish procedures for gradual release of inmates.

Juvenile
Intake and
Detention

Juvenile crime is one of the nation's most troubling problems and it appears to be on the increase in rate per capita and seriousness of offense. Of relevance here is the widely held belief that the first contact young persons have with the justice system may be one of the most significant events in their lives. As a result, resource investment at this crucial point seems to promise the greatest yield, assuming that what happens to a child apprehended for his first offense may well decide whether or not he becomes a full-fledged delinquent.

Intake services, therefore, should be formally organized under the court to receive and screen all youths referred by police, public and private agencies, parents, and other sources. Intake services should divert as many youngsters as possible from the juvenile justice system and refer them for court action only when necessary. Court referral on a delinquency petition should not involve youngsters who have committed acts that would not be considered crimes if committed by adults. Additionally, intake services should function in close cooperation with other private and public agencies, such as youth service bureaus and family and mental health services, toward the goals of delinquency prevention and crime reduction.

Once court intake personnel have sifted out nondelinquent and social problem cases that can be served better in other programs, a number of other avenues to minimize penetration into the justice system should be explored. Since more than half of all juvenile cases presently referred to the courts are being handled nonjudicially (without formal hearings), it is estimated that improved intake services could substantially reduce the number of cases referred for adjudication by increased use of nonjudicial alternatives. Through this process, inappropriate complaints would be kept from the courts, fewer children would experience the official or informal sanctioning process of the judicial system, and more children would be diverted into delinquency prevention and social service programs. In speaking of informal sanctions or "adjustments" is meant empowering the intake staff to dismiss complaints that seem arbitrary, vindictive, out of proportion, or against the best interests of the child. Informal probation, which is another method of nonjudicial handling of juvenile cases, should be used. It permits informal supervision of young persons by probation officers who wish to reserve judgment regarding the necessity for filing a petition until after a child has had the opportunity for some informal treatment.

In view of the consensus of most jurisdictions the well documented proof that long detention periods are both unnecessary and counterproductive to the interests of the juvenile, it is essential that the detention period be kept to a minimum, and that the environmental setting should be nonpunitive in orientation and architectural design. Quarterly inspection should occur in order to maintain appropriate standards of housing and processing.

The expressed concern over juvenile intake and detention creates a basis for the recommendations cited below.

- Authorize police to divert juveniles.
- Establish a juvenile court intake unit.
- Apply total system planning concepts to juvenile detention centers.
- Evaluate juvenile intake and detention personnel policies.

Local Adult Institutions   Jails are the intake point for our entire criminal justice system.[11] There are more jails than any other type of "correctional" institution. Indeed, the current trend toward the decreased use of confinement in major state institutions promises to increase the size and scope of the burden jails must bear. Perhaps this is a short-term expedient that will not become permanent; there are some faint stirrings of hope that it will not be so. Nevertheless, it remains that local control, multiple functions, and a transient, heterogeneous population have shaped the major organizational characteristics of jails. Typically, they are under the jurisdiction of the county government. In most instances, the local area has neither the necessary tax base from which to adequately finance a jail nor sufficient size to justify even the most rudimentary correctional programs. Besides the problem of local control, the principal problems facing the nation's jails today are condition of physical facilities, inadequate personnel, poor administration, and underutilization of alternative programs and dispositions. New jails have been built, but they now present the same problems as those they were built to replace. History shows clearly that only a different attack on the problem holds real promise. The new approach must involve all components of the CJS.

Fundamentally, the answer to the major portion of the above problems resides in "total system planning." The "service area" concept is basic to total system planning. Service areas are demarcated by the scope of a particular problem that frequently crosses jurisdictions. Underlying the concept is the realization that social problems and their solutions do not confine themselves to geopolitical boundaries. Each service area may have distinct problems and resources, but there is sufficient commonality to warrant subsystem coordination.

The result of such planning should encourage the development of community correctional centers on either a regional or network approach. Briefly, such a center would furnish a variety of services ranging from short-term incarceration to in-community reintegration programs. It is therefore recommended that communities:

- undertake total system planning for community corrections,
- incorporate local correctional functions within the state system,
- formulate state standards for local facilities,
- establish pretrial intake services,
- upgrade pretrial admission services and processes,
- upgrade the qualifications of local correctional personnel,
- protect the health and welfare of adults in community facilities,
- provide programs for adults in jails,
- develop release programs for convicted adults,
- evaluate the physical environment of jails.

Probation The movement away from institutionalization has occurred not only because institutions are very costly, but also because they have debilitating effects on inmates who have great difficulty in reintegrating themselves into the community. Therefore, it is essential that alternatives to institutionalization be expanded in use and enhanced in resources. The most promising process by which this can be accomplished in corrections, i.e., probation, is now being used more as a disposition. Even greater use can be projected for the future.

Although probation is viewed as the brightest hope for corrections, its full potential cannot be reached unless consideration is given to two major factors. The first is the development of a system for determining which offenders should receive a sentence of probation. The second is the development of a system that enables offenders to receive the support and services they need so that ultimately they can live independently in a socially acceptable way. Yet, probation has failed to realize either of these objectives. Probation is not adequately structured, financed, staffed, or equipped with the necessary resources. A major shift of money and manpower to community-based corrections is necessary if probation is to be adopted nationally as the preferred disposition.

In corrections, the word probation is used in four ways. It can refer to a *disposition, a status, a system or subsystem,* and a *process.* Probation as a court disposition was first used as a suspension of sentence. Under probation, a convicted offender's freedom in the community was continued, subject to supervision and certain conditions established by the court. A shift is now occurring and probation is being used increasingly as a sentence in itself. Probation as a status reflects the position of an offender sentenced to probation. For the offender, probation status has implications that are different from the status of either free citizen or confined offender.

Probation is a subsystem of corrections, which is a subsystem of the criminal and juvenile justice system. Finally, the probation process refers to the set of functions, activities, and services that characterize the system's transactions with the courts, the offender, and the community. The process includes preparation of reports for the court, supervision of probationers, and obtaining or providing services for them.

The position of probation in the government framework varies among the states. The continuing controversy over the most appropriate placement of probation centers on two main issues: whether it should be a part of the judicial or executive branch of government; and whether it should be administered by state or local government. Arguments can be made for each position; presently, however, there appears to be greater weight being given to including probation within state unified correctional systems.

To implement an effective *system for delivering services to all probationers,* it will be necessary to:

1. develop a goal-oriented service delivery system,
2. identify service needs of probationers systematically and periodically, and specify measurable objectives based on priorities and needs assessment,
3. differentiate between those services that the probation system should provide and those that should be provided by other resources,
4. organize the system to deliver services, including purchase of services for probationers, and organize the staff around workloads,
5. move probation staff from courthouses to residential areas and develop service centers for probationers,
6. redefine the role of probation officer from caseworker to community resource manager, and
7. provide services to misdemeanants.

Further, to implement a *system for delivering services to the courts,* it will require that probation . . .

1. provide relevant information upon which accurate decisions can be made,
2. be circumspect and adhere to safeguards regarding the prepleading of investigations,
3. disclose confidential information as subjected to court control,
4. establish intake guidelines which are carefully monitored by the courts, and
5. furnish or assist in adult pretrial services such as the releasing of a defendant on his own recognizance.

Relatedly, it is recommended that . . .

- probation be placed under executive branch jurisdiction,
- a probation service delivery system be established,
- misdemeanant probation services be provided,
- a state probation manpower unit be developed, and
- release on recognizance procedures and staff be established.

Major
Institutions

Institutionalization as the primary means of enforcing the customs, mores, or laws of a people is a relatively modern practice.[12] In earlier times, restitution, exile, and a variety of methods of corporal and capital punishment, many of them highly punitive, were used. Confinement was for detention only.

Presently, *maximum security* institutions are geared to the fullest possible supervision, control, and surveillance of inmates' individual and social needs (which are responded to only in conformity with security requirements). Today *medium security* institutions probably embody most of the ideals and characteristics of the early attempts to reform offenders. It is in these facilities that the most intensive correctional or rehabilitative efforts are conducted. Here inmates are exposed to a variety of programs intended to help them become useful members of society. But the predominant consideration still is security. *Minimum security* institutions are diverse but generally have one feature in common. They are relatively open, and consequently custody is a function of classification rather than of prison hardware. The principal exceptions are huge prison plantations on which entire penal populations serve time. Minimum security institutions range from large drug rehabilitation centers to small farm, road, and forestry camps located throughout rural America. Also, youth correction centers, facilities, and reception centers typically are considered to be "minimum security" in design.

From the standpoint of rehabilitation, reintegration, and

eventual crime prevention, the major adult institutions operated by the states represent the least promising component of corrections. More offenders should be diverted from such adult institutions, much of their present populations should be transferred to community-based programs, and the construction of new major institutions should be postponed until such diversion and transfers have been achieved and the need for additional institutions is clearly established. However, the need for some type of institution for adults cannot be denied. There will always be a hard core of intractable, possibly unsalvageable offenders who must be managed in secure facilities, of which there are already more than enough to meet the needs of the foreseeable future. These institutions have and will have a difficult task indeed. Nevertheless, the nature of imprisonment does not have to be as destructive in the future as it has been in the past.

The planning for new institutions should concentrate on improved concepts, designs, operations, locations, and size that in combination will "treat" as compared to injure the inmate. Thus, it is proposed that . . .

- alternatives to new state institutions be sought,
- modifications be made to state institutions to serve inmate needs,
- modifications be made to the social environment of institutions,
- institutional programs be individualized,
- programs for special offender types be devised,
- provisions be made for constructive programs for women offenders,
- a full range of institutional religious programs be developed,
- recreation programs for inmates be provided,
- individual and group counseling for inmates be offered, and
- labor and industrial programs that aid in re-entry into the community be put into operation.

Parole   Most offenders released from a correctional institution re-enter the community on parole. Though some jurisdictions impose limitations on parole use, offenders generally can be released on parole and repeatedly returned to confinement for parole violation until the term of their original commitment has expired. The relative importance and power of parole determinations vary markedly from one jurisdiction to another and within jurisdictions from one offense category to another. While the power and functions lack consistency, the basic purpose of parole remains constant: reduction of recidivism and thus the prevention of criminal activity.[13]

Most persons concerned with parole decision making for juveniles are full-time institutional personnel. Only a few juvenile jurisdictions have noninstitutional personnel determining parole releases. Different circumstances prevail in the adult area. For example, adult boards tend to carry many more direct state level administrative responsibilities than do releasing authorities for juveniles. The former is likened to an institutional approach, while the latter is independent in nature. An alternate system has gained considerable support in recent years, tending to cut the ground away from both major models. This system is linked with a general move toward consolidation of all types of correctional services into distinctive departments of corrections that subsume both institution and field programs. The consolidation model, emerging from the drive toward centralized administration, typically results in parole decisions being made by a central decision-making authority organizationally situated in an overall department of corrections but possessing independent powers. Regardless of the model used, it is imperative that consideration be given to criteria for decisions, appeal procedures, qualifications of decision makers, tenure, training, *grant* and *revocation* hearing procedures, due process, representation, and the role of the courts in revocation matters.

One of the clearest trends in parole organization in the last few years is consolidation of formerly autonomous agencies or functionally related units into expanding departments of corrections. Some of these departments have been made part of still larger units of state government, such as human resources agencies, which embrace a wide range of programs and services. One indication of this trend is the number of states that have shifted administrative responsibility for parole officers from independent parole departments to centralized correctional agencies. Nevertheless, distinct divisions and departments of juvenile correctional services are emerging. There is less agreement about whether such departments should be combined with agencies serving adult offenders; yet it is widely agreed that separate program units should be maintained, even if adult and juvenile programs are combined in a single agency. Statewide juvenile correctional services embracing both institutions and field aftercare represent an established trend that should be supported.

A significant number of parolees can do very well without

much official supervision, according to repeatedly validated research. Many offenders can be handled in relatively large caseloads simply by maintaining minimum contact and attending to their needs. Most of these parolees probably should be released from any form of supervision at all. Outright discharge from the institution would be an appropriate disposition and should be used much more frequently than it is. Failing that, minimum supervision can and should be employed for a significant group. In either event, the parolee should be assisted in acquiring financial assistance, employment, residential accommodations, and an ability to comply with parole rules (conditions). As a consequence, it is recommended that . . .

- independent state parole boards be established,
- qualifications of parole board members be specified,
- procedure and requirements for granting parole be specified,
- parole revocation procedures and alternatives be specified,
- institutional and field services and functions be coordinated,
- community services for parolees be developed,
- parole conditions be individualized, and
- parole manpower and training programs be developed.

Structural/Functional Considerations

The following subjects are covered as they explicitly and implicitly influence the potentiality of corrections to prevent crime. Four topics are discussed: (1) organization and management, (2) personnel, (3) research and information, and (4) statutes.

Organization and Management

Actual observation and/or a statistical description of correctional services confirms claims of fragmentation, isolation, and multiple levels of delivery of services. Rather than dwell on the deficiencies, however, let us analyze some of the means for improvement. To begin with, there can be a more rational and coordinated distribution of tasks and missions among the various governmental jurisdictions involved. The federal government should relinquish most direct correctional services for offenders, retaining only those which cost-benefit analyses indicate are inappropriate for state and local governments. At the same time, the federal level should greatly increase its role in providing financial, standard-setting, technical assistance, and manpower development to the correctional services carried on locally. This is to say that the major arena for reintegrative programs is the local community. There is, moreover, a major opportunity for regional solutions to problems which no single jurisdiction can meet unilaterally. It is essential for our CJS to have intergovernmental agreements and flexible administrative arrangements that bring offenders to the optimal location for supervision and rehabilitation. It is suggested by some that the unification of all correctional programs within a state will allow it to coordinate programs that are essentially interdependent, to better utilize human and fiscal resources, and to build more effective programs across the spectrum of corrections. The tactics for developing and maintaining a more viable administrative framework are: management by objectives (MBO); organization development (OD); organizational analysis; short, intermediate, and long range planning; and an adaptive management style.[14] It is proposed, therefore, that we . . .

- improve correctional management,
- develop a correctional planning process, and
- train management in offender and employee relations.

Personnel

People are the most effective resource for helping other *people*. In corrections, as in most other fields, they also are the most *underutilized* and *misappropriated resource*. Out of the changes occurring within the correctional system and within our society as a whole, numerous issues have emerged with actual profound effects, and potential serious effects, on correctional manpower.

Although institutions quarter fewer than one-fourth of all convicted offenders, they employ more than two-thirds of all persons working in corrections, and in turn they spend more than seventy cents of each dollar allocated to corrections. This excessive maldistribution of human and financial resources has strong implications for restructuring the corrections system. With transitions toward community programs, new and different manpower demands will develop. It is predicted that staff now engaged in helping inmates will do so in community settings. Also, new requirements will bring persons into the field who may help provide an improved profile for corrections. The profile of the staff member oriented to the military and to law enforcement will give way to that of the community correctional worker. He will be armed with different skills. He will not be preoccupied with custody, control, and regimentation, but he will be intent on using community resources as the major tool in his rehabilitative mission. Most basically, he will be equipped to cope with racial strife and political activism among offenders. Also, he will be involved in a career development system that repeatedly updates his job-related skills, and fulfills his job-related needs (recognition, self-esteem, belongingness, and so on).

In due regard for correctional staff, it is suggested that this system . . .

- discontinue unwarranted personnel restrictions,
- recruit and employ minority group individuals,
- recruit and employ women,
- Recruit and employ ex-offenders.
- Recruit and use volunteers,
- revise personnel practices to retain staff,
- adopt a participatory management program,
- plan for manpower redistribution to community programs,
- establish a state program for justice system education,
- implement correctional internship and work-study programs, and
- create staff development programs.

Research and Information

Research and information alone cannot create a new day in corrections. It offers the administrator opportunity to learn from the mistakes of others. The administrator's task in attempting to meet needs as they arise is to utilize all tools with which innovations are forged.

Research is the process of acquiring new knowledge. In all science it begins with description of the objects of study. In most social sciences, description calls for measurement of events and processes. Description of a prison, for example, might require description of an enormous number of events related to the flow of offenders through the institutional process. As events and processes are accurately described over an extended period, it becomes possible to attempt an explanation of the interaction of persons with sets of events so that outcomes may be predicted.

An information system for corrections must supply data for an enormous number of individual decisions. Decisions about the classification of offenders—their custodial requirements, employment, and training—are common to every correctional agency. In prisons and reformatories, decisions must be made about housing, discipline, work assignments, and control. Many are so routine they hardly seem to be decisions at all, but each action requires certain information for fairness and efficiency. In turn, new concepts and technology for the delivery of information to management have been considered. But research and statistics constitute only two uses to which information must be put. Historically, supplying information for management has been primarily the responsibility of the statistician. Today, the statistician becomes a user, rather than only the processor, of information. It is therefore important to distinguish between the functions of an information system and the professional services of the statistician. Irrespective of the distinctions involved in such a program, the paramount factors remain research and innovation. Together they offer hope for the future of corrections as it relates to crime prevention. It is, therefore, suggested that corrections . . .

- maintain a state correctional information system,
- provide staff for systems analysis and statistical research,
- design an information system to supply service needs,
- develop a data base with criminal justice system interface,
- measure recidivism and program performance.

*The
Statutory
Constraints*   It is perplexing to define statutory reform in crime prevention terms. Legislation can authorize or prohibit—it cannot accomplish. Correctional statutes must seek to authorize an effective correctional system and proscribe the abuse of individual rights. In developing standards for correctional legislation, it is essential to bear in mind that correctional "law" has three components in addition to legal statutes. These are: constitutional enactment, court decisions, and administrative rules and regulations. Thus all three branches of government have a hand in shaping the structure of correctional "law." The first problem in recommending a statutory framework, therefore, is to decide which component can best handle the particular issue being considered. If the decision is that the matter should be covered by statute, the question then becomes one of the intent and content of the law.

Correctional legislation has one primary mission—allocation and regulation of governmental power. In the context of criminal corrections, the power to be allocated and regulated is substantial. An individual who violates criminal law subjects himself to possible deprivation of those attributes of citizenship which characterize free societies. A secondary mission in legislating for corrections is to create and organize the instruments for correctional decision making. The goals of correctional agencies and the quality of their personnel are decisions only the legislature can make. Only after the correctional system's goals and methodology are determined can the nature of the instruments for their implementation be considered adequately.

The most critical issues facing corrections involve the exercise and control of correctional power. To the extent that correctional programs are to provide an individualized response to criminal offenders, correctional decision makers require broad discretionary power. Legislatures generally have conferred such power. Sentencing statutes are delegated without real direction to the sentencing courts. Parole boards are instructed to grant or deny parole in the "interest of the public." This discretion has given correctional administrators vast and often unchecked power over the lives and property of offenders. Hence, discretion has played, and no doubt will continue to play, an important role in the correctional process. No system of government has been devised that can be operated solely by rules without the exercise of discretion. The exercise of power without restraint certainly can be counterproductive. But the issue facing legislative reform efforts is not *whether* discretion should be granted—for its authorization is inevitable—but *when* and *how much*.

One method of limiting discretion is through *legislative decision making*. Here the legislature makes some decisions itself through statutory enactment, often in setting policy on matters of importance, such as determining the public policy of corrections. This form of decision making provides what is referred to as statutory criteria. Through *statutory criteria* the legislature can delegate a particular correctional decision to a correctional agency and, in addition, provide criteria and guidelines governing the agency's discretion. Most legislative delegations of power include some broad direction for its exercise. However, these are generally ineffective and authorize such wide discretion that it becomes almost impossible to determine whether the direction is followed. Statutory criteria for decision making should be specific enough so that a review of particular decisions can be effectively undertaken to assure compliance. Such guidance allows sufficient discretion for individualizing justice while assuring some protection against arbitrary or inappropriate decisions.

Two decisions are appropriate for development of detailed statutory criteria. The first is the trial court's selection of the sentencing alternative to be imposed initially on the offender. The broader the range of sentences available, the more important become criteria to protect against disparate results. In most jurisdictions, the major decision for the court is between probation and confinement. The second decision deals with parole, another sentencing decision susceptible to detailed statutory criteria. It is fundamentally similar to criteria for initial sentencing.

The penal code includes the statutory criteria or provisions that designate an activity as criminal and prescribe the applicable criminal sanction. The penal code has a direct and influential effect on the corrections component of the criminal justice system. The penal code defines the clientele of the correctional process. It determines in a general way the type of person who will journey through the correctional system. Also, statutes that define criminal conduct generally specify the limits of the sanction that may be imposed for violations. In many states, these limits are phrased in confinement terminology.

In due regard for the penal code, the most immediate and sweeping impact that a legislature can have in reforming prison conditions and the correctional process in general is to develop and enact a code of administrative justice along the lines just discussed. A consistent and fair approach to structuring and reviewing discretionary decisions will serve the interests of the offenders, the public, and the correctional system. Fair decisions based on adequate procedures and sound factual information are good correctional decisions. Decisions that appear fair to those affected are good correctional decisions. Good correctional decisions are essential if corrections is to have any effect in reducing recidivism and thus preventing crime.

It is recommended that in conjunction with one another, the court and corrections systems should . . .

- enact a correctional code,
- enact regulation of administrative procedures,
- legislate definition and implementation of offender rights,
- legislate the unification of corrections,
- define personnel standards by law,
- ratify interstate correctional agreements,
- define crime categories and maximum sentences,
- legislate criteria for court sentencing alternatives,
- restrict court delinquency jurisdiction and detention,
- require presentence investigations by law,
- formulate criteria and procedures for probation decisions,
- legislate commitment, classification, and transfer procedures,
- lift unreasonable restrictions on prison labor and industry,
- legislate authorization for community-based correctional programs,

- clarify parole procedures and eligibility requirements,
- establish pardon power and procedure, and
- repeal laws restricting offender rights.

Learning Exercises

1.   Divide the class into site-visitation teams of four to six members each. In turn, classify each team as either institutional (I) or community-based (CB). The I teams are to arrange on-site tours of different adult and juvenile institutions. Similarly, the CB teams are to schedule on-site visits with different adult and juvenile community-based treatment programs. Each team is to deliver a fifteen minute oral presentation to the entire class on their observations and opinions of the various programs that they visited.

2.   Compose a panel of correction officials that represents: (1) adult institutions, (2) juvenile institutions, (3) adult community-based efforts, and (4) juvenile community-based efforts. Request that they present to the class a ten minute overview of their mission, responsibility, and role in the correctional system. Also ask that they allow sufficient time for twenty minutes of group interaction. The total process should take sixty minutes.

Endnotes

1.   Major portions of this chapter are excerpted from the National Advisory Commission on Standards and Goals, *Corrections* (Washington, D.C.: U.S. Government Printing Office, 1973). It is recommended that those readers desirous of a comprehensive discussion of contemporary corrections (goals, state-of-the-art, and problems) see the above report and the texts by Vernon Fox, *Introduction to Corrections* (Englewood Cliffs, N.J.: Prentice-Hall, Inc., 1972); and Paul K. Clare and John H. Kramer, *Introduction to American Corrections* (Boston, Mass.: Holbrook Press, Inc., 1976).

2.   A most enlightening discussion of changing the correctional system is included in the mimeograph by Clarence Schrag, *Crime and Justice: American Style* (Washington, D.C.: U.S. Government Printing Office, 1971), pp. 9–124.

3.   An outstanding article on the goals and future of corrections is written by John Conrad, "Law, Order, and Corrections," *Public Administration Review* 31 (November/December 1971), pp. 596–602.

4. This thinking is examined by Edwin H. Sutherland and Donald R. Cressey, *Criminology* 9th ed. (New York: J. B. Lippincott, Co., 1974).

5. For further information see The President's Commission on Law Enforcement and Administration of Justice *Task Force Report: Corrections* (Washington, D.C.: U.S. Government Printing Office, 1967), pp. 82–92.

6. Louis P. Carney provides a brief yet comprehensive discussion in the use of diversion in his text *Introduction to Correctional Science* (New York: McGraw-Hill Book Co., 1974), pp. 365–369. Also see the National Institute of Law Enforcement and Criminal Justice, *Exemplary Projects* (Washington, D.C.: U.S. Government Printing Office, 1975).

7. A more in-depth review of this subject can be found in Part 3 of the text edited by Leon Radzinowicz and Marvin E. Wolfgang, *The Criminal In the Arms of the Law* (New York: Basic Books, Inc., 1971), pp. 389–687.

8. Ibid.

9. Specific recommendations are contained in the monograph by the American Correctional Association, *Manual of Correctional Standards* (Washington, D.C.: American Correctional Association, 1966), pp. 361–365.

10. A comprehensive series of articles devoted to community-based correctional programs is continued in the text by George C. Killinger and Paul F. Cromwell, Jr., *Corrections in the Community: Alternatives to Imprisonment* (St. Paul, Minn.: West Publishing Co., 1974).

11. A companion volume on the subject of prisons is co-edited by George C. Killinger and Paul F. Cromwell, Jr., *Penology* (St. Paul, Minn.: West Publishing Co., 1973).

12. Ibid.

13. An intensive overview of probation and parole standards and practice is presented in a series of mimeographs published by the American Bar Association's Project on Standards for Criminal Justice.

14. Correctional management is the subject of an article by Vincent O'Leary and David Duffee, "Managerial Behavior and Correctional Policy," *Public Administration Review* 31 (November/December, 1971), pp. 603–615. Related to this topic is one evaluation. See Law Enforcement Assistance Administration *Evaluative Research in Corrections: A Practical Guide* (Washington, D.C.: U.S. Government Printing Office, 1975).

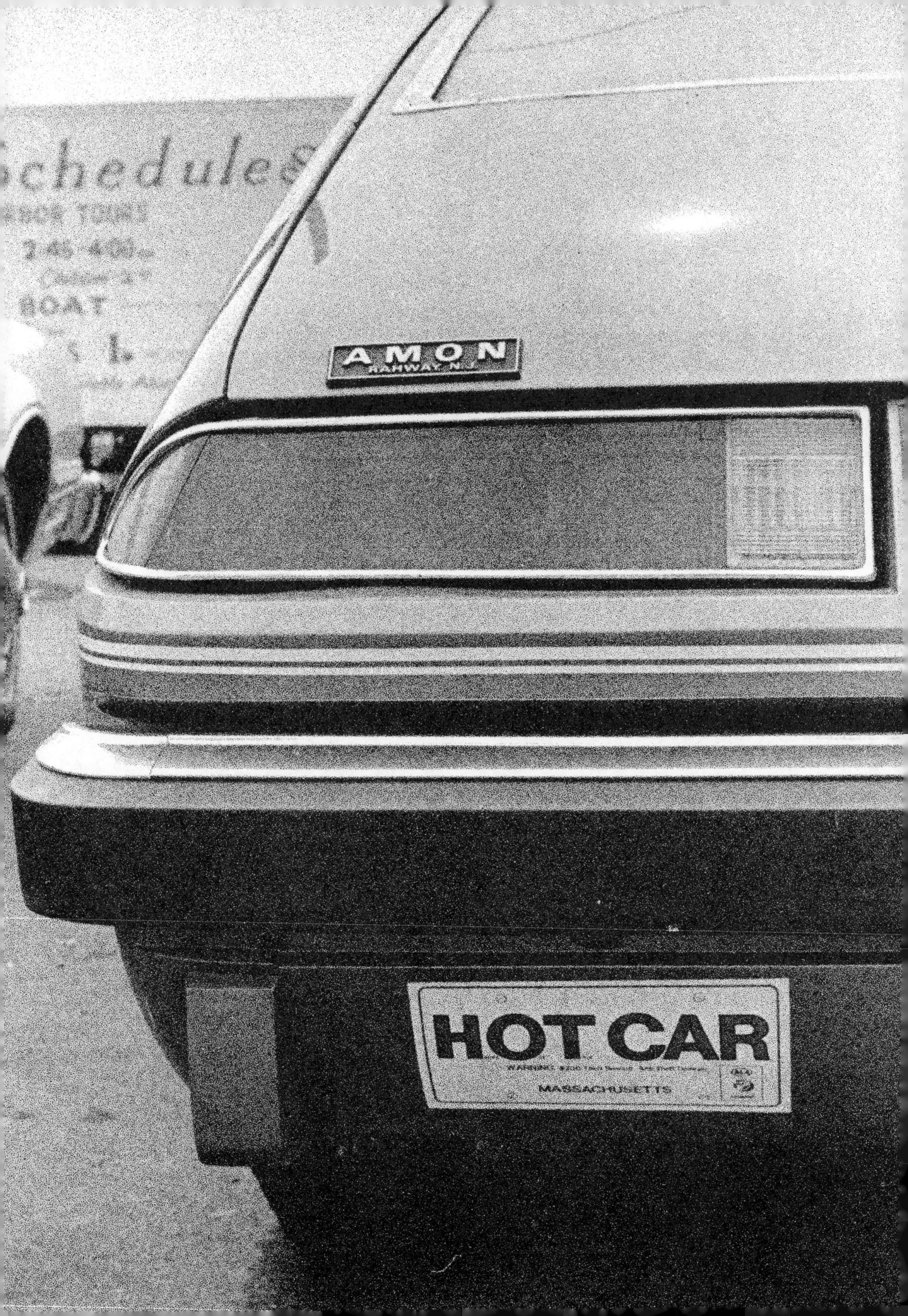
BOAT
AMON
RAHWAY N.J.
HOT CAR
MASSACHUSETTS

PART FOUR

The Fourth Subsystem: The Community

Along with the recommendations relating specifically to police agencies, however, it should be recognized that police effectiveness is also dependent, in the long run, upon:

1. the ability of government to maintain faith processes as the appropriate and effective means by which to achieve change and to redress individual grievances;
2. the willingness of society to devote resources to alleviating the despair of the culturally, socially, and economically deprived;
3. the development of effective ways of dealing with drug addiction; and
4. the improvement of the criminal justice, juvenile justice, mental health, and public health systems as effective ways of dealing with a wide variety of social and behavioral problems.*

You will soon see that the fundamental thrust of Part Four is devoted to involving the citizen in programmatic endeavors intended to reduce his risk of being victimized. Chapters 12 and 13 expand upon concepts and programs contained in preceding chapters that dealt with the subject of community crime prevention. Chapter 12 speaks to the importance of community *partici-*

*Special Committee on Standards for the Administration of Criminal Justice, *The Urban Police Function* (New York: American Bar Association, 1973), p. 25.

pation in the design and use of preventive measures. Further, the CJS is envisioned as a *delivery* system that encompasses other noncriminal justice agencies. Finally, it depicts a variety of pertinent experimental programs along with a discussion of the local government official's responsibility for promoting crime prevention activities. More specifically, this chapter will review the potential role of youth service bureaus, employment agencies, educational institutions, recreational programs, religious bodies, physical planning, and drug abuse programs in improving the *pre* in "preventing" crime.

Finally, Chapter 13 discusses the volatile issue of integrity in government. It purports that there is a distinct and indelible relationship between honest politicians and public administrators, and criminality in the community. You will find that a wide range of potential abuses are covered including conflicts of interest, public finances, procurement practices, land use, organized crime, and white collar crime. A strong case is made for us to become more alert, dedicated to, and proactive in establishing and sustaining probity in government.

12

Community Crime Prevention

A formidable problem faced by the nation's criminal justice system is insufficient citizen involvement. Indeed, why not leave the crime problem to the professionals who are paid to cope with it? Perhaps the most pragmatic answer is that the professionals themselves are keenly aware and readily admit that without citizen assistance they do not command sufficient manpower or funds to shoulder the monumental burden of combating crime in America.*

In short, "decentralization" of administration is in the air every-where. While it is sometimes defended on grounds of efficiency, it is more frequently justified in terms of effective popular participation in government. *Reformers of earlier generations succeeded in raising the level of expertise and professionalism in the bureaucracies, and to a lesser extent in improving capacity of chief executives to control the administrative arms of government. Now, people are once again turning their attention to representativeness, and are trying to elevate it to a more prominent place in the government scheme of things.*†

Preview

Our communities have been perceived recently as being inextricably linked to the criminal justice system. In fact, the very success or failure of the CJS is now viewed as being **dependent** upon the involvement of the community in CJS efforts to reduce crime. Hence, the phrases "citizen involvement," "community participation," "citizen action," and "community representation" are omnipresent in CJS

**Marshalling Citizen Power Against Crime* (Washington, D.C.: Chamber of Commerce of the United States, 1970), p. 3.

†Herbert Kaufman "Administrative Decentralization and Political Power," *Public Administration Review* 29 (January/February, 1969), p. 8.

and administrative writings. Undoubtedly, the 1970s will record a multitude of programs and an infinite number of activities intended to involve the public in preventing crime.

One of the programs that appears to be in line for increased resources and expansion is the youth service bureau concept. The youth service bureau is a single service center for children in trouble, about to cause trouble, or causing trouble. Similarly, drug abuse and treatment centers will be enhanced in order to better support the diversion of offenders out of the CJS and into community assistance programs. Further, employment and educational opportunities will be approached as they pertain to crime prevention. Recreation, religion, and the physical design of our cities will be exploited and channeled in accordance with removing either the motivation or opportunity to commit a criminal act. In combination, such community and citizen action programs hold considerable hope for increasing our ability as a nation to prevent crime.

Crime Prevention and the Public

Effective crime prevention is attainable only through broad-based community awareness and involvement. Indeed, if our country is to reduce crime, there must be a commitment on the part of every *citizen* to give of himself, his time, his energy, and his imagination to this end.[1] Additionally, we can reasonably assume that *private and public agencies* outside the CJS influence rises and declines in crime rates. Hence, a dominant concept of this chapter is to be that the more efficient and responsive the delivery of general services (education, manpower development, recreation, and other social services including drug abuse treatment and prevention programs) the less will be our feelings of alienation. It also should increase our confidence in public and private institutions, thus fostering our cooperation with these institutions— including those of the CJS.

Finally, crime prevention efforts must include benefits for institutions and agencies that have other primary goals, yet secondarily seek to reduce crime. Thus, an employer who sponsors a drug education or treatment program for his employees should anticipate both advances in his own economic interests and a decline in the incidence and dangers of drug abuse in his community. School-sponsored job counseling and referral services can reduce the number of dropouts, enabling many young people to avoid the idleness and boredom that can cause juvenile delinquency and classroom disruption. Churches and community clubs willing to make their facilities and personnel available on an extended basis can draw new members to their programs while providing enhanced recreational and social opportunities to many who typically are not interested.

Citizens, community organizations, agencies, and facilities must recognize that the degree of imagination, efficiency, and enthusiasm they bring to their own work has a direct impact on crime prevention. As a consequence, this chapter provides testimony to numerous cases in which communities already have recognized this fact and acted on it. Examples are cited of crime and delinquency prevention programs and other projects that have reduced crime, augmented existing criminal justice resources, found jobs for juveniles and ex-offenders, and influenced people to return to school and complete their educations. The remainder of the chapter is divided into four sections dealing with: (1) citizen and community participation in crime prevention efforts; (2) the CJS delivery system as it interacts with the citizen; (3) programmatic efforts; and (4) the local official's responsibility for supporting crime prevention programs.

Citizen Responsiveness

Individual and collective responsiveness to crime preventive efforts is not a luxury for us but rather a fundamental ingredient in a concerted program to reduce crime.[2] However, this thinking on our part has merely resulted in limited and sporadic attempts by citizens to assist the CJS in preventing crime. At the same time, the average citizen's response to the crime problem is a demand for more action by the police, courts, correctional institutions, and other government agencies. The citizen asks far too seldom what he can do to help; and when the public does decide to act, its activities often are short-lived outbursts in reaction to a particularly violent crime. Fortunately, this state-of-affairs is yielding to a citizenry that is more committed to the exertion of positive action in preventing crime. It is being recognized that while crime prevention may *not* be the main purpose of an organization, crime prevention opportunities still may exist. For example, tenant patrols may help prevent burglaries in apartment buildings, and cargo security councils formed and supported by local transportation companies may reduce the number of cargo thefts. Programs geared to increasing the employability of the jobless, furthering the education of the dropout, supplying adequate medical treatment for the alcoholic and drug addict, and providing adequate recreational and other constructive activities for youth are all preventive in nature. Moreover, group endeavors by citizens may focus on strengthening the crime prevention activities of government agencies (e.g., courts, corrections, and law enforcement agencies) or at supporting anticrime measures undertaken by the private sector. For instance, the focus of a block crime prevention association is often on self-help measures that are designed to improve the safety of persons and property over and above the protection afforded by local police. Other citizen groups, such as local chambers of commerce, may concentrate on the CJS by sponsoring surveys of police effectiveness, proposing more effective methods of selecting judges, or promoting support for community-based corrections facilities. Nevertheless, it remains that *organized efforts to reduce crime do not replace individual action; they result from it.* Organizations do not relieve a citizen of his crime prevention duty; they offer a most valuable vehicle for him to exercise it.

Still, in the desire to attack the crime problem, there is too often a failure to generate adequate consideration over such crucial questions as: How do we organize? How do we establish priorities? How do we obtain funding, assistance of other citizens, and cooperation from public officials? How do we sustain a crime prevention program once it is underway? To begin with, regardless of the reason sparking citizen action, the natural tendency is to form an organization. This is fine, providing no other group in the community is actively and effectively engaged in the same activity. Duplication of effort is expensive. If those wishing to organize find another organization engaged in what they had planned to do, they should check to see if it needs more members or assistance from another organization. In any case, coordination between groups is essential in order to avoid counterproductive or duplicative activities.

Dissipation of energies and resources can be avoided by organizing according to priorities. Thus, it becomes important to ascertain what others consider to be significant problems. The staffs of social agencies and of criminal justice agencies, and clients of these agencies (e.g., poor people, persons held in pretrial detention, court witnesses, jurors, inmates, ex-offenders, and juvenile delinquents) can provide valuable insights on the major crime problems. Once the problems are identified, priorities must be selected, for the opportunities will outstrip the available resources of any organization. First, the course of action selected should fall within the scope of interest of the organization's members or potential members. Second, the problem selected for attack must be tractable within the organization's geographical base and its available manpower, funding, and other resources. A third concern in determining priorities is to be sure that the action program selected does not create more problems than it solves. Mr. Newburg supports the above thinking:

> Any suggested action in a crime prevention program should be first tested by determining if the objective of that action is obtainable and looking to see if the action will contribute effectively to the desired result. Attempts to solve unreachable problems at the outset is not only frustrating but will lead to the failure of the program.[3]

Word of mouth, publicity by media, and talks before community organizations are among the many ways the initial members of a crime prevention effort can elicit added manpower. Programs that seek to prevent specific crimes have fairly well defined recruitment targets. A campaign against shoplifting, for example, might require the involvement of merchants. Programs pertaining to self-help protection against burglary, for example, would enlist the participation of each neighborhood resident. It is advisable, however, that our citizens not be recruited for a crime prevention effort unless they have the time to fulfill these responsibilities and unless they are prepared to serve for reasonable periods. High turnover and failure to be productive typically destroy the program.[4]

Citizen groups, far from regarding public officials as adversaries, usually attempt to work with them and rely on their assistance to achieve goals of common interest. In most cases, the relationship is mutually supportive and productive. Yet, it is alleged that although almost all citizen crime prevention organizations stress the need for cooperation and cordial relations with officials, there is substantial opinion that public servants should not be admitted as members.[5] At the same time, if official support is not acquired, then citizen action effort will be hampered. Other limiting factors are: (1) a lack of needed funds, (2) inadequate training of the volunteers, (3) waning enthusiasm once the project is established, (4) a means of evaluating their results, and (5) the absence of a feedback mechanism.

The Delivery of Public Services

This section concentrates on the involvement of citizens in the delivery of government and social services to the community.

Further, it focuses on the use of youth service bureaus as a primary vehicle for delivering social services to young people.

Citizen In-volvement in the Delivery of Services

Nearly every Presidential or national commission report in recent years cites compelling arguments that citizen alienation, inaccessibility of governments, and the quality and quantity of the services provided are not conducive to respect for the laws of this nation. There is evidence to suggest that when governments are unresponsive to citizens' needs, there is a tendency to seek redress and to fulfill needs through extralegal means.[6] This is not to say that government may have caused the problems of the inner city, but most citizens feel that it is incumbent upon government to solve the cities' problems.

In the area of municipal services, there is widespread agreement that the political system has failed to correct the inequalities that exist in predictable patterns throughout the country. Ghetto residents live with the fact that city governments do not pave, repair, clean, and light the streets and sidewalks in their neighborhoods as systematically as they do in white, middle- and upper-income areas. Also, ghetto residents witness police departments permitting narcotics traffic, prostitution, and gambling operations to flourish, and failing to respond quickly to calls for help in stopping assaults and batteries. Every day these same citizens experience losses of life, liberty, and property—losses more serious and more widespread than those that occur in higher income neighborhoods.

Most people now realize that the immediate priorities for improving the responsiveness of government must center on the aspect of government that will cause our citizens to view government in a positive light; namely, the delivery of services. To that end, the following goals are stated:

- to achieve equitable and more effective municipal services;
- to improve methods of access to government services and program information;
- to improve citizen complaint and grievance response mechanisms; and
- to promote maximum community involvement and participation in the governmental process.

The methods of achieving these goals are reflected in the following recommendations, which include proposals for: reallocating resources, establishing complaint and information offices, utilizing the public media more effectively, improving channels of communications, decentralizing city halls, establishing multiservice centers, and developing partnership citizen councils.

- Distribute public service on the basis of need.
- Dispense government services through neighborhood centers.
- Enact public right-to-know laws.
- Broadcast local government meetings and hearings.
- Conduct public hearings on local issues.
- Establish neighborhood governments.
- Create a central office of complaint and information.
- Broadcast local Action Line programs.

Youth Services Bureaus
    Neighborhood agencies or Youth Services Bureaus which provide community services for our young people can be important elements in the prevention and reduction of crime and delinquency. An effective service delivery system, in addition to upgrading the quality of life for its clients, can reduce the feelings of alienation many of our citizens have, increase the confidence of these citizens in public and private institutions, and foster citizen cooperation with these institutions. Youth Services Bureaus (see Figure 12.1) for the most part were the result of a recommendation by the 1967 President's Commission on Law Enforcement and Administration of Justice, which urged communities to establish these bureaus to serve both delinquent and nondelinquent youth referred by the police, juvenile courts, schools, and other sources.

    We find that the youth services bureau concept seeks to resolve the problem of fragmented services by integrating the services available to the individual through a central intake unit, which analyzes the individual's needs and refers him to the appropriate agency. It is critical to the success of these programs that the clients be involved in the actual development and operation of the programs, both in an advisory role and as employees. The integrated nature of the youth services bureau approach and the multiple functions of the bureau are portrayed graphically in Figure 12.1. A youth can walk into the youth services bureau on his own or be referred by his family or by a number of community agencies. Figure 12.1 shows how the bureau itself utilizes a number of existing resources to help to develop a program appropriate to the individual youth. The program might involve direct assistance such as counseling, education, training, and health checks. Also, it might offer activities in which the youth can become involved, such as social or issue-oriented activities. For youth with particular difficulties, it involves utilization of drug programs, hotlines and crisis centers, and other resources.

Since 1967, we have witnessed youth services bureaus being established across the nation in large cities and small, in over-crowded inner city neighborhoods, middle-income suburbs, and sprawling rural counties—joining the few pioneering youth services bureaus that had preceded the Commission's recommendations. Relatedly, a national census in 1972 identified 150 youth services bureaus currently in operation in many states and territories throughout the country.[7] While the Task Force in 1967 suggested exploring the feasibility of federal funding for establishing youth services bureaus, the national study in 1972 was only able to identify *less than $15 million* annually in federal dollars supporting the youth services bureau movement.

The goals for youth services bureaus suggested by the President's Commission in 1967 were primarily to establish and coordinate programs for our young people. As more bureaus have come into operation, the basic goals have been expanded. Youth services bureaus have at least five goals. These include: (1) diversion of juveniles from the justice system; (2) provision of services to youth; (3) coordination of both individual cases and programs for young people; (4) modification of systems of services for emphasizing the needs of youth; and (5) involvement of youth in decisions that promote the development of individual *responsibility*. The following suggestions are in concert with the five goals:

- Coordinate youth services through youth services bureaus.
- Operate youth services bureaus independent of the justice system.
- Divert offenders into youth services bureaus.
- Provide direct and referral services to youths.
- Hire professional, paraprofessional, and volunteer staff.
- Plan youth program evaluation and research.
- Appropriate funds for youth services bureaus.
- Legislate establishment and funding of youth services bureaus.

Programs for Community Crime Prevention

We find that a large number of crime prevention activities are aimed at what many view as the *infrastructure* of crime (e.g., insufficient education, inadequate job skills, and lack of recreational

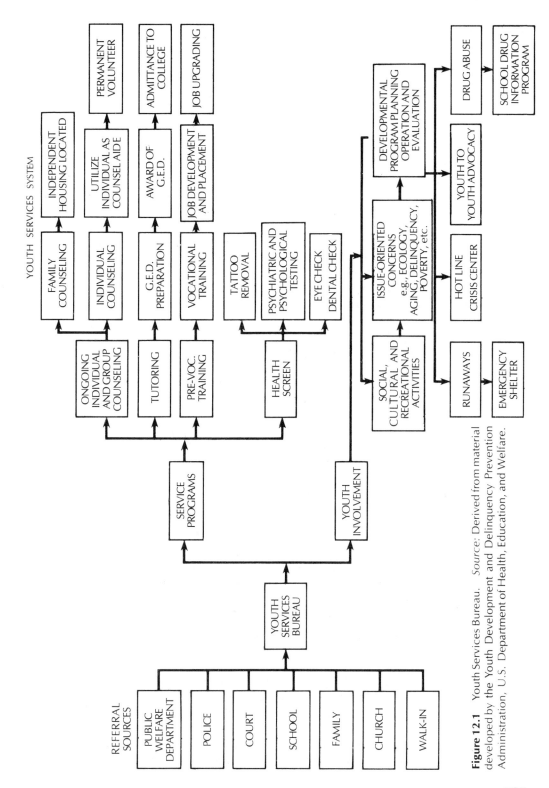

Figure 12.1 Youth Services Bureau. *Source:* Derived from material developed by the Youth Development and Delinquency Prevention Administration, U.S. Department of Health, Education, and Welfare.

opportunities). Citizen action in these areas is brought to bear outside of the CJS and is designed to reduce significantly the need to utilize the sanctions of that system. This section presents a series of programs that seek to attack the infrastructure of crime. The programs are: (1) drug abuse, (2) employment, (3) education, (4) recreation, (5) religion, and (6) physical design of the cities.

Drug Abuse and Treatment

The concern here is primarily with treatment and prevention of drug abuse rather than with law enforcement efforts to prevent drug trafficking.[8] (While it is recognized that illicit trade must be stopped, the present discussion will be limited to abuse and treatment of the drug problem.)

The "multimodality" approach to drug treatment provides a broad range of services to treat all drug users. This approach permits addicts to be treated in programs suited to their individual health needs so that they may regain their status as functioning members of society. Consequently, a broad number of programs should be contained in a comprehensive drug treatment program. Among the elements of comprehensive drug treatment systems are:

- crisis intervention and drug emergency centers;
- facilities and personnel for methadone maintenance treatment programs;
- facilities and personnel for narcotics antagonist programs;
- therapeutic community programs staffed entirely or largely by ex-addicts; and
- closed and open residential treatment facilities as well as halfway houses staffed primarily by residents.

Voluntary treatment of the addict-defendant before prosecution can be most helpful. Eligibility requirements should be liberal, and treatment made available early in the criminal justice process. Besides treatment programs, comprehensive drug abuse prevention programs should be developed. Children should be informed about drugs at an early age by parents and teachers. Peer-group influence also should be utilized in prevention strategies. Materials in prevention programs should focus on individuals as people, as well as on drugs and their effects. Young people also should be given alternatives to drug use, such as meaningful recreation and education programs. Communities desiring to establish a far ranging drug treatment and prevention program should start by surveying the drug problem in their communities. A central agency to coordinate programs should be developed, and a study made of funding sources. States and local units of government should seek available aid from the federal government in designing their particular multimodality drug treatment and prevention centers.

- Adopt multimodality drug treatment scene.
- Create crisis intervention and drug emergency centers.
- Establish methadone maintenance programs.
- Establish narcotic antagonist treatment programs.
- Create drug-free therapeutic community facilities.
- Organize residential drug treatment programs.
- Encourage broader flexibility in varying treatment approaches.
- Enable defendants to refer themselves voluntarily to drug treatment programs.
- Establish training programs for drug treatment personnel.
- Plan comprehensive, communitywide prevention.
- Coordinate drug programs through a state agency.
- Coordinate federal, state, and local drug programs.

Employment   Opportunities for work are most often inequitably allocated among various groups. Hence, we see young people, members of minorities, residents of depressed urban areas, and individuals who have been denied a fair chance to obtain educational credentials or marketable work skills with higher unemployment rates, fewer opportunities for promotion or advancement, and lower earnings than other members of the community. Any success they achieve in the world of work is gained against great odds. Significantly, there are correlations between individual failure in the labor market and criminal behavior, and similar correlations between high local unemployment rates and high local crime rates ought to suggest that unequal economic status is a major cause of crime.[9]

The immediate institution of measures to eliminate unequal opportunity and to reduce economic deprivation is justified on the basis of "social fairness" alone. The prospect that such measures will also serve the self-interest of the community by reducing levels of crime indeed adds a special urgency to the need for them, and for committing the necessary resources in their design and implementation. Can it not be concluded therefore that changing labor market conditions are sufficient to explain increasing crime rates for youth? Crime rates could be explained not only by the raw unemployment rates but also by "participation rates" which represent the proportion of each age group in the labor force.[10]

Other studies have demonstrated that property crimes are more likely to be committed by those in the lower socioeconomic classes.[11] The cause-and-effect relationship cannot be proven beyond question nor quantified precisely, but it appears reasonable that unemployment reduction will have a significant impact on criminal conduct. Thus, one way to prevent crime is to assist those with severe employment problems. To maximize the impact, these efforts should concentrate on those most likely to commit crimes. Inner city, low-income males between sixteen and twenty-four are an obvious target group, especially those who have not completed high school. In 1967, 369 out of 100,000 non-whites were arrested for robbery, as opposed to 23 of every 100,000 whites.[12] Further, two other target groups in need of employment assistance are the more than 5 million individuals arrested annually, and those who have formerly been convicted of a crime. The FBI's *Uniform Crime Report* statistics indicate that a majority of those who are arrested are likely to be re-arrested within six years. Many arrestees already have employment problems, and when they are released in the community again with a record, their employment problems are intensified.

It should be noted that the above material centered on the economic problems of particular groups in the community who pose high risks of criminal behavior. Just as present and potential offenders have problems that can be addressed by programs serving these individuals, so do neighborhoods display typical economic problems. To solve these problems it appears that two things are needed: (1) programs of systematic reform that will impact the levels of criminal activity of all residents, including those not singled out as members of any identified target group, and (2) more effective programs designed to reach the target groups by improving the environment in which program participants will make their venture into the world of work.

- Expand job opportunities for disadvantaged youth.
- Broaden after-school and summer employment programs.
- Establish pretrial intervention programs.
- Expand job opportunities for offenders and ex-offenders.
- Remove ex-offender employment barriers.
- Create public employment programs.
- Expand job opportunities for former drug abusers.
- Target employment, income, and credit efforts in poverty areas.
- Require employers' compliance with antidiscrimination laws.

- Increase support of minority businesses.
- Alleviate housing and transportation discrimination.

Education   Unfortunately, the American educational system has not separated sufficiently its responsibility to provide learning conditions for the development of people from its concern with *operating schools*. It has not seen itself as part of a process of providing differential experiences for people maturing into adults. As a consequence, it has not perceived itself as a mechanism contributing to either the prevention or production of crime. It is readily apparent that very little is being done in the schools as a direct, intentional effort to discourage young people from criminal careers. Moreover, there is a definite impression that some of the existing conditions of our schools (which we often accept without question) actually create the antipathy, frustrations, and despair that lead people eventually to criminal acts.

The problems with our schools are chronic and profoundly complex.[13] The major problems are: (1) resistance to change, (2) a lack of specificity to the children's needs, (3) an over-emphasis on college education, (4) needless competition, (5) poor parental participation, (6) inadequate democratic processes, (7) ambiguity over the learner's objectives and instructor qualifications, and (8) an absence of supportive relations between the schools and other parts of the community. These factors plus others directly bear on the ability of the school to favorably influence children in their conduct as responsible citizens.

The school plays an integral part in the socialization process and therefore is in a position to positively affect the predelinquent and delinquent behavior of youth. In seeking to direct individuals to socially acceptable roles, changes in the school system must continually be implemented. A willingness to experiment and evaluate must be a major responsibility of all school systems. A great deal is known about crime, what precipitates it, and what a large part learning and conditioning play in an individual's social behavior. Schools can exert a strong crime-preventing influence on their students through improvements in the learning environment. They can also influence family, peer group, and neighborhood environments, and indirectly influence others. Moreover, schools must become more involved in the early years of students' lives. They need more information about their students; they need to design educational experiences that can adapt to the different needs, backgrounds, and environments of their students. The following recommendations are made in accordance with this thinking.

- Adopt teacher training programs for parents.
- Exemplify justice and democracy in school operations.
- Guarantee literacy to elementary school students.
- Provide special language services for bicultural students.
- Develop career preparation programs in schools.
- Provide effective supportive services in schools.
- Offer alternative education programs for deviant students.
- Open schools for community activities.
- Adopt merit training and promotion policies for teachers.

Recreation   In its *Task Force Report on Juvenile Delinquency and Youth Crime,* the President's Crime Commisson cited a goal for recreation:

> If recreation programs are to have relevance in today's world, they must merge with others to create a total environment serving a central goal of human development .... It would appear that certain types of recreational opportunities may deter our young people from delinquency, but this effect is largely dependent on the nature of the activity and cannot be attributed to recreation as an entity. [14, 15]

In respect to the inconclusive relationship between recreation and delinquency prevention, an evaluation component should be included in recreation programs that attempt to prevent crime.

Recreation is common to all people and cultures. In its most fundamental sense, the term implies for us a pastime, a diversion, a respite from labor. Whatever serves to refresh or renew the person's physical or psychic energies is properly termed recreation and answers a completely human need. Recreation does have a part to play in the prevention or reduction of crime and delinquency, and recreational planners will need to weigh the social and economic aspects of making recreation a strategy of intervention.

Because recreation activities have a strong appeal for young people, delinquency is less likely to flourish in those communities where opportunities for wholesome recreation are abundant and attractive, as opposed to cities or neighborhoods where adequate facilities are lacking. Simply put, young people engaged in recreation activities on the playground cannot at the same time be robbing a bank, breaking into a home, or perpetrating some other crime.[16] Yet, the provision of adequate recreation facilities is a minimum goal and will require aggressive followup in the form of innovative programing and flexible scheduling to attract and hold the interest of youth. Many recreation programs and facilities never reach the poor, the inner city resident, or the minorities; and while there is no statistical evidence to confirm a relationship between recreational deprivation and higher rates of delinquency among these groups, the existence and significance of such a relationship cannot be dismissed. Clearly, delinquency prevention programs must react to the specialized needs of those youths with special problems. Unfortunately, many of our youths are excluded from agency and institutional assistance if they have had behavior or academic problems in school, or have been disruptive in recreation groups. The delinquent population is thus excluded de facto from the programs it needs so much. Delinquent youths require special services and therefore constitute a special target group. However, providing specialized services while avoiding harmful labeling and stigma is a central dilemma in the delinquency prevention area.

In conclusion, special emphasis must be placed on programs that reach out to those young people who in the past have rejected or ignored established recreation programs, and the *effectiveness* of such efforts needs to be assessed. Further, youths whose behavior typically precludes their participation in recreation programs should be encouraged to take part in programs that are designed to cope with disruptive behavior in the recreation setting. Obviously, counseling may be necessary to help change that behavior, and thus should be directly connected with the program (either as part of it or on a referral basis). It is, therefore, recommended that recreation programs for delinquency prevention be developed.

Religion   The religious centers of our nation can well be a part of a massive new effort to reduce and prevent crime. The spiritual community is a significant part of society, and hence it has invaluable resources to commit. Indeed, religious institutions could list many other reasons that would reinforce the challenge to its members to become explicitly involved in crime prevention efforts. In responding to that challenge, these institutions have unique resources to apply in an effort against crime. In addition to their spiritual resources and moral influence, they have buildings in strategic locations; trained personnel with specific counseling skills; organizations with competency in planning and action; and access to large numbers of volunteers. The religious community also has facilities and equipment for educational and recreational activities; relationships with community organizations and communications networks; and links with state, regional, and national associations.

Most basically, the religious community should be encouraged to ask its congregations across the country what they can do to reduce crime, and more specifically, what individual members can do. Such questions usually stimulate a flow of ideas and an indepth reassessment of the resources available in the crime prevention effort. Specifically, then, the religious community should[17]:

- enlist religious community participation in crime,
- encourage religious institutions to educate their constituencies about the crime problem,
- enlist religious institution support of crime prevention,
- open church facilities for community programs, and
- promote religious group participation in the justice system.

Reduction of Criminal Opportunity   The reduction of the opportunity for a person to commit crime through control and design of the physical environment is an integral part of any crime prevention program. In this approach, crime must be seen not as a symptom of other factors to be corrected but as an act that must be prevented. Direct controls include only those that reduce environmental opportunities for crime, such as security hardware, street lighting, surveillance, and building design. The environment should be structured so that the individual considering a criminal act thinks that there is a good chance he will be seen and recognized, that he will be identified immediately as an intruder, that someone will take action, and he will be *apprehended*.

Physical targets can be made sufficiently crime-proof to deter an individual from perpetrating a crime. This approach, often referred to as "target hardening," involves use of security hardware. Proper use of such hardware can prevent some burglaries, or at least increase the time it takes to complete the criminal act (thereby increasing the chances of the offender's being detected and apprehended).

The physical design characteristics of residential complexes and housing—e.g., architectural features such as the grouping of dwelling units or the design and placement of elevator doors and lobbies—can increase or decrease the probability that crimes will occur. The importance of building design in crime control was emphasized by the Violence Commission:

Modern architectural features such as elevators, enclosed stairways, pedestrian underpasses, and underground parking garages, offer seclusion and screening from public view. Hence, they are often settings for violent behavior. This kind of problem can be overcome. In at least one case, the stairways of a public housing project were enclosed in glass and well illuminated. Crime in these stairways virtually ceased. Visibility also has been improved by selecting, locating, and trimming trees and shrubbery, by better street lighting, by using closed circuit television systems, and eliminating places of concealment.[18]

Oscar Newman, a New York city planner and architect, has identified certain spatial arrangements that promote feelings of proprietorship and increase the sense of community among tenants in public housing, which in turn lead residents to control their own security and encourage their defense of certain areas. This self-policing is facilitated by designing a housing complex so that all areas of that complex can be naturally and conveniently observed by tenants, the surrounding community, and police patrols. It is Newman's hypothesis that surveillance opportunities, or the ability to observe certain public areas of a residential complex, can reduce the fear and anxiety felt by residents and can contribute to the image of a safe environment.

Many communities are currently trying to reduce residential and commercial crime through the adoption of security codes or the revision of building codes to include security measures. Some states are preparing statewide security standards for most buildings. These codes can serve as guidelines for architects and physical planners, and can make security a primary consideration in the design and construction of buildings. For example, in 1971 the Governor of California signed into law Sections 14050 and 14051 to the California Penal Code. They require the State Department of Justice to develop and recommend to the legislature, and thereafter continually review, building security standards for the purpose of reducing the likelihood of burglary in California.

The Building Security Law was a legislative recognition of a strong feeling among many in law enforcement that serious target hardening could make burglary less desirable as a way of life. The regulations eventually adopted will appear in the State Administrative Code. They provide all of the necessary information for enforcement groups and for building owners. When considered together with technical guidelines developed by the California Crime Technological Research Foundation, they also provide sufficient information for producers to manufacture, construct, or assemble products to meet the regulations. Further, the purpose, scope, design specifications, and performance tests for each building component or system required under the new regulations will be specified, including drawings and technical references and descriptions where necessary for clarification. Detailed test reporting procedures for proprietary construction materials and equipment listings are also set forth. Each mandatory provision of these new requirements will be included as a part of the Minimum State Building Standards of the Administrative Code.[19]

Although the record of crime reduction due to these codes has not been totally confirmed, it is reasonable to assume that the codes can help prevent certain types of crime. In addition, security ordinances can:

- lay the ground work to legitimize crime prevention as a responsibility of the community;
- reassure the citizens of the responsiveness of government to their needs;
- increase citizen awareness of different means of crime prevention; and
- bring pressure upon the security industry to improve its products.

It is recommended that:

- buildings be designed to incorporate security measures,
- security requirements be included in building codes,
- street lighting be improved in high crime areas,
- shoplifting prevention techniques be adopted in retail establishments,
- car theft prevention programs be legislated, and
- citizens be involved in law enforcement.

Community Crime Prevention and the Local Official

This section presents remarks made before the National League of Cities' Public Safety Policy Committee Seminar on "Community Crime Prevention and the Public Official" in December, 1973.[20] It both supplements and reemphasizes the concepts and practices covered in the preceding sections of this chapter.

Introductory Remarks

Mayor James J. Eagan
Florissant, Missouri

Our topic today is Community Crime Prevention and the Public Official. The need to develop effective community crime prevention programs in one of the problems with policing in the United States is that in too many places policing is too independent. That means that too many mayors either don't know how, or have not wanted to completely fulfill their responsibilities as elected officials responsible for policing of their cities. By the same token, there are too many mayors who want to run their police department and don't know how to run them. And there are too many mayors who want to get their cottonpicking political fingers into their cotton-picking police departments; and that's not always good.

But on the whole, police departments aren't quite independent in the United States. One of the reasons may be that the administration and the management of a police department is much more complex than we may be inclined to think on the face of it. Unfortunately, too many people—not only mayors, city managers, budget directors, controllers, and legislators, but the man or woman on the street—think they understand the problems and the intricacies of policing. Too often, simple solutions are provided and recommended because not enough work or time is spent on learning what the issues in policing are.

Crime has become a national problem only within the past few years. During the presidential election campaign of 1960 there was no mention of crime worth repeating; but in 1964 as you will recall, Senator Goldwater talked in his campaign about crime in the streets and the need for safe streets. Then Congress found, for the first time, that crime was a national problem. We've now seen the creation of a federal law enforcement assistance program that many of the cities are unhappy about and many of them for good reason. Crime has been elevated to the status of a national problem and the solutions to this terrible problem of crime are going to be dependent upon national policy and some kind of national thrust.

We're not here today to talk about that subject, but I think it's not fair to you city officials to make you bear too much responsibility for the control of crime. Presidents of both the Democratic and Republican parties have said that crime is basically a local problem. The people on the national level want to keep it on your back by saying that crime is a local problem. I think you'd make a mistake if you tried to accept too much of this responsibility. I urge you not to repeat the mistake of police chiefs who have said, "Give me more police and I'll reduce crime." That's suicidal talk because the police certainly cannot influence crime that much, no matter how good they are. There are too many other factors involved in the crime problem.

Some of you may have read a story which appeared a few weeks ago about a police patrol experiment in Kansas City, Missouri; this carefully planned and designed experiment had the support of the Police Foundation and was under the direction of then-Chief Clarence Kelley. Incidentally, the final results are not in yet but an enterprising reporter for the *New York Times* was picking up some information about the experiment and asked a lot of the right questions and then did his story. The headline said something to the effect that "Value of Police Patrol is Challenged." The experiment was intended to test the effect of police patrol on crime. And the preliminary results suggest that, if patrol is decreased or increased, it seems to have very little effect on the level of crime in any part of the city where this experiment is underway.

Now, I made reference earlier to the fact too many chiefs tend to say,

our cities is obvious and often repeated. In 1967 the President's Commission on Law Enforcement and Criminal Justice saw citizen involvement as a necessary foundation for any crime control program. "Controlling crime," the Commission reported, "depends to a great degree on the interaction between the community and the criminal justice system." Now, six years later, the National Advisory Commission on Criminal Justice Standards and Goals has stated the case even more strongly: "The Commission believes that effective crime prevention is possible only through broad-based community awareness and involvement."

I think it accurate to say that each of us, as public officials, is aware of the potential of an involved and supportive citizenry in helping to prevent and reduce crime. Moreover, most of us can probably document instances in which communities have recognized ways that they can become involved and have acted upon them. To give just a few examples: community delinquency prevention programs; volunteer programs in courts and corrections; citizen-sponsored-and-run drug and alcohol abuse programs; and education programs to assist citizens in securing their homes and their belongings.

But I think we must also recognize that much more remains to be done to achieve widespread and productive use of the citizen resource. What we would like to explore today is the way in which the public official should be involved in developing community crime control efforts and helping to integrate those efforts into the traditional criminal justice system. Our objective here should be not to hammer out any particular crime control program, but to carefully discuss the issue of how the public official should and can serve as a bridge between expressed community needs and capacities and the operation of criminal justice agencies.

There are good reasons, I might add, why we should be concerned about this topic. It's the local official to whom the citizen turns for resolution of the crime problem. It's the local official who makes final decisions about the allocation of criminal justice resources. As the demand for community crime prevention efforts increase, the same official will again be called upon to help meet that demand.

Our three speakers this morning have been charged with helping us to discuss the potentials of community crime prevention and the implications for local governmental officials.

Let me introduce all these gentlemen at the very beginning and then turn the program over to them individually.

The first speaker will be Mr. Patrick Murphy, President of the Police Foundation in Washington, D.C. Mr. Murphy has a distinguished career in law enforcement. Most recently serving as Police Commissioner of New York City, he was also Police Commissioner of Detroit, and Chief of Police in Syracuse, New York. Mr. Murphy began his career as a patrolman within the New York Police Department. He will discuss our topic from the perspective of the criminal justice agency—the benefits and disadvantages of community involvement and appropriate roles for the local elected official.

Our second speaker, Mr. Oliver Lofton, is an attorney and the President of Priorities Investment Corporation, Newark, New Jersey. Mr. Lofton's experience in criminal justice and his work in the Newark community well qualify him for this topic. Mr. Lofton has been a federal and local prosecutor. He then became the Administrator of the Newark Legal Service Project and was the Associate Director of the Community Relations Service of the U.S. Department of Justice. For the last two years, he has served as a member of the Community Crime Prevention Task Force, National Advisory Commission on Criminal Justice Standards and Goals. Mr. Lofton will offer us a citizen's perspective on appropriate roles for the citizen, the police, and the local government official in the area of community crime control.

Our final speaker is Mr. Joseph Coates, Program Manager in the Office of Exploratory Research and Problem Assessment at the National Science Foundation. His professional training is in industrial organic chemistry and he worked for a number of years in that field. Prior to joining the National Science Foundation, Dr. Coates was a senior staff member for the Institute of Defense Analysis. He describes himself as having both a professional and an avocational interest in the future and in the impact of technology on society. Among other works, he has authored a paper entitled "The Future of Crime in the United States from Now to the Year 2000." Mr. Coates will round out our discussion by addressing the issue of future changes in the criminal justice field and relate these changes to the development and the implementation of community crime prevention techniques.

The Police Perspective

Patrick Murphy

We're here this morning talking about involvement of citizens in crime control because crime continues to be a problem of great concern to all Americans.

We must recognize the value of citizen involvement. This is particularly the case for the police, the largest component of the criminal justice system. It's estimated that the cost of policing constitutes 70% of the total cost of crime control, with 20% for corrections and the remaining 10% for courts and prosecution and some ancillary services. So the police are the big part of the system; and the police part is the part most dependent upon citizen involvement.

One of the reasons why the police have not involved citizens sufficiently in my opinion, is that we continue to follow the military model.

Of course, the concept of democratic policing is a relatively new concept. It's only a few hundred years old and it hasn't been perfected; although in England and some other countries the quality of policing is quite high. The concept is one that is slow to reach us but the concept of democratic policing is, frankly, that the people will police themselves.

If you look at the kind of policing we have in our communities and try to apply that test to it, you may quickly observe that the people aren't policing themselves very much. For instance, one of the complaints that we've heard over and over again from the so-called ghetto communities of the country where Blacks or Puerto Ricans or Mexican-Americans live is that the police come in as representatives of the power structure of the government and they function like armies of occupation. No matter how overstated that may be, I think we'll all have to agree that in large parts of the city where the population is more than 90 or 95% black and the police department is more than 90 or 95% white, in that part of the city

we have a problem. The civil service system is certainly another contributing factor in this issue of minority recruitment.

We see, then, something less than the democratic ideal of policing and we see a lack of adequate representation of minorities in our police departments. These things contribute to some degree to the lack of citizen participation.

Another reason why police departments have resisted proposals to involve citizens more is that, like all bureaucrats, police are happier doing their job on their own. And they're not particularly pleased with the notion of having a citizen volunteer come into the police station and snoop around, as the police might see it, looking over their shoulders as to what they are doing. They are not altogether happy about the proposition that it would be useful to have citizens patrol with police, either as a second or third rider in a police car or on a foot patrol accompanying an officer. And the police are not comfortable having citizens patrol on their own without police officers.

So in city after city, we've seen resistance to bringing citizens into the department as volunteers of one kind or another. And the police have tended to be slow in using citizens in other ways. For instance, in New York City a few years ago, we began a program called the Block-Watchers; a very successful program, especially in the minority neighborhoods of the city where crime is at its highest. Crime has always been at its highest, and it continues to be, where we see the social and economic problems of the society: poverty, unemployment, racial discrimination, bad housing and the rest of it. In those parts of the city, the department's Block-Watch Program calls upon citizens to observe suspicious activity and to come to the local police station for a few hours one day or evening for a very brief course of instruction as to how they could rapidly report to the police any criminal or suspicious activities. Not only was the program quite successful in providing to the police information about criminal activity, but we thought we could see an almost measurable increase in the citizen spirit of cooperation with the police department.

Let me say another word as to why some police departments have resisted bringing citizens into police departments and involving them more with the day-to-day work of the department—it's the problem of corruption. Corruption is not an East Coast phenomenon or a Mid-West phenomenon; it is a United States phenomena. During the past six to twelve months, I don't think any state in the Union has avoided some kind of police corruption scandal and/or corruption scandal in other parts of the criminal justice system. I suppose it's kind of obvious on its face that if there is a problem of corruption of any significance in the police department, there will probably be resistance to any citizen involvement with the department because it could cramp the style of some people.

Now, the police cannot do the job alone. It takes a team, as some of the public relations talk has put it—the citizen and the police working together. Obviously, the police are very dependent upon citizens for reporting crimes, for reporting suspicious activities, for being willing to appear as witnesses in cases and to just be supportive of the police.

By being supportive I mean to understand the police and to cooperate with them. I don't mean it necessarily in the sense that the bumper sticker says, "Support your Local Police and Keep Them Independent." In fac

"Give me enough police officers and I'll reduce crime." Their assumption is that putting more police officers out on patrol would reduce crime. And as you probably know, the great effort to putting more police officers on the streets occurs in the nation's capital. That's where the federal government's great effort is being implemented. Washington, D.C. now has six and one-half police per thousand population. The police department was increased 65% in size during the first two years of the Nixon administration. Those of us in police work like to kid Jerry Wilson, the great Chief in Washington, and tell him he has wall-to-wall cops. But, they still have a very high crime rate, one of the highest in the country.

So the experiment in Kansas City was intended to test this assumption that by putting more police on routine patrol, crime could be reduced. And if the final results indicate that routine patrol does not have the impact most of us in police work thought it did have, then it raises many questions for us. One question revolves around the fact that the police function is a very expensive function, probably the most costly function of most cities. I am not suggesting for a minute that, when these final results come out and you read about them, you cut the size of your police department but it does raise questions about how better to use police officers and specifically the officers on patrol.

My own view of it is that the routine patrol concept is not valid (it's part of the military concept) but that the officer doing street work—the officer in uniform or the marked police car—will be much more valuable if a share of his time is spent in interacting with citizens, in introducing himself to the people, in learning the community.

Many of you have read about the team policing program and experiments that are under way in the country. Most of these team policing programs have these concepts. First, that it makes sense to assign police officers to one neighborhood and, as far as possible, keep them in that one neighborhood. Second, to involve the police officers with the citizens as much as possible because the officers will then be much more effective. They will receive more information, they will get greater cooperation from the citizens and they will be much more effective in controlling, preventing, and reducing crime and in providing the many, many other services that the police provide for citizens. Incidentally, more than 80% of the time of the police is spent in providing service rather than in enforcing the law. But much of that 80% of the time is devoted to activities that do have an impact on crime prevention.

As these new models of policing and patrolling are experimented with, it is my belief that we will see police work become more effective; we will see the police more acceptable to all citizens; and we will see an increase in citizen participation and cooperation which I think are essential ingredients to good crime patrol.

The Citizen Perspective

Oliver Lofton

I'd like to thank the National League of Cities for inviting me here and giving me the opportunity to share some of my thoughts and observations. I don't know how many answers we'll be able to arrive at today but one thing is for sure: we are certainly in the midst of one of the most serious problems facing this country—that of crime and its potential prevention.

My first observation is on the name of this seminar—Community Crime Prevention and the Local Official. Now this title might seem to suggest that community crime prevention was what was left after a thorough treatment of the problem by the police, the courts, the correctional institutions and the city halls. But I think that if that were to be gleaned from the title, then we would be failing to recognize the essential dynamic: the criminal justice system itself is not a "separate part of the community" but is a part of that total community and exists to serve that community; and not the other way around. And I begin with that kind of an outlook as an approach to the whole issue of community crime prevention.

I would define "community" as that community which is necessary to effectively combat and prevent crime, as the broad encompassing prospective of the family, the town, the state, the nation, with all of the criminal justice institutions in assistance. I also recognize that it is popular to use the term "community" to mean the minority community.

I think that what we first have to recognize is that it is impossible for the minority community, or any other segment of the total community or the formal criminal justice system, to promulgate anything approaching a meaningful crime prevention program. This is true because, from a sociological and psychological point of view, the total community is responsible in the final analysis for the crime that exists in society.

Now this is not to say that a society, or the total community with all of its institutions and groups, can effectively eliminate all crime. I don't believe in such a societal utopia. Some individuals will commit deviant antisocial behavior simply because they are individuals. And when I say crimes or deviant antisocial behavior, I mean antisocial behavior that has a victim.

So the total community is responsible for the crime that exists within its structure. It is the total community that sets the opportunity, or lack of opportunity, for positive self-image development through access to the mechanisms for the delivery of the goods and services that society can render. A negative self-image developed through nonequal access to opportunity will, in my judgment, produce antisocial criminal behavior in one form or another.

Now this is not to say that all criminal behavior is related to this variable of negative self-image. However, I do believe that a substantial amount of such behavior is so related. Therefore, one of the ways for the total community to significantly reduce or prevent crime is to make sure that the idealistic concept of equal opportunity becomes a reality. I'd just like to quote, if I might, from the National Crime Commission in its report entitled *The Challenge of Crime in the Free Society*.

> The Commission finds that America must translate its well-founded alarm about crime into social action that will prevent crime. It has no doubt whatever that the most significant action that can be taken against crime is action designed to eliminate slums and ghettos, to improve education, to provide jobs, to make sure that every American is given the oppor-

tunity and the freedoms that will enable him to assume his responsibilities. We will not have dealt effectively with crime until we have alleviated the conditions that stimulate it. To speak of controlling crime only in terms of the work of the police, the courts, the correctional apparatus, is to refuse to face the facts that widespread crime implies a widespread failure by society as a whole.

Now another way to reduce or prevent crime in this country is for the total community to insist that the criminal justice system redefine what is in fact a crime. And the redefinition or the definition suggested by others which I would embrace and offer is, "behavior that is deviant and which has a specific victim or a clearly deleterious effect upon the total society." While I can see some imprecision on this definition, I think that it is better than the current one employed by the criminal justice system. This redefinition would decriminalize such activities as gambling, prostitution and marijuana use when engaged in by adults. One of the ways to reduce crime, in other words, is to redefine what is in fact crime.

It can be said without fear of much contradiction that in most communities across the country the relationship between the citizens and the police is less than satisfactory. This problem is accentuated and is most acute, in the urban areas. I think that this negative relationship between the police and the people is one of the most critical factors militating against an effective crime prevention program being inaugurated in those communities. So it doesn't do much good to talk about specific programs or projects to be undertaken to improve citizen participation in crime prevention without first dealing with the attitudes of the average urban citizen toward the police and vice versa.

Community crime prevention depends to a very large extent upon a healthy attitude existing between the people and the police. It depends upon a high level of confidence and trust that the people have in their police. As long as the confidence and trust level remains low, the people will frequently not notify the police of situations that require enforcement or prevention. And the public will avoid involvement in or interfering with criminal conduct.

Here's an example of what I'm talking about. During a recent trip to Los Angeles, I picked up the paper and read about one of the efforts in community crime prevention. It involved a team of plain clothes black police officers working out of a store-front center in Los Angeles. The center functioned as a mini-police station. But there was no writing on the building or on the windows to indicate that the building was a police station. It did have a mural painted over the door which depicted a black police officer shaking hands with what would obviously be described as one of the black community residents.

The long and the short of the article was an interview with the officers who manned that center. They related the fact that the center was enjoying minimal success because the people were apparently hostile and suspicious of the officers. And this hostility, this suspicion, this lack of trust existed even though these officers were black, in plain clothes and functioning in this low-profile and helpful manner in that community.

I think that this example of a minimally successful community program, or crime prevention program, is reflective of the results of most such programs. What I'm really attempting to say here is that they are really band-aid efforts which deal with the symptoms of crime and potential criminal behavior and not with the root causes. Now this is not to say that such efforts at segmented community crime prevention should be discontinued, but it does suggest that the expectation level for success should be kept within a realistic parameter of evaluation.

We will not have a very successful segmented community crime prevention program unless and until the total society, or in the very broadest sense, "the community," deals effectively with removing the root causes of crime that I have alluded to earlier in this discussion—poor housing, unemployment, discrimination, and lack of equal upward mobility opportunity. My experience in the lower socioeconomic level or element of the minority community leads me to conclude that they perceive the police, just as Mr. Murphy indicated, as the enforcers of an establishment of which they, the people, are not a part. As long as this negative perception exists, there will be but minimal cooperation between the police and that segment of the population whose cooperation is essential to community crime prevention.

Now, I recognize that I have not dealt here this morning with specific crime prevention programs but this omission has been conscious and purposeful. I believe that our energies and our attention should be directed toward the removal, and stimulation of the removal, of the root causes of most criminal behavior. That is the most effective method or approach to crime prevention.

To summarize, I have attempted to make four points. They are: (1) community crime control programs will enjoy minimal success until the root causes of most criminal behavior is removed; (2) there is a direct connection between the socioeconomic level of people and their cooperation with the police in any effort at community crime prevention; that is, the lower the socioeconomic level, the less cooperation; (3) in order to reduce or prevent the high level of crime we should decriminalize certain acts which are now classified as crimes; and (4) the total society must accept the responsibility for crime prevention and not attempt to relegate that responsibility solely to the criminal justice system.

A Future Perspective

Joseph F. Coates

There is a widespread tendency to bad-mouth crime. I think to limit your perspective to that is unfortunate and misleading. After all crime is a source of fun, a means of profit, a source of occupation, and a mainstay of entertainment.

Many of you probably either see or read yourself to sleep with some criminal activity. Crime is a mainstay of daily news. It's a source of employment for some half million people, including a significant fraction of the 317,000 lawyers in the country, 20,000 people in the judiciary, and 125,000 people in corrections.

Crime is also, unfortunately, the source of much misfortune. On the other hand, it is a very human activity. What other kind of collective activity is there which so well reflects those most human characteristics of envy, lust, greed, avarice, and fear? The propensity to crime is part of our human nature and it's not likely to be dramatically changed until we learn to dramatically change people.

There is, however, a widespread hope or belief that somehow or other criminal behavior can be changed.

There is an even more widespread belief that public action, particularly through the implementation of its strong arm, the police, can have an influence on the rate and nature of crime. I think the latter is a particularly false assumption. Mr. Murphy has made the point: the notion that the police can have a primary impact on crime is almost certainly false.

By the nature of crime the police cannot have a primary effect on its characteristics, its nature, its frequency, or its location. One doesn't have to go to Washington, with its wall-to-wall police, for evidence. Looking at the data across the country in more conventional police departments, there is no clear relationship between the number of police per capita and the rate of crime.

The converse ought not be accepted as true. As we've learned from the Kerner Commission and other studies, the police can have an extremely deteriorative effect on community relations and can be a factor promoting antisocial behavior. So the police are not an indifferent factor in regard to crime. It's just that they can't be a major factor in reducing it.

Before we get into any serious discussions of the factors influencing crime, it is important to turn to the number magic associated with crime, because that number magic is a major source of political game playing, of hysteria, and of misleading articles in newspapers.

Virtually nobody knows what the crime rate is in his community. One of the few reliable studies, the 1966 National Opinion Research Center Study, showed that many major classes of crime are committed at a rate far higher than that reported to the formal system. For example, something like only 30% of forcible rapes are reported through criminal justice channels.

This under-reporting leads almost to a paradox when coupled with a long-term trend in our society, the trend toward middle-classification. Everyone is becoming middle-class: the rich, the poor, and the middle-class. One of the characteristics of the middle-class is that they report things and use public systems. So as we promote the long-term social objective of middle-classifying America, we will find this hidden figure of crime becoming more public. The irony if not the paradox is: as we become more middle-class, all things remaining equal, we can expect an increase in the reported rates of crime.

Take another feature associated with the number magic of crime. It has to do with the age cohorts of our crime-prone cities. It's well known that the ages 16–24 are crime-prone ages in our population. Well over half the crimes are committed by that age group. And yet there's nothing we can do about that age cohort pattern because we are experiencing a postwar baby boom which is coming to a culmination. With no increase in turpitude, with no increase in moral deterioration, just more young people, one would automatically expect an increase in crime. Similarly, as this surge in the population ages, one should expect a decrease in crime. One should avoid the temptation to attribute this to actions of the police or politicians or any other external variable.

Another factor related to the number magic in age cohorts is the fact that we are an aging population: people are living longer and that surge of youth will eventually become a geriatric explosion. The result will be, not a wave of ancient criminals, but a very large number of new victims of predatory behavior.

But look at the long-term implication. For the last two generations, we have tended towards smaller and smaller families, what are known as nuclear families: Mom, Pop, and a couple of kids. The old folks—the aunts, uncles, friends and lodgers—are no longer with us. Well, one can anticipate that, if the aged get pushed into living by themselves, they are going to be more easy prey for crime.

Your police cannot have a primary influency here. But you can, if you alert the community, your state government, and Washington with the need to take some basic actions in our society to reintegrate the aged into family units. Whether those family units are geriatric communes or foster grandparent programs or more basic structural changes to make young people want to have old people around, I don't know. But if you don't get to the structural basis, in twenty years you're going to be the inheritors of the geriatric crime explosion.

I want to talk with you this morning about what I call structural factors, influencing the future of crime. By a structural factor, I mean something that is built into our society which has the characteristic of being stable, relatively slow changing, and is a major influence on an activity. Examples outside the field of crime of the structural elements in our society are: right-hand driving down the street; deference to women; four-year high school for everyone. These factors may be institutionalized or mandated by law or customary, or they may be explicit or implicit in our world. The structural elements are principle determinants of the makeup and characteristics of our society. Let us look at some of them in relation to the future of crime.

The movement I spoke of earlier, towards middle-class attitudes and the general middle-classification of American society, is the central structural factor which you ought not lose sight of.

One of the other characteristics of America is a kind of cultural homogeneity. That's not to say that we have a classless society, but rather to say something different. This room here in San Juan could just as well be in Tacoma, Washington; New York City, or Arizona; it could be in any part of the United States, and you couldn't tell where you were by any of the things that surround you: The same vinyl rugs, the same chairs, the same food, the same waste of electric energy, the same drapes, the same ties, clothes, hats, haircuts. Even regional accents are rapidly disappearing in the United States, as we become more mobile and culturally homogeneous.

What goes along with that cultural homogeneity is a unique opportunity for experimentation. The same problems literally repeat over and over again, which opens up an opportunity for action taken in one city to have an influence or an effect, good or bad, positive or negative, throughout the country. So this is another feature you ought not to lose sight of. There is a real opportunity for information transfer that didn't exist 50 years ago.

Along with this homogeniety and middle-class attitude is the great politicization of many issues that until quite recently no one would ever have thought of politicizing. Consumer affairs and environmental impacts are just two of the most recent ones; civil rights was an earlier one; and women's liberation is one that will be with us for quite a long time. This politicization of new issues will have a primary effect on your political future and the organization and management of your local government.

Now let's look at a different structural factor: the reclassification of antisocial behavior which has been going on in America for well over a generation. Alcoholism, drug addiction, even many classes of violent behavior are no longer seen by many as matters of moral corruption. Rather they are seen as the consequences of environment, of genetic defect, of a variety of factors outside the control of both the individual and, to a substantial extent, of society as it's now structured.

The result in the short run is going to be a custodial crisis. As one shifts the auspices from criminal justice to medicine, one would hope that the doctors had something better to offer than the police and the judges. But the simple fact is, they don't. So, the custodial problem will still be there; who's going to collect, handle, manage, organize, and take care of these people under shifting ground rules. If you don't integrate this development into your planning, there will be a lot of trouble ahead in the short run. In the longer run, it will undoubtedly stimulate the search for better means of rehabilitation, prevention, and control of antisocial behavior.

Another long-term factor in our society is the redistribution of population, particularly the movement from countryside to city, and the immigration of foreign population into the United States. We have a jargon term for the result: culture shock. We know the movement of rural people to the cities, and the movement of alien people into American cities, tends to create dislocation across generations. The dislocations are such that the canons of behavior that mother and father brought with them are inappropriate for city life. Young people very quickly perceive this and, in an attempt to emulate the life of the city, they get caught in all sorts of difficulties, many of which end up in crime.

It will be a continuing factor in our society. It is no comfort, but instructive, to see this happening in Europe now. For the first time in England there are books coming out with titles like "Black Power and the Police." In Northern Europe there are riots involving Greek and Turkish immigrant laborers. It is important to recognize that these factors are outside the control of any particular local police authority. Something more deep-seated needs to be done to deal with deep-seated causes.

Another feature of our society, however, is the rejection of information and knowledge by organizations. As public officials you probably are as guilty of it as anyone. Let's illustrate this historically. In 1938 the Department of Agriculture did a study on the mechanization of cotton agriculture and its consequences. The study effectively predicted the mass displacement of black farm workers in the south. It only missed by a small degree predicting the exodus to the northern cities with the consequent problems we've known for the last 20 years.

What happened to the report? It was ignored as a basis for long term planning. That's rejection of knowledge, with a vengeance. We had in our hands the kind of knowledge that would have undercut, or have lead to more effective management of what is a central problem to the largest cities in the United States today.

An interesting article appeared in the New York *Daily News* sometime during the summer. It was reported that a group of New York policemen beat nine homosexuals. You might say, "What's new?" What is new is that it was at baseball. Structural change in attitudes and values will continue to affect job expectations and performance.

The movement towards decriminalization, particularly decriminalization of sexual crimes and gambling crimes, is a major trend in our society. I noticed that nobody protested the casino upstairs. Nobody was particularly taken aback by the fact that gambling is legal here and becoming legal in many places in the States.

The effect of this decriminalization on the criminal justice system will be quite interesting. For one thing it ought to free up labor, and secondly it ought to reduce corruption, the perennial bane of police departments. If for no other reason, moderating corruption would be a major reason for wanting to reinstitutionalize prostitution and gambling.

But reinstitutionalization introduces its own problems. Let me illustrate. If you really want to get a hook into crime and deal with gambling, you have to come to grips with the problems of penny-ante gambling. In the slums it's not fifty cent to three dollar bets, it's nickel and dime bets. Yet the labor force structure in the United States wouldn't permit you to pay $2.25 an hour to a local runner. Somebody will have to develop a labor schedule to permit hiring large numbers of runners at a rate commensurate with the one they are now earning. What that effectively means is that they may have to be hired by the civil service. In a few years, you may see the hooker and the corner bookmaker join us in the civil service, and enjoy the same employment rights and privileges of other organized labor.

The physical environment is another structural factor influencing crime. I'm sure you would herald as a great step forward anything which could promise with some reliability to bring about a twenty or twenty-five percent reduction in crime in a given community. Oscar Newman has effectively done this in some of the high-rise multiple slums in New York. He has analyzed the relationship of buildings and crime, and has shown how one can reorganize the physical structure so as to have a major and dramatic effect on the incidence of crime. Any public official who permits a housing development to be built in his city without drawing on the kinds of evidence that Newman has generated is almost derelict in his duty. In Newman's work we have a major structural factor that is just beginning to be adequately explored. But if most cities roll along their customary way, city planning will continue to build criminogenic structures.

The central determinant of the whole future of our society, and the factor from which all these others I have mentioned flow, is technology. And the two technologies which will have the most dramatic effect on crime are transportation and telecommunications. Take the case of skyjacking. It was worldwide news, millions of people knew about it. An epidemic— one could have plotted it just like an epidemic of measles—was initiated around the country and around the world.

Technology, however, offers major new opportunities for crime that are largely outside the present span of authority of local officials. For example, in San Francisco there's the Bay Area Rapid Transit system. As an exercise, a group of Cal-Tech students figured out some 15 ways to cheat the system and to get free transportation. What happens when trained people are really motivated to undertake crime? What happens when we use electronic banking? What happens when every supermarket, department store, and drug store in your community is wired into the bank and tied to credit cards? You're going to have new kinds of crime which your whole structure will be totally unprepared to deal with if it does not plan ahead.

Let me illustrate another kind of technological crime potential that could result from most benign intentions. The British corrections system is planning to introduce a sexual depressant into its prisons. As you know, homosexual activity is a major problem in jail; and one would think that something that suppresses sexual desire would relieve custodial problems and open up opportunities for more constructive rehabilitative activities in jail. Well, aside from challenging that argument, what happens when this cute little product gets onto the black market? What happens with every cuckolded husband or betrayed wife? What happens when you have an irate, discontented junior employee? What happens when the hellraisers of the world get hold of it? The opportunity to generate a new kind of antisocial or criminal behavior as a byproduct of what is a benignly-intended development, is the sort of thing that you should be sensitive to.

Let me quickly tick off some of the characteristics of the criminal justice system itself which are impediments to effective action and planning for its new future.

First, there is an almost complete present-orientation. I know of only three papers in the criminal justice literature that have "future" in their titles. This is one rough measure of how the system is locked to the present.

The second issue is the social class structure in the criminal justice system. It's an uncongenial subject for Americans to discuss, but the class origins of lawyers, judges, policemen, and corrections officers may be a major inhibitor of change in the system. In the police world, one finds a peculiar brotherhood attitude, an attitude of closure, or secretiveness. This works against openness and receptiveness, not just to citizen participation, but to new modes of action.

Another feature of the criminal justice system, and of our society, is bureaucratization. You can't get away from bureaucracy, and the problem is to learn to control it in new ways. Any mature bureaucracy, and they mature in about three years, has a number of characteristics. They do not primarily address the function for which they ostensibly exist: bureaucracies instead exist predominantly to perpetuate themselves, to keep themselves safe, funded, and adequately employed. They reject new information. They have no memory. They have no adequate reward system. And they tend in general to shy away from bad news, or if it is thrust upon them, to go into paralysis or worse.

They also tend to be susceptible to a condition I call "functional lying." That's different from the kind of lying a ten-year-old experiences. The ten-year-old says, "No, I didn't take the cookies." You slap him, and that's the end of that. He learns he'll be punished if he steals a cookie. But the bureaucracies are different. They functionally lie, very often because one end of the system does not know what the other end of the system is doing. Then the system retracts into its shell; it denies that it lied; it ends up saying, "we didn't do it, and we promise never to do it again," rather than facing the issue squarely. Police brutality is an excellent issue in which to explore this phenomenon.

An adequate reward structure is essential to effectively influence bureaucracy. Just take the police department in your community. Do any of you have a police department that could be characterized as having a special, or an unusual, unique, or particularly effective reward system for effective performance? In a room of 100 people, there will be one or two who claim that they do have such a system. Yet, the reward system is the one way in which change can be brought about in a stable bureaucracy.

The way to challenge a bureaucrat on this issue is to ask him the following questions: Do you have a system for rewarding effective performance? If he says, "No," you proceed in one direction. If he says, "Yes," then you lay it to him in the following way: "Name the last five people you have rewarded and tell me precisely what they did." That usually sets him into a trance.

The lack of reward structures is directly related to the general crisis in authority in our society. Nobody should fully trust a public official, because by and large the public experience is that some public officials up and down the bureaucracy are not trustworthy in performing their duties, i.e., their primary focus is not on understanding and doing their jobs. If you doubt this, let me suggest the following experiment—if you have the gall to try it.

Get a relative—a cousin, an uncle, somebody who is not publicly known—and have him register a complaint with the police, have him try to have the garbage picked up, have her report a rape. Make ten routine challenges on your bureaucratic system, anywhere, the way a citizen would, and see what happens. Try to get information. Try to put yourself in the position of an ordinary citizen and you'll see some of the second-rate aspects of the system your community is undoubtedly functioning under. And that can only be changed through the manipulation of reward systems.

Question and Answer Session

QUESTION: Mr. Murphy, you made a statement that crime control is not a local level responsibility. Where do you think that responsibility lies?

MURPHY: In its 1967 report, the President's Crime Commission referred to the need for each of the 50 states to serve a more active role as the coordinator and standard setter of the crime control system within each of the states. In the six years since that report, I think we've made little progress.

The reason why crime is so bad in the United States and why the crime control system is not working very well, in my humble opinion is that we have permitted the states to get off the hook all these years. Policing in the United States is fragmented by any account. There are between 25,000 and 40,000 police departments in the United States. They don't work. They ain't going to work. Crime control problems and policing are going to be very serious problems for us until we find out how to set standards for this crazy-quilt pattern of policing.

I'll try to be diplomatic and not step on toes, because I know police consolidation is a very delicate issue. The Standards and Goals Commission, as you probably know, just proposed that in a few years there no longer be police departments of fewer than 10 people. Most of the police departments in the country of course have less than 10 employees in them.

Aside from the consolidation issue, federal money, LEAA money, should be forcing the states to accept responsibility for setting standards for policing within each state, for providing those centralized services that the small department can't provide economically (training, laboratories, communications, and other functions) and to make the whole thing work together as a system.

We can think about crime control as a sort of production line. The people who feed into the system are the police when they make their arrests. The police tend to deny that they have discretion. Well, believe me, they have very broad and powerful discretion in deciding what they are going to arrest people for and what they are not going to arrest people for. And that's how the process begins. And after that, the district attorney has his function. And he has an awful lot of discretion; he has a lot of hidden discretion. He has corruption problems, just as the police force, the judges, and the corrections system have corruption problems.

Now the only way we can make this begin to function as a system is to have the states accept more responsibility in setting standards for all parts of the system and in developing coordinating mechanisms to make the system work in each jurisdiction.

But what's happening? The President proposed taking LEAA out of its present mold and putting it into revenue sharing early this year, and Congress reversed that. Well, I guess if I were the President, I wouldn't want to be blamed for the crime control problem. The states don't want strings on that federal money because they don't want to accept that loser of a problem that you're all familiar with. The bane of existence of so many mayors in recent years is the crime problem. So it continues to be stuck at the local level; maybe you feel that's the way it should be. Why should we give it up? Well, it's going to be a loser for about 10 or 15 more years at least, and I think you ought to share the responsibility.

I don't want a national police force. I attended Mr. Hoover's National Academy, I learned there that we don't want a national police force. But we do need to change the structure. It has to be reorganized because, with this terrible fragmentation both geographically and functionally, it's not working. We need some new mechanisms and I think they should be at the state level.

QUESTION: I address my question to Mr. Coates. You mentioned a reward system of some sort for police officers. Can you suggest some things for which we might reward them and what would be a typical reward?

COATES: The answer is obvious: Ask them. But let me illustrate the problem. This may be an apocryphal story. A man took over a U.S. Employment Service office. As you know, the U.S. Employment Service tries to employ the employable and the marginally employable. He decided he would do a better job than anybody else in the system. And within three months his office had the best record of any U.S. Employment office in the country. That was his downfall, because he immediately attracted the attention of the system. "What about this guy? He's got the best system going." So they came to the office and questioned him about his methods. He had set up a reward system. For every four people that a member of his staff got employed for three months or more, the staffer got a day off. Now, the first thing that the investigators said was not, "Great job! How could we institutionalize this and make it work across the country?" Their response was, "It's illegal, cut it out!" After a few months his office drifted back to having an ordinary record.

The problem is, find out what's important to the people who are employed in the system, determine the goals that you want to implement, and set up a reward system that will relate those two. The people in the system will often tell you what they want. Ceremonial functions, handing out certificates, and so on, don't amount to anything. The reward has to be tangible, or something that's negotiable, or something that's held in esteem and prestige or has psychic value. It should give the man a capability he didn't have before. It might involve a trip to Washington to shake the hand of the President, it might involve a trip to Puerto Rico, or it might involve a moose hunt to Canada, or new freedom on the job, or an opportunity to try other new things.

The other side of the problem is, how do you measure what you are going to be rewarding? If I were a public official, I would use one social scientist's self-anchoring scale system as a way of measuring performance. It takes a minute to describe how the system works. You survey the community and you ask each person three questions. "Imagine a scale of zero to ten. With zero as the worst possible life you can have and ten as the best possible life, where are you now?" He may answer, "Four." "Where were you five years ago?" "Three." "Where do you plan to be, expect to be, five years from now?" He may say three, seven, two or whatever. That sense of movement up or down is a measure of optimism. You can apply the same concept to the problems of sanitation in the neighborhood; to interactions with the police; to attitudes toward the mayor. It's a system which gives you real time measures of what people feel and their sense of change. This could be tied to a reward system.

QUESTION: What are the standards by which you determine who gets the reward? Specifically, with police work, are we talking about number of arrests, number of arrests which lead to conviction, or a decline in the crime rate? And can't these standards, crime statistics, be manipulated in the reporting?

COATES: The question was, "How do you know what to reward." First of all one has to get better data than just incidence of crime. There's no reason why a local community can't conduct its own opinion research study on a continuing basis. In other words develop the real figures on crime in your community as opposed to the official figures. That sort of thing incidentally will put you on the map if you're interested in being put on the map. With more objective data on the rate of crime, or with the self-anchoring scale technique to assess the responsiveness and satisfaction of the community with your performance, you can then address the question of reward.

But I think you've already lost half the value in the concept by seeking to routinize it. The thing missing from most local government is any spontaneity, any vitality. There's no reason why the reward system itself cannot be shifted from year to year and person to person. The whole notion of breaking out of the bureaucratic approach to rewards, penalties, and form-filling, ought to be central to any good reward system.

Basically, you can go back to the people you are trying to reward, and have them innovate the kind of awards that would be appropriate to them. On the first pass, you're going to get dull answers. But once you make it clear that you're going to innovate, and provide substantial and significant rewards, the departments, the courts, and corrections themselves will tell you what would comprise good rewards. My answer is not avoiding the question, but rather is in the spirit in which the proposal was put forward. Go to the people you are rewarding to find out what makes them run.

QUESTION: If gambling is legalized, who will run it? Also, wouldn't legalized gambling lead to economic and social harms.

LOFTON: If we legalize gambling, the idea is that the state or the local government would then run the gambling. In that instance, there would not be any built-in protections against excessive gambling. I happen to think that if a person wants to gamble, he should be allowed to, irrespective of what the local officials feel is best for that particular person. I think it smacks a bit too much of paternalism to say to a family, simply because they are at the lower economic level, that they can't gamble or that certain restrictions have to be placed on when they gamble. This just perpetuates the dichotomy between the "in" persons and the "out" persons, which in itself facilitates a certain kind of antisocial behavior that produces crime.

You know most states have race tracks, which is a form of gambling, but it requires a car to get there and a certain amount of income to play the horses. But when a person in the midst of the ghetto who has a dollar or a quarter, plays single action numbers, this suddenly becomes a crime. And that is hypocritical. I, for one, would not be at all in favor of putting restrictions as to who could gamble and who couldn't.

MURPHY: Let me follow up on that, as it relates to organized crime. Millions of Americans are gambling every day. And organized crime is getting richer and richer and more and more powerful until now it's become almost a subgovernment in parts of the country. I certainly agree with Mr. Lofton that it's the height of hypocrisy to say that when you step inside the fence of a race track it's moral, but when you're outside that fence or you can't afford to get there, it's immoral. This is the kind of hypocrisy that troubles us not only in gambling, but in our approaches to the drug problem as well.

QUESTION: I think you missed my question. I wasn't saying that the poor shouldn't gamble and the rich should. And I don't think I can go along with the philosophy that says, because everybody is doing something, it's right. What I'm concerned about is that in gambling there are always some people that are much sharper than others. There always are sharpies who systematically separate the gullible and the innocent from their money. A lot of people are hurt by gambling. Paychecks are lost and money is embezzled. I'm concerned about the innocent person, the victim, and there are victims.

QUESTION: I'd like to get a reaction from Mr. Murphy. There's been some attention given to protecting poor and powerless people as it relates to gambling and the victimless crimes. I would like to ask your reaction, not necessarily to decriminalizing, but to reprioritizing, our thinking so as to really protect these people. For instance, institutional discrimination, consumer relations, the relationships that poor people and powerless people have to landlords, and to supermarket owners who jack the prices up, just before welfare checks are given out. We should concentrate on these crimes, not waste time arresting gamblers, pimps, and prostitutes.

MURPHY: I don't think the police can ignore organized crime, although it's frustrating to the police administrator to put only two, three, five percent of his resources into organized crime control. But, as you know, they are the greatest of exploiters. Some of them own the grocery stores and the appliance stores in the poor neighborhoods and exploit the people in many ways. This is another example of the kind of law that is almost unenforced, the consumer fraud.

In minority neighborhoods in city after city across this country, many of the people believe that it is a failure of the police and a part of police corruption that the consumer laws are not being enforced. Now the fact of the matter is that most police departments try to avoid responsibility for the enforcement of consumer laws because they are so overburdened with street crime, organized crime, delinquency, and other problems. Some prosecutors have done the job. But to generalize, the consumer laws are not enforced in this country.

It's no wonder that there is frustration and hostility toward the government, the establishment, and the police. It is the police officer, the only visible representative of the government in many places, who bears the resentment and the hostility for the failure of the general government and the whole society. This obviously suggests a need for more citizen involvement. When citizens become more involved, when they understand the problems of the police, they can be extremely valuable in communicating to other citizens that this isn't a police failure nor is it police corruption.

QUESTION: No one has mentioned the lifestyle of the family, which I think is a primary function of society. Now, I've worked with young people and I found the parents don't care half the time what they're doing. They're both working, they're not at home. The children only have a place to eat and a place to sleep. Now how do we, as officials, work to help them?

COATES: Let me suggest that practically everything you've done in the past is sterile. So we've got to start fresh. What's been done doesn't work, and one must look for new and innovative approaches. This ties back to a point I made earlier—that city officials tend to reject knowledge. For 40 years we've been doing studies on the source of delinquency. A fairly reliable corpus of knowledge is available that allows one to identify the crime-prone delinquent, the one who is going to become, so to speak, a full-time delinquent or criminal. And as you point out, it's the disruptive family behind this. Yet how many cities have a program of extracting the child from that family at a very early age, and not putting him in an institution, but putting him in a foster family. The program should be well enough funded that that foster family not only is a good family, but one which has the incremental resources to take care of that kid and provide a new kind of environment for him. If I were setting up a delinquency program, I'd want to identify that six percent of the delinquents who are going to contribute 50 percent of the delinquent behavior and extract them from the system and put them in foster homes. Not on a three-month basis, but on a ten-year basis where they could acquire a whole new life.

The city official who can carry that one off will make his mark in the world. He will become a national figure of prestige and importance on the question of delinquency.

QUESTION: What the hell you talking about, pull them out of here and plug them over there? What are you thinking of, cattle? I'd like to know what your view of people is.

COATES: It's a common difficulty that one can't look past the term to the concept. Now, I think, as public officials, you have had a great deal of experience in pulling people out of a family. As public officials, you've been involved in sending tens, hundreds, and thousands of delinquents to reformatories, and in sending thousands of people to jail and to prison. That's pulling them out. I'm using the same kind of terms to suggest that it can be done differently. It can be done under different auspices with a different goal and intention. If you let the terminology stand in the way of the concept, then you've built up an obstacle to taking effective action. Now, would you prefer me to rephrase it in terms that would sound very genteel and very supportive? I can do that. Yet the fact is that we know how to identify with high reliability the high delinquency-prone child. We know that the methods of counseling and support now offered by local government doesn't work. The hope is to do something new, imaginative, and different.

QUESTION: I'd like comments on what effects plea bargaining and the removal of the death penalty have had on the increase in crime rates.

MURPHY: I think the death penalty change has had almost no impact because we had not been imposing the death penalty in this country for many years. Prior to that time we were imposing the death penalty only for a tiny fraction of all the crimes. So I don't have much confidence in the death penalty, although I think it's debatable in cases of premeditated murder, murder of police officers and corrections officers.

Plea bargaining is certainly one of our problems. People are not going to trial for their crimes. To some extent, this reflects the prosecutor's use of discretion. Of course, police administrators use discretion, too. The police could make five or ten times as many arrests as they now make if they enforced all the laws. Obviously all police departments attempt to arrest murderers, rapists, robbers, and burglars, but some don't try too hard to arrest auto thieves. When we get down to the misdemeanors— petit larceny, shoplifting, disorderly conduct, and public drunkenness— there are great varieties in the policies of various jurisdictions.

Plea bargaining is also a symptom of the breakdown in our crime control system. We're not spending enough money on crime control. With all of its weaknesses, with all of its waste, inefficiencies, and lack of integrity, we're still not spending enough money. I think it's interesting that in the past year, the Committee for Economic Development, a blue-chip organization of businessmen and educators, proposed that the federal government provide half the support of our crime control system. To have this radical view coming from a conservative quarter is probably a symptom of the frustration about crime.

LOFTON: With respect to the question of plea bargaining I take a diametrically opposed view to Mr. Murphy's. I don't think plea bargaining has had much effect on crime rates. But let me make some other observations about it.

First, the police discretion Mr. Murphy mentioned sometimes affects the prosecutor's decision to prosecute: the question is whether there is the evidence to prove the crime for which the police officer charged the individual.

Plea bargaining usually takes place when a person is charged with a more serious offense. The defense attorney discusses it with the prosecutor and he in turn discusses it with the judge, to determine whether or not there will be a plea of guilty to a lesser offense. We talk about congestion that now exists in the courts, but if there was no plea bargaining, the courts would just be astronomically overrun. I don't have any specific statistics, but I'll hazard to say the judicial budget would have to be doubled or tripled. I don't think that plea bargaining has a serious nondeterrent effect upon the future commission of a crime by a defendant.

MURPHY: Let me correct a wrong impression. I'm for plea bargaining but let me tell you that in New York City and in other cities the plea bargaining process is so used today by the criminal and the criminal lawyers, that they are expert at defeating the system. It is a revolving door, with the criminal going back out on the street over and over again. I'm not opposed to bargaining, but we need the resources to use it effectively and fairly. And we don't have them now.

QUESTION: What can be done about the discrimination against poor in relation to arrest and plea bargaining? Let's take the question of shoplifting. For the poor it's shoplifting and for the rich it's a fancy name. Another point: By and large there's a language barrier and other barriers that go with being poor. Under the bargaining system they simply parrot what is agreed upon by the prosecutor and a court-appointed attorney who doesn't see the client until it's time to go to court.

LOFTON: I would certainly echo that sentiment. This kind of representation should not be the case in our judicial process and I must admit that, in too many instances, it does take place. This is just another instance of economics dictating the kind and quality of justice in this country. But until basic things—poor housing, education, and so on—are dealt with, we are going to have double standards of treatment and of effective representation.

QUESTION: Your colleagues on the panel, Mr. Murphy, have mentioned the so-called "victimless" crimes. I'd like to hear your comments.

MURPHY: Certainly. Coates put his finger on a problem that plagues us in this country and that is the "pass a law" phenomenon. State legislators have a tendency to pass an awful lot of laws, and they never ask, "Can the police enforce them and where are the resources for enforcement?" So we have the traditional unenforceable law problem, gambling: twenty million Americans bet on football every week, all criminals, but they go on doing it. Prostitution is another kind of problem, marijuana, all the blue laws, Sunday closing, on and on ad infinitum. These are laws that the police can't possibly enforce even if they had five times the resources they now have. It doesn't make sense, and it causes a great disrespect for the police and government generally. We ought to decriminalize a lot of these things, especially the gambling. The criminal law is not a very good tool for controlling private morality.

QUESTION: We have started an innovative citizen participation program for predelinquents. But I sometimes get the feeling that the citizens aren't really supported by the police and probation departments. And then the citizens get discouraged. Any comments?

COATES: The question is, how do you deal with a situation in which the citizen isn't sure of his effectiveness or is put off by subtle threats like, "You'd better not let that bad kid out." I think that the response has to go back to the basics of the movement toward middle-class society in America and the fact that there are a large number of very well-intended people in the country, some of whom are businessmen, large numbers of whom are women. They get caught up in activities that reflect middle-class attitudes and middle-class myths. They fail to diagnose in sufficient depth what the problem is they are dealing with and where they can have effective leverage. As a result, enormous amounts of time and effort are squandered in peripheral, marginal, ineffective, guaranteed-second-rate, but benevolently intended, activities.

If I were a concerned citizen dealing with a probation authority I would want to know what their performance record is, what I would like them to do, and how, as a citizen, I could facilitate better rewards within that system. That would be a far more effective mode than attempting to provide ancillary, band-aid help.

The central dilemma is that you are dealing with a bureaucracy. In order to effect change in a bureaucracy, you must apply external pressure. You don't change them by cooperating with them; you don't change them by helping them; you don't change them by asking them what they want. You change bureaucracies by applying muscle to them. Muscle sometimes is money.; sometimes it's public display; sometimes its revelation. But you only initiate change in bureaucracy by external force.

QUESTION: What are your positions on the control of handguns?

MURPHY: My position is clear. I've testified a number of times before Congress on the need for national handgun control. I know it is a difficult and complex problem. One of the difficulties is that we have different laws in each of the 50 states. But, law enforcement is beginning to shift its position. Sheriff Pitchess of Los Angeles County, a life member of the National Rifle Association, is beginning to come out in favor of national gun control. So many police officers are being killed by handguns.

We're the only well-developed country in the world that doesn't have tight control on weapons, especially handguns. This so underlies our violent crime problem and the number of deaths in family quarrels and accidents that I think we have to begin to bring the possession of guns under control. But I admit that it's an emotional, complex, long-range problem.

LOFTON: I would certainly come down at the bottom line where Mr Murphy does—in favor of effective gun control legislation. At that same time, I also recognize the concern of citizens who feel that violent crimes are rampant and are uncontrollable by the criminal justice system. People feel that if guns are taken out of their hands, the guns are not going to be taken out of the criminals' hands, and they are going to be left defenseless. What is not recognized is that the very thing they want to utilize to protect themselves is the very instrument that precipitates many of the crimes about which they are concerned. We have come to a position in civilized society where we are going to have to live without these instruments of death and destruction.

COATES: I'm inclined to think that the handgun control issue is one so cloaked in middle-class miasma as to be essentially not worth any serious discussion here.

Along the lines of innovation, how many city officials with ghetto gun control problems have ever thought about setting up a shooting gallery? Don't ignore the central fact—guns are fun, they're associated with drama, with interest, and with entertainment. Ever think of going to IBM and having them generate a photo-electric marksman system? Set up something constructive whereby kids are brought in wholesale to learn what handguns are like, and to learn that a Saturday night special is dangerous, discharge their interest in shooting in a constructive public program. But the important point I want to make is the following: how many people in the room think that within the next 35 years, there's a fair chance of a coup d'etat or an attempted coup in the U.S.? You have one, two . . . well, if you ask a different group, it comes out as high as 50 or 60 per cent. I think one ought not to lose sight of a basic constitutional right, a safeguard to democracy, in the right of the citizenry to defend itself. One of the things the citizenry ultimately must be prepared to defend itself against, is its government. So let's not throw out the long-term benefits of an informed armed citizenry for short-term needs, probably miscast in terms of middle-class myths.

Learning Exercise

1.   Divide the class into seven equally numbered task forces. In turn, each of the task forces is to be assigned one of the following field survey missions: (1) youth service bureaus, (2) drug abuse, (3) employment, (4) education, (5) recreation, (6) religion, and (7) physical design of the cities. Each of the assigned missions is to be developed in terms of the present state-of-the-art of its programs in preventing crime. Hence, the task forces are to make on-site visits to the various centers that are responsible for providing such programs. Before visting the respective agencies, each task force should create a list of questions to be asked of the agency personnel. For example, one task force may be given the topic of "recreational programs that have either an intentional or indirect impact on crime prevention." A brief set of questions then should be generated by the group. Next, the task force should identify community recreation agencies (city, county, and private). Singularly or in pairs the task force members then visit three to five agencies in order to ascertain if there is a *concern* and *activity* devoted to the prevention of crime. Once the site visits have been completed, the task force should assemble and write a three-page "staff report" on what they discovered. Finally, each task force is to make a five-minute presentation to the entire class on their *findings, opinions,* and *recommended actions.*

Endnotes

1.   An example of this thinking is reflected in the article by George T. Hart, "Home Alert: Crime Prevention Through Police-Citizen Cooperation," *Crime Prevention Review* 1 (July, 1974), pp. 18–24.
2.   An expanded treatment of this subject can be found in *Marshaling Citizen Power Against Crime* (Washington, D.C.: Chamber of Commerce of the United States, 1970).

3. Herbert B. Newberg, "Building Local Citizen Alliances to Reduce Crime and Create a Fairer and More Effective Criminal Justice System," *Journal of Urban Law* 21 (February, 1972), p. 470.
4. Ibid., p. 81.
5. Ibid., pp. 79–80.
6. National Advisory Commission on Civil Disorders, *Report of the National Advisory Commission on Civil Disorders* (Washington, D.C.: U.S. Government Printing Office, 1968).
7. William Underwood, *A National Study of Youth Service Bureaus* U.S. Department of Health, Education and Welfare, Youth Development and Delinquency Prevention Administration, (Washington, D.C.: U.S. Government Printing Office, 1972). Further, it should be noted that the youth service bureau concept is in concert with the growing movement to eliminate status offenses from the juvenile court. See Board of Directors, NCCD, "Jurisdiction over Status Offenses Should be Removed from the Juvenile Court," *Crime and Delinquency* 21 (April 1975), pp. 97–99.
8. For those interested in a comprehensive overview of this subject see the monograph by Alan L. Switzer, *Drug Abuse and Drug Treatment: Community-Center Drug Program* (Sacramento, CA.: California Youth Authority, 1974). In a more comprehensive sense, the community is being asked to increase its responsibility for accepting sentenced criminals and *preventing* their return to the CJS. A case in point is the article by H. Richard Lamb and Victor Goertzel, "A Community Alternative to County Jails: The Hopes and the Realities," *Federal Probation* 39 (March 1975), pp. 33–38.
9. Robert Taggart, *The Prison of Unemployment* (Baltimore, Md.: Johns Hopkins Press, 1972), pp. 502–503.
10. Llad Phillips, Harold L. Votey, Jr., and Harold Maxwell, "Crime, Youth, and the Labor Market," *Journal of Political Economy* (May/June 1972), pp. 502–503.
11. E. H. Sutherland and Donald R. Cressy, *Principles of Criminology* (New York: J. B. Lippincott Company, 1966), pp. 235–238.
12. Fred P. Graham, "Black Crime: The Lawless Image," *Harper's* III (September 1970), pp. 64–71.
13. For details on the problems associated with education see Charles E. Silberman, *Crisis in the Classroom* (New York: Random House, 1971).
14. President's Commission on Law Enforcement and Administration of Justice, *Juvenile Delinquency and Youth Crime* (Washington, D.C.: U.S. Government Printing Office, 1967), p. 339.
15. Ibid., p. 334.

16. George D. Butler, *Introduction to Community Recreation* (New York: McGraw-Hill, Inc., 1967), p. 26.
17. The author would not want the reader to place a value judgment on the potential import of the religious community in preventing crime that is based on the space allocated to this subject. For one, personally I am convinced that the ethics and sense of justice professed by the various religions is directly applicable to the social problems at hand. If we emphasized moral obligations more, we would be able to lessen our emphasis on locks and a host of other items designed to protect us from those that are ignoring laws and the common good.
18. *Crimes of Violence* A Staff Report to the National Commission on the Causes and Prevention of Violence (1969) Vol. 12, pp. 710–711.
19. Donald R. Hughes and Eric E. Younger, "California's Answer to Building Security Legislation," *Crime Prevention Review,* 1 (January, 1974), pp. 33, 38.
20. Thomas E. Kelley, ed., *Community Crime Prevention and the Local Official* (Washington, D.C.: National League of Cities—United States Conference of Mayors, 1974).

13

Probity in Politics and Public Administration

There is not space to discuss the crisis in confidence about American values. Suffice it to say, there is a serious and familiar literature that argues that the extant American value paradigm—based for the most part upon utilitarian prescriptions—has now outlived its usefulness and that it must be changed or it will bring about the decline and collapse of contemporary society. If such contentions are even partially correct, it becomes imperative that we deal with questions of what alternative values should be adopted and how the process of change should be accomplished . . .*

Among the most important results sought by public services are: (1) providing services to individuals who are unable to obtain them through the free market mechanism in the quantity or quality deemed essential by society, e.g., adequate education, police and fire protection; (2) providing services to individuals which will give them an equal opportunity to compete for and occupy all positions in society, including the most attractive ones, e.g., compensatory education, job training, physical rehabilitation; (3) providing services which insure that people will receive the benefits they are entitled to under law, e.g., public defender services, outreach activities to notify people of their rights to program benefits; and (4) providing services which allow individuals to meet approximately minimum survival needs, e.g., food stamps, public housing, cash payments.†

Preview   Ethical misconduct on the part of politicians and public administrators indirectly, if not explicitly, influences our

---

*David K. Hart, "Social Equity, Justice, and the Equitable Administrator," *Public Administration Review* 34 (January/February 1974), p. 4.
†Stephen R. Chitwood, "Social Equity and Social Service Productivity," *Public Administration Review* 34 (January/February 1974), p. 32.

society's ability to prevent crime. While the strength of this relationship is debatable, it is undeniably clear that street crime and government corruption are linked to one another. Both are preventable; however, any effort to do so must, to be effective, deal with both simultaneously. The community has a responsibility for coping with both. In turn, the government has a responsibility for encouraging and organizing their involvement.

Violations of governmental integrity range from the flagrant (a la Watergate) to the minor infraction (a la free coffee for the patrol officer). Within this broad spectrum, one can observe conflicts of interests, irregularities in public financing, improper procurement procedures, unethical land use and licensing decisions, haphazard attacks on organized crime, and an insensitivity to white-collar crime. The indicators of each are more overt than not to even the most casual viewer. Most fundamentally, their presence depends upon: the absence of management; sloppy management; vague standards; inoperative codes of ethics; a lack of external audits; and weak investigative agencies. Once these are improved, we will, in all probability, see their injurious effects upon our quality of life disappear.

Probity and Prevention

Honesty in government is related to crime prevention programs.[1] While we might debate the strength of the connection, few of us would question that a relationship does in fact exist. You will find that the sections comprising this chapter deal with the fundamental importance of integrity in government and with the problems posed by official corruption, particularly as those problems affect the prevention of crime. Indeed, confidence in public institutions and public officers is critical to the success of crime prevention efforts. Official corruption—actual or suspected—undermines confidence and exacerbates the inability of the CJS to elicit the support of the community. Notably we find, in 1971, the Advisory Commission on Intergovernmental Relations concluding that:

> The willingness of citizens to become involved in crime prevention and control efforts, as well as the extent and effectiveness of their participation, depends a great deal on the status of law enforcement and criminal justice agencies in the community's eyes. If they are viewed as being corrupt, as a means

> of minority suppression, or as tools of a political machine,
> than many citizens will not become involved.[2]

In this sense, therefore, it is apparent that the paramount crime prevention activity appropriate for citizen action is the consistent pursuit and encouragement of governmental integrity.

Obviously, the burden for maintaining official integrity and combating corruption in our government cannot be left solely to those of us who are paid to cope with the problem. The professionals themselves openly admit that without citizen assistance they lack the resources to do what is required. This is especially evident where white-collar crime flourishes. Some may fail to associate white-collar crime with government integrity; but it is in three most critical ways. First, a large percentage of the white-collar crimes would remain completely undetected if it were not for the vigilance of the private business firms in monitoring the probity, as well as propriety, of their operations. Second, when white-collar criminals are discovered, the CJS is typically requested to assist in resolving the problem. Third, where prevalent, white-collar crime can either taint, or destroy government integrity.

The public can serve as the most comprehensive source of feedback available to those in government who are concerned about integrity. Citizens can perform an immeasurable service by informing the appropriate public officials, a private crime commission, or the media, of misconduct or inefficiencies that may have been caused by corrupt government and business practices. Concern by citizens regarding public and private misconduct can produce results: (1) through the ballot box, by removing slow acting officials, and (2) through its mere existence, by creating an overall climate that facilitates the successful implementation of needed reforms.

Official public and private business corruption does exist; however, we must also recognize that most people in public service and business are honest and dedicated. Hence this chapter is structured so as to: (1) support the many public officials and private businessmen who are honest and dedicated; and (2) encourage others to enter occupational careers, and to do so with an awareness of the significance that attaches to the integrity of public institutions, public officials, and private business firms.

Corruption, as it is viewed here, is not limited to its most infamous and sensational form—cash purchase of official decisions. We will approach corruption as including all of the circumstances in which the public officeholder, government employee, or businessman sacrifices or sells all or part of his judgment in return for personal gain. Further, corruption can be seen as also including more implicit conditions in which the bargain is latent. Such conditions—usually described as conflicts of interest—include any and all circumstances in which the officeholder or government employee is or may become the beneficiary of favor from persons with business that comes before him in his official capacity. Frequently we find such conflicts of interests involving the officeholder whose business or professional pursuits (e.g., insurance firm or law practice) service or represent those who may benefit from his official conduct. Finally, corruption, as defined here, may flow from the electoral process itself. The payment, or promised payment, of campaign contributions in return for official conduct constitutes a bribe. Here is the link between the white-collar criminal and the guilty official in a conspiracy to commit a crime.[3] Moreover, dependence on a source of campaign funding probably represents the most pervasive and constant pecuniary shackle on the judgment and action of the elected official.

The following examples describe the types of corruption. A trash collection business wins a municipal contract by corruptly obtaining confidential information enabling it to be a low bidder. A developer secures favorable zoning for a building project that will increase the cost of municipal services. The residents of a housing development which violates building code regulations suffer expense, discomfort, and physical danger because the city engineers moonlight as draftsmen for the developer. At times government services and supplies are procured but never delivered. The appropriations votes for an expensive government program are influenced by needed campaign contributions from the contractors who will flourish financially if the program is funded. Deposits or investments in state-regulated institutions are lost because the regulators are in the pay, directly or indirectly, of the regulated.

No one can fail to realize the impact that public corruption and white-collar crime have on street crime. The gas station robber, the burglar, and the mugger know that their crimes are pale in comparison with the larger criminality "within the system." And nowhere, unfortunately, is the cynicism greater than in this nation's prisons, where convicted offenders are supposed to be rehabilitated. A feeling of injustice occurs among prisoners, and it stems mainly from the inmates' belief that they are the unlucky victims of a hypocritical system that tolerates lawlessness among its official and businessmen but makes scapegoats of less fortunate offenders. Under these circumstances, we find that rehabilitation is impossible. In short, can we not agree that official corruption presents a serious impediment to the task of reducing criminality in America? Can we not also agree that as long as official corruption and white-collar crime are tolerated, the war against crime will be perceived by many as a war of the powerful against the powerless? As a result, "law and order" will be merely a hypocritical rallying cry, and the voicing of "equal justice under law" will be but a hollow sound.

Indicators of Corruption

For those of us looking, the evidence of corruption is the same everywhere. Where it exists there are signs of favoritism and graft, of "sweetheart" contracts and padded public payrolls, of open illegal gambling and bribes for public licenses and permits. These signs may flourish in full sight of citizens and government officials, but their significance may be lost on the unsuspecting or the naive. In turn, the following questions are offered to assist in determining whether official corruption or an atmosphere that is conducive to official corruption might exist in your state or city government. Each question is so worded that an affirmative answer tends to indicate the presence of corruption or an atmosphere that is conducive to corruption. *It is emphasized that one, or even a few affirmative answers, does not constitute a conclusive showing of corruption, however.* Further inquiry into laws and regulations would be necessary for that. And only official investigation and prosecution could affirm the existence of criminal activity.

Questions

1. Do respected and well-qualified companies refuse to do business with the city or state? Yes___ No___
2. Are municipal contracts let to a narrow group of firms? Yes___ No___
3. Is competitive bidding required? Yes___ No___ On contracts above what dollar amount? Amount_____
4. Are there numerous situations that justify the letting of contracts without competitive bidding? Yes___ No___ For example, are there frequent "emergency contracts" for which bids are not solicited? Yes___ No___
5. Have there been disclosures of companies that have submitted low bids but were disqualified for certain unspecified technical reasons? Yes___ No___
6. Do turnpike or port authorities or governmental departments

operate with almost total autonomy, accountable only to themselves and not to the public or other government officials? Yes___ No___

7. Does the mayor or Governor have inadequate statutory authority and control over the various departments of the executive branch? Yes___ No___

8. Are certain government employees frozen into their jobs by an act of the city council or state legislature? Yes___ No___

9. Is there not an effective independent investigation agency to which citizens can direct complaints regarding official misconduct? Yes___ No___

10. Are kickbacks and reciprocity regarded by the business community as just another cost of doing business? Yes___ No___

11. Is it customary for citizens to tip sanitation workers, letter carriers, and other groups of government employees at Christmastime? Yes___ No___

12. Is double parking permitted in front of some restaurants or taverns but not in front of others? Yes___ No___

13. Do some contractors keep the street and sidewalks reasonably free from materials, debris, etc. while others show little concern about such matters despite ordinances prohibiting litter? Yes___ No___

14. Is it common knowledge that architects add a sum to their fees to cover "research" at the city's planning and building department? Yes___ No___

15. Is illegal gambling conducted without much interference from authorities? Yes___ No___

16. Do investigations of police corruption generally result in merely a few officers being transferred from one precinct to another? Yes___ No___

17. Is there no special state unit charged with investigating organized crime and the conduct of public employees? Yes___ No___

18. Does one encounter long delays when applying for a driver's license, for the issuance of a building permit, or for payment in connection with services rendered the city or state? Yes___ No___

19. Are government procedures so complicated that a middleman is often required to unravel the mystery and get through to the right people? Yes___ No___

20. With each new administration, does the police department undergo an upheaval—the former chief now walking a beat, and a former patrolman now chief, etc.? Yes___ No___

21. Are zoning variances granted that are generally considered detrimental to the community? Yes___ No___

22. Is there a wide gap between what the law declares illegal and the popular morality? Yes___ No___

23. Are officeseekers spending more of their personal funds campaigning for political positions that the cumulative salary they would receive as incumbents during their term of office? Yes___ No___

24. Do city or state officials have significant interests in firms doing business with the government? Yes___ No___

25. Would officials benefit financially from projects planned or underway? Yes___ No___
26. Is there a lack of qualified government personnel to supervise and monitor public works projects? Yes___ No___
27. Is there no merit system incorporated into civil service procedures? Yes___ No___
28. Are patronage appointments extensive? Yes___ No___
29. Do government salaries fail to approximate what could be earned in comparable private sector positions? Yes___ No___
30. Are vice operations in certain sections of the city more or less tolerated by authorities? Yes___ No___
31. Is moonlighting by government personnel not regulated? Yes___ No___
32. Is it common knowledge that jury duty can be avoided or a ticket fixed? Yes___ No___
33. Have public officials accepted high posts with companies having government contracts? Yes___ No___
34. Has a legislator or councilman introduced legislation by which he would benefit financially? Yes___ No___
35. Is there no effective bribery statute that embraces all government personnel, not just department heads? Yes___ No___
36. Do officials use government equipment or material for personal projects? Yes___ No___
37. Do the media fail to report the existence of organized crime within the community or state? Yes___ No___
38. Is there a high turnover rate within municipal departments? Yes___ No___
39. Do the police discourage citizens from making complaints or pressing charges? Yes___ No___
40. Have certain prisoners been known to receive special favors while in jail? Yes___ No___
41. Does the police department have no internal investigation unit? Yes___ No___
42. Are state police with statewide investigative authority not authorized to operate in municipalities if there is reasonable suspicion of corruption there? Yes___ No___
43. Are an extraordinary small percentage of arrested organized crime figures convicted, and, of those convicted, are sentences insignificant in relation to the crime and criminal? Yes___ No___
44. Are complainants in judicial proceedings frequently not notified of the date they are supposed to appear in court? Yes___ No___
45. Are court fines regarded as a source of revenue for the municipality? Yes___ No___
46. Are there part-time prosecutors? Yes___ No___
47. Are key public officials not required to disclose sources of income and the nature of their investments? Yes___ No___
48. Is the presence of organized crime repeatedly denied, even though no one has really looked for it? Yes___ No___
49. Are records of official government agencies closed to public inspection? Yes___ No___
50. Are archaic laws still on the books? Yes___ No___

51. Are public employees not required to answer, under penalty of removal from office if they decline, questions pertaining to their official conduct? Yes___ No___

52. Are records of disciplinary action against government employees closed to inspection? Yes___ No___

53. Is it common knowledge that if the press prints unflattering, though truthful, stories about the police, delivery trucks are ticketed and sources of information for reporters within the department dry up? Yes___ No___

54. Is it common knowledge that candidates for judgeships and for police positions of lieutenant and above must be accepted by ward committeemen? Yes___ No___

55. Is morale among public servants low? Yes___ No___

56. Are citizens barred from public meetings and from access to what should be public records? Yes___ No___

57. Do laws protect from public scrutiny information that should be public, such as ownership of real estate? Yes___ No___

58. Do projects for which money has been authorized fail to materialize or remain only partially completed? Yes___ No___

59. Can city employees represent private interests before city boards? Yes___ No___

60. Do state workers have to contribute a percentage of their wages to the party's campaign chest? Yes___ No___

61. Are machine politics an inherent part of the system? Yes___ No___

62. Are bribegivers, as well as bribetakers, arrested and prosecuted? Yes___ No___

63. Do public officials attend conventions at the expense of private sector groups? Yes___ No___

64. Do civil services regulations inordinately impair the hiring, disciplinary, and firing latitude of public officials? Yes___ No___

65. Do large campaign contributions follow favorable government rulings? Yes___ No___

66. Are ethical codes not institutionalized to any significant degree? Yes___ No___

67. Are those arrested for narcotics and gambling violations primarily bottom rung violators (street pusher and numbers runner vs. wholesaler and numbers banker)? Yes___ No___

68. Do bail bondsmen flourish within the community? Yes___ No___

69. Are public positions filled when there is no need for such jobs, such as the post of swimming instructor at a location where there is no pool? Yes___ No___

70. Do business establishments give certain public employees free meals, passes, discounts, and the like? Yes___ No___

71. Are sheriffs permitted to pocket the difference between the sum they are authorized to spend on food for jail inmates and what they actually spend for this purpose? Yes___ No___

72. Is it well known that dedicated police personnel do not relish assignment to vice or plainclothes units? Yes___ No___

73. Is there no mechanism to monitor court testimony of building inspectors, liquor inspectors, and other enforcement per-

sonnel to determine whether their court testimony differs from their original reports to the extent that defendants are thereby freed? Yes___ No___

74. Can public employees who wish to retire receive their pensions despite pending charges of misconduct? Yes___ No___

Prepared by the National Advisory Commission on Criminal Justice Standards and Goals for its Report on Community Crime Prevention.

Conflicts of Interest

"Conflict of interest" is an issue that comes occasionally to our attention (usually when large lettered headlines appear in the newspapers). But, the problem is one that our public officials and students of government confront every day. Where does one draw the boundary between private interest and public duty? Who is to determine standards for ethical conduct? What body can be entrusted to judge very complex cases involving a public official's outside income and employment? These are questions of major import, yet questions not easily answered.

Conflicts of interest can be a problem whenever public officials exercise power and discretion over decisions that affect many citizens. It may be the city building inspector who decides whether or not a permit shall be granted, the state legislator whose vote will decide the passage of off-track betting legislation, or the criminal justice planner who votes on LEAA grant awards and then serves as a consultant on the project. Basically, a conflict of interest arises whenever an official intentionally disregards the public interest in favor of some other interest, personal or otherwise; likewise, a conflict exists whenever, because of personal financial interests or pressure exerted by outside interests, an official is incapable of performing his official duties impartially, or chooses not to perform them impartially. It should be underscored that the categorization of who is or who is not a public official lacks preciseness. In general, however, two factors determine which officials should be included: (1) the degree of discretion exercised by an official, and (2) the susceptibility to pressure from outside interest groups that the particular position affords. Elected officials at the state and local levels—state legislators, mayors, city councilmen, and county officials—are necessarily included because of the critical policymaking positions they hold. The majority of state and local government employees, including employees of the CJS, make discretionary decisions.

There are three major potential conflicts of interest inherent in public service.[4] First, the income of many officials, particularly legislators, comes mainly or in part from their outside professional work. Dependence on a sizable income apart from legislative salaries increases the likelihood of a private interest conflicting with official duties. Second, the representative function of elected officials results in an inescapable conflict. Officials are faced with the sometimes incompatible duties of: (1) representing the interests of their constituents, and (2) acting in an impartial and detached manner. The representative function can be undermined and public trust abused when the official assumes the role of a broker for special interest groups; (3) as a professional, the legislator usually has developed expertise in a specific field. As a consequence, often the legislator is appointed to committees on which his professional knowledge will be useful. In such cases, his official action may have an influence on matters affecting his finances.

An appropriate system of controlling conflicts of interest and a code of ethical principles to guide officials are imperative! Why? First, because potential conflicts always exist and thus might constrict the official in performing his duties. Second, because such conflicts increase the probability of crime. Nevertheless, we should be careful that the system of controls neither modifies the essential nature of representative government nor strays from the citizen-legislator ideal. An official cannot detach himself completely from political concerns, and he is expected to share both the financial and political interests of other citizens. Hence, the system of regulation must balance these rights of the official against the public's right to have officials who can be held accountable for their conduct. As a consequence, the primary goals of conflict of interest regulation should be to maintain a high standard of ethical conduct that will protect the integrity of our public offices.[5] Subordinate objectives are: (1) to prevent the use of public office for private gain, (2) to minimize the effect of external financial interests upon an official's judgment, and (3) to insure that public office attracts the most qualified personnel.

Clearly, no single law or type of law is sufficient to deal with the gamut of ethical problems that underlies an official's conduct. Indeed, a *system* of various types of provisions—criminal laws, ethical guidelines, an enforcement body, and disclosure of financial interests—is critical to assure us that our public officials will act with integrity. Further, carefully worded and consistently enforced provisions will protect the official's privacy and his legitimate economic and professional pursuits. They will also increase the attractiveness of public office. Either the complete absence of, or the presence of ambiguous provisions that can be abused in their enforcement, degrade public service and discourage ethical persons from seeking public office.

The following courses of action are recommended.

- Adopt an ethics code for public officials and employees.
- Create an ethics board to enforce the ethics code.
- Disclose public officials' financial and professional interests.
- Include conflicts of interest in the state criminal code.

Political Finances

The regulation of political finances is at the forefront of contemporary issues in our nation. Plainly, corruption in political financing not only increases public cynicism about political money but also affects basic citizen attitudes toward politicians and the entire political process. To the degree that unhealthy attitudes persist, parties and candidates have difficulty raising sufficient funds from legitimate sources, and hence may be forced to turn to funds from inappropriate sources.

Large donations from individuals or organized interests do more than aid candidates whose views are compatible with those of the contributor.[6] They expand the unrepresentativeness of politics by substantially aiding candidates whose programs are acceptable to such interests. To the extent that parties depend upon large contributions from special interests or persons seeking favors, they must take into consideration the views of these interests. This reinforces the tendency to succumb to institutional obstacles and individual pressure. A citizen's perception of what can be accomplished through regular channels may lead to an activism outside party channels. His perception of the role of the special interests of large contributors, whether real or imagined, may lead him to abandon hope of accomplishing his ends through approved channels of political participation. Such alienation breeds frustration which can generate militancy and, at times, illegal activism—*thus the connection of crime prevention to the prevention of unethical political financing.*

To develop respect for the law from both practitioners and the public, regulations must account for the financial needs of parties and candidates, while encouraging means of financing that avoid obligations to special interests. Part of the problem of regulation in the United States has been the lack of serious enforcement. Whatever the reasons for nonenforcement, an urgent criterion is the establishment of a process giving statutory responsibility to officials isolated as much as possible from political pressures. This entails providing for a bipartisan Registry of Election Finance or similar agency to monitor the law, but it also means that the registry must be able to prosecute directly, going to the appropriate courts without referring cases to the regular enforcement agencies (which are partisanly staffed and administered). In addition, there should be a mechanism for the protection of community interest, permitting individual citizens to bring actions before appropriate courts.

Keep in mind that corruption stems from the system itself, from the lack of realistic laws, from indifferent administration and enforcement, or from all three. Only as political finance becomes better understood, and attitudes toward political finance change, will attempts at its regulation and more salutory management in the political system have a greater chance to succeed.

It is recommended that . . .

- candidates' receipts and expenditures be disclosed,
- political campaign spending be limited,
- campaign contributions from government-connected businessmen be prohibited, and
- campaign gifts from unions, trade groups, and corporations be prohibited.

Government Purchasing

In governmental purchasing, as well as purchasing for other public agencies, the cost of corruption is passed on to the taxpayers. If state and local government purchases increase in volume, or costs rise unnecessarily because of corruption, tax increases are then paying for the perpetuation of the corrupt practices. Whenever a government official or employee must make a decision that carries economic consequences, the conditions automatically exist for personal gain. At times those affected by the decision are willing to pay for a favorable decision or even for the expeditious handling of a routine matter. Bureaucracies sometimes create such onerous problems for the private sector that the only viable means to overcome delays is to find an "inside track" to a favorable action.

Any public official or purchasing officer who bends or breaks the rules for his own gain exerts a corrupt influence. He is in a position to be approached both by organized crime members and by legitimate businessmen who, like the unethical public official or purchasing officer, seek to promote their own cause at the expense of the public. What may appear to be a request from a legitimate business, on a deeper level, may be an approach by a member of organized crime.[7]

Centralization has fostered greater efficiency and economy in purchasing as well as professionalization of purchasing agents. A centralized purchasing agency is able to make use not only of volume purchasing, but also of: (1) specialized personnel; (2) increased mechanization or computerization; (3) development of specific products to fit precise needs; and (4) reduction of the necessity for packaging, handling, and storing small quantities —all of which help reduce duplication thereby lowering costs.

The need for accurate and prompt auditing of all purchasing transactions is obvious. Auditors are able to find errors made either through negligence or deliberate attempts to defraud the government. Any mishandling of purchasing records can be detected and exposed, frequently before the agency incurs major losses.

The most frequent type of bribes are nepotism, political contributions, honorific appointments, the sale of property below fair market value, direct payment to a third party of some loan or indebtedness, and (the most wrongful of all) direct cash payments. The official, for his part, can find equally varied ways by which to repay a bribe. Perhaps the most obvious is to select arbitrarily the vendor who is to receive the bid. The official may or may not later attempt to justify the award of the bid to a vendor who was, perhaps, the highest bidder. In summary, it is recommended that a state procurement agency be established.

Zoning, Licensing, and Tax Assessment

The three areas of zoning, licensing, and tax assessment are highly susceptible to corruption. We can only estimate the extent and cost of corruption in these areas, however, because little has been done to document known occurrences. Conditions contributing to corrupt practices unfortunately exist in governmental jurisdictions of all sizes. Moreover, further urbanization is going to involve increasingly complex financial operations of great magnitude. Yet planning and zoning functions include fairly *small* public expenditures to cover the cost of personnel and other administrative services. Consequently, we usually pay less attention to them as compared to public safety, sewers, parks, or any of the larger, more visible services of local governments. Nevertheless, government decisions in the low visibility areas are of major economic importance to private interests. Paradoxically, the same, if not more, incentive for corruption exists here as in other areas of government operation. To this end, the National Commission on Urban Problems wrote:

> In some communities, there is a very real problem of corruption in zoning decisions. A property owner who could build a shopping center or a high-rise apartment suddenly discovers that his property is worth many times as much as the property owner who is relegated to low-density development. The values at stake are enormous, so it is not surprising, therefore, that the zoning system is subject to enormous pressures by landowners and developers and that outright corruption is more than simply an occasional exception.[8]

Zoning is only one element of concern to urban developers. Building and construction codes and tax assessment policies of local jurisdictions affect costs and are integral parts of corporate and development planning. Favorable regulatory and tax conditions are as important as favorable purchase arrangements, and developers usually look for jurisdictions responsive to their interest for the best arrangement possible on taxes and services. Indeed, the most sensational abuses and perhaps the most complex ones occur in the area of property taxation. The prevention of corruption in tax assessments is more than a legal or moral issue—it involves the financial solvency of already hard-pressed cities.

Government zoning, licensing, and tax assessment processes share several characteristics that contribute to the occurrence of corruption. A basic factor contributing to malpractice in these areas is the lack of precisely stated public goals. Most jurisdictions define the actions that may be taken in these target areas and may even do so with some specificity. There is a large difference, however, between what action *may* be taken and *why* it is to be taken.

A lack of planning and management goals provides a basis for substantial arbitrariness in day-to-day governmental decisions. The legislative benchmark for granting zoning variances, for example, may well read like the Standard State Zoning Enabling Act, which permits variances if they:

> ... will not be contrary to the public interest, where, owing to special conditions, a literal enforcement of the provisions of the ordinance will result in unnecessary hardship, and so that the spirit of the ordinance shall be observed and substantial justice done.[9]

Language this vague not only makes the work of honest zoning boards difficult, but also it actually invites abuse.

Pressures on both private groups and public officials to achieve special ends are going to intensify. Thus, the need for administrative reforms, can be expected to grow as the pace and complexity of government planning, regulatory, and revenue requirements increase. Most of this problem could be resolved through sound management. Applications should be centrally controlled with review deadlines specified for the various evaluations; evaluations (specified review element approval/disapproval) should be required in writing from the reviewing official; and the application pipeline should be audited regularly by an external agency, particularly field inspection reports.

Hence, it is recommended that communities

- develop equitable criteria for zoning, licensing, and tax assessment,
- formulate specific criteria for government decision making, and
- publicize zoning, licensing, and tax assessment actions.

Attacking Organized Crime

On the one hand, to recommend that a single state or local approach will lead to successful detection and prosecution of all types of organized crime both within and outside the CJS would be erroneous. On the other hand, the large number of state and local agencies, each with different statutory powers, administrative organization, social and political histories, and available tools for prosecution, makes it difficult to set standards that would be useful and appropriate for every jurisdiction. Thus, local and state law enforcement agencies should first conduct very careful analyses of the conditions that suggest actions necessary to ferret out and prosecute corruption and organized crime. In turn, among the variables that state and local jurisdictions must consider to determine the nature and extent of their corruption problems are the following:

1. the history and structure of state and local law enforcement;
2. the complexity of state and local government structure;
3. patterns in the sources of corrupting influences;
4. the history and extent of organized crime and corrupting influences on government;

5. the nature or level of the government service compromised; and
6. the complexity of the corruption scheme.

When these factors are analyzed, both for long-term CJS planning and for devising ways to pursue individual corruption cases, logical and feasible methods for attacking cases of official corruption can be devised. Jurisdictions can accumulate the histories of such cases—from preliminary investigation through court disposition—and analyze why certain cases failed while others led to convictions and to significant sentences. This type of knowledge is invaluable in order that the prosecuting attorney can convince the legislature that he needs additional or more sophisticated statutory powers; and for use in analyzing why progress is or is not being made in investigating and prosecuting successfully the most difficult cases. This approach, in conjunction with county grand juries and state investigative commissions, presents a triangular attack and overlapping accountability for eliminating corruption in public affairs.

*   Set capability and integrity standards for local prosecutors.
*   Create a state office to attack corruption and organized crime.

White-Collar Crime

Written across an official poster warning businessmen and government employees that bribery is a crime are the added words, "It's only a crime when you get caught." This too-prevalent attitude, among many other contributing factors, explains why white-collar crime is considered by many CJS officials as the fastest growing sector of crime.[10] This is not to imply that most of those in business, industry, and the professions are unethical or dishonest; the opposite is true. It just so happens that a few are "sharp," blatantly unethical, or just plain crooked. But clearly more is required than a preponderance of honest people; they must take *positive action,* not merely sit passively on the sidelines. Unfortunately, honest executives and professionals are often asleep at the switch. The definition of "white-collar crime" is not purely an academic matter but has a very significant bearing on how best to combat the offense. White-collar crimes are "illegal acts characterized by guile, deceit, and concealment"—and are not dependent upon the application of physical force or violence or threats thereof. Further, they may be committed by individuals acting independently or by those who are part of a well-planned conspiracy. The objective usually is the obtaining of money, property, or services; avoiding the payment or loss of money, property, or services; or securing business or personal advantage. By describing white-collar crime as "illegal acts," the implication that only criminal proceedings and sanctions should be directed at such offenses is avoided. Civil proceedings and remedies can be equally, if not more, effective.

White-collar crime can not only result in an immediate and direct financial impact on citizens but also, and even more important, it generates nonfinancial and long-term consequences. Careful consideration of these effects will help demonstrate that the response to white-collar illegalities should be considerably more than just writing them off as another cost of doing business. For those interested (and well the public should be), as for a total dollar figure for those white-collar crimes falling within the scope of the *Handbook* some offenses are not covered herein), the "ballpark" figure for the short-term and direct dollar loss is estimated at $40 billion annually, excluding the costs of price-fixing illegalities and industrial espionage (satisfactory measures of these offenses were not found).[11] Although the direct, short-term dollar cost of white-collar crime is of great importance, the long-term and/or nonfinancial consequences are even more serious.

A major long-term impact on white-collar crime is loss of public confidence in business, industry, and the professions and debasement of competition. In addition to debasing competition, insensitivity to ethical practices has, in some instances, retarded economic growth. In one state where payoffs to government officials were expected, many companies refused to conduct business there. Also of the interest of investigators and prosecutors in white-collar crime is the realization that investigation of one such offense is often tied to, and can help solve, other crimes. An investigation of a credit card fraud, for example, could lead to the arrest of not only the immediate possessor of the card but also a pickpocket, burglar, cargo thief, or fence. Arrests in connection with an advance fee swindle (fees are paid for loans that do not materialize) may lead to the discovery that the assets of the "lending company" are really stolen, counterfeit, or bogus securities, which might be traced back to a fence, a dishonest broker's employee, or a number of other criminals or illegal operations. Law enforcement officials can be expected to become increasingly attentive to white-collar crime when the citizenry views the arrest and conviction of those involved in intricate and complicated white-collar schemes as being as important as the investigation and prosecution of robbery or murder.

Whether organized along national, regional, or local lines or structured to focus on inter- or intra-industry problems, collective action by business and the professions can be, and is, a key ingredient in an informed response to white-collar crime. What a firm acting on an individual basis may lack in financial resources, expertise, perspective, manpower, or just plain clout can be supplied by an organization that all belong to and support, from which all benefit, and through which goals can be achieved jointly.

Listed below are some of the many types of collective action in which business and the professions are, or could be, engaged.

How to Take a Common Stand Against Bankruptcy Fraud

With over 3,000 indictments and more than 1,800 convictions to its credit, the Fraud Department of the National Association of Credit Management is a good example of how joint action by companies enables business to implement anticrime efforts that are either too costly or too impractical to conduct by any one firm. For instance, the Department can add to the scope of a bankruptcy investigation by collecting pertinent information from every part of the nation. Also, the cost of an investigation to develop evidence of fraud is spread among member companies—a cost that a lone firm would not assume because the price tag would most likely far exceed the fraud-related loss.

Joint Action Against Bribery, Kickbacks, Payoffs

Detailed codes and statutes which entangle business can be the rain forest of corruption. The outsider is usually bewildered and frustrated. Nothing he does seems to be quite correct. Reasonable efforts at compliance seem inadequate. There always seems to be something in writing somewhere with which he did not comply or which is an absolute bar. When a building inspector receives $15,000 yearly and has the power of life and death in his summons book, the temptation is too great. The result, in too many instances, is systematic solicitation of payoffs by building inspectors and an equally systematic payment of bribes by contractors.

Computer-Related Crime

One of the more recent examples of collective action occurred in June, 1973, when the First National Invitational Conference on Computer Abuse convened at the Stanford Research Institute. Numerous facets of computer-related fraud were discussed and many courses of action probed. One of the recurrent themes was concern that ethical and moral values are not yet well-formed by many of those engaged in computer technology. Yet substantial trust is being increasingly placed in EDP personnel. Also in mid-1973, a joint effort by those in the data processing field resulted in a Code of Ethics and Code of Conduct for EDP Holders. One provision states that because of the privileged capability of computer professionals to gain access to computerized files, especially strong strictures will be applied to those who have used their position of trust to obtain information from computerized files for their personal gain.

Consumer Fraud   There are various industry-supported attempts at self-regulation to protect consumers. These include Better Business Bureaus, special divisions within local Chambers of Commerce, centralized sources for referrals of consumer complaints (in such areas as appliances, advertising, and home improvements), and programs centering on product standardization, certification, and seals of approval. The extent to which the self-regulatory approach can be pursued without running afoul of legal or regulatory provisions is currently being studied by the FTC's staff.

A consumer protection program that seems worthy of emulation is administered by the Better Business Bureau of Western New York, in Buffalo, which operates what might be called a consumer affairs clearinghouse. Publicity alerts consumers that if they have complaints, the Bureau is the place to call. This avoids (1) consumer confusion over which of several possible agencies to contact, and (2) consumer frustration over being bounced from agency to agency before finally, if ever, reaching the right source.

Collective Action Against Credit Card and Check Fraud   Through a contract with a private agency, the American Bankers Association provides a free crime investigation service to its member banks. Free preliminary investigations are available in connection with such offenses as swindles involving the use of stolen or fraudulent credit cards and the forgery of checks. The Association also publishes a protective bulletin alerting readers to various frauds and criminals. Local banks could collaborate to conduct clinics which highlight countermeasures for credit card and check fraud. Such clinics, geared to commercial customers, could utilize the educational package available from the Travelers Cheque Division of the American Express Company.

Insurance Fraud   Illustrative of the type of collective action possible against insurance fraud is the Insurance Crime Prevention Institute, which is supported by member casualty insurers. The organization seeks to deter fraudulent claims through the investigation of important cases and presentation of evidence to prosecuting authorities. According to the Institute's policy statements, it does not participate in the actual settlement of claims and does not advise members about the disposition of any claims.

> Eight persons have been indicted by a Cook County grand jury for allegedly defrauding insurance companies of about $2 million last year through phony auto accident claims.
>
> Named in the 15 indictments Thursday were an attorney, a doctor, an insurance claims adjuster, and four others. The charges included theft, forgery, perjury before the grand jury, and presenting fraudulent claims.
>
> A spokesman for State's Attorney Bernard Carey said the indictments were the first phase of a massive investigation started in July of phony accident insurance claims.[12]

Industrywide Efforts Against Pilferers and Receivers

Within the transportation industry, for example, there are several associations whose activities are directed against pilferage and other forms of cargo theft. Programs have been developed to achieve the following:

* screen prospective employees for member companies,
* maintain and analyze theft statistics, and
* develop and enforce performance standards.

Coordinated Action to Reduce Securities Theft and Fraud

The principal goal of the New York City-based Joint Industry Committee (JIC) is to reduce securities theft and increase recoveries by stimulating and facilitating cooperation between law enforcement agencies and members of the securities industry. Members of the JIC include representatives from New York area banks, New York and American Stock Exchanges, National Association of Securities Dealers, and brokerage houses. In effect, JIC serves as a liaison between law enforcement and the financial community. Among other activities, JIC has issued theft-prevention suggestions to its members; provided law enforcement officials with an introduction to brokerage office operating procedures; supplied funds for police to use as rewards, "show money" or "good faith money" in their undercover attempts to recover stolen securities; provided expert witnesses for court testimony; and "opened doors" to put law enforcement agencies in touch with key industry officials who could supply needed information.

Among the potential recommendations of collective action are the following

* Funnel criminal intelligence to law enforcement agencies and to participating firms.

- Conduct investigations and compile evidence that involves expertise, time, and personnel not always available to hard-pressed police and prosecutors.
- Upgrade the ethical code of the profession.
- Serve as a central source of information that has heretofore been scattered and difficult to obtain on a timely basis.
- Screen prospective employees for members.
- Initiate and support legislation.
- Settle consumer complaints.
- Develop performance standards and procedures to be implemented by constituent companies.
- Assist law enforcement (which generally begins with the "bad guy" and works toward identifying "the front") by identifying the front and attempting to locate the crook.

Learning Exercise

1.   Divide the class evenly into seven task forces. Each of the task forces is to be assigned one of the following topics: (1) questionnaire completion, (2) conflicts of interest, (3) regulation of public finances, (4) government procurement practices, (5) land use and licensing decisions, (6) organized crime, and (7) white-collar crime. The task force assigned the first topic is to take the questionnaire on corruption that appeared earlier in this chapter and complete it. The members of this task force should individually interview people from differing professions and backgrounds (e.g., court judge, housewife, business purchasing agent, city council person, minister). The data should be compiled, analyzed, and prepared as a graphic presentation to the class. The other task forces are to: (1) review the last thirty daily editions of the local newspaper for any articles pertaining to their subject (e.g., conflict of interest), (2) locate a recent court case that has been adjudicated and brief it, and (3) prepare a three to five page written presentation of your findings. Finally, all of the task forces are to share with one another their *findings, opinions,* and *recommendations.*

Endnotes

1.   Portions of this chapter were drawn from the National Advisory Commission on Criminal Justice Standards and

Goals, *Community Crime Prevention* (Washington, D.C.: U. S. Government Printing Office, 1973).

2. Advisory Commission on Intergovernmental Relations, *State-Local Relations in the Criminal Justice System* (Washington, D.C.: U. S. Government Printing Office, 1971), p. 263.

3. I had anticipated at this point to furnish a singular noteworthy citation concerning "the politics of crime" or vice versa. However, the existing literature is so rich in case examples and prescriptive packages that the reader needs only to go to the library reference service to find a plethora of pertinent information.

4. It is widely understood that organized crime can thrive only through the acquiescence or active assistance of public officials. Because public officials act on measures that affect the regulation and conduct of state and local government agencies and businesses, they are prime targets for organized crime influence.

5. For example, Florida's laws on conflicts are dispersed throughout four statutes, three senate rules, two house rules, and one section of the state constitution. Details are contained in the report by the Council of State Governments, *Conflict-of-Interest and Related Regulations for State Legislatures* (Washington, D.C.: Council of State Governments, 1971), Appendix 2.

6. Case illustrations of wrongful political finances are cited by Michael Dorman, *Payoff: The Role of Organized Crime in American Politics* (New York: David McKay Company, Inc., 1972).

7. There is no question that many businesses have been, and continue to be, infiltrated by organized crime. Influence with government officials on all levels benefits organized crime both monetarily and through the protection that can be obtained from such officials. The involvement of organized crime with procurement offers: (1) legitimate outlets and fronts for money obtained through illegal activities; and (2) opportunities, for tax purposes, to draw off capital and bankrupt companies when so desired; and (3) opportunities to influence or corrupt public officials.

8. National Commission on Urban Problems, *Building the American City* (Washington, D.C.: U. S. Government Printing Office, 1968), p. 19.

9. Ibid., p. 226.

10. *White-Collar Crime* (Washington, D.C.: Chamber of Commerce of the United States, 1974), p. 1.

11. Ibid., p. 5.

12. Joe Foreman, "Eight Indicted in $2 Million Claims Fraud," *Chicago Daily News* (February 22, 1974), p. 3.

PART FIVE

Measurement and Evaluation

The biggest drag on overall productivity advances is not in manufac-turing but in the service field, which employs more than 60 percent of the nation's workers and is hard to automate. Simply measuring—much less improving—the productivity of policemen, pilots, teachers, or symphony conductors is far tougher than assessing the output of an assembly-line worker. Even so, adept use of computers has raised productivity in such fields as medicine and sales management.*

The ideal organization would be self-evaluating. It would continu-ously monitor its own activities so as to determine whether it was meeting its goals or even whether these goals should continue to pre-vail. When evaluation suggested that a change in goals or programs to achieve them was desirable, these proposals would be taken seriously by top decision makers. They would institute the necessary changes; they would have no vested interest in continuation of current activities. Instead they would steadily pursue new alternatives to better serve the latest desired outcomes.

The ideal member of the self-evaluation organization is best conceived as a person committed to certain modes of problem solving. He believes in clarifying goals, relating them to different mechanisms of achievement, creating models (sometimes quantitative) of the relationships between inputs and outputs, seeking the best available combination. His concern is not that the organization should survive or that any specific objective be enthroned or that any particular clientele be served. Evaluative man cares that interesting problems are selected and that maximum intelligence be applied toward their solution. While he often does have strong social preferences, his central commitment is to solve problems in the right way.†

*"Troubling Dip in Efficiency," *Time* (June 3, 1974), p. 71.

†Aaron Wildavsky "Evaluation As An Organizational Problem," A paper delivered at the American Society of Public Administration Convention, (New York: March 24, 1972), p. 1.

The issue of measuring and evaluating the impact of social services on its clientele is of profound importance today. With limited resources and the constant threat of "stagflation" we see a concerted interest on the part of government officials and citizens alike to maximize the value received from the public dollars spent. As will be seen in Chapter 14, productivity and measurement are inextricably tied to one another. Together they provide a foundation upon which reliable cost/performance decisions can be made over both the short- and long-range. Suggestions on what can and should be measured in terms of crime prevention activities are covered in this chapter.

Chapter 15, the final chapter, addresses the ultimate question —what is the degree of success or failure that we have or are achieving? In essence, the focus in on the planning for evaluation which includes the establishment of objectives, measuring devices, data requirements, obstacles to data collection, and methods of analysis. Project monitoring is also reviewed. All are related, in turn, to the primary concept at hand—the prevention of crime.

14

Improving Productivity in Police Crime Prevention Services

State and local governments are challenged to provide more effective police services at a time when the growing desire for public safety is surpassed only by the increase in police costs. For a police department to create one or more round-the-clock post, actually requires adding five officers to the force at a cost that may exceed $80,000 a year. To place an officer in a police car with a partner 24 hours a day may exceed $175,000 in annual costs to the community.

These costs are reflective in the growing nationwide expenditures for police services. In response to the mounting fear of personal harm, loss of property, and public disorder in recent years, municipal police expenditures increased 70 percent from $2.1 billion in 1967 to $3.5 billion in 1971. Total federal, state, and local expenditures for police services reached $6.2 billion in 1971, a 20 percent increase over the previous year. Those funds went principally to cover the compensation for over 530,000 law enforcement officers employed full-time in over 10,000 public police agencies at all levels of government.

These fiscal facts of life have forced many communities to recognize that the demand for more police services cannot be met simply by expanding the police force. Rather, police departments must learn to use more effectively the personnel and other resources currently available to them. That means increasing their productivity.*

Productivity improvement is among the practical approaches government is taking to achieve its objectives of effectiveness, efficiency, and economy. The concept of productivity improvement focuses on whether the right things are being done and whether they are being done without wasting valuable resources.†

*Report of the Advisory Group on Productivity in Law Enforcement on *Opportunities for Improving Productivity in Police Services* (Washington, D.C.: National Commission on Productivity, 1973), p. 1.
†*Personnel News*, 40 (September, 1974), p. 1.

Preview

Local government officials and municipal administrators, as well as schools of public administration, other academic institutions, the federal government, and national professional associations have expressed considerable interest in the question of local government productivity. For example, as far back as 1928 the National Committee on Municipal Standards developed means of measuring the effectiveness of government services. Of late, an interest in increasing productivity in police services has been widely and strongly voiced. Most basically, augmenting police productivity denotes an endeavor to achieve greater levels of performance per unit cost. Since the police deal with people there is a concern not only for quantity but also for the quality of the services provided. Improving productivity involves five functions: establishing objectives, assessment of progress, better operating methods, experimentation, and implementation.

The concept of productivity quite logically includes the function of measurement. It is generally held that existing police measures are at best limited in scope. Typically only a very small part of what the police do is counted and reported—and seldom are the figures compared to the goals of the agency. One means of measuring work planned as related to that accomplished is through the creation of a crime analysis unit. Such a unit is responsible for counting and assessing activities and recommending optimal patterns of human resource deployment to control and prevent crime.

The measurement of crime prevention activities and results is confronted by ambiguity—i.e., what ought to be measured? Some agencies are now accepting the challenge and taking action. Early results are more promising than not. Three indicators found worthy of measuring are: amount and percentage of fiscal resources spent on crime prevention; extent of volunteer manpower used; and amount of crime prevention training. Further, it is encouraging to note that the level of research and specific organizational commitments (specialized units) to preventing crime appears to be on the increase. The challenge of measuring crime prevention is being approached by many as an opportunity to improve the productivity and overall effectiveness of the police delivery system.

Productivity: A Nationwide Concern

Increasing our nation's productivity has been given top priority among the economists, elected leaders, businessmen, and others who share an interest in our economic well-being.[1] Indeed, many realize that improved productivity is a means of avoiding the constant threat of inflation and unemployment. To this end, the National Commission on Productivity was formed in 1970. Because public employment has been growing sharply in relation to that in private industry, the Commission was charged with looking into productivity in the public as well as the private sector. In 1970, nearly one out of every five wage and salary workers was a government employee, and 80 percent of all public employees worked for state and local governments.[2] Projecting the current trends of governmental growth and decentralization of federal programs inherent in the revenue-sharing concept, many experts foresaw continued sharply rising expenditures and employment at the state and local levels. Thus we find that a basis was laid for examining the opportunities for enhancing the productivity of public service employees.

Since a large share of local government's revenue is expended on police services, the Commission established in 1973 an Advisory Group to assist them in conducting a study on ways to increase the productivity of police. In order to maintain creditability and relevance, the Advisory Group was selected from a cross section of progressive police administrators, criminal justice planners, and academicians, as well as representatives from relevant professional and funding organizations. The staff consisted of a select group of police officers, criminal justice planners, and consultants assembled by the Commission. The Advisory Group wisely recognized the diversity of police departments and the uselessness of trying to prescribe solutions that could be universally applied. Each department in the country is unique. Local conditions vary, governments are structured differently, community priorities respond to local needs, and expectations of the police department are diverse. Indeed, productivity analysis is in part a response to that diversity, recognizing as it does the need for each government and police manager to respond individually to the special local needs.

It is commonly held that productivity tools for the public sector in general, and for police services in particular, are in their infancy. Because of the complex factors involved, these efforts are not likely to reach maturity in the near future. However, even though the state-of-the-art is obviously imperfect, this fact *must not* deter police managers from experimenting with new techniques, tactics, and tools designed to raise productivity. The days of the police chief or sheriff being able to cite an increased crime rate as sole justification for additional resources are coming to an end. Policy makers, in conjunction with budget analysts, are asking in many cases, "What will we get for our money? How much more productive will you be?" The traditional response of "We don't know because we can't measure noncrime," is not only begging the issue but is erroneous today. Through the use of victimization studies, many cities are able to predict their actual crime rates as compared to only those crimes brought to their attention.[3] Consequently, *productivity* and the related function of work *measurement* are upon us and will be with us from now on. In fact, one local police agency has tied salary increases for their police officers to their productivity.[4]

The Advisory Group decided initially to emphasize limited areas of police work. Three areas were selected because they were believed to be both of great importance to most police departments, and subject to significant productivity improvements through existing techniques or knowledge. The areas studied were:

- *Patrol:* direct services to the public in both crime and noncrime situations.
- *Crime Prevention:* specific programs—aside from those associated with traditional patrol activities—designed to anticipate and prevent crime.
- *Human Resources:* the management of people—including recruitment, selection, assignment, training, and organization development—to maximize their potential in meeting department goals while increasing the satisfaction they get from their work.

In line with the particular focus in this text we will explore increasing police crime prevention productivity.[5]

Productivity and the Police

Productivity denotes the return received for a given unit of input. To increase productivity means that a greater return must be realized for a given investment. The concept most often is used in reference to the production of goods, e.g., more agricultural products, automobiles, or tons of steel per man-hour. Specialists argue over the precise definition of the term "productivity," but it can reasonably be assumed to be a ratio of "output" (or what results from an activity) to "input" (or the resources committed to the activity). It is granted that police services are not as easily defined as the process of producing a television set. In general, higher police productivity means keeping the police department's budget constant and improving performance, or keeping performance constant and reducing the size of the budget. Productivity gain can also mean increasing the budget but improving performance at an even higher rate. But the concept of productivity cannot simply be transferred in a theoretical form from the economics of production to the operations of a state or local police department. Thus, it is proposed that increasing productivity in police services be considered in the following four ways.

First, *increasing police productivity means improving current police practices to the best level known in order to get better performance without a proportionate increase in cost.* This means doing the things that are considered to be a necessary part of good police work, but doing them as well or as efficiently as the best current practices permit. For example, officers assigned to patrol spend a great deal of time on such activities as filling out unnecessarily long reports, or on activities that are important but that would require less time if they were better coordinated (e.g., the long hours spent waiting to testify at a trial).

Second, *increasing police productivity means allocating resources to activities which give the highest return for each additional dollar spent.* A police department carries out a range of activities, many of which are non-crime-related most of which are necessary to its overall responsibility to the public. Beyond a given scale, however, expanding certain activities will give the force less value than initiating or expanding others. For example, experiments already in progress tend to support the contention of some criminal justice analysts that random patrol has a limited effect in deterring criminals. Thus, it may be possible to take, say, 10 percent or more of the patrol force off random patrol without any significant negative effect and shift them to activities that focus on preventing crime such as "hardening" likely crime targets (e.g., improved building security).

Third, *given the uncertainties of police work, increasing productivity means increasing the probability that a given objective will be met.* The professional police officer—from the chief to the patrol officer—must deal constantly with many unknown or ambiguous factors. He is constantly assessing the likelihood that this or that may happen, and consequently the more skillful he becomes at increasing the probability that each activity will result in useful accomplishment, the more productive the overall operation becomes. The clearest example of increasing the probability of achieving the intended impact is having personnel assigned when and where crime is highest or the calls for service are heaviest. Simple observation can indicate the "when and where" in general terms; careful analysis of available data can more accurately pinpoint likely times and places of crime occurrence, thereby significantly increasing the probability of putting officers where they are needed.

Fourth, *increasing productivity in police work means making the most of the talents of police personnel.* Sworn officers are better trained and more expensive than ever before. This means that they are capable of higher performance, that economy requires they be used more effectively, and that they expect to be treated with greater respect and intelligence.

Examples of better human resource development and management abound and can be expected to become increasingly important to police managers. They may include making patrol officers responsible for following through on investigations; permitting advanced patrol officers to avoid promotion, but yet receive a higher salary as a patrol officer. This latter concept is in line with the notion of a "police agent."

Productivity And Effectiveness

For any police activity, productivity must be viewed as it relates to effectiveness. Admittedly the two concepts are closely related and at times may be difficult to differentiate. Basically, effectiveness can be defined as a measure of the extent to which a goal is achieved. In this sense, then, it does not include any notion of resources committed to the activity. Productivity, however, includes not just what was accomplished but also what resources were required to accomplish it. It is important for us to recognize that productivity does not necessarily indicate the extent to which the result actually accomplished a given goal. Productive performance (was the job done efficiently?) should also be seen in terms of effective performance—how well was the job done and how significant was the activity in contributing to agency objectives?[6]

One element always found to be common to both productivity and effectiveness is "output," or results. Under the weight of growing demands for service and accelerating costs, government is being forced to identify more exactingly what it is trying to accomplish, and what the real results are from its activities. The former requires a clearer identification of objectives, and the latter a more precise way of assessing the results of activities that contribute to those objectives. We can readily see that better *measure-*

ment of results leads to better *productivity assessment.* And, better productivity assessment, in turn, is an important step in the process of productivity improvement.

The Process
of
Productivity

Getting a greater return for our tax dollars is not a "one-shot" activity. It is an ongoing, long-term process that should be an integral part of police management. The road to productivity improvement includes five milestones.

One: Establishment of Objectives.   Ideally, each police department establishes its goals in concert with the political and professional leadership of its government and the people it serves. It then proceeds to identify intermediate objectives, the achievement of which will contribute to the attainment of the broader goals. Unfortunately, in practice, the process of setting objectives is often reversed; instead of determining the mission of the department and then organizing to accomplish it, more often the apparent aims of ongoing activities are described and are built into departmental goals. It is important that the different levels of objectives be systematically related and understood. For example, police agencies usually have a broadly defined goal of reducing crime. An intermediate objective would be to reduce the incidence of a specific crime during a specific time period. A police department can then choose various strategies such as reducing the opportunity for burglary by a citywide campaign on building security or by increasing the visibility of the police in areas of high burglary rates.

Two: Systematic Assessment of Progress.   Police management needs to know how well it is doing in meeting its objectives. Most police chiefs, mayors, or managers have some judgment on how their police force is doing (good, better than before, about the same, not quite up to par, or, it appears that we have a problem).

In today's police work, effective assessment requires more precise measurement. This is not to say that all assessment must be derived from quantified information, but without more reliable measures it is difficult to determine how much better or worse a particular unit, strategy, or piece of equipment works.

Three: Search for Improved Operating Methods.   The many improved operating methods, types of equipment, and ideas being used in certain police agencies could and should be made known to and transferred to other jurisdictions. While numerous journals, conferences, and other communications media provide information on innovative and improved methods, unfortunately some are not presented clearly enough to be usable by busy police managers. Often the most valuable ideas come from within an agency, but people familiar with staff and line problems either are not asked for suggestions for improvement, or are asked to address themselves to the wrong questions. Similarly, nonpolice agencies within the same government, such as management analysis staffs, are too often ignored.

Four: Experimentation.   Most police executives are cautious when it comes to doing something unusual. "Innovation" often results in a price many police departments feel they cannot afford; however, they also can not afford to hold the *status quo* while their surroundings change.

Undoubtedly, a balanced approach to risk-taking is needed. It is important to recognize that useful information often comes from ideas that did not work as expected. Managers must also learn how to take reasonable and controlled risks. Experiments should be designed in such a form as to make evaluation possible, to determine whether or not they are successful, as well as why and by what margin of quality or cost they are inferior or superior to existing methods, techniques, equipment, and ideas. In addition, those who ultimately are to use a new idea should be involved with the development and testing process.

Five: Implementation.   Any new method that has been tested and proven feasible must then be implemented. At this point, the resistance to change that might result from department leadership, typically extends throughout the department, the government, and the citizenry as well. Overcoming this resistance requires involvement of those people at the experimentation stage, as well as thorough preparation, patience, cooperation, close monitoring of the innovation, and clear accountability.

The measurement of police services is not new; in fact, it may be more familiar to police managers than to many other state and local government officials.[7] Nevertheless, most police managers would concur that many of the measures currently being applied to police services do not provide information they need to help them evaluate and improve operations.

The most common data used for assessing overall police performance are crime rates—such as those compiled in the *Uniform Crime Reports (UCR)*, published annually by the Federal Bureau of Investigation.[8] However, because the incidence of crime is a function of many factors unrelated to police activity, crime rates alone provide a very poor measure of police performance. Police managers repeatedly ask for other measures that more accurately report the amount and type of police activities. The *UCR* has other deficiencies as a management tool. The most critical of these is the fact that the UCR is not a totally reliable reflection of crime; it documents only *reported* crime, which as several surveys have shown is only a fraction of crime actually committed.

As referred to earlier in this chapter, recent surveys of "victimization" have indicated that reported crimes may represent, in some jurisdictions, as little as 25 percent, and rarely more than 75 percent, of the actual incidence of crime. One reason many types of crime go unreported is the victims' fear of embarrassment, of family or personal involvement, or of retaliation on the part of the offender. In some cases victims failed to report crimes because of lack of confidence in the police. Some hope is offered for getting more accurate crime data through victimization surveys (confidential and detailed surveys of scientifically selected samples representative of the population as a whole to detect the true number of crime victims). Scientifically and consistently administered, victimization surveys may provide new measures for crime control and crime prevention programs.[9] They may reveal not only the true incidence of crime but also the reasons why crimes were not reported and the victims' attitudes toward the police and police service.

Unfortunately, victimization surveys are expensive if conducted properly, primarily because a large sample is needed for the data to be valid. Additionally, in the FBI's Crime Reporting Program, data are not published on both offenses and arrests for all categories of crime. The *UCR* identifies "Index crimes," which include the major crimes of murder, forcible rape, robbery, aggravated assault, burglary, larceny $50 and over in value, and auto theft. It then groups offenses into two categories: "Part I" offenses, which include the Index crimes, and "Part II" offenses, which while they are lesser crimes consume much of every police department's time and effort. The *UCR* reports both offense and arrest information for Part I offenses, but only arrest information for Part II offenses. The distinction between major and minor offenses is all the more a problem since many police agencies do not adhere strictly to *UCR* definitions. Some, for example, classify

a burglary attempt as a malicious destruction of property, thus de-
moting it to a Part II offense.

Besides the data obtained in the *UCR*, there are several other
types of data upon which police rely to help them monitor their
workload and evaluate their performance:

- numbers of arrests by crime category,
- the clearance rate, (As used in the *UCR*, police "clear" a
  crime when they have identified the offender, have sufficient evidence to charge him, and actually take him into
  custody. The arrest of one person can clear several crimes,
  or several persons may be arrested in the process of
  clearing one crime.)
- the exceptional clearance rate, (Once again using the *UCR*
  definition, crime solutions are recorded in exceptional instances when some element beyond police control precludes the placing of formal charges against the offender,
  such as the victim's refusal to prosecute after the offender is
  identified, or local prosecution is declined because the
  subject is being prosecuted elsewhere for a crime committed in another jurisdiction.)
- complaints received from the public about the department
  or about specific actions by officers,
- activity measures (called-for-services) of field operations,
  and
- workload measures of clerical functions (e.g., number of
  additions per month to the fingerprint files).

All of the above data are useful, but they are limited in the
amount and quality of information they supply. Activity and workload measures can be usefully integrated into an information
system to help managers estimate the demand for additional manpower resources or to identify concentration of clerical or administrative activity. Arrest data provide crude estimates of the activity
of the patrol force, and the clearance rate is thought to provide
some indication of a department's ability to solve reported crimes.
While many police agencies have a solid base for gathering information regarding police activities, the data as presently aggregated
can be misleading. One reason that existing data are not put to
better use is that the police mission is complex. The specific objectives of the force are not always known, nor is it always clear what
some police activities are contributing, or how they relate to
broader agency goals. Pointedly, it is difficult to know what to
measure! Therefore, the initial step to improved measurement is
to recognize how the various functions of police work relate to the
broader mission of the department and in turn the goals of state
and local government.

Improving Measure-ment of Police Services

The measurement of police activities, as is true for most government organizations, is confused by the absence of goals and objectives that are easily quantifiable. While agreement may be found on the broad goals of the police force, the specific activities that appropriately fall under the purview of a police agency are subject to debate.[10]

The Realm of Police Management.   Among the services delivered by the police agency are the following:

- criminal justice, which includes (depending upon one's definition) the courts, correctional institutions, probation, parole, and many other public and private agencies concerned with crime and the criminal offender;
- maintenance of public order;
- emergency response for fire, accidents, natural disaster, medical emergencies, etc.;
- community relations, which affects the community's feeling of confidence in or alienation from the government; and
- nonemergency general services. Police are called upon for a variety of non-crime-related tasks which do not fall under the responsibility of any other public agency, or which, because of the 24-hour nature of police duty, befall them when other agencies are closed. This may range from directing a stranger to a historical landmark, to registering bicycles, or to stoking the town hall furnace.

The relative amount of time and resources a police department devotes to meeting responsibilities within each of these systems naturally varies from community to community. But more important is the fact that the police both affect and are affected by other elements of the several systems of which they are a part. Effectiveness in preventing crime, for instance, depends in part on how well the corrections agency performs in rehabilitating felons. Or, whenever patrolmen spend time in court beyond the minimum required for efficient assistance in the judicial process, they have less time available for crime-related work. On the other hand, police skill in investigation and apprehension increases the likelihood that district attorneys can obtain convictions of arrested persons. Thus, it is axiomatic that measures of police performance must take into account the other system components that affect the outputs of the police delivery system.

Measurement to Support Management.   The principal purpose of measurement, once again, is to provide sufficiently precise information to enable police managers to: (1) evaluate their agency's performance; (2) identify and diagnose problem areas; and (3) design solutions. But measurement has still other advantages. For example, measures frequently stimulate constructive thinking—e.g., measurement of crime deterrence requires indepth analysis of the nature of deterrence—thus increasing the understanding of police activity. Measurement also may provide a device for linking one activity to another, or one part of the management process to another—e.g., relating resources to output.

Measurement does have certain limitations. It is not a substitute for sound professional judgment; it is meant to assist the manager, not to dictate his actions. Furthermore, care must be taken to guard against measures that provoke negative activity. To use a familiar example, measuring a police officer solely on the basis of arrests made without considering whether or not the arrests are valid, can result in rewarding him for the apprehension of innocent people. Nor should blind acceptance of measures result in meaningless and costly measurement activity. Some measures may require data gathering that is more expensive than their value would justify and therefore should be avoided.

There are many types of measures, and as many ways to describe them as analysts have time to devise. Given the state-of-the-art of measuring public services, a few basic distinctions should be made. There are two fundamental types of measures that may be used separately or in combination to provide useful information: measures of results (or output), and measures of resources used (or input). Police departments, traditionally have been more concerned with measures of resources than with measures of results.[11] The budget gives the most basic measures of what resources are being used for what activities. Resource use might also be measured in terms of man-time, or units of equipment. Results are generally more difficult to define and measure. Traditionally, police departments have relied upon easy-to-quantify results such as miles driven by a patrol vehicle. Such measures (often referred to as workload) have some use as indicators of intermediate results, but they clearly do not provide an adequate assessment of whether higher level objectives are being met. A comparison between results achieved and results intended gives a simple measure of effectiveness.

Result and resource measures can be compared to indicate productivity. A productivity measure indicates the cost (in money, men, and/or equipment) of accomplishing a given result. Such a measure can apply to a whole police department, a division of the department, or a unit within a division. It should be noted that the results of a smaller division may be meaningless to overall departmental goals; the productivity of that division may increase (it gets more results per unit of resource) but with no improvement in the department's overall productivity. Thus, it is essential that *the measurement of individual activities or organization components always be understood in the context of overall departmental goals and performance.*

Crime Analysis: A Technique For Improving Measurement.   The creation of crime analysis units within police agencies is underway and probably will increase over the next few years. They are destined to serve as a major cornerstone from which improved measurement techniques can be constructed. Of equal, if not greater importance, is that they also offer a predictive capability for our police. Some form of crime analysis exists in every police agency. However, in most agencies the individual officer or investigator conducts the analysis of limited crime data in an informal way. Formal crime analysis exists when a specific unit has been established to collect and analyze all of the available crime control and prevention data and disseminate the "distilled" crime information to operational user groups.

The operation of a crime analysis system that is geared toward crime prevention requires several basic elements.[12] These include a definition of goals and objectives, crime data input, analysis of crime data, crime information disseminated as output, and feedback and evaluation. In addition, several fundamental prerequisites must be considered. These include formal administrative support, organizational placement, staffing, and a method of guaranteeing the integrity of crime and offender input information. Most of the crime data collected by a crime analysis section is received from the operational units within the agency. This data consists of offense reports, supplemental reports, arrest reports, field contact reports, special analysis reports, agency records, and statistical data. In addition, to this structured data, the crime analysis section also collects informal data (such as soft intelligence) from other units within the agency. Outside data sources contribute information to the crime analysis section regarding status and records of known offenders, other law enforcement agency crime problems, and collateral information.

The collection of data for the crime analysis operation requires a determination of the accessibility of data sources, an evaluation of the data validity and reliability, standardization of data elements, and systematic collection methodology. The actual data collection and the format in which data is received is dependent upon the sophistication of the system, the communication vehicle (such as direct routing vs. computer terminal), and the functions performed by the crime analysis operation.

A crime analysis system requires the maintenance of specific records and data storage. It is important to keep in mind that the analysis section files are *operational,* since they are based on non-duplication of other departmental records and stored data accessibility or retrievability. The storage of crime analysis data may be either manual, mechanical, or both. Naturally, computer storage has numerous benefits. The necessary crime analysis records include: crime description files, known offender files, crime target files, criminal history files, suspect vehicle files, and property files. These files require periodic purging, based on data utility and record storage methodology.

A crime analysis unit is specially designed for measuring and defining offenses with a high probability of recurrence and is directed toward those criminal offenses the police are most capable of suppressing, or those offenses in which the perpetrator can be apprehended. Some benefits may be gained in analyzing nearly all types of crimes; however, the crimes selected for extensive analysis must be based on priority considerations. The analysis and measurement of different crime types hinges on the information available to the analyst for extraction, collation, comparison, and correlation. Several informational factors can be considered universal such as crime type, geographical factors, chronological factors, victim target descriptors, suspect descriptors, vehicle descriptors, and property loss descriptors. However, these universal factors are only variably available when analyzing a specific crime type. Thus, the analysis of a particular crime type presents *specific problems* with *alternate solutions.*

In addition to the universal factors, there are a number of factors that may be considered specific to a particular crime type. These are almost always present for the specific crime to be analyzed. The specific crime factors represent the information with which the analyst will usually connect crime by unique characteristics and identify crime and criminal offender patterns. The suitability of the various crime types to analysis typically includes residential and commercial burglary, armed robbery, strong-armed robbery, and theft from persons, auto theft, general theft classifications, forgery and fraud, rape and sex crimes, aggravated assault, and murder.

Geographical analysis is the examination of crime type relative to actual location or within prescribed areas. This analysis is performed to identify geographical crime patterns and trends, and is accomplished by utilizing mapping and graphical or statistical methods. Specific mapping methods include various manual-visual techniques and computer mapping. In addition to crime type maps, it is recommended that crime analysis also maintain known offender and other special maps. Further, the collation and correlation of crime analysis data is dependent upon the expertise of the analyst, the analytical techniques utilized, and the availability or retrievability of recorded crime data. Crime analysis is especially suited to correlative listings of possible suspects for particular crimes or listings of crimes having a common offender.

One of the most important functions of the crime analysis operation is to identify crime trends, predict criminal activity, and establish estimated productivity patterns. By effectively analyzing crime data, the analysis section can determine similarities which make these targets most attractive to the criminal, and productivity goals can be reached.

For crime analysis to be effective, the analyzed information must be disseminated to *operational user groups*. Crime analysis information is disseminated by either formal or informal means. The majority of information is routed by the analysis section in the form of formal reports. The various formal dissemination techniques are utilized for purposes of crime prevention, suppression, and suspect apprehension. The publications should be tailored to user needs, should function to increase officer awareness, and should facilitate short-term special manpower deployment. Information on criminal offenses is distributed daily, weekly, monthly, and on an as-needed basis. These publications take the form of crime recaps, information bulletins, crime summaries, and analysis section reports. Information on criminal offenders is given either routinely or on an as-needed basis. Of particular importance are crime pattern information bulletins, investigative lead reports, and productivity figures. A crime analysis operation also should communicate information to user groups on an "event-triggered" informal basis. Informal dissemination of crime analysis information takes place during discussions between analysis and operational personnel, and during examination of the analysis section by information user personnel. Several law enforcement agencies have attempted to increase informal dissemination of analysis information with successful results.

A crime analysis operation can be evaluated by a number of methods. Utilizing conventional planning techniques, the police manager can determine to some degree the areas of increased effectiveness that should result from the implementation of an analysis section. The analysis section activities also require evaluation on a cost-effective basis. This can be largely accomplished by determining costs per output unit, and by measuring user reliance or opinions of information recipients. Additional forms may be designed to determine the user utilization of crime analysis information.

A manual crime analysis system is one in which all methods of data collection, data storage, data analysis, and information dissemination are done "by hand." The manual system has several limitations when compared to semiautomated or fully automated systems; however, most of these limitations can be overcome by increasing analysis staffing levels. The manual methods remain best suited to agencies serving populations below 200,000. The semiautomated crime analysis system is one in which much of the data is captured by automated data processing. In addition, stored and recorded data is filed mechanically for easy retrieval. The semiautomated system requires fewer personnel actually assigned to the unit, but receives support from other departmental units. The semiautomated system may still require manual data extraction and manual analysis. Finally, the fully automated crime analysis system utilizes extensive data capture by electronic means. The analysis function is carried out primarily by computer, with special analysis capabilities programmed for use by the analyst as the need arises. The storage of data is completely mechanical and the analyst can employ a wide variety of analysis techniques and search criteria.

Productivity in Crime Prevention Programs

The factors affecting crime prevention are extremely difficult to isolate and measure. For example, can one measure the number of robberies which did not take place because of a policeman's time spent working on recreation programs for inner-city youth? Or the number of burglaries that did not take place because of advice given to the community on building security? It is not surprising, given the difficulties of answering such questions, that police performance usually is judged on the basis of apprehensions rather than on their apparent success in holding down the rate of crime increase.[13]

Program Attributes Facilitating Measurement   Keep in mind that a number of difficulties must be overcome before reliable measures of productivity in crime prevention can be devised. For example, the most commonly used measure, the rate of reported crimes, represents only a fraction of all crime committed, and variations in the rate can be caused by a variety of factors other than crime-specific prevention programs. Also, as mentioned before, victimization surveys and careful design and control of crime prevention programs offer promise of overcoming the weaknesses of this measure. Because productivity is a comparative concept, care must be taken to avoid the "measuring of apples against oranges" and other statistical fallacies. It may be easier, for instance, to achieve a 10 percent reduction in a small number of burglary occurrences than in a relatively larger number. It may also be easier to reduce burglaries in an area that has suffered temporary police neglect than in one where patrol and other activities have been intense.

Crime prevention activities have, in many instances, been effective; however, most have been subjected to little scientific evaluation. Encouraging measurement of crime prevention activities does not mean to suggest that only those activities that can be quantitatively measured are valuable. The point is that it is unlikely that one would be able to make judgments about priorities and resource allocations among various crime prevention activities unless it is known *how* productive or effective they are in comparison to each other. *Measures* are simply a tool for better *evaluation.* But for us to accomplish this, crime prevention programs and activities should be structured so as to yield as much useful information as possible. This is not to suggest that ease in measurement should be the principal criterion in the design of a crime prevention program. Sometimes rigor in design for measurement purposes can dilute the effectiveness of the program. Fortunately, however, there are several factors which can both facilitate evaluation and enhance the effectiveness of crime prevention programs. These include:

- specific objectives with relation to type of crime, location, and period of time;
- specific *strategies* for achieving the objectives; and
- specific *resources* and manpower allocated to the strategies.

Specific Objectives.   In fiscal year 1973, one police department spent $102,000 on 18 crime prevention programs. As far as could be determined, none of them had specific objectives, and as a result, it was difficult to evaluate the worth of each program or to identify where improvements could be made in subsequent years. On the other hand, the departments in St. Petersburg, Florida, and Oakland, California, did set objectives and can measure progress toward those objectives in crime prevention programs. Using its own funds, St. Petersburg is trying to reduce residential burglary citywide by 20 percent over the next ten months. Through individual security checks, lectures, burglary prevention brochures, radio and TV "Prevention Tips" broadcasts, a Burglary Security Ordinance already drafted, and efforts by the city's Citizens' Crime Committee, it hopes to measure a reduced incidence of this crime. (Results are not yet available.) Oakland, also using local funds tried to reduce burglary by 10 percent in a selected census tract over a three-month period by persuading residents and merchants to keep lights burning in front and in back of their houses or business establishments all night at a cost of about 2 cents per night. They managed only a 3 percent reduction.

Specific Strategies.   One state developed a federally funded Six-City Model Burglary Prevention Program. To date, it remains one of the most carefully designed crime prevention programs to be implemented. (A consultant firm was used as an independent program evaluator for all six participating law enforcement agencies.) Each law enforcement agency involved was free to develop its own strategies and abatement techniques with respect to the following five categories:

1. increase public awareness and involvement through education,
2. improve security (target-hardening),
3. improve patrol and surveillance,
4. improve investigation and suspect handling,
5. decrease the market for stolen goods.

Preliminary results are presented in Table 14.1, i.e., those relating specifically to nonpatrol crime prevention. The program also involves the monitoring of such other areas as the characteristics of the burglars apprehended (mean age 18, median age 16) and of the local character of the crimes (57 percent are committed within a mile of home). The fundamental point to note is the way in which measures have been chosen to reflect specific program activities, which in turn can be instrumental in the planning and goal-setting of other similar burglary prevention programs.

Specific Resources and Manpower.   The commitment of funds to explicitly defined crime prevention programs is estimated to range from 0 to 1.6 percent of the police budget.[14] Unless the costs to carry out these programs can be isolated, productivity improvements will be difficult, if not impossible, to measure. Further assessment of any program will not be possible unless the results can be related to the skills, methods, and manning brought to the program. The National Crime Prevention Institute, which is part of the Southern Police Institute of the University of Louisville, Louisville, Kentucky, believes that it is both desirable and feasible for police agencies to aim for a 2 percent budget allocation to specific crime prevention programs.

A Few Useful Indicators   In the end, the results of measurement must enable our police managers to distinguish between crime prevention programs that yield a lasting improvement and those whose effect is only temporary. Measures must also be arranged so as to relate the improvement directly to specific activities carried out in the program and to a determination as to whether or not the program has simply pushed crime into neighboring areas or jurisdictions. Consequently, as more experience is obtained through experiments in specifically designed programs (such as the six-city plan just mentioned) and better crime data are developed, it should become possible to devise more definitive productivity and effectiveness measures for crime prevention. For those departments that cannot perform such ambitious projects, a number of indicators still can be used as a start toward developing meaningful measures. These include:

- the relationship between the *fiscal resources* spent on crime prevention activities and the total departmental budget;
- the extent to which *volunteer manpower is* used;
- the extent of *crime prevention training;* and
- the development of *new data* sources.

Fiscal Resources.   Comparisons of the resources devoted to crime prevention programs from one period to another, or between comparable jurisdictions, is a rough indicator of a department's relative priorities. The greater the proportion of the police budget devoted to specific crime prevention activities, the greater the commitment to crime prevention. As noted below, however, more money is not the only indicator of commitment.

Volunteer Manpower.   The use of volunteer community resources to augment police manpower is an important component of crime prevention programs. The greater the resources that can be marshalled at minimal cost, the more productive the enterprise is likely to be. Again, however, the real test is the extent to which the volunteer manpower is engaged in effective work and/or the efficiency of sworn personnel increases. The number of man-hours devoted to a particular program by nonpolice community volunteers is an indicator to the police manager not only of his crime prevention effort but also the state of police-community relations.

Training.   Specific crime prevention training generally has been a low priority in most agency training programs. In data obtained in a survey of six police departments,[15] crime prevention training averaged from 0 to 8 hours per year for personnel attending regular inservice and supervisory training programs. Of course, more important than the time spent in training is the quality of the training. Another useful indicator is the number of personnel sent to external institutions for courses concerned with crime prevention. The survey data showed that although the numbers are small in comparison to the size of the departments, personnel trained externally in crime prevention increased by a factor of 10 over the last three years. Thus, it is safe to surmise that crime prevention training will continue to grow over the coming years.

Table 14.1. Preliminary results from California 6-city model burglary prevention program

Category	Measure	4-Month Period for Which Data Have Been Examined Beginning	End	Percent Change
OVERALL	Monthly burglaries per thousand population	1.52	0.72	—53
	Dollar losses from reported burglaries per thousand population	$70	$25	—64
PUBLIC EDUCATION	Number of no-force entries per thousand population	0.48	0.24	—50
	Percent burglaries reported by nonvictims	9.9	13.1	+32
TARGET-HARDENING	Number of minor-force entries per thousand population	1.15	0.54	—53
	Number of aborted or unsuccessful attempts as a percent of all burglaries per month	5.0	6.4	+28

SOURCE: System Development Corporation, Santa Monica, California.

Table 14.2 Measurements for basic productivity measurement system, police crime control

A. Currently available[1]
1. Crime rates for reported crimes
2. Clearance rates relative to reported crimes
3. Arrests per police department employee and per dollar[2]
4. Clearance per police employee and per dollar[2]
5. Population served per police employee and per dollar[2]

B. Requiring significant additional data gathering[1]
1. Crime rates including estimates of unreported crimes from victimization studies
2. Clearance rates based on victimization studies
3. Percent of arrests that lead to convictions
4. Percent of arrests that "survive" preliminary hearings in courts of limited jurisdiction
5. Average response times for calls for service
6. Percent of crimes cleared in less than "X" days
7. Percent of population indicating a lack of feeling of security
8. Percent of population expressing dissatisfaction with police services

[1] These (except for A-5, B-7, and B-8) should be disaggregated by type of crime. We recommend initial attention on index crimes.
[2] Resource inputs should to the extent possible be developed to exclude noncrime control functions such as traffic control.

New Data Sources. To the data currently being collected, processed, and analyzed should be added other categories of information. Examples of such data are presented in Tables 14.2 and 14.3.

Improving Productivity In Crime Prevention Programs
In spite of the difficulties encountered in designing crime prevention programs, several new programs have been accompanied by significant decreases in reported crime, or by the reduction or elimination of inefficiencies. Some of these are discussed below for the purpose of suggesting ideas on where to begin. (Not all are equally applicable; each department must determine its own needs and limitations.)

Utilizing Community Resources. Nonpolice resources in our communities, whose use is often less expensive than the addition of sworn and nonsworn personnel to the payroll, can be directed toward increased crime prevention productivity. These include volunteer manpower, cooperation of commercial and private vehicles with radios, block security programs, identification of property, referral services, and building security audits. Examples of these in specific communities are:

- *Volunteer Manpower.* In New York City and in Los Angeles County, special men and women reserves, paid only $1 per year, are trained for specific work performed on call. They serve as a second officer to the uniformed officers in radio patrol cars; do special duty at fairs, parades, and youth programs; assist in traffic and crowd control; and provide special skills such as electronics, photography, and horsemanship.

- *Citizen Eyes and Ears.* In Oakland, the Citizens' Crime Prevention Committee, which helps the department involve the community in crime prevention activities, assisted in organizing the Radio Alert Program. By 1971 this comprised 31 companies with more than 1,700 radio-equipped vehicles such as tow trucks, taxis, utility trucks, and ambulances. Drivers are instructed to call in if they notice crimes in progress or unusual occurrences. In one month, the department received eighty calls, some of which resulted in successful apprehensions.

- *Block Security.* In New York City, the municipal government is setting aside $5 million to provide technical and financial support for local residents and groups willing to work together to make their blocks and homes safer. One resident in each block is to serve as block security officer. After receiving special training, he will be responsible for designing and implementing the block security program and will act as liaison between the block and the department on crime prevention programs.

- *Identification of Property.* "Operation I.D." is being used in many communities. This encourages residents, using a pointed steel-tipped vibrating pen, to mark their valuable possessions with either a driver's license or social security number to assist in proper identification and speedy return of stolen items.

- *Referral Services.* In both Oakland and Los Angeles, extensive use is made of community referral services. The Oakland Police Department's Family Crisis Intervention Program has secured the participation of eight public and private social service agencies. In Los Angeles County, the Juvenile Referral and Resource Development Program of the Sheriff's Department has used the services of about 100 community-based agencies since the inception of its referral program in 1970. In Richmond, California, a juvenile referral program is aimed at increasing the number of youths who are apprehended, "processed," and passed to an appropriate referral agency, and who do not revert to crime, presumably within a specified period of time.

- *Building Security Audit.* A crime prevention program in Sunnyvale, California, includes a comprehensive security audit of all commercial multi-dwelling apartment complexes. A unique feature of the program is the use of firemen[16] to conduct the security inspections while they are gathering information about fire hazards in the same buildings. A separate file is maintained for premises that have been burglarized. The ultimate intent of the program is to recommend worthwhile security strategies and techniques based on the data gathered in this broad security audit. The city obtained $25,000 in federal grants and added $80,000 of its own funds to conduct the security audit. The program was completed toward the end of 1973.

Table 14.3   Minimum data requirements for suggested police productivity measures

Data	Source[1]	Generally currently available	Basic data often available but some modifications needed	Requiring significant additional data gathering
Crime control effectiveness-related data[2]				
1. Annual number of reported index crimes (homicide, rape, burglary, robbery, auto theft, aggravated assault, larceny above $50, and total)	UCR	X		
2. Annual clearance data on each index crime and in total	UCR	X		
3. Estimates of "true" crime rates including unreported crime	Victimization survey			X
4. Estimates of true clearance rates for index crimes including unreported crimes ..	Victimization survey			X
5. Annual arrests for each index crime	UCR	X		
6. Annual adult convictions associated with each index crime	UCR		X	
7. Arrests for index crimes that pass preliminary hearing in court of limited jurisdiction..	Court records		X	
8. Number of days between report of incident and clearance for each index crime ...	Police records		X	
9. Citizen feeling of security data	Citizen surveys			X

Table 14.3 (continued)

Data	Source	Generally currently available	Basic data often available but some modifications needed	Requiring significant additional data gathering
10. Citizen expressed satisfaction with police service	Citizen surveys			X
11. Response time (minutes) between receipt of crime call and police arrival at scene— by crime and whether in progress or not	Police records		X	
Expenditures and manpower data				
12. Police employment for crime-control related activities	UCR local records		X	
13. Police expenditures for crime-control related activities	Local records		X	
Background data				
14. Population: Total, by race, and by age groups (15-24) . . .	Census, local reports	X (decennially)	X (other years)	
15. Percent unemployed—by race	Census, local reports	X (decennially)	X (other years)	
16. Percent households under $5000 income	Census, local reports	X (decennially)	X (other years)	
Reporting system				
17. Changes made since prior report	Police report	X		
18. Method of data audit or review	Police records	X		
19. Special data gathering procedures	Police records	X		

[1] UCR refers to the FBI's *Uniform Crime Reports.*
[2] Though the analysis in this study focused on Index Crimes, full productivity analysis should be expanded to cover other crimes, particularly certain others of special interest to society such as narcotics dealing.

Municipal Year Book 1973 (Washington, D.C.: International City Management Association, 1973), p. 41.

Research Related to Crime Prevention

Many basic questions remain unanswered in the field of crime prevention, such as:

- What are reasonable crime prevention goals?
- What behavior patterns can be changed or encouraged to decrease the likelihood of crimes being committed?
- How can the changing sociocultural profile of a community be described, and how does this affect ongoing crime prevention programs?

Although each crime prevention program launched involves a search for answers, systematic research is needed to make possible the planning and design of more effective programs. Such research, of course, will probably be limited to the larger police departments, which are able to devote their resources to research. Universities, research institutions, and state and federal agencies working to prevent crime share a responsibility in this area. Three examples of research which demonstrate the value of increased knowledge in designing strategies to meet crime prevention objectives follow.

An Assessment of Criminal Justice Priorities.   In Ventura County, California, a survey of all criminal justice agency heads in the county was conducted.[17] They were asked to rank forty separate types of crime on a scale from 0 to 100, using criteria such as the cost per offense to the system and to each major part of it, and its impact on victims and the community in general. These data were compared to objectively measured data on the impact and characteristics of these offenses. The purpose was to assess criminal justice priorities. The results were voluminous and informative, although not conclusive in the sense that one type of crime stands out. Some specific data for decision making were revealed, however. The victimization rate for burglary in the county, for example, was more than twenty-five times the conventional reported rate per 1,000 population. The odds of a business being burglarized were 1 in 2.5 compared to 1.4 for shoplifting. Most burglars are male (83 percent), young (75 percent under 25), single (58 percent), unemployed (66 percent), and, of those employed, 80 percent are categorized as semiskilled or unskilled. Of relevance here is the fact that crime prevention planning should be able to make use of such crime-specific data in setting priorities and devising prevention strategies.

An Econometric Study of Crime Factors.   An econometric study[18] of the factors contributing to crimes against property and the factors determining the effectiveness of law enforcement activity directed against these crimes was carried out in 1969. Among its findings, which are supported by substantial statistical evidence, are the following:

- Deterioration of labor market opportunities for youths, particularly nonwhites, was one of the principal factors responsible for rising per capita offense rates for economic crimes.
- Increasing school enrollment rates for youths have had an ameliorating effect on the rise in crime rates for some types of crime.
- The decline in police effectiveness, as measured by the ratio of offenses cleared by arrest to known offenses (clearance ratio) commencing in the late 1950s and early 1960s, has encouraged criminality and induced higher rates of growth in per capita offense.

For each of the age groups studied (16–17, 18–19, and 20–24-year-olds), the report found that "approximately 98 percent of the rising trend of economic crime is explained by the worsening of economic conditions as measured by the age group's unemployment and participation rates."[19] The report implies that two strategies—namely, increasing labor market opportunities for youths and increasing school enrollments (with their potential for greater earning power)—would have a substantial impact on reducing the amount of property crime.

An Exploration of Police Inputs to City Planning.   A Police Foundation planning grant was awarded jointly to the police departments of Fremont and Richmond, California, to explore the potential of police inputs to city planning. Specifically, the project was intended to:

1. demonstrate actual changes in planning practices as a result of police inputs:
    - in building, street, and park design and construction,
    - in adoption of minimum security codes or guidelines for business and residences;
2. collect data needed to convince planners and developers that security-related modifications are worth the costs involved; to show city officials how the modifications can diminish calls for service;
3. disseminate the results of the project to other jurisdictions. The results of this kind of project will have significant impacts on cities engaged in substantial rede-

velopment, or those that are growing very rapidly. Illustrations of the crime prevention thrust of this work are the attention paid to:

- patrol access to backs of houses in cul-de-sacs and those bordering on wooded sites,
- the visibility of entrances to buildings,
- the visibility of entrances to apartments on a floor of a multi-apartment unit—they should all open onto a common space where every entrance is visible from any other; and in instances where corridors are necessary, no crooked corridors.[20]
- design of cargo-loading areas—prior work led to the reduction of cargo thefts in one firm by 40 percent following the redesign of the loading bay into the shape of a large "U," with centralized surveillance at the head of the "U" and controlled access at the other end.

Organiza-   For a department concerned about crime prevention, the
tional Status requisite activities need visibility, emphasis, competent direction,
for Crime   and commitment. The effectiveness of such activities suffers when
Prevention   they are performed as an adjunct to other activities such as patrol,
and when people are put to work on such programs with inadequate training. These principles were applied by one large-scale police agency in February 1970, when it established a Preventive Service Division. It consolidated three related units into a more effective managerial structure. There were the Crime Analysis Unit, the Building Security Section (formerly the Security Section), and the Special Operations Section (formerly the Crime Prevention Unit). The merger of these units into a cohesive group reflected a commitment by the chief to these activities and a realization that performance can be improved through a unified structure.

In Conclusion: A Challenge

In regard to *productivity,* quantitative measures can take an endless variety of forms. At some future date it will be useful to establish a more precise system and language of public service measurement. For the time being, these simple distinctions should suffice. The critical objective is to formulate quantitative measures that provide better information to management, and to constantly be alert to what those measures are and are not exposing.

In regard to measuring crime prevention, the problems are formidable, but the opportunities for developing new programs geared specifically at the prevention of crime appear to be great. The volume, patterns, and methods of crime have changed faster over the past years than police departments have altered their operations to keep up with the change. Therefore, there exists a potential for diverting departmental resources from marginally productive activities to higher leverage programs of proactive and predictive crime prevention.

Learning Exercise

1.   Admittedly, this chapter is slanted toward one (although the largest) component of the CJS. Divide the class into six task forces. Assign to each task force one of the following topics: (1) police crime prevention productivity, (2) court crime prevention productivity, (3) corrections crime prevention productivity, (4) police crime analysis, (5) court crime analysis, and (6) corrections crime analysis. I would caution you to be flexible in your approach to the acquisition of information about these functions. The titles may differ, or the function may be divided among two or more agency units. For example, you may find some using the term "productivity" as being synonymous with crime "statistics." In any event, develop a state-of-the-art paper of five to seven pages on your *findings, opinions,* and *recommendations.* This paper is to be predicated on your site-visits to the above mentioned agencies. Finally, the task forces are to present their papers orally to the entire class.

Endnotes

1.   A case in point is seen in the 1974 International Conference of the International Personnel Management Association whereby one full day was devoted to the following topics:

   • Productivity—Organizational and Motivational Aspects
   • Productivity and Costs—The Budget and Budget Cycle
   • Productivity and Organizational Effectiveness
   • Productivity—The Technology of Its Measurement
   • Productivity—Case Studies in the Public Sector
   • Productivity—Bargaining Productivity in the Public Sector

2.   *First Annual Report* (Washington, D.C.: National Commission on Productivity, 1972), pp. 13–14.

3. For one example, see the Law Enforcement Assistance Administration, *Advance Report: Crime in Eight American Cities* (Washington, D.C.: U.S. Government Printing Office, 1974).
4. In this instance the city is Orange, California, and the productivity factor centers on crime rates.
5. For those interested in reviewing the other two areas, see the Report of the Advisory Group on Productivity in Law Enforcement on *Opportunities for Improving Productivity in Police Services* (Washington, D.C.: National Commission on Productivity, 1973). The remainder of this chapter draws upon much of the Report for information pertinent to crime prevention productivity.
6. While conceptually it may be useful to assume that effectiveness does not concern itself with resource input or cost, in practice the term "effective" often is used in a way that assumes a reasonable economy of resource use. This consideration, and the relationship between effectiveness and productivity, may be clarified in the following example.

   Suppose that one measure of police productivity is the number of valid arrests per patrolman per year. If in a year, a force of 100 men made 500 such arrests, then its productivity for that activity would be 5.0 arrests per patrolman.

   However, if the force were reduced by 20 men, and if the remaining 80 men made 480 arrests the following year, then the productivity of the force would increase to 6.0 arrests per patrolman. But while productivity increased, the actual number of valid arrests made decreased. In that sense, the effectiveness of the force in apprehending criminals (assuming the same level of criminal activity) has declined.

   Whether effectiveness actually declined, of course, depends upon how the goal of the police department is defined. If its goal is to apprehend as many criminals as possible commensurate with a reasonable degree of public order and cost, then perhaps the slight decline in arrests is acceptable, (especially in light of the apparently large cost savings that resulted). In this type of case the goals of increasing productivity and increasing effectiveness become intimately related.

   The ideal productivity gain, of course, is where the same force of 100 men is able to increase its number of valid arrests from 500 to 600. In this case, both the productivity and effectiveness of the force—by this measure—are increased: more valid arrests are made with no increase in manpower.
7. For a brief discussion of the history and current trends in local government productivity see the article by George P. Barbour, Jr., "Measuring Local Government Productivity," *The Municipal Year Book: 1973* (Washington, D.C.: International City Management Association, 1973), pp. 38–46.

8. The full title of the latest *UCR* dated August 1974, is *Crime in the United States, 1973—Uniform Crime Reports*. Since it was first published in 1930, the *UCR* has been the only nationwide data source on crimes committed throughout the United States. The report has been improved over the years by refinements in data collection, comparison, and dissemination, and it will undoubtedly continue to be used in the future as an indication of crime rates and police performance.

9. See Anthony G. Turner, "Victimization Surveying—Its History, Uses, and Limitations," Appendix A of the National Advisory Commission on Criminal Justice Standards and Goals *Criminal Justice System* (Washington, D.C.: U.S. Government Printing Office, 1973).

10. Currently one finds two highly reputed sources that deal with police goals and standards: (1) the National Advisory Commission on Criminal Justice Standards and Goals, and (2) the American Bar Association. In regard to the latter, the American Bar Association's Project on Standards for Criminal Justice (which was also approved by the executive committee of the International Association of Chiefs of Police) ranges from such general goals as safeguarding freedom and developing a reputation for fairness, civility, and integrity, to more specific goals such as identifying and apprehending offenders and facilitating the movement of people and vehicles. The Advisory Group did not attempt to define the overall police responsibility or to develop an authoritative list of police goals and functions. Rather, it decided to focus its attention on selected activities which are of top concern to police chiefs. The debate over proper police goals no doubt will, and should, continue. And efforts to measure police activity must be attentive to the changing perception of police responsibilities.

11. For instance, see Walter Pudinski, "Management By Results In The California Highway Patrol," *Journal of California Law Enforcement* 8 (April, 1974), pp. 194–199.

12. Details on crime analysis units and functions can be found in *Crime Data Analysis Handbook* (Sacramento, CA.: California Crime Technological Research Foundation, 1973). Relatedly, you will also find of interest Peter B. Block and Cyrus Ulberg, *Auditing Clearance Rates* (Washington, D.C.: Police Foundation, 1974).

13. With the complexities and difficulties surrounding productivity and measurement in the police service, one should not be alarmed over resistance to its implementation. This problem is reviewed along with recommended solutions by Walter L. Balk, "Why Don't Public Administrators Take Productivity More Seriously," *Public Personnel Management* 3 (July–August, 1974) pp. 318–324.

14. See Chapter 3 in Advisory Group on Productivity in Law Enforcement.
15. Departments that provided data were Oakland, California; Washington, D.C.; Kansas City, Missouri; St. Petersburg, Florida; Cincinnati, Ohio; and the Los Angeles Sheriff's Department.
16. The city consolidated its police and fire agencies in 1950, and a recent 1973 study showed that, while their performance in both fire and police areas was significantly better than the average of the 12 comparable Bay Area cities included in the study (measured according to indicators of fire damage in dollars and *UCR* statistics, respectively), the weighted police-fire cost per capita was 20 percent less than the average.
17. Robert W. Poole, Jr., *Crime and Criminality Matrix*, Report 012–005 Public Safety Systems, Inc., prepared for the Ventura County Model Criminal Justice System Development Project, Board of Ventura County, Ventura, California, February 1973.
19. Ibid., p. 41.
20. For a discussion of this and other design techniques that reduce criminal incidents, see Oscar Newman, *Defensible Space: Crime Prevention Through Urban Design* (New York: The MacMillan Co., 1972).

15

Evaluation of Crime Prevention Programs

*The Government is very keen on amassing statistics. They collect them, add them, refer them to the nth power, take the cube root, and prepare wonderful diagrams. But you must never forget that everyone of these figures comes in the first instance from the . . . (village watchman), who just puts down what he damn pleases.**

Preview

We see crime in this nation as being either close to, or perhaps at the top of, a rank-ordered list of "problems to be solved." Subsequent to an intensified concern over the rate and types of crime, a genuine hope for an effective attack on its threat and harm has arisen by both aware citizens and dedicated criminal justice managers. To this end, an accelerated commitment can be seen to the evaluation of ongoing projects. It is because of evaluative efforts that we can reasonably anticipate an improved rationale for the allocation of scarce resources within the CJS.

To "evaluate" a phenomenon is a most challenging activity for us. Far too often, due to the challenge presented, certain deficiencies tend to surface. Half-hearted designs, insufficient data, fear of failure, and lack of expertise are potential problems. As a consequence, a number of considerations crop up relative to the accuracy of evaluative designs. Critical among these considerations are: type of evaluation, program design, program size, choice of evaluators, and data reliability.

*Sir Josia Stamp, *Some Economic Factors in Modern Life* (London: P.S. King and Son, Ltd., 1929), p. 258.

The fundamental steps comprising *evaluation planning* for the *implementation of a project* are:

- quantify the objectives and goals;
- determine a quantifiable objective/goal relationship;
- develop evaluation measures;
- develop data needs considering requirements, constraints, and reporting; and determine methods of analysis.

Also, there are a variety of additional factors that we should consider in carrying out the evaluation plan and the special care required to evaluate multiple projects and programs. The concepts of evaluation presented here can be adapted to social programs other than crime prevention efforts. Further, the techniques used to show a quantifiable relationship between projects might also be used to assess the relative worth and/or to allocate resources among competing projects.

Sustaining a project's quality and internal strength is fostered through continuous *monitoring*. Project monitoring is basically an activity that seeks to insure "quality control." As such it is heavily dependent on visual and written status reviews. Of equal importance is the strategy adopted for implementing the evaluation component. We find that of prime significance are the input *data* and the *output* analysis. Together they furnish the foundation for measuring the degree of success or impact of the project on the intended problem area.

Finally, the project and police manager alike must share in the responsibility for project evaluation. Jointly they should be alert to: goal specificity, evaluation measures, data requirements, data analysis, and milestone reporting. This responsibility is linked to present and pending decisions pertaining to the allocation of resources for improving our capability to prevent crime.

General Underpinnings

When attention was directed in the middle 1960s to crime as a great social issue, it seemed natural to most people (including most criminal justice managers) to elicit the assistance of criminal justice agencies and in particular the police. The other thing it seemed reasonable to do was to provide the police, courts, and corrections with additional resources. So municipal, county, and state budgets for criminal justice functions, especially the police, went up and new federal agencies were created—the most prominent being the Law Enforcement Assistance Administration (LEAA)—with funds to massively and rapidly inject into our CJS.

Now and in the coming years, police and sheriff departments, along with other elements of the CJS, will be spending billions of dollars to reduce crime. Indeed, such funding support and increased attention for crime problems has encouraged local law enforcement agencies to initiate action-oriented programs which could not have been undertaken without federal assistance. Thus, innovations have been and are being tried in the state and local agencies comprising the CJS, in all types of their activities. In police departments, we see that many of the programs were initially directed toward the control of crime. Currently, sizeable sums of monies and resources are being committed to the prevention of crime. For criminal justice practitioners, researchers, and politicians have come to the realization that the reduction of crime necessitates a two-dimensional approach to control *and* prevention. The latter approach recognizes, for example, that the victim or target of crime can also be of importance. Many crime targets are poorly or inadequately protected; people who insure their property may become careless in securing it; city planning, building architecture, and store layouts may ignore the most fundamental tenets of designing for security, simply because security was not considered. These causes relate more to the opportunity for crime than to the motivation of the offender. We can categorize programs in nature.[1]

Basically, this chapter describes a methodology for planning and evaluating crime prevention programs. (Keep in mind that the proposed evaluation strategy can also, with minor modifications, be utilized in the assessment of crime control programs.) The term evaluation has been defined as: "The process of determining the value or amount of success in achieving a predetermined objective. It includes at least the following steps: formulation of the objective, identification of the proper criteria to be used in measuring success, determination and explanation of the degree of success, recommendations for further program activity."[2] An elaboration of this definition will follow to explicate the elements of each of these steps, the problems and pitfalls in carrying them out, and the way they relate to the context of crime prevention programs. It is concerned with crime prevention programs whose results are short-term. The concepts discussed are not new; many of the problems and procedures have been discussed by others in different contexts. What "newness" there is resides in the fact that they are, or can and should be, applied to crime prevention programs.

The guidelines proposed herein are directed primarily at two *user* audiences. First, they are designed to give the evaluative researcher an understanding of the characteristics of police operations and data that can affect evaluations. Second, they should give the police manager an understanding of the intricacies, requirements, and problems of evaluations, without getting too involved in technical and statistical matters. Further, it is noted that this chapter contains information and recommendations on what is to be either counted or measured during the evaluation process.

Finally, it is apparent that the police, perhaps more than any other public agency today, are experimenting with new technologies, techniques, and theories that are intended to reduce crime. It is up to each agency that implements a program to develop the evaluative information on how and how well it worked. It is apparent that the potential value of each program will not be realized if it is not evaluated or if its evaluation is kept isolated from similar evaluations in other jurisdictions. It is through the assessment process that we can generate reliable answers to the question, "What are we accomplishing with our money and efforts?" LEAA is encouraging and supporting state planning agencies, plus local and regional criminal justice coordinating councils all over the nation, to make use of the evaluation guidelines and regulations they have had all along to attain valid measurement of results for the projects they fund under block grants. Hence, there are questions—and money for answering them—continually coming from each of these hundreds of funding and planning agencies. Coincidentally, the question of effectiveness is not delimited to those that are supplying funds. On the contrary, the public, academics, and media are inquiring as to what is being achieved by the CJS in its pursuit of crime prevention. But, most importantly:

> The police themselves are asking more and more questions. And not just because they are being pressed by others, although that is a fact to which they are responding, but because they themselves need and want to know some answers. Why are so many supposedly smart people telling us to do so many conflicting things? If people think we ought to do this job, why don't they support us when we try? Maybe we should worry less about improving our efficiency and more about whether we're doing the right things? But how do we know that any particular new thing we might want to do would make people fear crime less, or help us more, or be more satisfied with our service? How would we know which

of the things we now do could be stopped without affecting crime, or fear? If we don't know that, how do we know it would be wise or safe to change? How do we find these things out without taking reckless and foolish risks? Who can help us?

An increasing number of police are working hard on those last two questions as the keys to all others. To the first of these, police leaders are saying: Let's try it out and see. Let's test it. We'll try it for a while and keep it, if it works. We'll try it in one area first and then adopt it departmentwide, if it works. What they are saying isn't new, but in today's setting, with all these pressures to *know* what we're doing and what works, it takes on a new meaning. It means experiment and measure. We know it's tough, they say, but it's the only way to go.[3]

Briefly, a lot of money is being spent to control and prevent crime. Moreover, the amounts will probably increase during the 1970s. Many citizens now are requesting an *evaluation* of accomplishments to date in order to justify a continued, if not enlarged, commitment of our funds.

Deficiencies in Evaluating

The fundamental reason for performing an evaluation is to *assist* in making the best possible decision. Plainly, police agencies need to determine which programs are effective, whether to continue or modify them. A criminal justice coordinating council or SPA must determine whether the program should be supported after the evaluative phase. An SPA or LEAA must, in turn, determine the best way to allocate money among competing problem areas, and among different programs focused on the same problem area. Many of the past evaluations were not adequate for these purposes—worse still, in many instances, there were not any evaluations conducted.

There are many reasons for not evaluating at all or for having poor evaluations. First, in such cases the agency often feels that the evaluation is superfluous, another bureaucratic demand, not requiring serious consideration. Second, many evaluations are based on insufficient data sources. To explain, it is assumed that since police records are extensive they must also be adequate; that somewhere within the vast files are all of the right data necessary for the evaluation. When these are not found, the evaluator tends to fall back on the existing data rather than searching for more pertinent information. Third, the evaluations are avoided, or superficially conducted and controlled. Four, there is at times a lack of expertise of those called upon to perform the evaluation.

The rapidly increasing budgets of our police agencies, coupled with the decline of funding in other sectors of government, has brought an onrush of individuals and firms ready to take on such work, but with inadequate background in evaluating activities in the CJS. Although experienced in performing research and conducting projects, most have little knowledge of peculiarities of the agencies comprising the CJS. Conversely, many of the evaluations are performed by practitioners in CJS agencies who have little training in program evaluations. Where these evaluations may be weak in methodology and may have limited validity, they at least express an understanding of the problem.

The remainder of this chapter recommends corrective action on some of these described problem areas. The proposed guidelines are intended as a "cookbook" for evaluations that can be used by an evaluator turning to the appropriate page and following the recipe. However, it more closely resembles a general guide to the kitchen, thus identifying some of the problems of evaluation for the police-oriented readers and some of the problems peculiar to crime prevention programs. It provides a framework for conducting evaluations, but not all kinds or on all levels of sophistication. We should make modifications, additions, and deletions as new evaluation strategies and new problems occur. Additionally, it should not be interpreted that a complete evaluation should be performed for all programs; it is entirely unrealistic to perform a thorough evaluation of a small or trivial program. Regardless of the extent of the evaluation performed, there should be an awareness of the shortcomings of the evaluation to avoid reaching unsubstantiated conclusions, and consequently making expensive mistakes.

Evaluation Considerations in Crime Prevention Planning

This section describes some of the ingredients of program planning that are crucial to evaluation. They include the choice of the type of evaluation to be performed, the justification for selecting the program, the scope of the program, the choice of the team to manage and evaluate the program, and the provision for valid and reliable evaluative data.

Types of Evaluation   The type of evaluation used most often has its basis in social science research.[4] Primarily, this model seeks to determine the relationship between two variables. For example, if we manipulate the independent variable (the dosage of a drug), the effect on the dependent variable (pulse rate) is determined, while all other variables and conditions (food intake, mobility) are held constant, constrained, or otherwise accounted for. It is assumed that the dependent variable does not influence the independent variable. This assumption is true in determining the effect of a drug on a population of white mice; however, it is far more complex to determine the effect of, say, team policing on crime. An evaluation plan in the former case can be designed in a straightforward manner. The number of mice can be determined by the degree of accuracy (or level of confidence) desired. An experimental sample is given the drug and a control sample is given a placebo (both samples are drawn from a population with known characteristics). Many experimental samples may be used to determine the effect of different dosages of the drug. The outcome of the experiment on each mouse is determined, and statistical tests are then applied to the data to determine the outcome.

Although more sophisticated in form, the same model can be used in evaluations of complex programs, e.g., education and public health programs. Experimental and control groups can be selected and "treatment" regimes can be administered by the researchers or by those taught by the researchers. The results can be analyzed for their statistical significance. However, since we are dealing with human subjects, complications arise. The degree of success may have nothing to do with the efficacy of the program, but only with the way it was introduced or with the personal predilections of the group involved. There is no "standard" population; human beings are not standardized as mice are for laboratory purposes. In fact, often a program that is found to be successful in one city may be indeed a failure in another.

These considerations also apply in the evaluation of crime prevention programs. Such evaluations are even further complicated by another problem. The people whose behavior is to be modified (i.e., the offenders) are difficult to separate into experimental and control groups. Although public health programs often encounter this problem, they often deal with physical cause-and-effect links between treatment and improvement: the same is not true for crime prevention programs. The effectiveness of these programs is usually determined by looking at statistics of reported crimes and arrests, which are more indirect and riddled with errors.

In a crime prevention program, it may be impossible to categorically classify variables as dependent and independent; for, they may all affect and be affected by each other. Furthermore, because of the difficulty in determining why people behave the way they do, a number of intervening variables may go unnoticed. Paradoxically, police programs designed to reduce crime may have their most direct effect on the behavior of the general public toward the police, which in turn affects the crime rate.

Evaluations are not always, nor should they be, restricted to analysis of objective crime data; they can also include subjective considerations and perceptions.[5] These subjective evaluations can be of significant benefit in augmenting the statistical analyses of the results of the program. They are especially helpful in assessing why and how a program worked, and whether a statistical outcome is actually evidence that the program was successful. Interviews of participating CJS agency personnel and residents of the area in which the program is constructed are usually used to furnish this data. They can give the evaluator new insight into the actual program operation.

The two evaluation types are referred to as "internal" and "external" evaluations. An internal evaluation of a crime prevention program involving the use of, for example, school resource officers would include the analysis of a juvenile delinquency control program and how it was effective in preventing crime, or why it was successful in one area and not in another. The external evaluation would focus only on the effectiveness of the program in reducing juvenile crime rates or solving crimes, not on how or why the methods under which the results were achieved proved to be successful.[6]

Program Design As It Relates To Evaluation

Connecting the program activities to the final outcomes is not a simple matter. Statistics cannot and do not serve as a substitute for a rational connection between the effect produced and the conditions that produced it. For example, in observing the recent increase in *police manpower* concurrent with the increase in *crime rates*, it could illogically be concluded that the former caused the latter. It is well known that public pressure due to the increase in crime brought about the increase in *police manpower*.

Discovering the actual relationships between cause and effect in crime prevention programs is made more difficult by the elusive nature of the population that is being "treated": the offenders. Reliable statistics on the effect of the programs on their behavior cannot be developed. Ironically, a program may deter half of the offenders from committing crime while it motivates the other half to become more criminally active. Relatedly, a causal connection can be inferred if, for instance, a reduction in the crime rate is accompanied by an increase in clearances. Even this inference should be verified, by determining how the program contributed to the arrests. The reasons for believing that Program A caused Result B should be specified. Saying, "I don't know how it worked, but it worked and that's all that matters," may satisfy the local administrator for a short time, but it will be of no use in estimating usefulness of the program under changed circumstances of time, place, or tactics.[7]

In most instances where a crime prevention program has been implemented, a bureaucratic thread does exist which forms the design for the overall program. This design should be well understood before the program is activated. The following outline can be used in most cases, to relate the program to the problem being addressed.

1. *Crime problem addressed:* its nature, its extent and importance, statistics relating to its occurrence, known information about offender characteristics and tactics which affect the type of program proposed,
2. *Present operations:* how the problem is presently attacked, deficiencies in this method of attack,
3. *Program operations:* how the program will operate, how the present deficiencies will be eliminated by the program, anticipated reactions of offenders to the program, how these reactions will affect the program,
4. *Evaluative data:* sources of required data and their sufficiency, problems in using these data sources, ways in which data reliability may be affected, steps taken to insure uniform data quality and reliability,
5. *Anticipated impasses:* problems which might occur, assumptions which have not been verified, conditions which may change.

Program designs should be developed with caution. The significance of the *design* of a crime prevention program is twofold. First, it provides a justification for conducting the program. Second, it structures and directs the *evaluation* phase of the program. In some cases it is very difficult to explain the logical connection between the problem and the solution. This is especially true when dealing with intuitive assumptions on the part of experienced police officers about the behavior of potential offenders and their probable reactions to new programs. "Gut feelings" are difficult to translate into cold logic, yet they are most important to assess. The final report of the program evaluation should contain an analysis of this *a priori* justification of the program. In summary, then, the program design must contain both a justification for its implementation, and a recommended means for its evaluation.

Program
Size
There is no guarantee that a program meeting with success in one city/county (or a section of a jurisdiction) would meet with the same degree of success in another area (or another section). Explicitly, the crime problems vary from city to city and may vary even more from section to section within a city. Different population distributions with respect to both race and age are found in different locales, and they react differently to similar programs; and the training, motivation, and community support of the police are far from uniform throughout the country or within a city. Thus, a program should be tried in a number of different locales with different characteristics in order to determine how externally valid the findings are under different circumstances. However, a limit should be established on the number of areas selected and the speed of expansion of the program to these areas. It has been predicted that a pilot program mounted for evaluative purposes could grow to such an extent before results are forthcoming that it loses its value as an evaluation program. One observer has called this phenomenon "The Iron Law of Political Dispersal."

> That "law" states that, in any democracy, there is a strong political pressure to expand every expenditure program to encompass a large number of geographic areas, and to spread the resources in the program across many of those areas, in order to build up a broad political base in support of the program.[8]

Programs initially designed to be tested in parts of a state may be diffused throughout the state, or to a number of cities. The financial resources may be increased commensurately, but the personnel resources necessary for coordinating program administration and evaluation should be curtailed. If not, the probable outcome of this situation is a large program in which it is impossible to determine its value and under what conditions it achieved that value. Awareness of this problem may cause moderation in planning programs.

Choice of
Evaluator
Evaluation problems related to the choice of an evaluator were mentioned earlier—lack of familiarity with police procedures on the part of outside evaluators, lack of research expertise by inhouse evaluators. An associated problem is the nature of the relationship between the evaluator and the program being evaluated, and between the evaluator and the agency conducting the program.

The most important determinant of the objectivity of the

evaluation is the attitude of the heads of the agency running the program. Some may want a fair evaluation of the program, others may feel threatened and want the program to be proved a success regardless of its merits. In the latter case the evaluation will be of questionable value. On the other hand, the program evaluator may have preconceived notions about the merit of the program that would distort his evaluation. He may be a fervid proponent of the program, or of a competing one. His professional pride may be affected by the outcome. These factors do not necessarily preclude unbiased evaluations. If they are not revealed by the evaluator, the findings may be open to question, despite their validity and reliability.

An outsider evaluator is usually considered more impartial than one selected from within the agency. The outsider does not have prior prejudices based on long association with the agency, and can judge the program on its merits. An evaluation performed by inhouse personnel is usually not free of these preconceptions nor free of the influence of the agency administrators. However, outside evaluators are not without their disadvantages. They start without sufficient knowledge of the agency's workings; time must be spent getting them to a point where they can contribute to the evaluation. A "symbiotic" relationship can develop between an agency and an outside evaluator who is dependent on funds from the agency, and objectivity is discarded in order to stay friendly with the agency.

Finally, one of the primary responsibilities of a manager is to evaluate the efforts of his agency. Hence, the criminal justice agency should seek to develop evaluative expertise. If such expertise is lacking in the agency, researchers can be retained with program evaluation experience. However, agency personnel must be included on the evaluation team. Indeed, they should be as involved in the evaluation as the consultants. (Complete reliance on outside consultants to conduct the evaluation will only perpetuate a dependency relationship, while contributing little of permanent value to the agency.)

Data
Sufficiency
and
Reliability

These evaluation tactics cannot be fulfilled unless sufficient data are developed during the program evaluation. These data will permit an assessment of the amount of resources expended in the program, and how efficiently and effectively these resources were used. They include the types of personnel assigned to the program, the number of man-hours of each actually spent on the program, the type and cost of special equipment and other inputs employed in the program, and the way each of these resource elements were used. Yet another data-related problem concerns the ability of the program personnel. For example, the more competent police officers may be pulled off an experimental program to deal with an emergency situation, to be replaced by fewer or less competent officers. (These personnel shifts should be documented in the evaluation report.)

An effort should be made to monitor the data collected for the evaluation on a continual basis to make sure that the quality of data is good and remains good throughout the evaluation. A decline in the standards of collection data may appear to be an effect generated by the program. Most commercial businesses submit their books to external audit as a quality control check on their own bookkeeping. I believe that police managers should also consider this practice, for routine operations as well as for the evaluation of special programs.

Evaluation Planning: Programmatic Steps

Evaluation planning provides to the police program managers information for: (1) assessing the potential value of projects and programs, and (2) blueprinting the evaluation efforts and requirements. Therefore, early and thorough evaluation planning and subsequent examination of the plan to determine its appropriateness are essential to good program management. Evaluation planning consists of five basic steps:

    (1)   quantify established goals and objectives,
    (2)   establish quantified goals/objective relationship,
    (3)   identify evaluation measures,
    (4)   determine data needs, and
    (5)   determine methods of analysis.

Quantify Goals and Objectives   The first step for those involved in evaluation is to quantify, if possible, the program goals and project objectives. (Again, as a reminder, a program such as crime prevention is typically comprised of a set of projects which are more precise in nature.) The goals and objectives should be quantified in terms of a measureable level or levels of achievement. Quantification of the goals and objectives will facilitate program and project success level measurements. For example, a ·quantified program goal and two possible project objectives for the program and projects could be as follows:

- *Program goal:* rehabilitate 400 known drug abusers in two years.
- *Project (1) objective:* enroll 500 known heroin abusers in methadone maintenance treatment over the next two years.
- *Project (2) objective:* reduce the unemployment rate for known drug abusers to 6 percent.

This example represents one possible set of quantified goals and objectives for the program and projects.

Establish Goal/ Objective Relationship

The second evaluation planning step is to show, whenever possible, the quantifiable relationship between: (1) the project objectives, and (2) the program goals. The purpose of this is to provide the means for determining the contribution of an individual project to a program goal, and an individual program to the overall mission of the police agency. Crime statistics, special studies, reports, and any other items that indicate relationship should be used to construct the quantifiable relationship.

To illustrate the construction of a quantifiable relationship between the police mission and a program goal, consider that the police, courts, prosecution, defense attorneys, and other elements of the law enforcement and CJS of a city perceive that an estimated 50 percent of the city's stranger-to-stranger crime and burglary are drug related ($50\% \times 8,000$ incidents/year $= 4,000$ incidents/year). Furthermore, suppose that these perceptions are confirmed by studies and statistics from other similar cities. If the drug program goal of rehabilitating 400 known drug abusers in two years was met, then crime and burglary would be reduced. The amount of the reduction would depend on the number of rehabilitated drug abusers who were involved in crime and burglary and the per capita number of criminal incidents.

To illustrate the construction of a quantified relationship between a program goal and a project objective, assume a survey of methadone maintenance treatment centers showed that such treatment is 55 percent effective (that is, 45 percent of those treated would continue to use heroin). These statistics indicate that if 500 of the city's heroin abusers were to receive methadone maintenance treatment, then 275 (computed by $500 \times 50\% = 275$) of the city's drug abusers would be habilitated. The result is that Project 1 would contribute approximately 69 percent (275–400) towards the achievement of the program goal.

These relationships are not as easily constructed as indicated by the drug project/program illustrations. For example, the relationships are predicated upon the identification of drug abusers (a) who are known to the authorities, (b) who are also criminals, and (c) who are criminals primarily to support their drug habit. These data may not be readily available.

The design of the project/program will greatly affect the construction of these relationships, e.g., is the program voluntary? If so, how do you know whether or not the volunteers are really impact crime offenders? Is there a control group so that the effectiveness of the project/program can truly be gauged?

Finally, evaluation planning steps (1) and (2) should be taken jointly because of the interdependence of city goals and those of the police.

Evaluation Measures   The third planning step is to develop evaluation measures for each project and program. Two types of measures are used for assessing levels of achievement: measures of efficiency and measures of effectiveness. To explain, measures of efficiency indicate how well a program is executed in accordance with its plan—in terms of time, allocation of manpower and equipment, program activities, and funds expended. Examples of efficiency measures are: (1) average response time to reach the scene of a crime (e.g., a command and control program), and (2) the allocation of resources for the performance of program activities vis-a-vis the results attained (i.e., cost/benefit considerations). Measures of effectiveness, on the other hand, are used to evaluate the impact of program activities upon the target problem. They are intended to be "end" rather than "means" oriented. That is, they relate to what is ultimately desired, not the way in which it is attained. Examples of effectiveness measures are rates which indicate the incidence of target crimes or recidivism.

Significantly, primary emphasis should be placed on using measures of effectiveness. That is, every effort should be made to measure project or program impact on the reduction of target crimes. However, certain programs do not directly relate to or directly affect the reduction of impact crimes. In the evaluation of these programs, measures of efficiency will be selected as alternatives for assessing the level of success or failure.

For example, it is assumed by the criminal justice community that excessive delays between arrest and trial enhance the opportunity for offenders to commit crimes while free on bail awaiting trial. Consequently, certain programs have been developed and aimed at reducing the elapsed time from arrest to trial in order to minimize the opportunity for criminal activity during this period.

Ultimately, the ability to correlate the reduction in court delay with a corresponding reduction in criminal recidivism would be highly desirable as a measure of program effectiveness. However, the ability to gather recidivism data on offenders while awaiting trial may not be feasible within the time frame of the evaluation program. Thus, a measure of efficiency would be selected to evaluate the program such as average elapsed time between arrest and trial, rather than a reduction in recidivism or crime rates.

Data Needs The fourth planning step is to identify the data needed to perform the evaluation. Most of the data will be directly associated with one or more of the evaluation measures. Some of the data, however, will not be associated with any evaluation measures, but will be required because, in the evaluator's opinion, they may be valuable to the evaluation analysis. There are three factors that should be considered in developing these data needs:

- data requirements,
- data constraints, and
- reporting systems.

Data Requirements/Constraints. Our first consideration should be that of data element identification. For individual projects and programs, the data requirements and constraints will be identified by the agency's unit. Additional data elements may be identified by other agencies' national evaluations of selected projects and programs. These data elements can be either quantitative or qualitative in value (e.g., crime statistics or a description of a project's environment). The second item to consider is that the definition of data elements be explicitly defined, especially when these elements are: (1) common to several projects and programs and/or (2) to be used in the other jurisdictions, and (3) difficult to collect, process, or control.

Reporting Systems. The final factor to consider in the planning of data needs is to identify how and when the data will be reported to the evaluators. To answer this question several important items must be identified. These are the:

- organizations involved in gathering and receiving the data;
- sequence of the data flow; and
- data frequency requirements.

The organizations involved in a single reporting system are often comprised of several local agencies, e.g., police department, the regional planning unit, the State Planning Agency, the state Attorney General, LEAA, and other branches of the federal government. Each of these organizations may have different requirements as to when the data are needed. For example, data could be collected daily by the local agency, reported monthly to the regional planning unit, and quarterly to LEAA. Hence, agreements between organizations may be needed to get the required data. If the data were required in one form but were being collected in another, procedural changes would have to be negotiated. For the observer, the sequence of the data flow shows *where* each organization fits into the reporting system so that a modification in the reporting system can be quickly assessed.

To minimize the data reporting system development burden, it is recommended that:

- a close coordination between the collecting and evaluating organizations should be established, and
- existing systems should be used whenever possible.

Methods of Analysis

The last planning step is to determine the analytical methods that are to be used for evaluation and to establish the management procedures to execute the analysis. The selection of an analytical method is highly dependent on each project and program. It is highly unlikely that one method of analysis will serve all projects and programs since the projects and programs typically vary over a number of dimensions.

Keep in mind that collecting the data represents only a portion of the data effort. Something must be done once the data start to arrive. This something is commonly referred to as data management: the storage, maintenance, processing, and reporting of the data. In order to provide for the management of data, several basic questions must be answered. First, how are the data to be stored—computerized or noncomputerized? Second, what data maintenance methods will be used to insure easy data accessibility? Since the data will be collected frequently over a long period of time, and management must be able to easily retrieve them to aid in controlling the direction of projects and programs, data must be stored in a manner to facilitate updating and access. Third, what processing of the raw data must be performed? Most data will be collected as raw numbers, but needed in terms of computed statistics. Hence, processing requirements for the data must be specified. Also, the means to perform the processing for the data must be specified (e.g., computer and/or hand calculations). Fourth, what reports will be needed for evaluation analysis and what is their reporting frequency? When all of these questions have been answered and their requirements fulfilled, project implementation is possible.

Data analysis is a multiphased function. It is a process that is to be performed frequently throughout the project or program evaluation period. Key points to consider are:

- It is a good practice to schedule an evaluation analysis on a periodic basis. In this way, project or program process can be continually appraised for management monitoring and directing purposes.

- The natural implementation of the project or program itself may generate certain milestones. Evaluation analysis should be performed at these natural review points to assess the past performance and determine the future direction of the project or program.

- Critical events both within and outside of the project or program should generate an evaluation analysis, e.g., the starting of a non-Impact Program project (directed toward the same target population as an Impact Program project) that also can reduce stranger-to-stranger crime and burglary. The purpose of this analysis is to establish a new reference point for future project and program analysis.

- To determine the outcome of the project or program, there should be an analysis at its completion.

There are four primary purposes for analysis defined as:

1. *Success level determination,* which ascertains the degree of project or program success (i.e., *effectiveness*) in meeting objectives or goals during their implementation and at their conclusion. Interim success levels, therefore, should be stated in evaluation components, as well as overall effectiveness measures.

2. *Management needs for monitoring and direction,* which involves providing program/project management with the information needed to make decisions regarding problems in program implementation, modification and redirection, and continuation:

    - How should problems in implementation be identified and resolved? The evaluation component should ideally contain a list of problems that may develop during implementation and the method that is planned for their resolution.

    - When and how should a project or program be modified or redirected? The conditions under which a project or program may need to be modified or redirected should be spelled out as part of the evaluation component. A discussion of the evaluation measures to be used and how the project or program may be changed also should be included.

An essential ingredient of any evaluation design is to describe the possible courses of action that may be taken if project objectives or program goals are not being achieved.

- When should the question of project or program continuation be considered? The evaluation component should contain a discussion of how the results of the analysis will be used to determine project or program continuation. Continuation is of concern when project/program success levels fall outside acceptable tolerances, when interim evaluation indicates failure at the end of the implementation period, or whenever subjective judgment indicates the anticipated impact goals will not be met. In the evaluation component, all three of the above questions should be resolved within the context of the particular project or program, with specific *milestones* indicated when the question of continuation will be considered.

3. *Contribution to the next level of evaluation,* which assesses the contribution made by projects to programs and by programs to the police mission. (This use of evaluation satisfies the requirement to measure the actual contribution discussed in *Goal/Objective Relationship*.)

4. *Diagnostic,* which focuses our attention on the reasons for the level of success achieved, and involves a quantitative analysis of the implementation and results of projects and programs. In addition, diagnostic evaluation of programs requires of us the measuring of the relative contributions of each of its constituent projects. This determination calls for us to analyze the project results within programs, how well each achieved its objectives, and the effect on program success. The analysis section of the evaluation component should include some comments on the flexibility of these levels of contribution and how not achieving, or over-achieving, project objectives might affect program results. A second use for diagnostic evaluation is analyzing the entire implementation of a project or program and weighing the influence of external variables. The inclusion of a list of external variables expected to contribute or restrain the project or program success in the evaluation component enables the participants to become more sensitive to developments that may relate to project or program success.

Evaluation Monitoring

Quite simply, the monitoring of an evaluation effort denotes a "quality control" routine whereby the integrity of the above described functions is sustained throughout the program and the composite projects. Program monitoring is best operationalized at the very moment that the program/project is implemented. Usually it entails the following tasks:

- on-site observations,
- time-triggered reports,
- exception-to-the-norm (event triggered) reports (as needed),
- conference, and
- milestone (progress) review.

Monitoring is, most logically, custom-fitted to the evaluation strategy; and, as mentioned earlier, the evaluation strategy is best tailored to the program under scrutiny. Evaluation infers constant and alert monitoring.

The Evaluation Component in Review: Equipments of the Police Manager and Program Evaluator

An adequate and successful evaluation component must be comprehensive and accurate. As a consequence, managerial review should be focused on ensuring that it possesses the following attributes:

1–2. *Statement of Goals and Objectives:* Does the evaluation component offer a clear statement of the goals or objectives of the project? Goals or objectives are summary statements which highlight what the program is designed to achieve. In order to be most useful, they should attempt to quantify desired results. As such, they provide the basis both for the evaluation planning and the evaluation analysis surrounding the project.

3. *Identification of Evaluation Measures:* Does the evaluation component clearly identify those measures appropriate to the project's stated goals or objectives? A project's goals or objectives are the key to the development of the overall evaluation component. Hence, the evaluation measures appropriate to a given project should follow from the project's goals.

4. *Specification of Data Requirements:* Does the evaluation component exhaustively specify the data required for developing the evaluation measures? Data from a variety of sources and dealing with diverse aspects of a project will often be required to form a single evaluation measure. The specification of data requirements,

therefore, involves the explicit determination of the data elements required for the evaluation. Further, does the evaluation component state how the required data will be collected? Responsibility should be assigned for reporting various required data elements. Specific reporting periods ought to be established, and designs for simplified, standardized forms should be included.

5. *Statement of the Data Analysis Approach:* Does the evaluation component present a data analysis plan? The project goals or objectives and their associated evaluation measures must drive any data analysis efforts. The analysis plan, then, should summarize how the data elements are to be combined to determine project results.

6. *Presentation of Monitor Reporting Schedule:* Does the evaluation component present an appropriate monitor reporting schedule both in terms of report content and timing? It is essential at both national and local levels to have a project evaluation reporting schedule to work from. At the local level, there is a need for timely reporting for project monitoring and continuation purposes. At the national level, there is a need to know what the results of project operation have been and how these results relate to project objectives.

Each of these attributes of an evaluation component are essential for a successful project evaluation. Each attribute builds and follows upon those which preceded it in the discussion. As a result, all of the attributes must be present in order to obtain an overall picture of the chances for a successful evaluation.

Concluding Remarks

We have covered some general evaluation principles. In turn, we have traced and postulated the processes which should be followed in the evaluation of a crime prevention program, from the program's initial conceptualization to its transfer from limited experimental basis, to full-scale operational mode.

Deficiencies in the available data present significant problems in crime prevention evaluations, but they *are not insurmountable*. Monitoring the data quality, more careful analysis of the data, and the collection of additional data will assist in minimizing the problems. However, these steps should be planned from the beginning of the program to achieve maximum benefits. Among the more important considerations in performing an evaluation is the need to maintain strong liaison between the groups within the police agency which are affected by the program. This will be of assistance in discovering problems while they are still incipient, and will facilitate the transition of the program from the experimental phase to other governmental jurisdictions. Finally, the theories initially used to justify the program should be tested and verified during the course of the evaluation.

A well-grounded evaluation will help both the federal government and the agency that is implementing the program to obtain a more valuable insight into the program's worth. Even if the program is *unsuccessful,* it can provide *useful* information for planning within the department and for other departments considering the same program. In order to achieve the greatest benefit, the tools of evaluative research should be applied realistically with due recognition of the unique characteristics of crime prevention program evaluations. The following quotation appropriately serves as a capstone for the central and commanding message of this chapter.

> As increasing sums of money have been infused into criminal justice programs, the need for evaluation guidelines has become more apparent. Evaluations are used at all levels of administration of criminal justice programs, from the Law Enforcement Assistance Administration (LEAA) and State Planning Agencies (SPAs) through local criminal justice coordinating councils and individual agencies. They are useful for a number of purposes: to determine whether to continue, stop, or modify a program; to determine whether local funds should be used to support the program after its experimental phase; or to decide whether the program should be promoted in other jurisdictions. Information obtained from evaluations can lead to general principles and guidelines to assist local administrators in setting their priorities for testing and implementing new programs.[9]

Learning Exercises

1.   Individually, each member of the class search the literature for criminal justice programs and projects that contain an evaluation component. (If possible, elect a topic that is related to crime prevention.) Analyze the material and present to the entire class a three-minute speech on its contents. Be certain to emphasize the evaluation *strategy* and *results.*

2.   Divide the class into six groups. Each of the groups is to be assigned one of the following study areas: police, prosecution, probation/parole, courts, corrections, and the community. Next, each group is to make an on-site visit to an agency in their assigned

area and assist in designing an evaluation plan for a particular ongoing or future project. Preferably, the project should pertain to a crime prevention effort. Finally, all the groups are to present to the entire class, in ten minutes, the projects and their evaluation strategies.

Endnotes

1. This chapter is the result of an electric process whereby numerous resources were drawn upon. Prime among the many were two in particular: Michael D. Maltz, *Evaluation of Crime Control Programs* (Washington, D.C.: U.S. Government Printing Office, 1972); and Ellen Albright, et al, *Criminal Justice Research: Evaluation in Criminal Justice Programs, Guidelines and Examples* (Washington, D.C.: U.S. Government Printing Office, 1973).
2. Edward A. Suchman, *Evaluative Research* (New York: Russell Sage Foundation, 1967), p. 28.
3. Joseph H. Lewis, *Evaluation of Experiments in Policing: How Do You Begin?* (Washington, D.C.: The Police Foundation, 1972), p. 4.
4. There are many excellent texts devoted to an explication of social scientific theories and methodologies. One in particular is commended to the attention of the interested reader. Fred M. Kerlinger, *Foundation of Behavioral Science Research* (New York: Holt, Rinehart and Winston, Inc., 1973).
5. There are numerous research methods, such as projective techniques, that lack objectivity, but are most useful in discovering or confirming the existence of predicted relationships among the research variables. An outstanding book on this subject is Eugene J. Webb et al, *Unobtrusive Measures* (Chicago, Ill.: Rand McNally and Company, 1966).
6. The documents by the National Advisory Commission on Criminal Justice Standards and Goals make repeated mention of the importance of evaluation. For example, note the sections devoted to this subject in *Criminal Justice System* (Washington, D.C.: U.S. Government Printing Office, 1973).
7. Possibly one of the most provocative program designs and evaluation to be reported during the 1970s is contained in the article by Richard Chackerian, "Police Professionalism and Citizen Evaluation: A Preliminary Look," *Public Administration Review* 34 (March/April 1974), pp. 141–148. Also, you will find of interest the series of articles on the study of the effectiveness of preventive patrol in the June 1975 issue of the *Police Chief*. See in particular the series of articles on the

Kansas City preventive patrol experiment, *Police Chief,* (June 1975), pp. 20–45.

8. Real Estate Research Corporation, *Possible Program for Counteracting Housing Abandonment* prepared for the Office of Research and Technology, U.S. Department of Housing and Urban Development (Washington, D.C.: U.S. Government Printing Office, 1971), p. 55.

9. Michael D. Maltz, p. 1.

Three other documents merit the attention of existing or potential evaluators: (1) U.S. Department of Justice, *Sourcebook of Criminal Justice Statistics—1974* (Washington, D.C.: U.S. Government Printing Office, 1975); (2) U.S. Department of Justice, *New York City Police Street Crime Unit: An Exemplary Project* (Washington, D.C.: U.S. Government Printing Office, 1975); and (3) Donald R. Weidman, *Intensive Evaluation for Criminal Justice Planning Agencies* (Washington, D.C.: U.S. Government Printing Office, 1975).

Index

HV   Whisenand
7431   Crime prevention
.W45

NOV 0 1 1990

AUG 0 4 2000

Schenectady Community College Library

PRINTED IN U.S.A.   23-363-002